Myanmar's
Transition

The **Institute of Southeast Asian Studies (ISEAS)** was established as an autonomous organization in 1968. It is a regional centre dedicated to the study of socio-political, security and economic trends and developments in Southeast Asia and its wider geostrategic and economic environment. The Institute's research programmes are the Regional Economic Studies (RES, including ASEAN and APEC), Regional Strategic and Political Studies (RSPS), and Regional Social and Cultural Studies (RSCS).

ISEAS Publishing, an established academic press, has issued more than 2,000 books and journals. It is the largest scholarly publisher of research about Southeast Asia from within the region. ISEAS Publishing works with many other academic and trade publishers and distributors to disseminate important research and analyses from and about Southeast Asia to the rest of the world.

Myanmar Update Series

Myanmar's
Transition
*Openings, Obstacles
and Opportunities*

EDITED BY

**NICK CHEESMAN
MONIQUE SKIDMORE
TREVOR WILSON**

LSEAS

INSTITUTE OF SOUTHEAST ASIAN STUDIES
Singapore

First published in Singapore in 2012 by
ISEAS Publishing
Institute of Southeast Asian Studies
30 Heng Mui Keng Terrace
Pasir Panjang
Singapore 119614

E-mail: publish@iseas.edu.sg
Website: http://bookshop.iseas.edu.sg

The responsibility for facts and opinions in this publication rests exclusively with the authors and their interpretations do not necessarily reflect the views or the policy of the publishers or their supporters.

ISEAS Library Cataloguing-in-Publication Data

Myanmar's transition : openings, obstacles and opportunities : papers from the 2011 ANU Myanmar/Burma update conference : 16–17 May 2011 / edited by Nick Cheesman, Monique Skidmore and Trevor Wilson.
   1.   Burma—Politics and government—21st century—Congresses.
   2.   Journalism—Political aspects—Burma—Congresses.
   3.   Law—Burma—Congresses.
   4.   International relief—Burma—Congresses.
   5.   Burma—Economic conditions—Congresses.
   I.   Cheesman, Nick.
   II. Skidmore, Monique.
   III. Wilson, Trevor.
DS530.4 B972 2011   2012

ISBN 978-981-4414-15-9 (soft cover)
ISBN 978-981-4414-16-6 (hard cover)
ISBN 978-981-4414-17-3 (e-book PDF)

Cover photo: Mandalay rush hour at sunset.
Courtesy of Shutterstock.

Typeset by Superskill Graphics Pte Ltd
Printed in Singapore by Chung Printing Pte Ltd

CONTENTS

LIST OF TABLES

LIST OF FIGURES

BACKGROUND ON THE ANU 2011 MYANMAR/BURMA UPDATE CONFERENCE

Committed since 2003 to its "Road Map" for national reconciliation, the military regime in Myanmar persevered with the adoption of a new constitution in 2008, then held multi-party elections in November 2010. Each of these steps was criticized for significant procedural and substantive flaws, and the overall process was neither democratic, transparent, nor inclusive. The freeing of opposition leader Aung San Suu Kyi in November 2010 was welcomed, especially her freedom to carry out political activities. Next, the new parliamentary assemblies were convened in January 2011, and the reins of government were formally handed over to a new, "civilianized" government on 30 March 2011. The new government under President (formerly General) Thein Sein began quickly to introduce some reforms and to set out its own agenda for change in line with the 2008 Constitution, and in its first twelve months in office released a large number of political prisoners. However, a number of substantive issues — such as the ongoing conflicts with several significant ethnic groups — remain unresolved, and some have even worsened. Government action in relation to the ending of human rights abuses continues to be manifestly insufficient, and the role of the military remains unchecked. No substantive measures for reforms to underpin the rule of law have been implemented, and the restoration of various freedoms, including freedom of the press and freedom of association, are being introduced only slowly and partially.

The eleventh Myanmar/Burma Update conference was held at the Australian National University (ANU), Canberra on Monday, 16 and Tuesday, 17 May 2011. It was supported by a grant from the Australian

Agency for International Development (AusAID). Co-conveners of the conference were Professor Monique Skidmore, University of Canberra, and Trevor Wilson and Nick Cheesman of the ANU. The conference was sponsored by the Department of Political and Social Change, School of International Political and Strategic Studies, College of Asia and the Pacific, ANU. The keynote speaker was Dr Thant Myint-U, historian and author, and formerly of the UN Department of Political Affairs.

ACKNOWLEDGEMENTS

The editors wish to thank the Australian Agency for International Development (AusAID) once again for its generous financial support for the 2011 Myanmar/Burma Update conference and for this publication of the conference papers. Without AusAID's assistance, neither would have been possible. We are most grateful for the steadfast support we have received from the Department of Political and Social Change at the Australian National University, which has always believed in the Update conference. Professor Paul Hutchcroft and Head of the Department, Professor Ed Aspinall, have been as solid supporters of the conference, and of Myanmar-related activities generally, as one could find. We would also like to thank the Institute of Southeast Asian Studies (ISEAS) in Singapore for once again being willing to publish the conference papers, and Christine Wilson for her copy-editing and indexing assistance. Finally, we wish to thank Karina Pelling and the ANU Cartographic and GIS Services for their assistance with providing one of the best and most up-to-date maps to be found for this publication.

CONTRIBUTORS AND EDITORS

Cheesman, Nick (Dr): Lecturer, Department of Political and Social Change, Australian National University, Canberra.

Egreteau, Renaud (Dr): Research Assistant Professor, Hong Kong Institute for the Humanities and Social Sciences (inc. Centre of Asian Studies), University of Hong Kong.

Farrelly, Nicholas (Dr): Research Fellow, School of International, Political and Strategic Studies, Australian National University, Canberra.

Hla Hla Win: Independent consultant, Yangon.

Horsey, Richard (Dr): Independent consultant. Formerly ILO Liaison Officer, Yangon.

Khin Maung Nyo: Senior Research Fellow, Centre for Economic and Social Development, Myanmar Development Resource Institute, Yangon.

Kyaw Min San: Independent lawyer practising in Yangon.

Lall, Marie (Dr): Reader in Education and South Asian Studies, Institute of Education, University of London.

Myint Zan (Dr): Professor, School of Law, Faculty of Business and Law, Multimedia University, Malacca.

Nwe Nwe Aye: Foreign Correspondent, based in Yangon.

Pe Myint: Writer and journalist. Editor in Chief, *The People's Age*, Yangon.

Pedersen, Morten B. (Dr): Senior Lecturer in Politics, University of New South Wales, Canberra.

Simpson, Adam (Dr): Lecturer in International Relations, School of Communication, International Studies and Languages, University of South Australia.

Skidmore, Monique (Professor): Pro-Vice Chancellor, International and Special Projects, University of Canberra.

Thant Myint-U (Dr): Historian and consultant. Author of *The Making of Modern Burma, The River of Lost Footsteps: A Personal History of Burma,* and *Where China Meets India.*

Thaung Tun: Visiting Senior Research Fellow, Institute of Southeast Asian Studies, Singapore.

Tin Htut Oo: Independent consultant based in Yangon. Formerly, Director-General for Department of Agricultural Planning, Ministry of Agriculture and Irrigation.

Turnell, Sean (Professor): Associate Professor of Economics, Macquarie University, Sydney; Editor in Chief, *Burma Economic Watch.*

Ware, Anthony (Dr): Research Fellow, Alfred Deakin Research Institute, Deakin University; Lecturer in Politics, School of Humanities and Social Sciences, Deakin University, Melbourne.

Wilson, Trevor: Visiting Fellow, Department of Political and Social Change, Australian National University, Canberra.

NOTE ON TERMINOLOGY AND GEOGRAPHICAL NAMES

In 1989, the former military regime changed the official romanized name of Burma to Myanmar and changed the names of states, cities, and towns from the names and spellings used prior to that date. Since then, the name "Myanmar" has been used officially by the United Nations, and inside the country today the revised geographical names and spellings are commonly used. The term "Myanmar" is still contested, however, particularly by activists outside the country, but in this publication the editors have decided to use the name "Myanmar" for the period since 1989, and "Burma" for the period when that was the official name of the country. Likewise, the current official geographical names are used for the period since 1989. The people of the country are throughout referred to as "Burmese", except where references are made to specific ethnic groups.

Nick Cheesman,
Monique Skidmore, and
Trevor Wilson

Map of Myanmar

I

Overview

1

INTERPRETING THE TRANSITION IN MYANMAR

Monique Skidmore and Trevor Wilson

The first elections in Myanmar since 1990, held on 7 November 2010, were a significant moment in the country's political life. Admittedly, the elections were organized to ensure continuity of ultimate military control, and to adapt and preserve such control rather than to make a break with the past. Moreover, as has been widely reported, the electoral process was neither free nor open, with unverified "early votes" brought in to decide results in favour of the government party. Another problem was the lack of inclusiveness, because opportunities for popular involvement in the election were restricted by the authorities, with many opposition groups at home and abroad — most notably the National League for Democracy (NLD) — boycotting them. Nevertheless, in spite of all these factors, the elections restored a degree of representative government for the first time in more than two decades, and ended the one-party system that had prevailed for more than four decades.[1]

The changes that followed the elections made the year 2011 even more momentous than observers could have predicted. The "new" civilianized government under President (former General) Thein Sein announced a series of policy changes that included relaxation of long-standing censorship arrangements; launched several initiatives to start a process of substantive reconciliation involving Aung San Suu Kyi as well as members of the expatriate pro-democracy Burmese diaspora; and supported various practical measures (such as open workshops and seminars) designed to foster participative public policy debate about more significant long-term policy directions for Myanmar. Some of these measures were immediately significant for what they meant for the character of the new government. Other changes, it is foreshadowed, will be gradual, will not threaten overall social and economic stability, and will speed up Myanmar's effective integration into regional cooperation arrangements (to which it had previously been largely a bystander).

The main reason why the elections, which marked the completion of the "Road Map" laid out in 2003 by the State Peace and Development Council (SPDC), were not recognized internationally as a substantial change is that more than two thousand prisoners of conscience remained in detention, including NLD leader Daw Aung San Suu Kyi (who was released a week later) and the leaders of the Shan Nationalities League for Democracy (the second-most successful party in the elections of 1990). It was widely expected that an amnesty would be declared by the authorities, as often happens in Myanmar, but initially the only concession announced was a one-year reduction of sentences, which resulted in a mere 112 political prisoners being released, and this was scarcely acknowledged internationally or in the media. The second reason was the collapse of the ceasefire agreement with the Kachin Independence Organization in June 2011 and the new government's inability to prevent the resumption of fighting between Kachin armed groups and the Burmese Army.

HOW ARE MYANMAR'S NEW POLITICAL ARRANGEMENTS EVOLVING?

New Political Architecture

Myanmar's 2010 elections established the basic composition of the new assemblies at national and regional levels, but left numerous pressing questions about how they would function and to what extent they would be able to exercise the powers vested in them under the 2008 Constitution. Over the period of the assemblies' initial sessions, some of the operating modalities evolved into the semblance of a system. Despite having only a handful of elected representatives, some opposition parties were able to use their positions creatively to bring about certain changes. It is still not completely clear to what extent the aspirations of regional and ethnic minority groups might be satisfied through the regional assemblies. The assemblies have so far had little impact on the continuing tensions between centre and periphery, which in some specific instances have worsened. It is increasingly evident, however, that the government wishes to effect further political, legal, and economic change through the new assemblies and other institutions.

What has emerged in the assemblies is a pattern of lively parliamentary debate that has included input of ideas and proposals as well as questioning, mostly from non-government representatives, with ministerial spokesmen being pushed by the Speakers to provide substantive and detailed answers to questions. Most of the proceedings are being reported at length in the official media, and other media personnel are no longer banned from the precincts of the assembly. Military representatives have sat more or less as "silent witnesses", neither contributing to nor blocking discussion. How long they will continue in this manner remains to be seen. This and many other questions remain to be clarified. Richard Horsey has been following the evolution of the new institutions closely and in his chapter offers a careful and objective analysis of their initial operations and their potential for development.

Political Space

As far as "political space" is concerned, surprising and welcome developments have been Aung San Suu Kyi's release from detention on 13 November 2010, her freedom since then to meet and communicate with both Burmese and foreigners, and her apparent ability to travel inside the country as she did in 2002–03. An unprecedented development is her freedom to be interviewed frequently by foreign media (although not always by the domestic media, whose coverage of her activities is still occasionally controlled) and her freedom to send video messages abroad, even to the U.S. House of Representatives Sub-Committee on Asia and the Pacific. Also unprecedented is that Aung San Suu Kyi now has personal access to the Internet, and that the National League for Democracy is able to operate a well-designed and up-to-date website (although it is unclear how readily ordinary Burmese people can access this website). This means that for the first time ever it is possible (theoretically at least) for any interested political observers or participants to understand the full extent of the NLD's operations.

Despite its initial refusal to register as a political party under the new Myanmar Election Law, after the elections the NLD was allowed to carry out a range of educational, training, and low-level capacity-building programmes, documented on its website along with other reports of NLD activity. While these activities are superficially consistent with what a social mobilization organization would carry out on behalf of its members, they are also manifestly political. This has led to high, and perhaps unrealistic, expectations among Aung San Suu Kyi's supporters at home and abroad about the inspirational role she might be able to play as *de facto* leader of the opposition.[2] The government's readiness to tolerate overt political activity by the NLD was unexpected, but it also had its limits, so it was hardly unexpected when, on 29 June 2011, on the eve of her first trip outside Yangon since being released in 2010, the Ministry for Home Affairs formally informed Aung San Suu Kyi that the NLD was engaging in activities that it was not permitted to conduct under the law, and warned that if her in-country travel caused tension, they could not assure her security.[3] Government spokesmen subsequently made it clear that the government wanted the NLD to register as a political party (thereby making these activities legal) and become part of the political process.

In a significant move, to make it possible for the NLD to agree to register, the government agreed to amend the 2008 Election Law to take account of NLD criticisms of the law. As a result, on 17 November 2011, the NLD revoked its refusal to register as a political party and stated that it would also put up candidates for future elections. When the government announced that by-elections for forty-eight seats that had become vacant would be held on 1 April 2012, the NLD announced that it would contest the by-elections and that Aung San Suu Kyi would herself stand as a candidate for the first time. It is difficult to overstate the momentous change in Myanmar's political future that these actions may bring, especially when one considers that twelve months earlier such actions were almost impossible to conceive. At this stage, how Aung San Suu Kyi and the NLD will carry out their role as a minority opposition party in the parliament remains to be seen, but there is no doubt that the political dynamics will change significantly. It will also bring Myanmar closer to "democracy", although building effective democratic institutions and habits across society and the country may take time to achieve.

Importantly, as far as politics is concerned, Aung San Suu Kyi and the NLD have already been allowed to disagree publicly with Myanmar government policy on some major issues, adding another new element of public policy debate not seen in Myanmar/Burma for many decades. Two specific issues, on which such open dissent would not previously have been tolerated, are the continuation of Western sanctions against Myanmar,[4] which the NLD publicly said should be maintained, and the International Commission of Inquiry on Human Rights Abuses, which Aung San Suu Kyi has announced she and the NLD supported.[5] In addition, Aung San Suu Kyi has called for an (unprecedented) nation-wide ceasefire with ethnic groups, and for urgent action to protect the environment, in particular the Irrawaddy River. Normally, on such major issues Burma's military rulers have not been willing to brook any opposition. The September 2011 announcement by President Thein Sein that he would suspend the Myitsone Dam on the upper Irrawaddy came as a surprise — for Burmese people perhaps more than anyone else — especially when the president justified his decision as needing to take account of the wishes of Burmese people, a statement not uttered in Burmese politics for at least fifty years.

At this stage, the NLD has begun to re-open the offices it set up across the country in 2002–03 as an integral part of its operations, but it is not entirely clear to what extent the NLD wishes to recreate a network of offices throughout the country. Aung San Suu Kyi is clearly holding back in her criticisms of government policy, but for how long is this sustainable? Presumably she will not be able to stand silent while the Burmese Army ruthlessly attacks insurgent groups, or tries to stamp out freedom of speech and assembly (which are supposedly permitted under the new constitution). If political activities continue to be permitted, to what extent will the NLD be able to influence national policies and national politics through these activities? If they are not permitted, what difference will this make, including for the NLD itself? The situation is constantly evolving during this rapid period of reform in the Burmese political space.

A major uncertainty is to what extent, and in what manner, the government will accept amendments to the 2008 Constitution. Aung San Suu Kyi has made clear in her victory speeches upon being elected to parliament that she intends ultimately to seek the removal of the role enshrined for the military in the political process by making changes to the constitution.

National Reconciliation

One of the longstanding demands of the government has been to set up a genuine process of national reconciliation. Until 2011 there was no clear indication of how the broader process of national reconciliation, in which all groups would participate, might be advanced in order to open up badly-needed opportunities for socio-economic progress at the grass-roots level. A most significant development was President Thein Sein's decision in August 2011 to meet Aung San Suu Kyi, something that had been consistently rejected by his hard-line predecessor, Senior General Than Shwe. In another important public statement in September 2011, President Thein Sein called on members of the exile community to return to Myanmar to participate in the national reconciliation effort. This is the first time such a public appeal has been made, but it has been taken up by a few leading critics of the military regime, including Dr Thant Myint-U, whose foreword in this publication sets out some views on how Myanmar's national reconciliation agenda might proceed.[6] Debate about national reconciliation and the possibility of a return to Myanmar of the Burmese political diaspora has raged through Burmese cyberspace over the past months. These incipient reforms have not yet gained the solidity and irreversibility that would be required to build trust among expatriate activists and yet this process proceeds apace.

It is now clear that one of the greatest problems inherited by the "new" government is the SPDC's failure to negotiate broader arrangements with the ethnic groups with which it had negotiated ceasefires in the 1990s. It failed to build on the preliminary understandings it had with some groups, such as the New Mon State Party or insurgent groups in Shan State. The serious consequences of the SPDC's ill-advised attempts to force groups such as the Wa and the Kachin to transform their militia into "border guard forces" without reassurances and guarantees about regional "power sharing" are now being felt. It is highly likely that tense situations in some ethnic areas could deteriorate further into civil war. Nicholas Farrelly, in his chapter on developments in Kachin State, correctly sees political, economic, and security issues as being intertwined, and suggests that the Kachin are not ready to agree to fundamental concessions along the lines insisted on by the Tatmadaw (the Burmese Army). If this pattern were repeated with other minority groups, it could leave a tenuous dual political structure in place for some time, parallelling the unworkable dual economic structure (formal economy vs informal economy), depending on the success or otherwise of the 1 April 2012 unification of Myanmar's multiple exchange rates.

For its part, the new Myanmar government has stated its wish to resolve outstanding differences with any ethnic groups through negotiation rather than by using force — although its readiness to deploy the army in strength, as in the past, has also been demonstrated. In addition to negotiations with leaders and groups in Kachin State, a series of high-level negotiations has been held with Mon, Shan, and Karen groups that still oppose the government, and several provisional ceasefires have been agreed. So far (as at time of writing), fighting has not necessarily stopped, and more comprehensive "peace" agreements have not yet been concluded. Realizing that its insistence on incorporating ethnic militia into the Burmese army was a key sticking point, the government appears to have dropped this 2010 proposal. It is more than fifteen years since the central government successfully concluded any significant agreement with ethnic groups, and over the period since then none of the parties has distinguished themselves as they strive to settle their differences.

The prospects for early, peaceful solutions to these long-standing ethnic tensions do not seem very good, and they could prove a major impediment to wider political progress. While Aung San Suu Kyi has called for a nation-wide settlement of these disputes, it is far from clear that she will be able to contribute effectively to finding a solution unless all concerned can agree on a new strategy for this purpose. The presence of ethnic representatives in the new assemblies, and the creation of regional assemblies, does not so far seem to have helped consolidate any "peace process."

MYANMAR'S ANTI-DEMOCRATIC INHERITANCE

Where is the Army?

It is reasonable to ask where the army stands in relation to all of these developments. It seems obvious that the army continues to play a key role in the background, at least exercising some kind of reserve power. While overseas activists continue to warn about the behind-the-scenes power still held by Than Shwe, there is no hard evidence for this; nor is there any hard evidence for the existence of a secret "Supreme State Council" through which ultimate military control could be systematically imposed.

One interpretation of the current pace of the reform is that President Thein Sein feels secure that he is not liable to suffer a coup from within the ranks of the military. However, the speech made by the head of the army, General Aung Myint, at Armed Forces Day ceremonies (27 March) made clear he sees an ongoing role for the military in the parliament.

Against the backdrop of the elections and the laborious work of building a new national assembly in the capital, Naypyitaw, the military has so far given no explicit sign that it intends to release its grip on the tools it has used to repress popular aspirations for genuine change and retain effective control over the state apparatus. Despite the absence of any manifest serious threats to state unity and stability, national security — which is equated with the predominance of the armed forces — remains the top national concern. This was made graphically clear when, just days before the new parliament convened, the SPDC announced as a *fait accompli* the budget that it had approved for 2010–11 and 2011–12, locking in military expenditures at more than 50 per cent of state outlays. Also the large military economic corporations — Union of Myanmar Economic Holdings and Myanmar Economic Corporation — continue to control large segments of the economy with little or no disclosure or accountability.

Building Foundations for Democracy

Most of the foundations for democracy do not exist in Myanmar: government in Myanmar is still heavily circumscribed by secrecy and lack of transparency; there is no developed sense of political rule as a participative process; and Burmese society in general still carries many signs of an authoritarian, "top-down" society. Consultative mechanisms and public policy debate remain alien concepts, and their absence underlines how far removed "democracy" is from Myanmar. The checks and balances that are now an inherent part of modern democratic societies, and which are not viewed as obstructive or problematic phenomena, are still regarded with mistrust by the rulers of Myanmar, and it is not clear how progress can be made towards building an understanding and acceptance that such measures are basically beneficial. Some of these features are now being developed, but there is a long way to go, and the highly restrictive "mindset" of decades of authoritarian rule is proving hard to throw off.

This is especially the case at lower levels, where, for example, in the recent by-elections, local vote-rigging occurred, in contradiction to statements made by President Thein Sein about the need for free and fair elections and despite the presence of international monitors.

Chronic features of most government processes in Myanmar — such as lack of transparency and accountability, non-responsiveness, and absence of integrity — continue to raise profound doubts about how quickly and how far the formal return to constitutional and parliamentary government might enhance prospects for improved governance. Few in the country have any memory or experience of participatory government or are acquainted with the types of consultative processes associated with democratic change in many other parts of the world. In her chapter, Lall describes how even the concept of citizenship has not yet fully evolved.

Although the country has formally returned to constitutional and parliamentary rule, it is still not entirely clear to what extent state agencies will adhere to the provisions of the constitution. In the absence of effective rule of law, the formal rearrangements of law-making and law-enforcing institutions under the new constitution will do little to bridge the vast gaps between what exists on paper and what happens in reality. The establishment of a National Human Rights Commission in September 2011 is an important first step, but effective mechanisms to protect basic civil rights are also needed. What further steps can be taken to protect fundamental rights? What meaningful measures can be taken at an early stage to establish some minimal conditions for the emergence of the rule of law? What can be done to ensure greater respect for property rights, so as to protect citizens against wanton confiscation of land and extortion of money and assets?

Moreover, the military as an institution operates largely above the law, and state security personnel still enjoy virtual impunity for human rights abuses carried out in the name of national security. So far there is no indication that army leaders will be prepared to negotiate over control of the state or allow for any true contest or verification of their policies and programs, nor is there as yet any sign that they will be disposed to tolerate compromises that might involve different parties conceding ground to ensure outcomes that can really command wider support. Can the new assemblies play any role in effecting changes that might lead to wider political and social reforms aimed at protecting rights?

STRENGTHENING CHECKS ON THE
EXERCISE OF POWER

Absence of the Rule of Law

Observers are increasingly focusing on the absence of the rule of law as a major unresolved issue for Myanmar. This problem has been singled out by the Special Rapporteur on the Situation of Human Rights in Myanmar, Tomás Ojea Quintana, as well as by Aung San Suu Kyi. Among the obvious problems, strong military influence is still exerted in relation to judges, as demonstrated by the appointments of new senior judges. It is not yet clear whether these judges will be better or worse than their predecessors, but any negative consequences in terms of independence and fairness of judgements will emerge in time. The large-scale amnesties of prisoners (including a number of political prisoners) by the new government during 2011 drew attention to the distorted pattern of sentencing "offenders" to excessively harsh sentences for relatively trivial, and often minor or technical, offences, and releasing some later at executive discretion, while other languish in prisons for years. (Some political prisoners who have been released, such as Ashin Gambara, the monk leader of the "Saffron Revolution", continue to be subjected to petty harassment by the security authorities.)

As a practising lawyer, Kyaw Min San looks at some of his direct experience with the functioning of the courts. He asks about the possibilities for change under the new administration, and draws attention to three key issues that require urgent attention: the status, composition and budget of the Supreme Court; the lack of authority of the courts, and the external pressures they face; and judicial corruption. Nick Cheesman takes up the last of these three issues and looks at the culture of corruption in Myanmar's courts through a discussion of the language used to buy and sell legal cases. From the point of view of a comparative legal scholar, Myint Zan considers the establishment of a Constitutional Tribunal in Myanmar — an innovation in a former British colony — and examines its role with reference to that of the Supreme Court. Their chapters are preliminary attempts at exploring some of the problems that will be faced in Myanmar by persons concerned to establish a rule of law.

It is disturbing to see how little international assistance Myanmar has received for capacity-building related to the justice system. Few international agencies have undertaken programmes on legal capacity-building, and no bilateral Western donors have dared to risk criticism from overseas Burmese activists by even contemplating such programmes. Perhaps some assistance in these areas may now be possible, especially since they have been flagged by Aung San Suu Kyi as being in need of urgent attention.

The Need for a Comprehensive Human Rights Strategy

The prevalence of serious human rights abuses in Myanmar is a continuing concern. Ordinary citizens are still at risk of being imprisoned for trivial acts of resistance or for acting within their legal rights to represent community and public concerns about the corruption and excesses of state officials. The new National Human Rights Commission faces a big challenge in investigating complaints from citizens and changing the pattern of violation of normal citizens' rights. Observers have expressed concerns about the Commission's independence and whether it will have the resources to function effectively, yet Western sanctions are not likely to be terminated until more decisive action is taken by the Myanmar government.

Myanmar's initial appearance in January 2011 before the Human Rights Council, to undergo its universal periodic review, was an opportunity to assess whether improvements in human rights practices were likely to be introduced any time soon. The result, however, was particularly negative — with ninety-nine of the Council's "recommendations" accepted by the Myanmar government and ninety-two rejected — and therefore quite disappointing.[7] This suggests that eliminating human rights abuses is not a high priority for the new government, and underlines how difficult it will be to move forward in this area where changing the behaviour of the army is the critical requirement.

The rights of workers to form unions, to strike, or to take other action to demand reasonable wages and conditions are now guaranteed under new legislation that entered into effect at the end of 2011. In the past two years, some workers have carried out strikes and won some wage increases in a way that has not happened in Myanmar for more than two decades. President Thein Sein identified workers' rights as important for ongoing development tasks, but it is not clear how any improvements in this area will be followed through and how thoroughly the new laws will be applied.

What steps can be taken to protect fundamental rights and establish some minimal conditions for the emergence of the rule of law? What can be done to ensure greater respect for property rights, so as to protect citizens against wanton confiscation of land and extortion of money or assets? Can the new assemblies play any role in effecting changes that might lead to wider political and social reforms aimed at protecting rights?

A Greater Role for the Media

Another key issue relates to concerns about the role of the media in Burma. Until now, scholars and observers of the various Burmese media have considered media inside the country and media outside the country as separate entities. This division of inside/outside is no longer relevant as an analytical paradigm, but it continues to aggravate differences and create tensions between aid donors. It is especially unhelpful as a framework for understanding the role of the media at the present time, when, since the beginning of the twenty-first century, technological change has introduced new forms of electronic media at a rate that has been almost revolutionary.

Under the old inside/outside paradigm, the Democratic Voice of Burma (DVB) is considered to be an expatriate media organization operated through foreign countries. However, when one considers that more than two-thirds of DVB's audience is inside the country, as are many of their journalists and reporters, it is clear that the paradigm no longer applies. In his foreword, Thant Myint-U describes a fracturing of the military's former political authority and practices. There is similarly a fracturing of the old authoritarian-style saturation propaganda on one hand and the crude and heavy-handed attempts to stop media leaking across national boundaries on the other. This is not a one-way process where media organizations outside the country broadcast inside the country. There is clearly a decentralization of the production and transmission of information through networked structures as citizen journalism and social media are combined.

In view of the expansion of information media in Myanmar over the past decade — characterized by fertile and diverse origins, new forms, widespread audience reach, portability, transmittability, and avid consumption — new analytical criteria, such as audience reach, persuasive impact, political impact, and degrees of censorship, are needed in order to understand the actual and potential effects of Burmese media as they operate today.

Over the past twelve months within post-election Myanmar all sorts of challenges to the media's traditional role have been occurring, often at the same time — a fracturing of the military state, parliamentary reforms, changes in the political economy, and the decentralization of information provision and control. During 2011 press controls were substantially lifted, and no longer represent the everyday problem they were in the past for all but internal political reportage. Nwe Nwe Aye and Pe Myint are experienced journalists, and their chapters illustrate the significant problems and issues facing the media in the period ahead.

Pe Myint writes of the widespread phenomenon of local journals in Burma and describes the stormy responses of Burmese readers of local journals, beginning in 2008, when well-known writers and writer-politicians began writing about the constitutional and electoral processes. Local journals began to introduce political affairs sections, and by 2010, Pe Myint writes, "journalists ... seized the chance to report political news for the first time". In analyzing the incremental press freedom of the past few years, Pe Myint speaks of the one true remaining censor, "the censor that has taken root in the minds of writers and journalists" — the kind of censor that it will take some time to fully remove.

In her related chapter, Nwe Nwe Aye describes issues that the media will not be able to report freely and fairly for some time. She concentrates upon corruption, mismanagement, criminal negligence, and the reportage of legal cases, and argues that the current weak link between freedom of expression and the rule of law could in the coming years be significantly strengthened through increasingly freer media.

The mooted abolition of the Press Scrutiny Board and the granting of new media licences suggest that further censorship reforms can be expected, and the lifting of much of the censorship surrounding reportage of the NLD and Aung San Suu Kyi has been widely welcomed inside the country. For each of the many significant post-election reforms, however, it is possible to find examples of increased or ongoing repression, and the jailing of *Myanmar Times* co-owner Ross Dunkley, the continuing censorship of certain political activities, as well as (from time to time) the jailing of journalists and writers, demonstrates how much further the country needs to proceed along the path of reform.

More opening-up of the media, including to normal international presence, seems likely to occur, and this could act as a more effective check on abuse of power than would have been imagineable before 2011. At the end of March 2012, in an unprecedented move, the Ministry of Information sponsored a conference of domestic and overseas Burmese media representatives to discuss many of these issues prior to redrafting the media laws. If this is followed through properly, it promises a new and more acceptable environment for journalists and proprietors alike, as well as substantially greater transparency.

ECONOMIC CROSS CURRENTS

Myanmar's economic development continues with little rhyme or reason and there is only minimum reform. It is hardly surprising that this should be one of a small number of areas where the new president has chosen to seek independent advice. Economists Sean Turnell and Khin Maung Nyo observe Myanmar from somewhat different vantage points, but agree on the policy failures that generate many worries about the future. Since 2005, the significant windfall from mounting off-shore gas revenues seems to have resulted in no transfer of financial resources to the national budget, although some skills transfers could eventually be beneficial for the oil and gas sector. Privatization seems to have been pursued opportunistically rather than strategically, leaving numerous state-owned enterprises under military control, and their loss-making nature is a significant drain on the national economy.

Ironically, the former military regime's business cronies continue to reap the benefits of receiving substantial transfers of state assets with little or no transparency, and apparently without any guarantees about ongoing governance or the realisation of financial returns for the people. Operating outside normal international rules and procedures, a situation that has been exacerbated by the operation of Western sanctions, these firms meet few environmental, labour, accountability, or fiscal requirements. The business "Wild West" that results is not effectively moderated by any Chinese or ASEAN presence in the economy. Egreteau describes how the jade industry has developed outside normal controls and despite sanctions. How these "lawless" businesses can eventually be integrated into the regional production supply chains or transformed into responsible investments remains unclear. The fundamental weakness and under-developed state of the financial sector threaten to undermine reform.

Such rapid changes pose particular challenges for international aid donors who need to understand their significance for current and future assistance flows. Thant Myint-U suggests that substantial international assistance for capacity-building will be needed in order for the necessary economic reforms and policy shifts to happen, pointing out how expertise in this area has been hollowed out. In his chapter, Adam Simpson suggests that the Asian Development Bank could have the ability to undertake a major coordinating and facilitating role, even though its role so far has been limited. While President Thein Sein's appointment of outside economic advisors is regarded as a positive move, the ability of these advisors to design and oversee the reformist policies cannot be taken for granted. In general, there is no dissent among observers from the proposition that economic capacity-building in any sector would be most beneficial.

The urgent need for a strategic approach to agricultural reform to allow full Myanmar's natural and workforce assets is spelled out by Tin Htut-Oo. The main economic challenge remaining — but not covered in this conference — is elimination of military dominance of the economy, through its control over state-owned enterprises and through its corporations, Myanmar Economic Corporation and Union of Myanmar Economic Holdings. Long known for acting beyond the law and for lack of transparency, the military-economic complex of Myanmar is increasingly contributing to corruption and the distortion of state finances. However, as yet no programme for removing this behemoth has been devised.

SHOULD THE NATURE OF INTERNATIONAL ASSISTANCE CHANGE?

Ever since 2008, when the ruling generals unreasonably and unwisely sought to block or restrict certain international assistance after Cyclone Nargis, pressures for ending such government interference and for allowing freer delivery of international assistance have increased substantially. Significantly, these pressures have come as much from inside Myanmar as from outside, witness the proliferation since 2008 of local humanitarian non-government organizations (NGOs), over which the authorities no longer exercise complete control as they did in the past. These NGOs — especially those like the assertive and controversial Myanmar Egress[8] — seem increasingly to be a permanent feature in the assistance world, are more openly than ever before pushing for change and reform, and are offering themselves as partners for international donors with a more activist reform agenda. The shifting or reprioritizing of aid funding has subsequently caused a sense of crisis within parts of the aid industry located on the Thai-Burma border, and this situation is likely to be exacerbated as the possibility that the Thai refugee camps may close looms over the next several years.

Meanwhile, continued formal insistence by the Myanmar government on maintaining its tight control of humanitarian aid deters many international donors, whose generosity will not outweigh their distaste for what they see as self-serving policies that do not give priority to alleviating the plight of ordinary people. Improved access for foreign media personnel and researchers could overcome chronic problems associated with a lack of reliable information and excessive government secrecy. Denial of freer access is counterproductive for everyone, since it results in mostly negative press for the government and hampers informed debate about the country internationally. The lifting of many of the restrictions on the flow of information could encourage agencies that have formerly been reluctant to get involved in Myanmar to consider initiating projects. Using the example of the European Union, Thaung Tun sets out why opportunities for more creative engagement should not be passed over.

Can international assistance contribute more effectively to encouraging an environment that might improve the prospects for genuine political, economic, and social change? To what extent can international agencies get involved beyond purely humanitarian endeavours? In what ways, and through which organizations, can assistance be delivered to strengthen capacity and enhance governance without providing unintended support for the military? Can strategically designed and targeted interventions realistically introduce or consolidate more far-reaching and sustainable improvements? The recent announcement that Burma will take the Chair of ASEAN in 2014 is clearly designed to encourage further reforms.

The many questions raised above speak to the main themes for the 2011 Myanmar/Burma Update. Morten Pedersen calls for "principled engagement" as a guiding philosophy for expanded future international assistance, while Adam Simpson and Anthony Ware demonstrate how multilateral agencies such as the Asian Development Bank, as well as non-government organizations, respectively, might expect to make a larger contribution in the future.

A consistent theme of all the contributors to this publication is the need for capacity-building in all forms. General indications are that the "new" Myanmar government may be prepared to consider assistance in areas that were previously taboo. Assistance that strengthens institutions, both government and non-government, would help to extend and embed reforms, and would simultaneously underpin democratic and participative processes for the future. It will take time for the results of such a transformation to become clear, but any delay in pursuing the transformation will only increase the human and practical costs.

Notes

1. Thirty-eight parties were registered in the 2010 elections and thirty-seven ran candidates.

2. For example, an opinion piece in the pro-democracy journal *The Irrawaddy* called on Aung San Suu Kyi "to reunite and reinvigorate the disparate groups that make up Burma's opposition movement and inspire the country's oppressed masses to once again actively participate in the cause of freedom and democracy". "Suu Kyi Must Return to Her Strength", editorial, *Irrawaddy*, 20 April 2011 <http://www.irrawaddy.org/article.php?art_id=21139> (accessed 24 July 2011).

3. See "Home Affairs Ministry sends letter to U Aung Shwe, Daw Aung San Suu Kyi informing they are to act in accord with law", *New Light of Myanmar*, 29 June 2011, p. 9. An accompanying article, "Right to make choice still in the hand", published under the name of Pyae Sone Aung, hinted at suggestions about concerns for Suu Kyi's personal security, and warned the NLD it should stop "trying to politically test the patience of the government", in order "to avert unnecessary consequences". *New Light of Myanmar*, 29 June 2011, pp. 8–9 <http://www.burmalibrary.org/docs11/NLM2011-06-29.pdf> (accessed 21 May 2012).

4. The NLD decision was announced on 8 February 2011 after the party carried out a review of their position and, in particular, of whether or not sanctions harmed the livelihoods of ordinary Burmese citizens. See <http://www.burmapartnership.org/2011/02/sanctions-on-burma/> (accessed 21 May 2012).

5. Aung San Suu Kyi's statement in support of a Commission of Inquiry was announced in the message she sent to the U.S. House of Representatives Sub-Committee on Asia and the Pacific on 22 June 2011. A report and links are available at: <http://www.burmapartnership.org/2011/06/aung-san-suu-kyi-supports-un-commission-of-inquiry-on-burma/> (accessed 21 May 2012).

6. One of the top activists to return to Myanmar after the 2010 elections was Dr Zaw Oo, former head of the Burma Fund in Washington. Articles by Zaw Oo have now been published in Myanmar for the first time. Another expatriate leader, Dr Zarni, visited Burma in 2004 in an early but unsuccessful attempt to create another channel of communication to the Myanmar leadership. Zarni now remains implacably opposed to any half-way measures for achieving democracy.

7. See the Human Rights Council official summary of Myanmar's position which is available at <http://www.upr-info.org/spip.php?page=backend-breves> (accessed 21 May 2012). These summaries are useful for comparison purposes, but do not necessarily describe the empirical human rights situation in any country.
8. According to its own website, Myanmar Egress "was set up in 2006 by a group of Myanmar nationalists committed to state building through positive change in a progressive yet constructive collaboration and working relationship with the government and all interest groups, both local and foreign". See <http://www.myanmaregress.org/about.html> (accessed 21 May 2012).

II

Introduction

2

WHITE ELEPHANTS AND BLACK SWANS
Thoughts on Myanmar's Recent History and Possible Futures

Thant Myint-U

George Orwell in *Shooting an Elephant* said that in Myanmar "a story always sounds clear enough at a distance, but the nearer you get to the scene of events the vaguer it becomes". As an historian by training, I am usually fairly reluctant to predict things. But today I am even more reluctant to predict very much, because Myanmar's future is less predictable now — even the very immediate future — than at any time since September 1988, when, as is well known, mass popular demonstrations nearly ended decades of military or military-backed dictatorship. Most people in this room are also familiar with the events of the past several months. We had elections in November 2010, the first multi-party elections in over twenty years, elections that were extremely controversial, with allegations of widespread vote fraud, particularly in Yangon. These were elections held under a new constitution, which reserves 25 per cent of the seats in national and local-level legislatures to the armed forces, as well as control of security-related ministries. They were also elections in which the junta-backed party, the Union Solidarity and Development Party or USDP, enjoyed a huge institutional and financial advantage, and in which many of the new and much smaller opposition parties were able to contest only a limited number of constituencies, in large part because they simply did not have the resources to contest more. And they were elections that the National League for Democracy (NLD), headed by Daw Aung San Suu Kyi, chose to boycott as inherently not free and not fair, and taking place under a constitution the NLD did not accept.

Since those elections, which led to the USDP winning a clear majority of seats, not only in the national legislature but in nearly all the local — State and Regional — legislatures as well, a number of things have happened. Daw Aung San Suu Kyi herself was released from several years under house-arrest, the new legislatures were convened in January 2011, and a new government was formed, taking office in March 2011, with retired General Thein Sein as the new president. About the same time, Senior General Than Shwe dissolved the old junta, the State Peace and Development Council (SPDC); appointed a new and much younger commander-in-chief of the armed forces; and removed himself from all public office.

Some will argue that, politically at least, not much has actually changed. General Than Shwe may still, some say, be pulling the strings from behind the façade of these new institutions, and even if he is not, that it is army men or ex-army men who remain in key positions, ruling in the same way as before. Others, however, will say that the country has taken at least its first tentative steps towards representative government: that multi-party elections, however flawed, have been held; that parliamentary debates, however restricted, have taken place; that whilst there remain ex-army men in key positions, there are as well new civilian faces in the cabinet; and that members of ethnic minority-based opposition parties have even been included in regional-level administrations. They will point as well to the policy speeches that President U Thein Sein has made since taking office, in which he has called for economic reform, political reconciliation, a strengthening of democratic practices, an end to ethnic conflict, an end to corruption, and for major improvements in the areas of health and education and environmental protection.

It is still too early to say where all this is headed. Even in hindsight, looking back at democratic transitions elsewhere, it is very difficult to say which early steps were important and in what way. Myanmar has certainly not embarked on a course that will lead automatically and irrevocably to democracy: that is for certain. But I would also suggest that Myanmar is at a clear watershed, that there is no turning back, and that what happens over the coming months may be critical in determining the nature of Burmese politics and society for many years to come.

What is taking shape today is a much more fractured system of power than what existed before — with a powerful presidency distinct from the army, as well as a ruling party leadership that is distinct from both. For more than two decades, until the end of March 2011, the country was ruled by a single hierarchy, with the junta — the State Peace and Development Council — at the top, and, more to the point, by the single individual who dominated that junta, Senior General Than Shwe.

But now that hierarchy is gone, and the junta has been abolished. In its place is a much more complex structure of power and decision-making. There is an entirely new army leadership, the degree of whose independence from their past commanders is unclear. There is a ruling party, led by some of these past commanders, but which includes, below the upper rung, a set of businessmen and local power-brokers new to the national political scene. Further, there is a government led by a president who is an ex-general, with ministers who are not (by-and-large) in the senior echelons of the party but who today wield day-to-day executive authority. There is a tension, a system of checks and balances, designed into the heart of the new system.

No one can know for certain what General Than Shwe's motivations were in stepping down from formal office and creating this more fractured system. Some say that it may have more than a little to do with his desire to avoid the fate of his predecessor, General Ne Win, who had left behind a pure army dictatorship only to see a new strongman emerge, and to find himself, on his deathbed, effectively under house-arrest and with many of his family members in prison. General Than Shwe may believe a more fractured political system will help him secure his retirement. He may even believe that a more civilian, broader-based, and perhaps even reform-minded, government will better help to secure his legacy. We do not know. Nor do we know for certain what residual powers Senior General Than Shwe may choose to continue to wield from behind the scenes — but that he, too, will one day leave the scene is beyond doubt. A new political system is being put in place and we need to enter imaginatively into the new dynamics that are emerging.

It seems increasingly clear that what is unfolding is a work in progress. Nearly all aspects of the relationship between, say, the new central structures and the new regional administrations have yet to be fully worked out, including the most basic fiscal relationships. Many of the institutions that had been key props of the old regime, such as the Trade Council, which controlled imports and exports, have been formally abolished. New institutions, such as the ruling party's own central organs and the parliamentary committees recently established, are just now (at the time of writing) beginning to start work. All these factors suggest the situation is extremely fluid.

There are, predictably, different views on how to interpret these developments — and behind these differences lie different assumptions. If one assumes that General Than Shwe was not all-powerful, but instead simply presided over a corporate leadership that had a corporate and set world-view, one may argue that this same corporate leadership, rejuvenated, will continue, collectively, along the same old path, no matter what institutional façades it works through. However, if one assumes that General Than Shwe was indeed able to concentrate over-arching power in his own hands, and if one assumes that many in the top rungs of government are motivated as much by self-interest as by a coherent ideology, the more likely it will seem that a fractured institutional landscape can only lead to greater intra-elite competition and rivalry, especially as General Than Shwe's personal involvement wanes more obviously.

I wrote and said more than two years ago that the way to see the elections and the implementation of the new constitution was to see them not necessarily as a step towards democracy but instead as the biggest institutional shake-up in at least twenty years, if not since the beginning of army rule in 1962.[1] The crucial issue was not whether there would be democratic change — as no one expected a fully-formed democracy to emerge — but to see which people from within the current establishment would wind up on top as successors to the old hierarchy, and how they would relate to one another. As with any big shake-up, new challenges and new opportunities will arise.[2]

Few will likely disagree with the progressive vision outlined by the new president, U Thein Sein, in his various policy speeches. Many, though, are sceptical about whether that vision can even begin to be realized. My strong sense is that the president would like to see this agenda realized, and there are several signs that he is trying to push ahead quickly, perhaps because he, too, feels that the next few months may be critical. Either his desired reforms will gain traction and momentum, or he will be overwhelmed by inertia and rival political interests. It is safe to say that, even if the new president and the government have the best intentions, the challenges facing them and the country are enormous.

One of the most important challenges will be to find a lasting end to Myanmar's many (and extremely varied) armed conflicts. There was a time, not long ago, when many countries in Southeast Asia were fighting wars far bloodier than Myanmar's, but Myanmar is now the last country in the region that still has large non-state militia groups who control sizeable territories, mainly in the north and northeast of the country. For example, the United Wa State Army, the biggest of these groups by far, claims to have no less than 20,000 men under arms, backed by armour and heavy artillery. Most of the ceasefires that have been in place now for nearly twenty years are still holding, but they are tenuous. Any slide back into all-out conflict would represent an enormous blow against whatever momentum exists towards more civilian and representative government and would propel the army back to centre stage. It is vital to maintain the ceasefires, to actively encourage peaceful solutions to long-lasting conflicts, and, not least, to protect civilians in the affected areas, who, as always, will bear the brunt of any new outbreak of fighting. (For an analysis of the political situation in Kachin State, see Chapter 4 by Nicholas Farrelly in this publication.)

An equal challenge, perhaps requiring even more urgent action, is the need to reform the economy. I have for more than fifteen years argued on the record against Western sanctions, which I believe have been incredibly counter-productive,[3] but I also believe that the Myanmar government's own economic policies need radical reform. Myanmar is now the poorest country in Southeast Asia — and needlessly so, hobbled by decades of ill-conceived policies and the emergence of rent-seeking business operations that have only entrenched the poverty of millions of ordinary people. Moreover, the middle classes have been weakened over the past fifty years, first from the extreme nationalist policies of the 1960s and 1970s, and then by the sanctions and boycotts of the 1990s and 2000s, from a lack of jobs and a lack of educational opportunities for their children. At least two million unskilled Burmese have migrated to Thailand, and hundreds of thousands of skilled workers and professionals have migrated to other countries all around the world.

The economy is in transition, and may soon become a major energy supplier to other Asian countries. In principle this is no bad thing, but the challenge of ensuring that the benefits from natural resource extraction go to the many and not just the few is a challenge few developing countries have been able to meet successfully.

Careful examination of the fiscal choices that are being made, both in terms of the processes being created and the budget allocations for the coming year, will be needed. For years the national budget has been at best opaque. The government's income from commodity exports, in particular from the export of natural gas to Thailand, will soon be complemented by gas sales to China, fees associated with the new oil pipeline, and, soon, revenue from the export of electricity to China as well. The question of how this revenue will be accounted for and used, and what will be the role of elected representatives as well as the president and his government in deciding fiscal priorities, may be the most important issues for the country over the coming year. Greater fiscal transparency would represent a meaningful step towards democratic government, a step that would be further enhanced if greater priority were given to the provision of basic social services.

There is, as well, the challenge of protecting the environment — which is not, I would argue, a second-order issue but one that should be absolutely a top priority. Myanmar is prone to natural disasters: as its population approaches sixty million and becomes more urbanized, the effects of future disasters could be nothing less than catastrophic. We saw the terrible impact of Cyclone Nargis. Earthquakes, cyclones, and tsunamis are not just a future possibility, but are among the events we know for certain will happen in an otherwise unpredictable landscape.

Yet another challenge will be to deal with widespread corruption. State institutions have been under-funded for decades, warped by mismanagement, and governed with little or no accountability. That this has to change is accepted by President Thein Sein, but, as has been seen in many other countries, any serious anti-corruption drive will be incredibly difficult.

None of these challenges, nor many other challenges I do not have time to mention, can be solved by the new government, even with the best political will, in a short period of time. Push too strongly, and hardliners within the system, as well as others with a stake in the status quo, may derail any further efforts. Nevertheless, at the same time my sense is that the new government must not move too slowly either, as many people, particularly people outside the system, doubt the sincerity of any commitment to reform. It is vitally important that the new government should get things right over the next few months. A major release of the more than two thousand political prisoners still held (at time of writing) may go a long way to demonstrate real change. Economic reforms targeted at alleviating poverty and creating jobs will help to do the same.

THE WIDER WATERSHED

It is obvious to me that all these changes — everything I have mentioned so far — are occurring within the context of a much greater set of changes in the wider region, and in Myanmar's place within the region.[4] The story of Asia's rise and the shift in economic power from West to East cannot be separated from any analysis of Myanmar's present and future. We will all have heard of the growing economic presence of China within Myanmar. China has now invested well over US$20 billion in transportation, mining, and energy-related infrastructure in the country. Over the next few years Chinese companies will complete the construction of a 1,000-mile-long set of pipelines, to carry Burmese offshore natural gas as well as African and Middle Eastern oil, as much as 800,000 barrels a day, from the Bay of Bengal across central Myanmar to China's energy-hungry interior. A new railway line will follow a parallel route, connecting China's southwest to the Bay of Bengal.

We know, as well, that the government of Myanmar has been making attempts (at least partially successful) to balance China's influence with closer ties to India, Russia, and the countries of ASEAN. But there is an additional story, only half-seen, but all-important. That is the creation of Myanmar as a new Asian crossroads, as ancient geographic barriers are overcome and the country is opened up in all directions — not just to China, but to India, Bangladesh, and Thailand as well. Late in 2010, Thailand and Myanmar agreed on construction of a new highway to connect Bangkok to Myanmar's Andaman Sea coast, and to create a massive US$8 billion deep-sea port and industrial complex at Dawei in Myanmar's far south. As borders open, Myanmar will be connected to the 2.5 billion people of India and China as never before in history. This development alone will change Myanmar's prospects, for better or worse, more than anything else that is happening at the moment.

I would argue that for all the peoples of Myanmar, there is no option of returning to the past, not even the recent past. We need to think creatively about the impact this will have, not just on politics or the economy, but even on notions of ethnic identity. A basic shift in geographic connections is under way. Think of the Wa hills, until recently Special Region 2 — once the back of beyond, now at the doorstep of the world's emerging superpower, China, and with economic, cultural, and military ties across the border. What was once the periphery will now be close to the new global centre.

Many observers had wondered how the insurgencies in Myanmar would end — whether the Burmese army would be victorious or whether it would be pressured into making concessions, perhaps even allowing a more federal system of government. But consider a different scenario, where what is developing in the border areas becomes part of a new norm — a mix of informal local autonomies with areas of government control, which then becomes an artery for supplying China's twenty-first century energy needs, as well as a frontier for Chinese consumerism and even tourism. Just on the other side of the border of Myanmar's northeast is Yunnan, which receives one hundred million visitors a year. Less than a day's drive from areas under the control of the Kachin Independence Army or the United Wa State Army respectively are Lijiang and Dali, each receiving millions of tourists a year. The new railway lines now proposed will soon connect both these cities straight to Mandalay.

If we continue to focus solely on the ongoing political contest in Yangon and Naypyitaw, we are missing the point — like people in a boat arguing over who is going to steer, about how to change or improve the boat, or even get a new boat altogether, all important things, but who fail to glance up and see that they are now in entirely new and uncharted waters.

REACHING A TURNING POINT

I generally make few predictions, but I will make one now — that the political picture in Myanmar will become immeasurably more complex over the coming years. This doesn't necessarily mean that life will be any better, or easier, or freer, for the ordinary person, but simple political divisions will give way to a much more diverse range of motivations, relationships to power, and access to profit. Regional variations will increase and the differences between different state institutions will become more pronounced.

We tend to think of political scenarios, but we need to think much more about scenarios for the underlying political economy. As new systems of power and patronage take shape, will we have a system that benefits only a very few at the top? Or one that will benefit a much broader group, but a group that is still only a minority of people? Or one that will actually begin to address the urgent needs of the tens of millions of Myanmar's poor?

We need a much more nuanced view of the political terrain. I am not sure at all that the terms we currently use — whether "the regime", "the state", "the opposition", "ethnic groups", "cronies" or "businessmen" or "civil society" are very useful for describing, much less for understanding, the sets of relationships that exist today. We miss not only the internal differences within these categories but also the ways in which they may overlap. And those terms miss, as well, a tangled web of intra-personal relationships that cross these lines, on a daily basis, in Yangon and elsewhere.

My sense is that we are at a turning point where we can't see at all the winding road ahead. It is quite possible that over the coming years we will see not only a lessening of the army's grip on power but also a lessening of state control overall. However, good things do not always come together. In the new environment, there may well be more room for an independent business community, for non-governmental organizations, for political parties, for outside aid, and even for freer media. My fear is that at the same time, much of the new environment will also be filled by an array of other, perhaps more informal, networks, criminal in their intent, and uninterested in popular welfare — gangsters and warlords.

It is possible that the problems of the future may prove to be less related to direct state repression than to the absence of well-managed and accountable state institutions. Issues such as the illegal confiscation of land or the local environmental impact of infrastructure projects, though not new to Myanmar, may increase significantly in the coming years in the absence of reforms. Later chapters talk about the courts — of course the eventual emergence of an independent and competent legal system, one that allows ordinary people access to justice, would mark a huge step forward, but, sadly, there is little at the moment to suggest that this will happen very soon. As in so many areas of institutional reform, the challenges appear overwhelming — even with the right political will, building or rebuilding viable and effective state institutions will need sustained effort over a very long period.

RESHAPING THE FUTURE

Those who are considering strategies to help Myanmar need to go beyond current thinking and formulations, especially in regard to aid policies. Myanmar is one of the poorest countries in the world, and it receives far less in international aid than any other poor country, a fraction of what is received per capita in, say, Laos and Cambodia next door. In recent years, aid levels have increased and are set to increase further, but aid is still limited to, primarily, humanitarian aid. There is little development assistance, and bilateral or multilateral assistance through government institutions is subject to tight restrictions. The argument of donor countries and organizations was that providing aid through the government would only strengthen repressive structures. But in thinking about the future, we need to rethink this equation.

I used the words "White Elephants and Black Swans" in my title. If the definition of "White Elephant" is "a burdensome possession that is difficult or costly to dispose of", then I would suggest that international policy towards Myanmar has many White Elephants. I do not foresee any major changes soon.

If there is one area where I feel the need for a rethink is even more urgent, it is the area of capacity-building for the country's public services, especially in health and education. Later chapters in this publication will discuss the role of outside assistance. In Myanmar today there is a profound need for technical assistance, advice, and help in practically all areas. The Myanmar people themselves may not be aware of how far behind the rest of the region they have fallen. It may be simply impossible for the government to move ahead in key areas of economic reform without some degree of outside support. Without support, economic reforms would falter, however strong the political will. Economic interaction with the outside world will grow, but the ability of any state institutions to manage these interactions will simply not be there. Even if there were a more-sudden-than-expected shift to democratic government, it is doubtful that democratic transition would be sustainable without urgent and immediate investment in the government's technical capacity. New representative institutions would simply be co-opted by corrupt and moneyed interests, as has happened in many other transitional societies.

In addition, it is not the case that there is a universal desire within the new Myanmar government for more outside aid. Far from it. In fact, it may well be difficult for the government to accept any technical assistance beyond current levels, given the deep distrust in some quarters of anything to do with the world outside Myanmar, in particular of Western governments or international agencies.

For half a century successive military and military-backed governments have not wanted, and have not been willing to listen to, the advice of civilian technocrats. This differentiated the Burmese military regime from military regimes elsewhere in the region, many of which were equally repressive but were at least able to manage their economies in a way that allowed for sustained development. In Myanmar there may now be a change — at last — with the appointment of new civilian economic advisors. This is a very welcome change, though it is too early to say for certain exactly what role and influence these advisors will have.

It should be understood that, in general, the denial of technical aid and development cooperation plays straight into the hands of the system's most hard-line, and often most corrupt, elements — who want to see neither economic reform nor any interaction with the West or the international community. Observers are well aware how complicated the politics of giving aid to Myanmar is for countries outside — but I would suggest that the politics of aid within the Myanmar government is equally complicated, with a wide array of views and anxieties.

This is not to say that outside aid should be the foundation for economic change. Not at all. In too many other situations the negative effects of over-reliance on outside assistance have been very clear, and there is absolutely no reason for a country as naturally rich and bountiful as Myanmar to become dependent on overseas aid. The goal must be instead to create jobs and opportunities for all parts of Burmese society, including through expanded trade and foreign investment. For this to be achieved, there needs to be a radically different business environment, official policies must become far more predictable, and legal institutions must be strengthened.

In the short term, outside help will have an important role in addressing urgent humanitarian needs and helping to reduce extreme poverty, but it will be equally important for outside help to encourage and support efforts at genuine economic reform. Over the period ahead, this is perhaps as important as anything else.

Whatever role foreign assistance may play in helping to move things in a better direction, there is a real need to encourage as broad a debate as possible on the future development choices the country faces. There are indeed many technocratic issues to be resolved, but there are also many more basic development choices, choices the Burmese people need to make themselves. I see little sign that this is happening. Development comes with trade-offs, as we all know. Would people in Myanmar, for example, be happy to accept a level of environmental destruction in return for more growth, more jobs? Would they prefer a more urbanized future, or one that preserves aspects of rural and agricultural society? Whilst Myanmar's chairmanship of ASEAN is often debated, there is barely any discussion of the consequences of Myanmar's integration into an ASEAN single market, something that will have far greater effect on ordinary people.

Take another issue — tourism. The tourism market may well grow quickly in the future. I have long advocated greater tourism in Myanmar. However, as the market grows, the people of Myanmar, understandably, will think about the potential negative effects of tourism, and will want to benefit from lessons elsewhere in the region and to decide themselves whether tourism should become as big a part of their economy as it is, say, in Thailand or Cambodia.

The role of the media in encouraging these debates will be critical. An economically literate citizenship that sees politics not as some abstract crusade but as something tied directly to their daily lives — to the availability of jobs and social services — is today almost entirely missing.

In closing, I underline again that the future is unpredictable; that we may well have at this moment the best window of opportunity for some time to see Myanmar move in the right direction; that this window may be very short-lived; and that whatever happens, the political landscape to come will be far more complex, and far more tied to the rest of the region, than ever before.

Myanmar is at a crossroads, both figuratively and literally, in its geographic position between the world's two greatest rising economies. There is a good scenario for what may happen next — the release of political prisoners, a serious push for economic reform, a relaxation of the restrictions on outside aid — all this could happen over the next few months, keeping open the window for further reform and political change. But as I said at the beginning of this chapter, the future is unpredictable. "Black Swans" — surprise events that have a huge impact — have happened many times before, and have very suddenly changed the course of history in Myanmar. It may well happen again.

Notes

1. See Thant Myint-U, "Prepared Testimony by Dr Thant Myint-U before the East Asia Sub-Committee of the Senate Foreign Relations Committee, Washington D.C., 30 September 2009" <http://foreign.senate.gov/imo/media/doc/Myint-UTestimony090930p.pdf (accessed 9 April 2012).
2. For an interview with the author, see Charles McDermid, "Missing the point on Myanmar", *Asia Times Online*, 4 July 2009 <http://www.atimes.com/atimes/Southeast_Asia/KG04Ae01.html> (accessed 9 April 2012).
3. "Trading With the Enemy", *Far Eastern Economic Review*, 10 March 1994.
4. See Thant Myint-U, *Where China Meets India: Burma and the New Crossroads of Asia* (London: Faber & Faber, 2011).

III

Political Update

3

MYANMAR'S POLITICAL LANDSCAPE FOLLOWING THE 2010 ELECTIONS
Starting with a Glass Nine-Tenths Empty?

Richard Horsey

The Myanmar/Burma Update conference at which this paper was presented took place six months after the elections, one hundred days after the convening of legislatures, and fifty days after the new government took over. It was thus a good moment to take an initial look at developments in the political situation. Of course, the danger of analysing current political trends in a paper that will be published a year hence is that it will inevitably be subjected to the harsh light of hindsight. Indeed, already in the two months between the conference and the finalization of this paper, significant events have occurred, including a resumption of fighting in Kachin areas, the prospect of tensions between the government and Aung San Suu Kyi around her planned travels in the country, and some jostling for authority and influence among senior members of the new power structures. Any of these could lead to developments that could significantly change the course of events in the next year.

Hence, this chapter will focus more on how developments in Myanmar should be assessed, rather than on giving detailed predictions on what developments can be expected. A broader perspective on change such as this, it is hoped, will better stand the test of time and will be most relevant in any ongoing consideration of where Myanmar is heading in this new period of "disciplined democracy".

THE NATURE OF POLITICAL CHANGE

In conducting any analysis of the situation, the most important question to ask ourselves is, What will political change look like in Myanmar, and how will we recognize it when we see it? This is important, because if we cannot answer this question, it is very difficult to assess the current political transition and what it means. There are indeed highly divergent views on the current situation: some analysts are saying that there has been no political change, and that it is merely a matter of "old wine in a new bottle"; others are saying that this is a key moment of transition. Resolving that debate comes down to answering the basic question that I have posed.

It is certainly the case that not much has changed. But I would suggest that if we are witnessing the early stages of a very slow, cautious transition away from fifty years of authoritarianism, we should not expect dramatic change. The most relevant approach is to focus on the small number of areas where the situation is different from before, rather than on the large number of areas where things are depressingly the same. The right approach, from an analytical point of view — though certainly not from an aspirational one — is to view the "glass one-tenth full" rather than the "glass nine-tenths empty". I argue that from this perspective, the developments that we are witnessing are consistent with what we might expect to see if slow and incremental — but nonetheless meaningful — change is occurring. This does not mean that positive change is certainly coming, or that any process of reform will be successful, but it does raise possibilities for change that have not existed in recent years.

There are many areas where circumstances are still bad:

- The human rights situation in general remains grave;
- There has been no major release of political prisoners (only one

hundred or so were released as part of the general amnesty of prisoners announced by the president after he took office);

- Brutal counterinsurgency operations continue in various parts of the ethnic borderlands, and there has been a very serious outbreak of fighting with the Kachin Independence Organization (KIO) in parts of Kachin State and northern Shan State;
- Corrupt and abusive practices by officialdom continue;
- Highly skewed budget allocations continue to be made in favour of defence and security (and natural resource exploration and extraction) at the expense of social services;
- ... and many, many more.

This must not be forgotten, and efforts must continue to push for such unacceptable things to change. But there are also a number of areas where things have changed, in interesting ways.

First, there are some obvious procedural changes:

- Senior General Than Shwe has retired and has withdrawn almost entirely from day-to-day political affairs. This is the single most significant thing to have happened in years, but its full impact has been ignored by many commentators;
- There are now elected parliaments with a (small) number of opposition members;
- A new process of decentralization has begun. There are now regional legislatures and governments, and some ethnic opposition representatives are State or Region ministers, a radical change;
- For all its flaws, a new constitution is in force, providing a basic legal framework for the country;
- A new government has taken over (albeit partly recycled, and only quasi-civilian), and the State Peace and Development Council (SPDC)/military junta has been formally dissolved;
- Opposition parties are legal.

These are, however, essentially procedural changes. The most important question is, What impact have they had? It is very early days, and therefore difficult to tell, but enough time has passed to have a tentative first look.

CHANGES IN THE FIRST WEEKS OF THE NEW GOVERNMENT

So what has changed? At first glance, the answer would have to be, "Not much". At second glance, however, the answer is, "Actually, there have been some interesting changes", as discussed below.

Activity in the Legislatures

The legislatures were convened twelve weeks after the elections, during the transitional period when the State Peace and Development Council continued to hold state power. The first sessions ended on or before the day of power transfer, which means that the legislatures have so far not met under the post-SPDC dispensation in Myanmar. At the time of writing, it was not clear when the legislatures would next meet, but under the constitution the maximum period between sessions is twelve months.[1]

The first sessions of the legislatures did not last long: the upper and lower houses (Amyotha Hluttaw and Pyithu Hluttaw) each sat on fourteen days in total, the Union Assembly (Pyidaungsu Hluttaw, the combined upper and lower houses) on eighteen days, and the region and state legislatures on only eight days.[2] On the days that they did meet, many of the sittings were short. Some of the sittings of the Union Assembly, in particular, were extremely short, lasting only a few minutes, earning it the epithet "the fifteen-minute parliament" among some activists. The first tasks of the legislatures were to elect Speakers, administer oaths of office, and then to elect the president and vice-presidents. The subsequent very short sittings mostly dealt with legislative approval for nominations to key executive and judicial posts — in almost no cases were any objections raised, so there was no discussion. The later sessions of the national legislatures were much more substantive, and lasted considerably longer, usually for several hours. These were the sessions that dealt with questions and proposals.

Although the procedure for representatives to submit questions and proposals was somewhat cumbersome, those issues that were raised, and the ensuing debates, were very interesting. Most of the debates were reported in some detail in the state media, but these accounts were rather dry. The actual discussions were far more lively, with the Speakers (particularly the Speaker of the lower house, retired General

Shwe Mann) allowing rather open and free-flowing debate, including interruptions and requests for clarification. Some sensitive topics were covered, including:

- Land tenure rights for farmers, and the problem of land confiscation by the government;
- The need for assistance from the state in cases of natural disaster;
- The need for reasonably-priced communications (mobile phone SIM cards and Internet connections), and request for clarification of why a mobile phone connection in Myanmar is fifty times more costly than in neighbouring countries;
- The poor functioning of the censorship board;
- The need to increase pension rates for retired state employees;
- The status of compulsory military service legislation;[3]
- The problems caused by state restrictions on the movement of produce from one region to another;
- The difficulty of registering associations and other local organizations, and a lack of clarity in the procedures for doing so;
- The need to allow registration of labour unions, in line with the provisions of the constitution;
- Discrimination against ethnic minorities in civil service recruitment;
- The need for teaching of ethnic minority languages in schools in minority areas;
- The concern that there had been no national census since 1983;
- Issues related to the relocation of populations as a result of hydropower schemes;
- The possibility of the government declaring a ceasefire in Kayin State;
- The problem of illegal gambling;
- The question of whether amnesty would be granted to Khun Htun Oo and other Shan political prisoners;
- The question of whether citizenship ID cards would be granted to Muslim residents of northern Rakhine State who are currently denied citizenship and have only temporary ID cards;
- The need to increase the rates of agricultural credit;
- The need for lower taxes on the importation of vehicles;
- Concerns about private-sector monopolies and manipulation of prices;

- Concern about the lack of government assistance to ethnic minority areas, and what the government intended to do to bring peace to ethnic areas.

Some of these topics are highly sensitive, and it was not possible in the past for people to question the government openly on such matters. While not all of the answers by relevant ministers were particularly encouraging, the fact that these ministers had to appear before the legislatures to answer such questions is striking, and brings a new level of scrutiny to governance in Myanmar. In some cases the Speakers pushed ministers rather hard to answer difficult questions that the ministers were trying to avoid, and on occasion chastised them for failing to address legislators (including those from opposition parties) with due respect. Some of the replies contained interesting information (such as the confirmation that the recently-enacted military service legislation will only come into force if the president issues a specific notification to that effect, or the details of village relocations in connection with new hydro-power dams). Others led to immediate action from the executive. For example, following the question on the difficulty of registering associations and organizations, twenty-five local NGOs, whose applications were pending, suddenly had their registrations approved.

In total, the national legislatures (lower house, upper house and Union Assembly) discussed ninety-seven questions and forty-one proposals. A majority of these questions and proposals were submitted by opposition legislators — that is, those who are not Union Solidarity and Development Party (USDP) members or military appointees. This is probably not surprising. What *is* highly significant, however, is that the agreement of a majority of legislators must be obtained in order for proposals to be discussed in the legislature (no such agreement is required for discussion of questions). This implies that a large proportion of USDP and military legislators have voted in favour of debating proposals tabled by opposition legislators, including some that deal with rather sensitive issues.[4]

The legislatures have also established a number of standing committees to deal with specific areas of legislative work, including during the periods when the legislatures themselves are in recess. Given the current uncertainty as to how regularly, and for how long, the legislatures will be in session, these standing committees could have a particularly important role. Under the constitution, the lower and upper houses are each required to form four committees, as follows:

- Bills Committee (for assessing draft bills submitted to the legislature);
- Public Accounts Committee (for scrutinizing the government budget and reports of the auditor-general);
- Rights Committee (to deal with the powers, rights, and breach of duties by the legislature, its committees or individual legislators);
- Government's Guarantees, Pledges and Undertakings Vetting Committee (for monitoring the implementation of pledges given by the executive to the legislature).[5]

All of these committees contain some opposition party members (approximately one-third of the membership); the rest are USDP members. No military appointees are included in these committees. Two joint Union Assembly committees (the Bills Joint Committee and the Public Accounts Joint Committee) were also formed, in each case chaired by the Deputy Speaker of the Union Assembly, and comprised of seven members drawn from each of the corresponding lower house and upper house committees. Again, about one-third of members are opposition party representatives.

Significantly, the head of the ethnic opposition Rakhine Nationalities Development Party was appointed chairman of the upper house committee tasked with monitoring the government's implementation of its pledges (the Government's Guarantees, Pledges and Undertakings Vetting Committee). Thus, while power may remain in the hands of the USDP, opposition representatives are being given some substantive legislative responsibilities.

President Thein Sein's Agenda-setting Speeches

Upon taking up his position as president, Thein Sein gave three key policy speeches outlining the agenda for his five-year term: his inaugural speech to the Union Assembly on 30 March 2011,[6] his speech to members of the new government on 31 March, and his speech to the Central Committee for Progress of Border Areas and National Races on 23 April (all carried in full in the state print media).[7]

These speeches were remarkable in the Myanmar context, because the very idea of setting out a public policy agenda had been anathema in the last fifty years of rule-by-fiat and because they offered a rather frank — as well as rather accurate — assessment of many of the serious problems facing the country.

In particular, the president:

- stressed the need for national unity and ending ethnic conflict and its legacy (which he described as "the hell of untold miseries"), including the need to "convince the people from the border areas of the government's goodwill efforts for peace and stability and development";
- recognized that "there are so many individuals and unlawful organizations inside and outside the nation that do not accept the State's Seven Step Road Map and the Constitution", a striking departure from previous official rhetoric, and he undertook to work together with "good-hearted political forces" outside of the legislatures (by implication, Aung San Suu Kyi and her National League for Democracy);
- highlighted the importance of economic reform, to grow the economy and "improve the socio-economic status of the people", promising to pass necessary legislation to this effect;
- provided a detailed policy statement on the state of the economy and measures needed to improve it;
- undertook to "work in cooperation with international organizations including the UN, INGOs and NGOs", reversing the previous regime's moves to shun multilateral engagement;
- promised to tackle corruption "in cooperation with the people", and to focus on creating "good governance and clean government [which] must be transparent, accountable and consistent with the constitution and the existing laws";
- finally, and rather strikingly, announced in his 31 March speech that the government and its leaders would not take their allotted salary increases for the moment, in recognition of the fact that "there are still many people whose life is a battle against poverty, whose life is a hand-to-mouth existence, and many unemployed people".

The content of these speeches gave a very different tone to governance compared with the past. Indeed, an unusually frank editorial in the *New Light of Myanmar* on 9 July 2011 pointed out that "it is a landmark of many years that a head of state [says such things] in a speech".[8]

These speeches significantly raised expectations for change. However, in terms of action to implement this agenda, achievements over the first one hundred days were somewhat mixed.

Progress in Policy Implementation?

Concrete implementation of the agenda set out in the president's speeches was always going to be far more difficult than expressing the political will to carry it out. Even with strong political will, the new government faces a formidable set of challenges: serious, interrelated problems in many different sectors; lack of capacity in the bureaucracy, including lack of an evidence-based policy-making tradition and competencies; and the risk of spoilers who have vested interests in the *status quo ante* or who are simply flexing their muscles to demonstrate their continued influence.

In such a situation, it is perhaps understandable that Thein Sein initially chose to move ahead selectively on those issues that will, in his estimation, generate maximum domestic political capital: economic reforms, improving basic living standards, and increasing pensions. While it seemed that his focus on these immediate issues had come at the expense of steps to address significant political and human rights concerns, such as a major release of political prisoners[9] and an amnesty for those in exile, or efforts to promote political solutions to ethnic grievances, these more complex issues were tackled in subsequent presidential initiatives.

Indeed, the resumption of fighting with the Kachin Independence Organization and some other armed groups cast a dark shadow over the first one hundred days, and raised the prospect that, far from the "national unity and ending ethnic conflict" promised by the president, there is a real risk of war returning to the northern borderlands. At the time of writing tensions had eased somewhat, but fighting could easily flare again, and durable solutions appear to be as distant as ever. (For an analysis of the political situation in Kachin State, see Chapter 4 by Nicholas Farrelly in this publication.)

While many of the problems facing the country are intractable, it is clear that Thein Sein wished to generate significant political momentum early on, given the risks of his agenda being challenged by powerful opponents with vested interests. This has proved difficult, however, and the president faced considerable resistance in pushing through the first phase of economic reform measures, although ultimately he was successful. Some of these measures will have a big impact, including:

- A reduction in export tariffs. This was a lifeline to many enterprises that were facing enormous difficulties as a result of the recent significant appreciation of the kyat against the dollar. (A reduction to 5 per cent had been proposed, but ultimately the lowest level that could be agreed in cabinet was 7 per cent.)
- Large increases in pension rates as of July 2011. This will greatly improve the lives of some 840,000 pensioners and, indirectly, several million family members reliant on those pensions. Pensioners were previously facing great hardship, as the real value of their pensions had eroded over the years to the point where the pensions were essentially worthless.
- Attempts to rein in public sector spending. In particular, non-core construction projects in Naypyitaw have been suspended.
- Moves to streamline government services. This includes faster and more efficient issuance of national registration cards, passports, and various government licences.

For a population that has, understandably, a high level of political disengagement and cynicism after decades of governance failures, only tangible improvements in living standards will convince them that anything has changed. Moves such as the reduction in export tariffs and greater fiscal discipline will please the business community and boost the broader economy, and the pension increases will certainly improve the lot of a large number of retired public sector employees and their families, but much more fundamental reform will be required in order for the general population to feel a tangible impact. Some such measures are in the pipeline — and, encouragingly, the government has recently reached out to the IMF for its advice — but these are by nature not quick-fix steps.

- Poverty reduction. In a U-turn from previous public positions, the new government has recognized the seriousness of poverty in Myanmar, and has shown a willingness to address the issue. On 20–21 May 2011, the president personally presided over a high-level workshop at which very frank assessments of the situation were presented and bold policy proposals put forward. Approval has been granted for the establishment of an independent and non-political Myanmar Development Resource Institute to provide the necessary academic and technical inputs.

- Microfinance. Moves are under way to lift restrictions on the operation of microfinance schemes, which could have a significant impact on the availability of credit at reasonable rates — including, crucially, to farmers.
- Exchange rates. By mid-2011, there was already speculation that gradual steps would be taken to unify the various official and semi-official exchange rate schemes, although no decision has yet been taken. Such a step would greatly simplify business operations and allow much greater transparency in private and public sector finances, as well as reducing the scope for profiteering and corruption.

The institutional challenges to moving forward should not be under-estimated. Poor human capacity and a context of weak institutions are serious impediments. There is also clearly an element of bureaucratic inertia: many civil servants are so accustomed to working in the old ways that they feel threatened by change. Partly this is caution — in the past, one could get into serious trouble for taking the wrong decision, but almost never for taking no decision, and that culture persists; and partly it is that officials feel threatened by reform, because they are worried that they lack the technical capacity to implement changes that the political level may order.

More significantly, there will continue to be strong resistance to these reforms from powerful forces — because if the reforms are successful, significant political capital could accrue to the president, shifting the balance of power away from reactionary elements; and because some of these reforms will have a direct negative impact on vested interests. Thus, the success of the president's reform agenda may have less to do with political will than with harsh political realities.

CONCLUSION

What does this all mean? How should these initial steps be assessed? The most important thing to keep in mind is the question this chapter began with — What will political change look like in Myanmar, and will we recognize it when we see it? There are essentially two ways change can come to the country: revolution or evolution. All the indications are that evolution is much more likely, and probably preferable. Revolutions have a rather violent and unsuccessful history in Myanmar. Although gradual reform may not be popular in some quarters, we should be cognizant of the fact that the most likely alternative would be a return to the autocratic, repressive, and isolationist tendencies that have characterized previous periods. That remains a possibility, given the continued power of certain vested interests and reactionary hardliners, but the more momentum these reforms build up, the less likely it becomes.

After half a century of authoritarianism, the challenges facing the country are huge. This is a legacy Myanmar will take many years to recover from, even in the best of circumstances. Add to this that the country is hardly an island of vice in a sea of tranquillity; rather, it is surrounded by countries that are grappling with many of the same problems and difficulties. It would be unrealistic to expect a Western-style liberal democracy to emerge overnight.

I would argue that what we are witnessing at the time of writing is more or less what we should expect to see if Myanmar were indeed in the early stages of a transition away from authoritarian rule. It is too early yet to reach a definitive conclusion either about the trajectory of reform or about whether it is likely to succeed. In any major political reorientation, there are risks of failure, but it would certainly be premature at this time to draw the opposite conclusion. We should be cautious about adopting what I think is the almost universal perspective that one gets from the international media and from many observers — that nothing has changed.

Notes

1. This subsection draws on material presented in Richard Horsey, "The initial functioning of the Myanmar legislatures", Conflict Prevention and Peace Forum briefing paper, May 2011.
2. The Chin State legislature sat for an additional day to consider a (successful) challenge to the credentials of a ministerial appointee.
3. In this respect, it was clarified that the recently promulgated law on military service would only come into force if a notification to that effect was issued by the president (which has not yet happened). See New Light of Myanmar, 12 March 2011, p. 6.
4. For an interesting discussion of these issues, see Kyaw Kyaw, "Life Behind Parliament's Stonewalls", Democratic Voice of Burma, 4 April 2011 (also carried on New Mandala, 1 April 2011, as "Burma's Parliamentary System

Explained" <http://asiapacific.anu.edu.au/newmandala/2011/04/01/burmas-parliamentary-system-explained/> (accessed 21 May 2012)).

5. In addition, the upper house, lower house, and the Union Assembly each formed a committee for vetting legislative representatives, monitoring their attendance, and related issues.

6. For a detailed analysis of the inaugural speech, see "President Thein Sein's inaugural speech", Euro-Burma Office, Analysis Paper 2/2011.

7. This subsection, and the following, draw on material presented in Richard Horsey, "The first 100 days of the new Myanmar government", Conflict Prevention and Peace Forum briefing paper, July 2011.

8. Banya Aung, "Hopes formed over past 100 days", *New Light of Myanmar*, 9 July 2011, p. 6.

9. Approximately 112 political prisoners were included in the general amnesty of over 14,000 prisoners declared by the president in May 2011.

References

Banya Aung. "Hopes formed over past 100 days". *New Light of Myanmar*, 9 July 2011, p. 6.

Euro-Burma Office. "President Thein Sein's inaugural speech". Analysis Paper 2/2011. Euro-Burma Office, Brussels, 2011.

Horsey, Richard. "Who's Who in the new Myanmar government." Conflict Prevention and Peace Forum Briefing Paper. Social Science Research Council, New York, April 2011*a*.

———. "The initial functioning of the Myanmar legislatures". Conflict Prevention and Peace Forum Briefing Paper. Social Science Research Council, New York, May 2011*b*.

———. "The first 100 days of the new Myanmar government". Conflict Prevention and Peace Forum Briefing Paper. Social Science Research Council, New York, July 2011*c*.

International Crisis Group. "Myanmar's Post-election Landscape". Asia Briefing No. 118. International Crisis Group, Brussels, March 2011.

Kyaw Kyaw. "Life Behind Parliament's Stonewalls". *Democratic Voice of Burma*, 4 April 2011 (also on *New Mandala*, 1 April 2011, as "Burma's Parliamentary System Explained" <http://asiapacific.anu.edu.au/newmandala/2011/04/01/burmas-parliamentary-system-explained/>. (Accessed 21 May 2012).

Transnational Institute. "Burma's New Government: Prospects for Governance and Peace in Ethnic States". Burma Policy Briefing No. 6. Transnational Institute, Amsterdam, May 2011*a*.

———. "Conflict or Peace? Ethnic Unrest Intensifies in Burma". Burma Policy Briefing No. 7. Transnational Institute, Amsterdam, June 2011*b*.

4

CEASING CEASEFIRE?
Kachin Politics Beyond
the Stalemates

Nicholas Farrelly

WAR AND ITS ALTERNATIVES

Myanmar carries the tragic distinction of hosting the world's longest-running civil wars. These conflicts — some of which commenced almost immediately after the Second World War — have frustrated attempts to bring about lasting and peaceful resolutions.[1] The civil wars colour relations between the country's ethnic minorities, who make up around one-third of the population, and the ethnic Burmans who are the majority. Inter-ethnic battles have seen countless casualties as all sides struggle to defend competing visions of pride, power, and position. But periods of relative stability, without regular violence, have also shaped the political landscape. For the past two decades, Burma's unresolved wars have been characterized, in large part, by ceasefire agreements that discouraged direct hostility and confrontation. The 1988 disintegration of the Communist Party of Burma generated a suite of militia groups, often labelled with the ethnicity of their respective leaderships, that the world came to know through the prism of their ceasefires with the Myanmar government.

Ceasefires with former Communist troops in the Shan State were followed by agreements with other ethnic militias in Kachin, Karen, and Mon areas that offered the government a modicum of nationwide "peace" to bolster plans for national "development".

A foundational characteristic of Burma's State Peace and Development Council period (1996–2010) was the preponderance of these agreements and the economic, political, and cultural responses that followed. In 2007, Martin Smith, a long-time analyst of ethnic politics in Burma, suggested that "[b]y any international standards, the achievement of ceasefires with so many insurgent groups, in one of the most conflict-torn countries in Asia, has to date been unexpectedly smooth and stable" (Smith 2006, p. 53). He argued that the "simplicity" of the agreements, the general concessions that accompanied most deals, and the prospect of almost immediate and unprecedented economic development, meant the ceasefires "quickly found popular support". Some ceasefire group leaders fully embraced economic opportunities under the ceasefire stalemates. They built lavish residences, sent their children to posh schools and cultivated commercial relationships well beyond their immediate mountain strongholds.

The ceasefires were designed by Myanmar government strategists to present strong disincentives for any ethnic leaders considering a return to hostilities. According to another long-time observer of ethnic politics, Ashley South, "[t]he regime's intention [was] said to be to promote disillusion with, and provoke disputes within, ethno-nationalist communities, causing armed organisations to lose support" (South 2008, p. 156). Perhaps as an unintended consequence of this effort, the ceasefires failed to be translated into final political settlements. In many ceasefire areas the resentments that originally motivated armed struggle never truly faded and the potential for the re-ignition of conflicts remained. For its part the Myanmar military leadership habitually avoided making concessions to support chances for lasting peace. In the final years of the State Peace and Development Council period, there was widespread disquiet about Myanmar government policies in ceasefire areas. The two years leading up to the November 2010 election were especially tense. Ceasefire groups were pressured to transform into what are known as Border Guard Forces: these are subordinate militias under the command of Myanmar military officers.

Some ceasefire groups such as the Kachin Independence Army/ Kachin Independence Organization (KIA/KIO) — a 10,000-strong force garrisoned across what they claim as "Kachinland" in northern Burma — rejected the government's directives. Throughout the ceasefire period, negotiations over self-determination in Kachin areas caused tension in the relationship between the government and Kachin leaders. The very notion of a "Kachinland" (which the Kachin call "*Jinghpaw Mungdan*") troubles the Myanmar authorities. The inability of the Kachin and the Myanmar government to reach final agreement meant that the 2010 election ended up disappointing those Kachin leaders who had been seeking a more broadly inclusive and participatory political system. In particular, the Kachin State Progressive Party (KSPP), founded by leading political figures associated with the KIA/KIO, was barred from running its candidates in the election. Instead, Kachin seats in the new legislatures were mainly captured by politicians affiliated with the government-backed Union Solidarity and Development Party.

Since the 2010 election, events in Kachin areas have moved very quickly. The KIA/KIO ceasefire, which had been in place since 24 February 1994, broke down on 9 June 2011.

It is under these new conditions that this chapter offers a preliminary analysis of post-ceasefire Kachin politics in the context of longer-term historical, social, and political dynamics in Burma's ethnic minority areas. It begins, first, by clarifying the context of the KIA/KIO ceasefire with the Myanmar government. Second, it describes some of the symbolic and cultural dimensions of ceasefire politics in Kachin State before the 2011 resumption of hostilities. This discussion helps to situate the re-ignition of the KIA war with respect to recent negotiations of political, cultural, and economic power. While much attention must necessarily focus on the politics of war and conflict, we must not forget that there was a long period when cultures of peaceful coexistence were trialled in Kachin areas. Third, this chapter describes efforts by the Myanmar government to negotiate with the KIA/KIO, especially during the election period of 2010 and then into the tense months that followed. The chapter concludes by examining the new conditions of conflict and exploring the difficulties that the Kachin and Myanmar leaderships face. The new conflict in this region means we may need to thoroughly reconsider inherited perspectives about the ceasefires that brought a pause in Burma's long-running civil wars.

KACHIN CEASEFIRES IN CONTEXT

From 1994 to 2011 the ceasefire between the KIA/KIO and the Myanmar government was integral to the security of northern Burma. It followed earlier ceasefire agreements between the government and the two other large Kachin militia groups — the New Democratic Army–Kachin (NDA–K, which agreed a ceasefire in 1989) and the Kachin Defense Army (KDA, 1991). Compared to the other Kachin militias, the KIA is a much more formidable political and military force. Its troops inherit a fifty-one-year-old movement that was first imagined, back in 1961, as the catalyst for an independent Kachin nation-state.[2] As geo-political conditions changed, and as more moderate perspectives gained authority, this political claim was widely, although never universally, re-conceived in terms of ethnic self-determination and autonomy in a democratic, federal union. Nowadays the KIA controls a set of strategic bases along the Sino-Burmese border and elsewhere in the Kachin and Shan States, although in 2011 it lost some of its key positions after heavy government bombardment. It has also created economic opportunities which mean that during the tense years at the end of the ceasefire period it managed to arm and train a new generation of Kachin fighters.

The conflict that re-ignited in 2011 will, naturally enough, test the more moderate and conciliatory political positions developed during the ceasefire period. During the KIA ceasefire years, collaboration with the Myanmar government became socially acceptable among the Kachin elite. It is unclear whether the pan-ethnic relationships developed during the ceasefire, many of which saw tremendous wealth consolidated in Kachin hands, will survive the new hostilities. The re-ignited war has already seen an unknown number of casualties, and there are impossible-to-verify reports of hundreds, even thousands, of deaths. According to KIO statements, Kachin ambushes have led to the deaths of many Myanmar government troops, including a number of officers. Roving KIA squads have also attacked bridges, roads, railways, and ships used by the Myanmar government forces for moving men and materiel. In response to the violence and tension, much ordinary business has ground to a halt; it is likely that any escalation of the conflict will see further depopulation of the major towns in northern Burma. Distrust between ethnic Burmese and ethnic Kachin in the region is set to increase for as long as the new war continues.

This re-ignited conflict presents immediate analytical difficulties, most of all because details from Kachin State emerge only gradually and because the future direction of hostilities and negotiations is unpredictable. It is too early to offer a final diagnosis of the new war's origins or to prognosticate on its possible outcomes, but the fact remains that this new war is re-shaping how we understand ethnic politics, not only in Kachin State but across Burma more generally. The prospect arises that the entire analytical architecture built to explain the ceasefires during the State Peace and Development Council period will no longer be relevant.

However, in order to better understand the conditions in the Kachin State in this situation of new conflict, it is particularly important to pay attention to the political and social changes that occurred under the ceasefires. Kachin areas are wealthier and far better connected, nationally and internationally, than ever before. Improved transportation links, and far more frequent opportunities for travel, have exposed many Kachin to a wide range of external cultural, political, and economic influences. Many Kachin have spent the ceasefire years exploring their prospects in other parts of Myanmar. Countless numbers work and study in cities like Yangon and Mandalay where they speak the Burmese language that was so strongly resisted by earlier generations of Kachin. Others have moved abroad, to Thailand, China, and India, to Malaysia and Singapore, and to countries like Britain, the United States, and Australia. This Kachin diaspora influences ethnic self-imagination in important ways, and serves to re-shape earlier Kachin nationalism for the conditions of a globalized and inter-connected world. At the same time the main pillars of Kachin identity — passionate defence of language and culture, supported by a widely-held Christian faith — motivate many to proclaim deep connections to the nationalist cause. The Kachin, and the KIA/KIO, cannot be dismissed as unsophisticated mountain dwellers, isolated from international politics and social transformations. They are, instead, an integral part of the complex social and political fabric of contemporary mainland Southeast Asia.

SYMBOLIC POLITICS UNDER THE KACHIN CEASEFIRES

It follows that the politics of the Kachin ceasefire and post-ceasefire periods present subtleties that require careful consideration. The symbolic levels of ceasefire and post-ceasefire politics are especially worth our attention. During the ceasefire period the most important annual celebration of the region's political status occurred in Myitkyina, the Kachin State capital, on 10 January each year. This is Kachin State Day, which marks the Saturday in 1948, only six days after Burma's independence, when the Kachin State was formally declared. The celebration was popularized during the years of ceasefire by a week-long Manau festival (*Manau Poi*) that brought together government and ethnic leaders, not to mention tens of thousands of people from across the Kachin and Shan States, as well as from further afield. That festival marked the symbolic apex of Kachin solidarity, punctuated by large-scale communal dances, feasting, and public activities of many other kinds.[3] It became an opportunity for the Kachin to perform the largest Manau dance of the year and to welcome visitors to the region. Kachin State Day celebrations showcased political, commercial, cultural, and religious interests from across the spectrum of Kachin society, and from many of Burma's other ethnic groups.[4]

While they should not be considered uncontested representations of Kachin identity and pride, Manau festivals did become the key public events for a conglomeration of ethnicities in northern Burma. Importantly, Manau festivals are now also held by "Kachin" groups in China and India, and by Kachin refugees who have found themselves in Thailand, the United States, or other countries. Notwithstanding this impressive proliferation of Manau festivals, the largest festival, the one held in Myitkyina on Kachin State Day, received special attention from the Myanmar military leadership *as well as* from the Kachin. During the ceasefire period, it became an annual opportunity for presenting a relatively harmonious and inclusive impression of ceasefire politics. While the event was regularly attended by other ethnic armies, including the NDA–K, KDA and the Lasang Awng Wa (Ceasefire) Group, it was the KIA troops that the people of Myitkyina would come to see.

The Manau festival grew to serve a number of related purposes. First, the Myanmar military leadership used the event to emphasize its dominant role under the KIA/KIO ceasefire. The Northern Commander of the Myanmar army, always a Brigadier-General or a Major-General, would offer a speech marking the occasion and participate in the most prestigious Manau dance. The presence of such a senior government figure among so many Kachin ensured tight security precautions. At the Manau festivals held during the KIA ceasefire period, the large contingent of bodyguards who travel with the Northern Commander were always augmented by hundreds of other military, police, paramilitary, and civilian security officials.[5] Second, the Manau was an opportunity for commercial and political relationships to improve in a non-confrontational setting. Prominent organizers of the Manau, often drawn from the class of Kachin known as *Sutdu* (tycoons), used the event for their own personal gain. Among the many layers of sociality at a Manau, the elite level negotiations were notable. Third, until 2011 the Manau provided an opportunity for the KIA/KIO and other Kachin political organizations to present themselves to a wider public. During the war with the government from 1962–1994, the KIA were rarely welcome in Myitkyina. The ceasefire period saw opportunities for re-familiarization with the Kachin State capital and its people.

These inter-related purposes for Kachin State Day Manau celebrations were given an abrupt shake-up for the 2011 iteration. On 10 January 2011 the people of northern Burma were invited to Myitkyina to celebrate the 63rd anniversary of Kachin State Day. However, the 2011 event reflected the striking changes in the local political climate. Compared to previous years, very few Kachin attended the Manau in 2011. Thinner-than-usual lines of dancers were matched by smaller crowds. To bolster the numbers — particularly for some of the main performances of "Kachin" solidarity — contingents from Myanmar government agencies and students from local educational institutions filled the ranks. Parts of the programme that previously drew tens of thousands of spectators saw only hundreds gather to watch. The overt and confident presence of troops from the Myanmar Army's Northern Command was not matched, as it had been in previous years, by large numbers from the Kachin side. The proud, uniformed, massed delegations of KIA personnel were notable by their absence.

In their stead, Kachin State Day 2011 was dominated by background chatter — whispers of dissatisfaction, talk of plots to sideline the real owners of the Kachin celebration, and disquiet about the behaviour of the Northern Commander and his troops. For the first time in my experience of life in northern Burma, I heard anxious expectations that war was, once again, right around the corner. Only weeks later, in early February, there was a brief period of greatly heightened tension. On a road outside Bhamo in southeastern Kachin State, a KIA squad was confronted with an apparent incursion by a Myanmar military patrol. In that engagement six Burmese soldiers were injured and one, their Battalion Commander, Lieutenant Colonel Yin Htwe, was killed. The death of the officer led to a period of sharp tension as the two sides traded fragments of information about exactly who deserved blame. The Northern Commander, Brigadier General Zeyar Aung, quickly issued a statement that he had not ordered the incursion. This released some pressure, but it did not mean the Myanmar authorities took a backwards step. Extra controls along the crucial route between Myitkyina and the Kachin Independence Army headquarters at Laiza were one immediate outcome.

After the tension of the 2011 Kachin State Day Manau, the political situation in Kachin State has changed, with quick movement through a period of re-fortification and military build-up, and now war has returned. After years off the radar, the political situation in Kachin State once again carries weighty implications for the nation. This is a test for the relatively new Myanmar government led by President Thein Sein and a challenge for ethnic Kachin politicians, commercial leaders, and military commanders. All are confronted with real risks as they seek to find a path towards a new configuration of post-ceasefire politics under the Myanmar government's new parliamentary system.

THE 2010 ELECTION AND MYANMAR GOVERNMENT NEGOTIATIONS

Once the former State Peace and Development Council headed by Senior General Than Shwe had launched the new parliamentary system, the need to manage the remaining ceasefire armies became ever more pressing. One of the government's initial hopes may have been to dissolve all other armed forces on Myanmar soil before the 2010 election. Indeed, the 2008 Constitution is quite explicit on this point. It states that "[t]he Defence Services [the *Tatmadaw*] is the sole patriotic defence force which is strong, competent and modern." For a country that has seen dozens of armed groups emerge under a bewildering range of ethnic and ideological banners, this is a statement of significant, and dangerous, intent. It is buttressed by the suggestion that all citizens can be called on for military service. In Chapter 8 of the 2008 Constitution [para. 386], "every citizen" is described as having "the duty to undergo military training in accord with the provisions of the law and to serve in the Armed Forces to defend the Union".

Since introducing this consolidated approach to national security, the Myanmar authorities have chalked up few victories in their negotiations with ethnic ceasefire armies. Despite sustained efforts to negotiate with all of the ceasefire groups — most notably the United Wa State Army, Shan State Army–North, New Mon State Party and the KIA — they failed to broker final peace agreements. This has led the government to take a more confrontational approach. In the Kachin State, increasing the pressure has proved to be the strategy of choice — a strategy that is supposed to change the complex set of political, economic, and cultural interests that have evolved under the Kachin ceasefires. The Kachin State Progressive

Party, which was designed by KIA/KIO leaders to contest the 2010 election, has been one prominent victim. Attempts to register the party failed as Myanmar government officials, frustrated by their failure to re-make the KIA as a Border Guard Force subordinate to central government command, sought to remove competitive threats from the local political landscape. Marginalizing the main Kachin ceasefire army, and seeking to imply its de-legitimization under the new constitution, held obvious appeal for government negotiators who had failed to generate a KIA surrender. Kachin resistance to government plans has been a constant headache throughout the recent nationwide constitutional transition.

The election of November 2010 gave the clearest indication of government priorities across the country. In essence, the election was designed so that the State Peace and Development Council could regenerate in a civilianized form, endorsed by a public process, and thus gain the potential for greater international acceptance. In the Kachin State, the election saw government-aligned parties win majorities at the National Assembly, People's Assembly and Regional Assembly levels. In the National Assembly, the only notable result for Kachin candidates was that former NDA–K chairman, Zahkung Ting Ying, won a seat as an independent (see Tables 4.1, 4.1A). In the People's Assembly, the dominance of the Union Solidarity and Development Party was even more marked (see Tables 4.2, 4.2A).

TABLE 4.1
Kachin State Representatives Elected to the National Assembly
November 2010

Name	Party
U Za Khon Tien Ring	Independent
U Gam Hsai	National Unity Party
U Brangshaung	National Unity Party
U J Yaw Wu	National Unity Party
U Sai Mya Maung	Shan Nationalities Democratic Party
U Khat Htein Nan	Unity and Democracy Party of Kachin State
U Sai Tin Aung	USDP
U Pe Thaung	USDP
U San Pyae	USDP
U Mya Ohn	USDP
U Tun Lwin	USDP
U San Tun	USDP

Source: Data from <http://www.mizzima.com/candidates/election-results-a-k.html>.

TABLE 4.1A
Summary for National Assembly

Independent	National Unity Party	Shan Nationalities Democratic Party	Unity and Democracy Party of Kachin State	USDP
1	3	1	1	6

TABLE 4.2
Kachin State Representatives Elected to the People's Assembly
November 2010

Name	Party
U N Phon Hsan (a) U N Htu Phon Hsan	National Unity Party
U Yein Borm	National Unity Party
U Zaw Tun	Shan Nationalities Democratic Party
Daw Dwe Bu	Unity and Democracy Party of Kachin State
U Zong Taint	USDP
U Zaung Khong	USDP
U Yaw D Dwe	USDP
U Gyee Phon Hsarl	USDP
U Khamai Mon Twam (a) U Khamai Tan	USDP
U C Khan Ram	USDP
U Thein Zaw	USDP
U Myo Swe	USDP
U Kyaw Soe Lay	USDP
U Phone Swe	USDP
U Ohn Myint	USDP
U Lun Maung	USDP
U Tun Thein (a) U Tun Tun	USDP
U Win Naing (a) U Phyu	USDP

Source: Data from <http://www.mizzima.com/candidates/election-results-a-k.html>.

TABLE 4.2A
Summary for People's Assembly

Independent	National Unity Party	Shan Nationalities Democratic Party	Unity and Democracy Party of Kachin State	USDP
0	2	1	1	14

Among other important officials, a former Northern Commander of the Myanmar army won a seat. Government-aligned parties also performed very well in Kachin State's regional assembly (*Pyi-ne Hluttaw*), one of fourteen around the country (see Tables 4.3, 4.3A). The Unity and Democracy Party of Kachin State, the only one with even a mild Kachin nationalist ideology, won only four seats across the three different parliaments. This was a very modest success.

TABLE 4.3
Kachin State Representatives Elected to the State Assembly
November 2010

Name	Party	Name	Party
U Yaw Na	Independent	U B Htaw Zaung	USDP
U Zaung Khong	National Unity Party	U Ra Wam Jon	USDP
U Ah Yi	National Unity Party	U Chan Tan Khin	USDP
U Htein Maung Tu	National Unity Party	U Ma Bu Da Gon	USDP
U Khin Lay Phon	National Unity Party	U Deng Khan Dawi	USDP
U Pa (a) U Khin Maung Shwe	National Unity Party	U Gwam Ring Dee	USDP
U Kaman Du Naw	National Unity Party	U Ah Hsi	USDP
U Mya Aung	National Unity Party	U Khin Maung Tun	USDP
U Htaw Lwan	National Unity Party	Daw Baukgyar	USDP
U Kyaw Swe	National Unity Party	U La John Ngan Hsai	USDP
U Tun Shein	National Unity Party	U Kwam Hsaung Hsam Ong	USDP
U Hsut Naung	National Unity Party	U Nyunt Aung	USDP
U Li Paw Ye	Shan Nationalities Democratic Party	U Nyi Lay	USDP
Daw Khin Pyone Yi	Shan Nationalities Democratic Party	U Soe Nwe	USDP
U Myo Aung	Shan Nationalities Democratic Party	U Kyaw Myint	USDP
U Sai Maung Shwe	Shan Nationalities Democratic Party	U An Fraung Gam	USDP
U Za Khon Yein Hsaung	Unity and Democracy	U Sai Myint Kyaw	USDP
U Alay Par	Unity and Democracy Party of Kachin State	U Tun Kyaing	USDP
		U Aung Naing	USDP
		U Pho Pa Kywe	USDP

Source: Data from <http://www.mizzima.com/candidates/election-results-a-k.html>.

TABLE 4.3A
Summary for State Assembly

Independent	National Unity Party	Shan Nationalities Democratic Party	Unity and Democracy Party of Kachin State	USDP
1	11	4	2	20

Now that the war between the government and the KIA has re-ignited, it is worth considering a question that has preoccupied many in the Kachin State — What would have happened if the Kachin State Progressive Party, headed by Dr Tu Ja, a former senior member of the KIO, had been allowed to run its candidates? The risk for the Union Solidarity and Development Party, and for others that ended up winning seats in the 2010 poll, was that many Kachin voters would have voted for KSPP candidates with an understanding that they represented the Kachin nationalism of the KIA/ KIO. Instead, there were few candidates in the election who explicitly spoke to the Kachin political demands that have motivated so much resistance over so many decades. The image that we are left with is one where much of the political space in the Kachin State has been starkly monopolized by the Myanmar military authorities, to the exclusion of almost all other voices. The Kachin State Hluttaw, which met for the first time from 28 June to 1 July 2011, is dominated by USDP representatives. When new ministers were to be decided, the government mouthpiece, the *New Light of Myanmar*, reported that "[t]he nomination was approved with one voice" (*NLM* 2011c).

KACHIN WAR IN 2011

The new war commenced on 9 June 2011, when a hydro-electricity development along the Sino-Burmese border, funded by Chinese investors, became the flashpoint for fresh hostilities. Myanmar government forces provoked a violent response from the KIA troops in the area. That led to the expansion of hostilities to areas near KIA-controlled territories in parts of Shan and Kachin States. Myanmar troops lobbed artillery shells into key KIA bases, while Kachin troops roamed throughout Kachin State attacking strategic targets, including in Myitkyina, the capital and home of the Kachin State Day Manau festivals and symbolic heart of ceasefire politics. Bridges and railways were bombed, and the Myanmar government was forced to seek alternative routes for bringing men and materiel to the fight. By the end of June there had been fighting all across northern Burma, with the KIA claiming dozens of Myanmar soldiers killed. In some cases senior officers appear to have been killed (such as a lieutenant colonel killed in July 2011).

Life in Myitkyina is now harder than before. Many families have prepared to leave. Some tens of thousands of refugees have already fled to KIA-controlled areas along the border. They are being supported by local non-government organizations and church groups, but reportedly receive very little international assistance.

One challenge for the Myanmar government is that the level of support for the KIA remains relatively high among the Kachin people, even in government strongholds such as Myitkyina. The KIA has not struggled to attract recruits. Ashley South points out that "[d]espite the alienation of sections of Kachin youth ... the KIO has still been able to attract fairly large numbers of young people to the nationalist cause" (South 2008, p. 159). From what I saw during my recent research trip to Kachin State, there are many examples that bear out the conclusion that the KIA is the most popular fighting force in northern Burma, and, one might speculate, perhaps in the country as a whole. As such, a long campaign against the KIA is likely to prove arduous for the Myanmar government. The government is faced not only with a well-disciplined and motivated fighting force, but also with the challenge of pursuing a war among a population that resents their presence. Violence against Kachin townspeople and villagers is likely to generate even more significant challenges, as it may produce the sort of underground resistance that could completely undermine the security of northern Burma. Attacks on economic infrastructure would likely follow, and there is no reason to expect the KIA would feel constrained to attack only the closest targets.

With conflict ongoing, it will be some time before there is an accurate tally of the political and military costs of the new war, and the apportioning of blame will continue for years to come. Accusations about who started the war have already been traded. In response, the KIA Information Office declared that: "[i]t is totally false propaganda published by the government saying the 'KIA started the war'".[6] The first Myanmar government statement after the re-ignition of hostilities with the KIA noted:

Concerning national reconsolidation, there are still personalities and organizations at home and abroad and underground organizations that are unwilling to acknowledge the seven-step Road Map [to democracy] and the constitution. Nevertheless, they should bear in mind that they are also Myanmar and should hold the concept that Myanmar is their motherland and the incumbent government is their own government constituted with own national races at different levels. (*NLM* 2011*a*).

According to the *New Light of Myanmar*, the "KIA is committing mine explosions on motor roads, railroads and bridges for killing and wounding the people in Kachin State due to the fact that the Tatmadaw opened limited fires for the sake of project and public security" (*NLM* 2011*d*).

Such statements have made the negotiation of a new truce difficult, with fresh animosities between the warring sides compounding their historical mistrust. Efforts to generate a comprehensive ceasefire commenced soon after the outbreak of new hostilities. These efforts faltered, however, and while both sides committed publicly to ongoing discussions, the KIA has been wary of government promises. Negotiations have continued, sporadically, with no sign of an early resolution. Ambiguities about the command of Myanmar troops in northern Burma have been especially difficult for the KIA to deal with; to maintain a strong negotiating position they have continued to call for nationwide discussions involving all ethnic groups. In December 2011 there was a revitalized government effort to launch peace talks with a new committee formed for that purpose under Railways Minister Aung Min. Aung Min has also been active in other ceasefire negotiations, most notably in the tentative January 2012 deal with the Karen National Union (KNU 2012).

In this uncertain context, one clear issue for Kachin forces is that the support they may once have enjoyed from across the border in China is no longer guaranteed. Instead, there is a strategic ambivalence on the part of Chinese authorities about exactly what style of political and social compact they are prepared to support in borderland areas. On 17 June 2011 the Chinese Ambassador to Myanmar, Mr Li Junhua, called on Union Minister for Foreign Affairs, U Wunna Maung Lwin. According to the Myanmar government's official media, "[t]hey frankly discussed bilateral relations and cooperation" (*NLM* 2011*b*). For the Chinese, the overarching priority is the stability and relative freedom of commerce and trade that benefited them so much during the ceasefire period.

MISMANAGING ETHNIC POLITICS

For the new Myanmar government, and its civilian leadership, a crisis in northern Burma has proven an inauspicious and awkward beginning to the new electoral system. Kachin interests are hardly in concert, but now that war has returned there is every chance that the bulk of popular sentiment in northern Burma will remain with the KIA/KIO. Batches of new recruits take its reported strength to around 10,000 uniformed personnel. Some of these are not yet deployable in combat roles, but there are still many thousands of Kachin fighters, some of whom are veterans of earlier periods of conflict, who have been mobilized for the contingency. There are also unknown numbers of KIA personnel who live and work in civilian roles across Kachin State. It would be unduly dramatic to call these people "covert operatives", mostly because they tend to be well known by local Kachin and probably also by the Myanmar authorities, but they need to be considered in any escalation scenario. Attacks by Kachin fighters in urban centres in 2011 and again in 2012, may, in some cases, be linked back to such networks.

On the KIA side, the leadership's inability to broker a final peace agreement during the ceasefire period ensures they will continue to face difficult choices. Depending on how long it lasts, the renewed conflict will see significant political, social, and economic ramifications, with the potential for large-scale dislocation and hardship. Kachin State's main towns such as Myitkyina and Bhamo, but also Putao and Hpakant, are now intimately tied to the national economy. It is only in a small number of Sino-Burmese border outposts that economic ties to China are more significant. The new war with the Myanmar government impacts the potential for further wealth creation among the entrepreneurial classes of the main towns, and a further retreat to highland forts would likely see the Kachin, especially fighting age men and women, deserting the economic hubs.

At this awkward time, there are also the political realities of the other Kachin ceasefire and militia organizations to consider.

New Democratic Army–Kachin

The largest of these ceasefire groups is the former NDA–K. In November 2009 it became a Border Guard Force. Its soldiers wear uniforms that subtly recognize their history, but now also carry the new flag of the Union of Myanmar. They are stuck, somewhat uncomfortably, between their Communist and Kachin nationalist roots, and a future where they will be expected to work closely with Myanmar authorities. Day-to-day command issues have already led to reported disquiet among rank-and-file members of this new organization. Some members of the Border Guard Force have been mobilized to take on the KIA in the new war, but there are early indications that some are unwilling to fight their Kachin "brothers". The leadership of the Border Guard Force will need to recognize these divided loyalties and manage the sentiments that see so many Kachin unwilling to work against the KIA. Under these conditions, tensions between the former NDA–K and the KIA are also likely to increase.

Kachin Defence Army

The KDA, formed from the old KIA 4th Brigade in the northern Shan State, is also relevant to this discussion. Their proximity to the potential flashpoint in United Wa State Army and Shan State Army–North ceasefire areas determines some of their calculations. Their fear must be that they could be annihilated by the government if they are left without support from other ethnic armies. Compared to the KIA they are a very modest fighting force. However, their leaders may opt to join an ethnic alliance to protect their interests against Myanmar government attack; they may also seek a path of least resistance by allying closely with government priorities.

Lasang Awng Wa Group

The other notable Kachin group is the one that coalesced around former KIA intelligence chief Lasang Awng Wa. His group's co-option as a Border Guard Force means that the KIA alone fills a void for those Kachin hoping to see the emergence of alternative political structures. It is unclear exactly where Lasang Awng Wa and his troops will sit in any reformulated, post-ceasefire Kachin political structure. The indications, however, are that they will be permanently absorbed into Myanmar government security arrangements.

THE CEASEFIRE ERA AND BEYOND

It is fair to surmise that the new war in the Kachin State signals the abrupt end of the ceasefire era, but does it mean a return to the pattern of conflict that shaped Burma's political and social terrain before the State Peace and Development Council sought to maintain the nationwide ceasefire system? There are reasons to expect different outcomes.

First of all, the Chinese government has shown no immediate appetite for ending the new Kachin war. The many ethnic militias that enjoy resupply from the Chinese side of the border could be strangled by a cross-border blockade. Aware of their power in this situation, the Chinese authorities have not, however, opted for such intervention. Instead they have so far only called for restraint. The ceasefires ensured that development in the country's border areas could proceed without the threat of sabotage or disruption. The Chinese government has, in particular, worked hard to guarantee political stability in many areas where its economic or security interests are at stake. In this context the Myanmar government's decision, in September 2011, to suspend the Chinese-funded Myitsone dam project in Kachin State received much attention. However, it is unclear whether that decision indicates any substantive or permanent change in the political economy, and international relations, of northern Burma.

Second, the Myanmar government faces much broader challenges. For the newly-elected, quasi-civilian regime of President Thein Sein, the risk is that new concessions to one ethnic group, such as the Kachin, could shatter any overarching sense of united destiny and obliterate the foundations of the national reconciliation project. The dilemma now facing the government is that, so soon after the 2010 election, the portfolio of ceasefire agreements inherited from the State Peace and Development Council period has begun to unravel. This is intensely problematic, not only because new wars are expensive in terms of both blood and treasure, but also because the KIA and others will now seek to push for generous terms if new ceasefires are to be agreed. Such terms were never on the negotiating table during the years of ceasefire.

Third, after largely disavowing the potential for secession from the Union, most Kachin nationalists, whether KIA sympathizers or not, have been inclined to work towards a federal structure which would provide them with significant autonomy. The goal, in their minds, was for a level of self-government that could offer security and prosperity, while also safeguarding their cultural and civil rights. This more moderate political position is not the only attitude expressed in Kachin political discussions. The new war is likely to embolden those Kachin nationalists who rejected the premise of the KIA ceasefire and who quietly hoped that the nationalism enunciated by the KIA back in 1961 could, once again, be harnessed to a broad-based political movement. The time for a breakthrough with the Myanmar government that sees satisfaction on all sides appears to have passed, and we are now confronted by the lingering tensions of a dispute about self-determination that has never been satisfactorily resolved. On all sides, there is a residue of resentment, ill-feeling, and fear, now joined by the prospect of even more comprehensive hostilities.

That prospect appears to be diminishing now that Aung San Suu Kyi and other National League for Democracy members have been elected to parliament and new truces are being agreed around the country. When this chapter was finalized, there was still no new ceasefire agreement between the Kachin Independence Army and the government. However, if President Thein Sein and his advisors can negotiate such a deal, then Burma will be moving into uncharted territory: a chance for comprehensive truces with ethnic minority armies. The new government probably still fears a future where ethnic Kachin, Wa, Shan, Karen, and Mon forces, not to mention a number of other ethnic and political movements, coalesce their anti-government agendas into a single fight. With so much now to lose in their transition process, they will hope to avoid that at almost any cost.

For decades, the dream for ethnic nationalists has been a fight where they are all talking together, and working together, in a networked fashion. Many continue to labour in the hope that a united front — a grand coalition of democratic and ethnic forces — can finally topple the government and dismember the military high command. This seems less likely by the day. However, the potency of such feelings is still at times on display. Even during the government-sponsored celebration of the Kachin State Day Manau in 2011 there was palpable dissent. At one moment, while the Northern Command sought to dominate festival proceedings, the author saw a young Kachin nationalist dancing provocatively, with crossed KIA swords, just out of sight of the Myanmar authorities. On that day he took his political statement right to the heart of government-controlled Kachin State. Now, the potency of such Kachin nationalism is being tested, and re-shaped, in the furnace of the new war and the post-ceasefire politics that will follow.

Notes

1. The war between the Karen National Union and Burma's central government commenced in 1949. At the time of finalizing this chapter, there is a very tentative ceasefire agreement.
2. The Kachin Independence Army was formed on 5 February 1961 in the northern Shan State. That "revolutionary" day is still commemorated each year with *Rawt Malan Poi* events.
3. Descriptions of contemporary Manau festivals are contained in my earlier work: Nicholas Farrelly, "Spatial control and symbolic politics in the borderlands of China, India and Burma", D.Phil thesis, University of Oxford, 2010. Mandy Sadan (2005) provides an important historical depth to analysis of Manau festivals in her own doctoral dissertation.
4. I attended Manau festivals in Burma, China, and India in the years 2007–2011. The two Kachin State Day Manau festivals discussed in detail in this chapter were attended in 2008 and 2011. There was no Kachin State Day Manau in 2012.
5. In 2011, commemorations of the 1985 killing of the government's Northern Commander, Brigadier General L-Kun Hpang, were a major component of the Kachin State Day Manau. Right at the symbolic heart of Kachin life, the government emphasized this attack and feted the family of the deceased. By one interpretation, the prospect of a repeat of that audacious Kachin raid helps justify the security precautions of senior government commanders in this region.
6. As quoted in "KIA denies starting war with Burmese Army", Kachin News Group, 24 June 2011 <http://www.kachinnews.com/news/1957-kia-denies-starting-war-with-burmese-army.html> (accessed 16 May 2012).

References

Constitution of the Republic of the Union of Myanmar (2008). Naypyitaw: Printing and Publishing Enterprise, Ministry of Information, Union of Myanmar. Available at: <http://www.burmalibrary.org/docs5/Myanmar_Constitution-2008-en.pdf>. Accessed 24 April 2012.

Farrelly, Nicholas. "Spatial control and symbolic politics in the borderlands of China, India and Burma". D.Phil thesis, University of Oxford, 2010.

Kachin News Group. "KIA denies starting war with Burmese Army". Kachin News Group, 24 June 2011. <http://www.kachinnews.com/news/1957-kia-denies-starting-war-with-burmese-army.html>. Accessed 16 May 2012.

Karen National Union (KNU). "Statement on Initial Agreement between KNU and Burmese Government". Karen National Union Supreme Headquarters, 14 January 2012.

New Light of Myanmar (NLM). "Tatmadaw columns inevitably counterattack KIA troops for their threats and armed attacks; Government opens the door of peace to welcome those who are holding different views if they wish to cooperate with the government in mutually concerned cases for the interests of the nation and the people and run for election in compliance with democratic practices to justly gain power; Tatmadaw counterattacks on KIA just to protect its members, nation's important hydropower project without even a single intention of aggression or oppression". *New Light of Myanmar*, 18 June 2011*a*.

————. "Union Foreign Affairs Minister meets Chinese Ambassador". *New Light of Myanmar*, 18 June 2011*b*.

————. "Kachin State Hluttaw meets". *New Light of Myanmar*, 29 June 2011*c*.

————. "KIA blows up rail tracks between Hopin and Nankhwin of Mandalay Myitkyina railroad Tatmadaw, MPF, officials focusing on security of life and property of people". *New Light of Myanmar*, 8 July 2011*d*.

Sadan, Mandy. "History and Ethnicity in Burma: Cultural contests of the ethnic category 'Kachin' in the colonial and postcolonial Burmese state, 1824–2004". PhD thesis, School of Oriental and African Studies, University of London, 2005.

Smith, Martin. "Ethnic participation and national reconciliation in Myanmar: Challenges in a transitional landscape". In *Myanmar's Long Road to National Reconciliation*, edited by Trevor Wilson. Singapore: Institute of Southeast Asian Studies, 2007.

South, Ashley. *Ethnic politics in Burma: States of conflict*. Oxford: Routledge, 2008.

5

PERCEPTIONS OF THE STATE AND CITIZENSHIP IN LIGHT OF THE 2010 MYANMAR ELECTIONS

Marie Lall and Hla Hla Win

The concept of citizenship is directly linked to the nature of the nation state. Whilst there is a debate about whether citizenship can exist under a military dictatorship (Heater 2004; Mitra 2011), the shift from Myanmar's military junta to a parliamentary system heavily dominated by the military does pose new questions about the concept of citizenship and about how individuals view the state, particularly with regard to rights, responsibilities, and political participation.

To date there has been no work (at least in English) on how the Burmese, whether of Bamar[1] or minority ethnic extraction, perceive the state and how they view their relationship with the state. The authors conducted research over a period of eighteen months, before and after the elections, as a first step towards exploring changing conceptions of citizenship in Myanmar. We focused on citizenship as an individual's relationship with the state, including his or her understanding of rights, responsibilities, and political participation, and how these were perceived in light of the creation of a multi-party system and the 2010 elections. In this chapter we discuss how young Burmese articulated their relationship with the state, focusing in particular on the perceptions held by those in their early to late twenties. Given that Myanmar, like many countries in the region, has a very young population,[2] the views of the younger generation are a crucial factor in determining how the country is likely to develop. In this chapter the authors also discuss the role (and perceived role) of education and educational institutions in building concepts of Burmese citizenship and nationalism. Despite rigorous state control of schools and universities, Myanmar's state education system has been in decline for some time; in recent years private education alternatives (for those who can afford them) have sprung up to fill the gaps.

The most interesting and, perhaps, significant aspect of this work-in-progress is that it has been possible to conduct our research in Myanmar without taking any extraordinary precautions. Before and after the elections people were happy to take part, by filling out the questionnaire or by attending the focus groups. This in itself points to changes in their conception of their relationship with the state — and of their citizenship. Only two years before the start of this research, such fieldwork would have been impossible.

CITIZENSHIP: A WORKING DEFINITION

The relationship between the individual and the state is linked to the particular form of the nation-state in which that individual lives — and this changes over time, often as the result of social movements or revolutions. Globalization has been seen to have altered the concept of citizenship, although scholarship on this topic has largely focused upon Western societies (Kuisma 2008). In low-income countries the concept of citizenship is likely to vary between democracies and military dictatorships. Even when there is no democracy, and consequently a lack of rights (as opposed to duties), there is still a form of citizenship, albeit a reduced form, as citizens will have a relationship with the state in some way or another. When a country moves from a military dictatorship to some form of limited or controlled parliamentary structure, as has happened in a number of Asian countries in the last three decades, the relationship between individuals and the state necessarily changes, as concepts such as rights, responsibilities, and political participation start to take on new meanings. In order to explore the concept of citizenship in Myanmar in light of the change from a military junta to a parliamentary system still heavily dominated and controlled by the military, we shall work with Joppke's definition:

> Citizenship as status, which denotes formal state membership and the rules of access to it; citizenship as rights, which is about the formal capacities and immunities connected with such a status; and in addition citizenship as identity, which refers to the behavioural aspects of individuals acting and conceiving of themselves as members of a collectivity, classically the nation or the normative conceptions of such behaviour imputed by the state (Joppke 2007, p. 38).

In Myanmar, citizenship as "status" existed throughout the time of military rule, as people carried ID cards and could apply for passports. They were, in effect, recognized as citizens by the state. Myanmar nationals resident abroad could secure continued recognition by the state by paying a certain percentage of tax on their foreign income. However, rights — including political participation and access to a "political life" — were largely nonexistent.

The issue of national identity in Myanmar is complex because the country is a multi-ethnic state. Many ethnic Bamar do not see a difference between the word "Myanmar" and the word "Bamar" (or "Burmese"). In contrast, a great many Myanmar nationals of ethnic minority extraction have come to view their identity as their ethnicity (Tun Aung Chain 2000; South 2008). The issues pertaining to ethnic identity versus an overall Myanmar identity have not yet been affected by the structural changes discussed in this chapter.[3] The focus of this chapter is, therefore, less on identity (although we do discuss "sense of belonging") but rather on the concepts of rights and responsibilities.

THE POLITICAL BACKDROP

The rate of social and political change in Myanmar is accelerating. Change is particularly evident in urban centres, with the development of civil society organizations across the country as well as the introduction of limited economic and political reforms. This process began with the dismantling of the old security and intelligence structures, in the winter of 2004, which allowed a very limited space for civil society to develop, and that space has been quietly growing. Local grassroots organizations that had formerly been under strict controls were suddenly able to develop and expand. Some middle-class leaders started to become involved in education and research, and think-tank organizations were created to fill the gaps of a faltering public education system. The same middle classes who were unhappy with the public school system started to set up alternative private schooling, both as a way forward for their children and as business opportunities. In December 2009 private schools were finally legalized, leading to a dramatic increase in the already growing non-state education sector.

In 2008 Cyclone Nargis brought death and destruction to many, but it also brought international aid and, most importantly, support for local development and local organizations. Many of these are now networked with each other and with the "outside" aid and development community. The influx of foreign aid has led to a small but increasingly active civil society in urban centres, spearheaded primarily by a small but influential non-military middle class.

There have been other changes that have had profound effects on society at large. Telecommunications have improved connectivity across the country, with mobile phones becoming increasingly widespread. At the time of writing, temporary SIM cards that cost around $20 allow millions to communicate with the outside world as well as with each other. The use of mobile phones is no longer limited to those who could afford the extraordinarily expensive permanent mobile phone accounts or those with good political connections. While the Internet is regulated, many Internet cafes manage to bypass the sensors through proxy servers. Communicating with the outside world is no longer unaffordable or impossible.

The availability of visas on arrival has helped increase the number of tourists coming to Myanmar compared with the number in the years prior to the elections, but tourist numbers remain small compared with the number who visit the other countries in the region, and few people from the West travel to Myanmar. However, this does not mean Myanmar is isolated in the traditional sense, since Myanmar's relations with countries to its east are good. Increased links with China have brought infrastructure and business investments, mainly to the border regions and Mandalay, although the Chinese presence (and significant Chinese migration) has also had negative consequences, as a result of the clear focus of the Chinese on accessing and exploiting Myanmar's natural resources and the environmental damage they have caused.

The November 2010 elections introduced some new factors, the most important of which was the restoration of parliamentary government. Voters elected representatives to two houses in the national parliament, and the new bicameral structure has for the first time allowed for some minority ethnic representation. Voters also elected regional assemblies in the seven States and seven Regions, each of which included a small number of seats reserved for ethnic representatives.

The main pro-regime party, the Union Solidarity and Development Party (USDP) "won" over 75 per cent of the seats across all assemblies, a result that surprised no one. The main opposition party, the National League for Democracy (NLD), decided not to stand in the elections due to its rejection of the 2008 Constitution and the unfair election laws, and their break-away faction — the National Democratic Force (NDF) did quite badly. However the ethnic minority parties, especially in Shan, Chin, and Rakhine States, did comparatively well nationally and are well represented in their own regional assemblies. Since none of the nation-wide pro-democracy parties adequately contested the regional assemblies, a large number of these seats in the ethnic states were taken by pro-democracy ethnic political parties. The regional assemblies are significant because they represent a potential new power base, with new members of parliament and a new civil service infrastructure to support the new institutions — in essence a new and legal political space where there was none before.

Despite the fact that the USDP has kept overall control and will be supported by the military members of parliament, this new parliamentary system represents a structural change, from a military junta to a presidential system that has new institutions and will require as a result changes in governance. The elected and non-elected elements of the new government will have to learn new ways of governance, and some level of discussion and compromise can be expected. The electorate, in turn, will also have to learn about the functions and functioning of the state apparatus. This chapter seeks to examine what citizens think about the state, its role, and their relationship with it, at the advent of the transformative process.

Among scholars who work on the Southeast Asian region it is widely understood that Western ideas about concepts such as citizenship may not necessarily be relevant or applicable in other contexts.[4] Other work on Myanmar has thrown up differences in the understanding of terms such as "politics". Hans Bernd Zoellner's work depicts how politics is perceived by Myanmar's traditional opposition (Zoellner 2012). He argues that debate and discussion do not necessarily form a part of the internal functions of a democratic party. Traditionally, Burmese party members will expect complete adherence to party leadership and principles — whether the party is in power or in opposition. The creation of the NDF was a case in point, as the disagreement over whether or not to take part in the elections split the NLD. After the elections such splits have continued, with the NDF expelling a sitting member of parliament over internal disagreements. Internal debate, especially across hierarchies, is not tolerated. Zoellner locates this issue in Myanmar's political history, starting with Aung San and anti-colonial political movements. In essence he argues that when Burmese people speak about democratic politics they mean something quite different from the Western concept. It would be reasonable to expect such basic differences to exist also in relation to the concept of citizenship, which is why it is important to look at public discourse on the concept before looking at how ordinary citizens think about it.

DISCOURSE ON CITIZENSHIP IN MYANMAR

Discourse on Citizenship in the Constitution

In the 2008 Constitution citizenship is described in Chapter VIII, "Citizen, Fundamental Rights and Duties of the Citizens", Articles 345–390. In principle, the constitution does enshrine rights and duties and, most importantly, the right to political participation — although the environment for such participation remains restricted by other laws governing Union and national security. While acknowledging these positive features, it must be kept in mind that how these rights and duties are observed in practice may differ from what might be expected from a literal reading of the text. However, the text seems to reflect the Western conception, defining citizenship within the concepts of rights and duties.

Discourse on Citizenship in the Press

More recently, the press has also been able to engage in some limited discussion on citizenship and the concepts of rights and duties. Previously all references to politics were oblique, and the avoidance of politics was essential for a journalist's survival (as described in Pe Myint's chapter in this volume). However, with the holding of the elections there has been a change in discourse, from fear to responsibility. Not only has politics become legal again, but the state media now depicts the elections and citizen involvement as a national duty:

> The success of elections is concerned with the image of the State as well as every citizen. So, the State, the people and the armed forces are to prevent those attempting to disrupt the elections. (Then Prime Minister Thein Sein, as quoted in *New Light of Myanmar*, 29 September 2010).

This 180-degree turn reflects Burmese cultural norms of politics and leadership, which do not accept dissent. After decades of having to actively avoid politics, citizens are now directed to support and protect the political process and to engage with the state. These elections are, in effect, not "optional" and a boycott (as advocated by the opposition) would be seen as an affront to the same powers who previously suppressed any form of political participation. In practice, the establishment of the new constitution, the holding of the elections, and the discourse in the press have led to a revival of politics. Political parties have been allowed to form and campaign, albeit in a limited way. Around election time, discussions on the elections were rife in teashops. But how far this will actually lead to a wider debate on issues pertaining to rights and responsibilities is as yet unclear. How this turn-around is being viewed by young, ordinary citizens is discussed below.

RESEARCH METHODOLOGY

The authors' research used a mixed-methods approach. During the year preceding the elections, a questionnaire in English containing qualitative and quantitative sections was distributed at a private higher education institution in Yangon, from which fifty-four questionnaires were returned, while a Burmese-language version was distributed to fishermen and farmers in seven villages in the Delta, from which forty-nine were returned. In both cases the ethnicity of participants was 75 per cent Bamar with 25 per cent of respondents from non-Bamar ethnicities.

The quantitative section of the questionnaire asked respondents to rate their sense of belonging to the state, their awareness of rights and duties, the role education had played for them in defining citizenship, and their political awareness. The qualitative section asked respondents to give short responses to explain and elaborate their views on the same themes, which allowed comparison with responses to the quantitative section.

A second set of data was collected in Yangon in February 2011, after the elections had been held and after the first sitting of the parliament on 31 January. Part of the data included responses collected from focus groups, in an attempt to find out what young people felt the new state structure could bring and whether they felt that their concept of citizenship was changing. While it was not possible in this second phase for the authors to collect data outside Yangon, care was taken to obtain the views of ethnic minority groups by working with a local non-government organization that sponsored young people from Karen State. One focus group was composed entirely of ethnic Bamar; one group had young people from a variety of ethnic backgrounds (including Bamar); and one was composed entirely of ethnic Karen.[5]

The timing of the research was also important. The changes that preceded the elections have increased space for political dialogue and debate quite markedly. Politics has once again become an acceptable topic of discussion. It would have been impossible to conduct such a survey or focus groups as openly as this even two years before the research began (when laws about political association and agitation were used to fill Myanmar's jails with political prisoners).

RESEARCH RESULTS

Results Relating to Citizenship

In the qualitative section of the survey carried out before the 2010 election, one question that participants were asked was, How do you understand citizenship? In the quantitative section respondents were asked to rate their sense of belonging and their awareness of rights and duties. The results, discussed below, show interesting differences between the responses given by urban and rural respondents.

When asked "How do you understand citizenship?", 70 per cent of urban respondents displayed a comprehensive understanding, relating the concept to rights and responsibilities, and around 30 per cent wrote about passports, identity cards, birth, and parents. Most gave examples of responsibilities, such as obeying laws and paying taxes, and of rights, such as the right to good education and proper health care, to equal opportunity, the right to consume natural resources, and the right to own property and land. A few participants mentioned political participation as a right, and protecting the country from abuse by its own people as part of a citizen's duties.

In contrast, the rural respondents had limited knowledge and understanding of citizenship. Sixty-one per cent of them identified the concept with identity cards, birth, and residency, while 17 per cent said they had no idea or had never thought about it. Only 22 per cent defined citizenship as being related to rights, duties, and social participation for the good of their immediate community. Some considered love for the country and emotional attachment to it as part of citizenship.

Differences between urban and rural responses to the qualitative section of the research were reflected in the two questions asked in the quantitative section. In relation to both a sense of belonging and awareness of rights and duties, urban respondents were much better informed and had a deeper understanding of these concepts (see Figure 5.1).

The fact that the urban sample was taken at a private education centre will have had an effect on the results, but it can be safely argued that most middle-class educated young people in Yangon would have had a similar understanding to their peers who took part. More than half of the urban respondents felt a strong sense of belonging, and 72 per cent of them had a high awareness of their rights and duties.

FIGURE 5.1
Urban Quantitative Responses

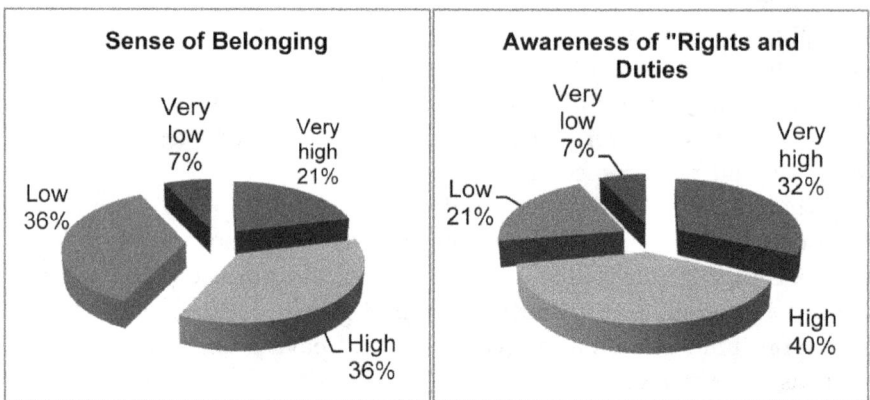

FIGURE 5.2
Rural Quantitative Responses

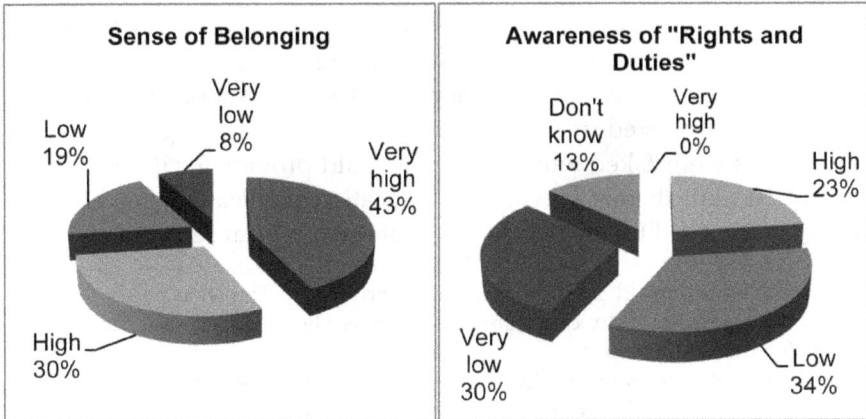

Among the rural participants, 73 per cent claimed to have a strong sense of belonging, yet only 23 per cent said they had a high awareness of their rights and duties (see Figure 5.2). Given the background of the rural respondents, it can be deduced that limited access to education would have had a particular effect on their awareness of rights and duties. That they showed a higher "sense of belonging" than the urban respondents is interesting, possibly reflecting the fact that identity is a more important measure of citizenship in the rural areas. In the focus groups, identity was mentioned by only one participant — but what he said found resonance with the others:

> Citizenship is a form of identity. A person needs a family; in the same way he needs to belong to a state. Otherwise he is a stateless person. Without the state there are no rights. Humans have rights — health, education, quality of life.

A second question in the qualitative section of the survey was, "What should the state do for you?", which was intended to elicit responses exploring the role of the state. Again there were marked differences between urban and rural respondents. The responses of the urban respondents focused on education (free; quality; capacity-building; human resource development) and on stable economic conditions. Rural respondents did mention education, but not as frequently as respondents in Yangon. They saw the state's role as also providing help with farming, agriculture and fisheries, with infrastructure, and with basic necessities such as clothes and shelter, while some mentioned health care.

Given the importance of the responses to the pre-election questionnaire, this theme was picked up again in the post-election focus groups, where participants were asked what the state should provide for its citizens. In general the same themes prevailed — education and health were the major themes mentioned by all groups. To quote two typical responses:

- The state should provide education and health. The state needs to be the organizer. Individuals are not effective. There needs to be efficiency for the whole country.
- The state needs to provide for its citizens. They need to have a sense of ownership. At the moment even if the state provides, we don't feel this is ours. We don't value.

It was also interesting to note that the role of the state was seen as potentially very valuable by most participants. The private sector was recognized — but was seen largely as something that would only help the middle classes. An active state was seen as essential for the benefit of the wider population, and the Western neo-liberal model with a reduced state was rejected outright in the discussions. Only one participant ventured to suggest that the middle classes who could provide for themselves should do so, and leave the state to fend for those too poor to do so themselves.

Beyond the role of the state and the fact that the state was seen as needing to improve its performance, the theme of education permeated responses. The main difference between the urban and rural participants was clearly access to education and the level of education. In both the focus groups and responses to the questionnaires, education was seen as the key to changing society and developing citizenship.

THE ROLE OF EDUCATION IN BUILDING THE RELATIONSHIP BETWEEN INDIVIDUALS AND THE STATE

Education is often used as a tool by the state to inculcate the "state's ideology" in the masses. This is particularly the case with the construction of national identity (Lall and Vickers 2009). Beyond this, however, education in general, and the school curriculum in particular, play a vital role in shaping the concept of citizenship in the minds of people. Kaltsounis and Osborne argue that "the *raison d'être* of social studies education in a democratic society is the preparation for citizenship" (Kaltsounis 1994; Osborne 1997). The skills acquired through a curriculum are often deemed necessary for "informed participation in a democracy" (Dean 2005). The concepts that Dean is referring to include those of rights, responsibilities, and political participation, all of which go beyond the construction of national identity.

Democracy demands active political participation from citizens. The 2010 election was the first election in twenty years and more than half the voters were voting for the first time. What sources of political knowledge have been available to voters, and what has been the role of the education system in fostering knowledge of political concepts such as citizenship? People living in urban and border areas are exposed to, and influenced by, the globalization process. They have relatively easy access to global news through media and the Internet. However, two-thirds of the Myanmar population live in rural areas where there is limited or no access to those sources. Therefore, the only common source of political knowledge for both the urban and rural population is through formal basic education provided by the government.

Under Myanmar's curriculum, the textbooks used describe the duties and responsibilities of individuals towards the state both explicitly and implicitly, and there is no expression of the notion of rights or of political participation (that is, of individual involvement in the political decision-making process). This contrasts with what is written in the 2008 Constitution described above — but then it has to be noted that the education system has not — not yet — been reformed in light of the structural changes that are occurring as a result of the establishment of the new political system. Current school textbooks reflect and describe the political situation of the last decades. Only the history textbook used for the most senior high school levels includes an update of the Myanmar political situation up to the State Peace and Development Council era. Most Burmese textbooks were written during the period of the socialist government. They were purposely and clearly created to promote social, cultural, and national integration and unity. The concept of citizenship they present is, therefore, quite different from what might have been written in more recent years.[6]

Results Relating to Education

In the pre-election survey, one question asked of respondents was, How has schooling contributed towards defining your concept of citizenship? The difference between the responses from the urban and the rural participants was striking. (It should be noted that the urban participants had finished secondary school or college and had access to informal education provided by the private sector. In contrast, the rural participants had had less education opportunity, most having barely finished middle school.) Sixty-two per cent of urban participants believed that education played a major role in defining their concept of citizenship, but less than half (47 per cent) of rural participants shared the same perspective (see Figure 5.3).

These figures raise the question of the role of education and the different types of education providers in Myanmar. Increasingly, urban middle class people look for education alternatives offered by private providers to either complement or replace state education (Lall 2009). The recent rise of civil society organizations alluded to in the initial sections of this chapter has markedly changed the education landscape in Yangon and Mandalay. This is happening at different levels, as some organizations focus on capacity-building for adults while others provide alternative

FIGURE 5.3
Urban and Rural Quantitative Responses

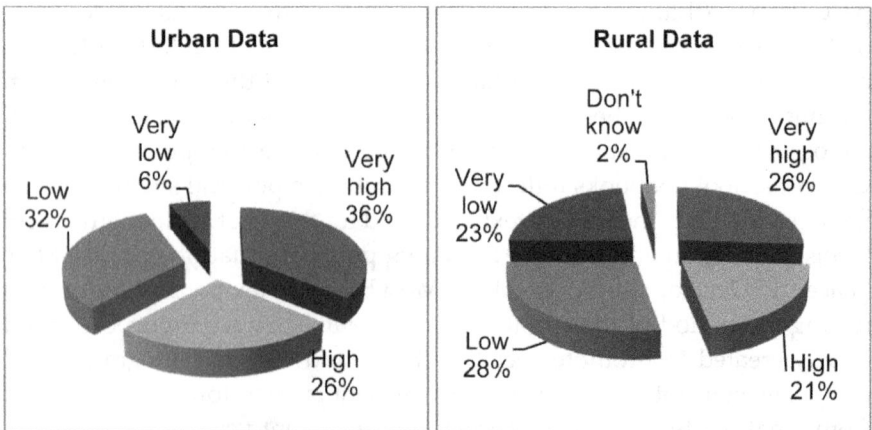

schools for children. Nevertheless, both types of organizations not only help to increase social and political space, they also help address the issue of low political literacy amongst the young. Many of the institutions that offer capacity-building teach their students about the constitution and the role of the newly-formed institutions, and therefore contribute directly to building the concept of citizenship. Such organizations could play an important role in building an understanding of citizenship and the role of the state, especially as state institutions do not currently appear to be developing such knowledge.

CONCLUSION

The authors' research aimed to investigate how Myanmar young people articulated their relationship with the state. The data pointed to significant differences between the urban and the rural respondents, leading to the conclusion that access to, and quality of, education are key factors in defining and developing the concepts of citizenship, rights, and responsibilities. Rights in particular are not well understood as a concept — but they are enshrined in the 2008 Constitution. In one-on-one interviews with ethnic civil society leaders, one of the ethnic leaders explained:

> With regards to rights — we feel we don't have much experience. Starting with the socialist government, health care and education were the state's responsibility. This perception stays to this day. This can also create obstacles. For example, if there is a school in a village and they [the villagers] want to set up another school — for example, a high school — then the education will only be one part. The other [such as the school building] has to come from the community [which does not have the means]. In order to build the school, you need to have the full funds. Otherwise the school will not be built. But our understanding was that this was the responsibility of the state.

In thinking about and discussing citizenship in light of the recent political changes, many participants made the point that differences between urban and rural populations — which were stark in the small sample collected — would be very difficult to overcome. Rights and responsibilities are seen as urban concepts that have little relevance in Myanmar's poor rural areas. Further, even in urban areas the divisions between the middle classes who have to private education providers and capacity-building centres and those who do not will result in different parts of the population having different conceptions of citizenship. In another, similar interview another civil society leader said:

> It [the concept of citizenship] will change it for some — for those who have political knowledge it might, but understood theoretically, not in an active way in the beginning. For at least one to one-and-a-half years people will feel not sure about what we can do / talk / where we can go and whom we can talk to as citizens. The system and structure is in place. People in the system are not able to function well because they still have to change their ways of working. This is a transition. The leaders will need to learn how to function. Politicians, political parties, all need training. From an ethnic perspective we need to think where we can find space for ethnic grievances. Once people learn, they can find gaps. There is need for further education.

In order to work properly, a democratic society needs responsible citizens who are able and willing to participate actively in the political process. It will be difficult for Myanmar to develop a concept of active citizenship as the majority of the Myanmar population live in rural areas and do not have access to the same educational resources as the urban population. It will be a challenge for the new government to provide the necessary citizenship education to both the urban and rural population, either formally through the national curriculum or informally with the help of the emerging private sector. Using the school curriculum to teach the concept of citizenship that has certain rights and duties attached would enable the state to build an active citizenry. There could also be an elaboration on participation in collective decision-making as both a right and a duty of citizens in a democratic society. These two steps are necessary for the country to transition to a more participatory democracy.

Notes

1. The term "Bamar" (Burmese, also called "Burman") refers to persons who are from the dominant ethnic group of Myanmar, constituting approximately two-thirds of the population. The Bamar live primarily in the Irrawaddy basin and speak the Burmese language, which is also the official language of Myanmar. Bamar customs and identity are closely intertwined with general Burmese customs and identity. The Bamar are frequently — imprecisely — called "Burmese" although the term in modern usage refers to a citizen of Myanmar of any ethnic background.

2. Information obtained from CIA website, <https://www.cia.gov/library/publications/the-world-factbook/geos/bm.html>:
    - 0–14 years: 25.3% (male: 6,193,263; female: 5,990,658)
    - 15–64 years: 69.3% (male: 16,510,648; female: 16,828,462)
    - 65 years and over: 5.4% (male: 1,121,412; female: 1,493,298) (2010 est.)

3. This could, however, change as ethnic minority parties become more active in the ethnic States, and as their representation, especially in the local legislative assemblies, engenders change at a local level with regard to, for example, the language of instruction in schools.

4. See Subrata Mitra's work on citizenship as a conceptual flow from West to East.

5. In order to be comprehensive and more representative, the research would have had to take into account the views of the various ethnic and religious minorities in their own states. This, however, was impossible, not because of travel restrictions or other structural problems, but because of lack of research funding.

6. In the Myanmar school curriculum there is no material intended explicitly for teaching about citizenship or such matters as political participation at the national level. This means that one needs to look at other possible sources of such material, and in this respect the Myanmar literature textbooks throughout all grades are crucial, because literature is studied by all students whether in the Arts or Science streams or in the combined Arts-Science stream. In addition, the literature curriculum teaches culture, fine arts, and history. Since the curriculum was written in and for a socialist era, volunteerism is promoted, and the importance of socially and morally responsible citizens who are active in community participation is greatly emphasized. Patriotism is another key theme throughout the curriculum, especially in the literature curriculum, which teaches culture, fine arts, and history. As one example, the poem "Our Blood", from the Grade Seven textbook, is presented to condition students to love the country and to be ready to fight against any intruders. The poem says, "run away evils, don't dare to test our blood, we will defeat any rebels". Militarism also is advocated in many poems and essays across the curriculum as a way of serving the country. Textbooks have thus promoted the idea of joining the military and being prepared to defend the country as a form of devotion to the country. Many essays, stories, and poems endorse the "Unity is Strength" theme that has been prominent in state propaganda for several decades now. In the Grade Ten textbook is an essay called "Union and Myanmar" which states that the Myanmar nation has been united since the Bagan dynasty of the eleventh century. It endorses the idea of being loyal to the country, suggesting that all ethnic minority groups need to be united under this broadest of identities. Another essay describes how a piece of firewood can be easily broken while a bundle of firewood is much stronger and is more

difficult to break. The vast majority of content in the current school curriculum thus reflects a militarized Bamar world view.

References

Constitution of the Republic of the Union of Myanmar. Naypyitaw: Printing and Publishing Enterprise, Ministry of Information, Union of Myanmar, 2008. Available at <http://www.burmalibrary.org/docs5/Myanmar_Constitution-2008-en.pdf>. Accessed 24 April 2012.

Dean, B.L. "Citizenship education in Pakistani schools: Problems and possibilities". *International Journal of Citizenship and Teacher Education* 1, no. 2 (December 2005): 35–55.

Heater, D.B. *A Brief History of Citizenship*. New York: New York University Press, 2004.

Hla Hla Win and Yan Ming Aung. *Educational Space in Myanmar in light of 2010 Election*. Marseilles: International Burma Studies Conference Press, 2010.

Joppke, C. "Transformation of Citizenship: Status, Rights, Identity". *Citizenship Studies* 11, no. 1 (2007): 37–48.

Kaltsounis, T. "Democracy's Challenge as the Foundation for Social Studies". *Theory and Research in Social Education* 22, no. 2 (1994): 176–193.

Kuisma, M. "Rights or privileges? The challenge of globalization to the values of citizenship". *Citizenship Studies* 12, no. 6 (2008): 613–627.

Lall, M. "Education in Myanmar: The interplay of state, civil society and business". In *Dictatorship, Disorder and Decline in Myanmar*, edited by M. Skidmore and T. Wilson. Canberra: ANU E-Press, 2009.

Lall, M. and E. Vickers, eds. *Education as a Political Tool in Asia*. London: Routledge, 2009.

Mitra, S., ed. *Citizenship and the Flow of Ideas in the Era of Globalization: Structure, Agency and Power*. New Delhi: Sanskriti, 2011.

Myint Aye and Tin Kyi. *National aspects of curriculum decision-making*. Paris: UNESCO Press, 1998.

Osborne, K. "Citizenship Education and Social Studies". In *Trends and Issues in Canadian Social Studies*, edited by I. Wright and A. Sears. Vancouver: Pacific Educational Press, 1997.

South, Ashley. *Ethnic politics in Burma: States of conflict*. Oxford: Routledge, 2008 [2010 reprint].

Tun Aung Chain. "Historians and the search for Myanmar nationhood". *16th Conference of the International Association of Historians of Asia*. Kota Kinabalu: International Association of Historians of Asia in cooperation with Universiti Malaysia Sabah, 2000.

Zoellner, H.B. *The Beast and the Beauty*. Hamburg: Abera Verlag, 2012.

6

THE BURMESE JADE TRAIL
Transnational Networks, China, and the (Relative) Impact of International Sanctions on Myanmar's Gems

Renaud Egreteau

Diamonds are a girl's best friend, as the song goes. So is Burmese jade for a Chinese, or for any gem and jade dealer settled along the China-Myanmar borders. Hard numbers are difficult to come by, but it is thought that today thousands of Myanmar-origin jadestones worth several million U.S. dollars are traded every year in China, most particularly in the border province of Yunnan. Myanmar has long been prized for its precious gemstones, but its own gem and jade industry has rather stagnated since independence in 1948. Over the past decade, however, it has witnessed extraordinary growth, mostly driven by extravagant Chinese demand. With rising Sino-Myanmar economic interaction in the decade from the year 2000, the construction of modern infrastructure in the borderlands of Yunnan, and the increased purchasing power of jade-crazed Chinese diaspora societies, all the signs are that the Burmese jade trade is roaring ahead. Yet Western countries have been calling for tougher economic sanctions on the Myanmar gemstone market. After the international outcry that followed the "Saffron Revolution", European Union (EU) and United States policy-makers determined on imposing "smarter" sanctions to target the profits that military-ruled Myanmar could scoop up from this thriving industry. Brussels subsequently, in November 2007, revised the EU Common Position to include a section on mining, timber, and gems, and in July 2008 Washington adopted the *Tom Lantos Block Burmese JADE (Junta's Anti-Democratic Effort) Act*. These moves have had little success, however, as the Burmese jade trade has continued to boom. At the root of the ineffectiveness of Western sanctions on that particular industry is a simple miscalculation: China is too big a player in the jade industry to leave outside the scope of such sanctions; moreover, cross-border trade in and around Myanmar has become increasingly viable and profitable in recent years.[1]

This chapter intends to explore and evaluate the impact Western "targeted sanctions" have had on the Myanmar gem industry. The research on which it is based is drawn primarily from a broader project the author has been conducting since 2010 on Burmese Muslim jade traders settled in Yunnan — mostly in the major market town of Ruili (Shweli in Burmese) (see Figure 6.1).[2] After a brief overview of the patterns and configuration of Burma's gem and jade industry and trans-border trade, and a description of the scope and instruments of international sanctions that target Myanmar gems, this paper will debate the (ir)relevance of the latter in the local context of the Sino-Yunnanese borderlands. It will argue that extensive trans-national networks of Myanmar and Chinese gem dealers, the critical impulse given by jade-hungry Chinese consumers, and the structure of Burma's gem and jade production and trade, will continue to favor extraordinary growth in this sector in coming years. The author argues, therefore, that if the aim of the international community is to better monitor the Myanmar gem markets, but without either killing off a thriving local industry or leaving it to the will and whim of Chinese businessmen and consumers and the oligarchy-controlled Myanmar economy, then the international community must review its global approach.

THE MYANMAR GEMSTONE TRAIL

"And the old Chinese broker cried: 'pigeon's blood'." (Kessel 1961, p. 81)

Myanmar has long been renowned for its natural gemstones. Burmese "pigeon's blood" rubies and sapphires, but also its amber and jade, have

FIGURE 6.1
Map of the Burma-Yunnan Border Areas

Legend:

◻ State Capital

△ Major Cities and Cross-border Towns

Mong Hsu   Major gems & jade mining site

— · — International Boundaries

Burma's States and Regions (formerly Divisions) of Burma

▨   1. Kachin State
2. Sagaing Region
3. Chin State
4. Arakan (Rakhine) State
5. Shan State
6. Mandalay Region

Source: Author's map.

been prized for centuries, especially in Chinese societies. Archival and archaeological research found that during the Mongol, Ming, and Qing dynasties Chinese people were indeed fond of Burmese gems (*baoshan* in Chinese) (Khin Maung Nyunt 1996; Chang 2003; Sun 2011). Polished stones have been discovered across archaeological sites in Myanmar dating back to the Pyu kingdoms (third to eighth centuries AD). Reports of Burmese jade (*feicui*) being traded into Yunnan by mule caravans can be traced back to the late thirteenth century AD. Chinese academic Sun Laichen even argues that when comparing the Burmese gem trade during the Ming and Qing dynasties with trade in more recent, contemporary periods, the most striking common feature is that it has largely remained a Chinese-inspired business (Sun 2011, p. 204). Whether under imperial, republican, or (post)-socialist governments, demand from Chinese consumers has been the main driving force behind the transnational Myanmar gem industry and, more specifically, the jade industry throughout the whole region.

Colonial and post-colonial writings also popularized the existence and trade of Burmese gemstones in the West (Ehrmann 1957; Hughes 1999; Kessel 1961; Turrell 1988; Walsh 2011). Journalists, notably Bertil Lintner, have provided in-depth coverage of the underground patterns of the industry in the context of Burma's post-independence civil war period (Lintner 1989; Clark 1999). Kachin, Shan, and Pa'O insurgents, as well as Chinese Kuomintang factions stationed in northeastern Myanmar and Thailand, substantially financed their rebellions against Burma's central government with revenues from mining and cross-border trade of rubies and jade (Lintner 1999; Chang 2009). Gems also sustained Burma's black market economy during the Ne Win socialist era, between 1962 and 1988 (Chang 2004 and 2006). Since the 1990s, despite losing their domination of the industry to Burman and state-controlled trading networks, a few ethnic militias that still enjoy creaky ceasefire agreements with the central military authorities — such as the Kachin Independence Organization (KIO) and the Pa'O National Organization (PNO) — have kept a visible hand in the industry (KIO, until June 2011).

The industry is mainly structured around remote gem-producing valleys in the Kachin and Shan States (see Figures 6.1 and 6.2), as well as the market towns of Mandalay, Taunggyi (Shan State), and Yangon in Myanmar, and Ruili (Shweli) on the Yunnan-Myanmar border. Mogok (200 km north of Mandalay), Nanyarseik (Kachin State) and Mong Hsu (Shan State) are the three main ruby and sapphire mining centres of the country (Clark 1999; Ehrmann 1957; Samuels 2003). The Kachin-dominated

FIGURE 6.2
Major Jade-producing Areas, Kachin State

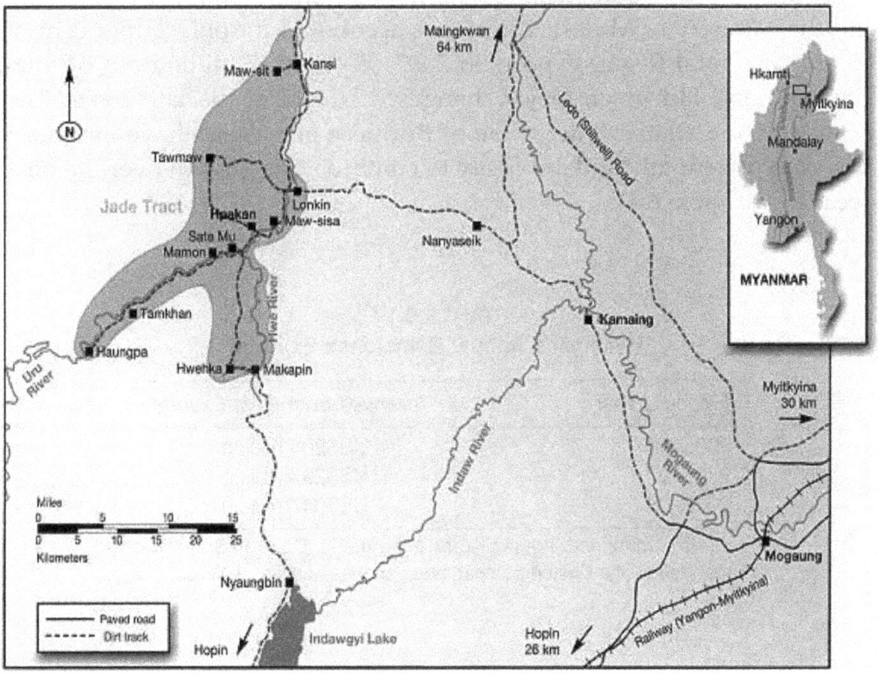

Source: Hughes et al. (2000). Reproduced with kind permission of Richard W. Hughes <www.ruby-sapphire.com>.

northern areas of the country (notably around Hpa'kant, along the Uru River) have historically been famous for their gem-quality jadeite,[3] and for amber mines near Noije Bum in the Hukauwng Valley (Hughes and others 2000).

Significance In and For Contemporary Myanmar

Conventional estimates underscore that today up to 90 per cent of the world's supply of gem-quality rubies are of Myanmar origin, while around 70 per cent of the world's jadeite is produced in Myanmar mines. Yet, while Myanmar remains an important gem centre and a major source for the world's most precious stones, its current official revenues from gemstones exports are far lower than those from other natural resources such as oil, gas, or timber. According to Myanmar government statistics (from the Central Statistical Organization, the Customs Department, and the Ministry of Mines), gemstones accounted for only 11 per cent of Myanmar's total (legal) exports in 2007–08 (US$647 million out of total US$6 billion). However, major changes occurred in the late 2000s. The extraction and trans-border trade of Burmese gemstones have increased almost exponentially and are likely to continue this growth over the next decade (see Table 6.1).

TABLE 6.1
Myanmar's Annual Gemstones Exports

Financial Year	Revenues from Gem Exports
2005–06	US$205 million
2006–07	US$297 million
2007–08	US$647 million

Source: Combined figures from Myanmar's Central Statistical Organization, the Customs Department, and the Ministry of Mines.

When private trading of commodities was legalized after the collapse of Ne Win's socialist regime in 1988, the Myanmar gem industry attempted to expand its legal networks. From that time individuals were allowed to extract and trade gemstones, including trading with foreigners, as stipulated by the *Myanmar Gemstones SLORC Law 8/95*. Enacted by the central government on 29 September 1995, this law purported to liberalize a sector that still lacked modern infrastructure and state support. Myanmar gem traders and mining companies needed only to be registered with the Ministry of Mines and the state-controlled Myanmar Gems Enterprise (MGE) to operate freely.

During the 1990s, the (relative) pacification of northern Myanmar under the auspices of various ceasefire agreements with Kachin, Pa'O, and Shan rebel groups, the expansion of Myanmar government control capacities, the emergence of a number of wealthy Myanmar businessmen (cronies of the military rulers), and increasing demand from China and various Chinese diaspora networks gave a considerable boost to the local Myanmar gem industry.

Interestingly, however, official figures for Myanmar gemstone export revenues were quite low during this period. Business was thriving, but it was out of the hands of the Myanmar government, being controlled mostly by black market traders and ethnic insurgent groups based in the border areas, and driven strongly by Chinese buyers in Yunnan, Hong Kong, and Bangkok (Chang 2004). Reportedly, only a few million U.S. dollars' worth of gemstones were traded yearly in the major markets of Yangon, Mandalay, and Taunggyi. According to a study by Japanese economist Toshihiro Kudo, official trade revenues from Burmese gems even declined in the first half of the 2000s (Kudo 2008b, p. 91).

Gradually, however, during the second half of the 2000s, this situation changed. With the development of an economic structure dominated by a number of military-owned conglomerates and private business empires run by cronies close to the ruling elite, the Myanmar government moved to exert greater control over the gem industry. Over the past few years, state-controlled companies and firms managed by a handful of business cronies have taken the upper hand in a reorganized system of extraction, production, and trade of the country's gemstones.[4] This trend has been even more obvious in the peculiar jade business, where domination by the Myanmar state apparatus increased markedly during the 2000s.[5] Production of the highly-prized jadeite from mines now owned by the Myanmar military-ruled state — which has largely displaced the local people and ethnic armed groups who owned most of the mines before the 1990s — reached around 46,000 tons in 2010–11, compared to an average of 20,000 tons in the mid-2000s and a meagre 10,000 tons in the early 2000s (see Table 6.2).

Revenues from Burmese jade sales have doubled every year since 2007, to reach US$1.75 billion in 2010–11,[6] according to Myanmar government statistics (see Table 6.3).

Key events — very useful for measuring the health of the Myanmar gem business — are the regular jade and gems emporiums held under the patronage of the Myanmar government. Annual fairs have been organized in Yangon every March since 1964. Mid-year fairs (held in October or November) were introduced in 1992 to boost the industry, while "special" fairs were introduced in 2004, and have been held sometime between May and July ever since, either in Yangon or Naypyitaw, Myanmar's capital since 2005. The rapid multiplication of these events and the large volume of trade realized during these one-week affairs highlight their significance for the government — which has been increasingly able to

TABLE 6.2
Myanmar's Annual Production of Jadeite

Financial Year	Production of Jadeite (in tons)
1987–88	c. 130
(...)	(...)
2003–04	10,754
2004–05	14,436
2005–06	20,390
2006–07	20,458
2007–08	20,235
2008–09	32,921
2009–10	25,795
2010–11	46,810

Sources: Combined figures from Myanmar's Central Statistical Organization, the Customs Department, and the Ministry of Mines.

TABLE 6.3
Revenue from Annual Jade Sales

Financial Year	Revenues from Jade Sales
2008–09	US$436 million
2009–10	US$953 million
2010–11	US$1,750 million

Sources: "The Future: Myanmar Business Report", Yangon: Yangon Publishing House, February 2011, quoted by the *Myanmar Times*, 7–13 March 2011.

levy taxes and to benefit from private trading activities (see Table 6.4). All are organized by the Ministry of Mines and its Myanmar Gem Enterprises, which levies a 10 per cent tax on each official gem sale made in foreign currency during these fairs (AKSYU 2008, p. 7). One has to add the usual 10 per cent in royalties paid to the local or national government on each declared gemstone extracted in the country (on appraised value, before the first sale) to measure the growing importance gems have acquired in the state revenues.

The March 2011 annual fair gathered 6,500 foreign merchants (mostly Chinese) for one week in Naypyitaw. It was a gigantic emporium, during which gemstones worth US$2.8 billion were traded, while foreigners were

TABLE 6.4
Revenues of Annual Fairs Since 2005

Annual Fair	Revenues
March 2005	US$29 million
March 2006	US$101 million
March 2007	US$220 million
March 2008	US$153 million
March 2009	US$191 million
March 2010	US$500 million
March 2011	US$2,880 million

Sources: Figures combined from material published by the Myanmar Times, New Light of Myanmar, Agence France Presse (AFP), and Reuters.

given free *wifi* access and pre-paid mobile phone cards for less than US$50, an unthinkable offer in normal times elsewhere in the country.[7] In November 2010, a mid-year emporium had already garnered an exceptional US$1.4 billion in revenue, while during another fair held in July 2011, sales reached US$1.57 billion, both results thanks to a growing reliance on deals made in Euro currency.[8] The extraordinary increase in China's demand for jade, plus the improved control of gem production and legal trade gained by the Myanmar state authorities in recent years, largely explain the striking figures. The expansion of cross-border trade also facilitates this particular commerce toward Yunnan (jade), Thailand, and India (rubies). However, in March 2012, the Naypyitaw gem emporium scooped up only some US$700 million. This sudden decrease can be explained by the falling value of the dollar against the Myanmar kyat, renewed tensions in Kachin-dominated areas and gem contracts signed in 2011 but not honoured afterwards by Chinese buyers.[9]

INTERNATIONAL SANCTIONS AGAINST MYANMAR: THE GEMS TARGET

With the apparent increase in official revenues from gems being earned by the Myanmar government, gemstones became an obvious target for the "smart" sanctions with which Western powers aimed to redefine their position towards junta-ruled Myanmar during the 2000s, especially after the outcry caused by Myanmar government repression of the so-called

"Saffron Revolution" of 2007 and its handling of the aftermath of Cyclone Nargis in 2008. Yet, although the rationale for imposing such sanctions was clear, observers remain sceptical about how effective sanctions are in operation and whether they are relevant for achieving policy objectives.

The Rationale Behind Sanctions on Gemstones

Since the first in-depth studies of sanctions, done in the 1960s, the literature on sanctions has been bogged down in Manichean debates revolving around their concrete policy relevance, usefulness, and effectiveness (Galtung 1967; Wallensteen 1968; Pape 1997 and 1998; Elliott 1998; Dorussen and Mo 2001). Nevertheless, particularly in the post-Cold War context, policy-makers have been increasingly using a wide range of complex financial and diplomatic sanctions, mostly construed as constituting a middle ground between mere dialogue (or inaction) at one extreme and military intervention to enforce law, secure interests, or compel the targeted state to action at the other (Marinov 2005). Myanmar is no exception. The question of whether American and European sanctions have achieved their aims in post-1988 Myanmar has been the subject of endless scholarly, activist, and diplomatic disputes (Pedersen 2008; Howse 2008; Kudo 2008a). Ostracization of the Myanmar pariah state is still a popular foreign policy instrument for many European and American governments (Steinberg 2010; Camroux and Egreteau 2010; Egreteau 2010). Schematically, they aim to cut off the Myanmar Leviathan-type military regime from international trade networks and financial opportunities in order, implicitly, to force it to open up, relinquish its authoritarian grip over the Myanmar polity, and eventually hand over power to a democratically-elected authority — ideally led by the charismatic Aung San Suu Kyi. Unless there is visible progress towards establishing some guarantee of the sacrosanct principles of human rights, of civil liberties, and of other globally-recognized democratizing values, the Myanmar military rulers — whether in uniform or not — cannot expect this foundation stone of the sanctions approach of Western countries to be questioned.

Since natural resources and other potential sources of wealth abound in Myanmar, but have long been either under-exploited as a result of poor state systems, or siphoned off by underground networks, the Western focus on limiting the potential revenue an increasingly dominant junta could gain seemed logical. Cutting off the linkages that the Myanmar state was developing with major international oil and gas companies as well as with lucrative timber and gemstones trans-national trading networks, and thus cutting off the resultant capital flows, became a policy priority for Western governments. Arguments in favour of targeted sanctions were based on how much nuisance they would create for Burma's rulers and their business "cronies".

Even more than the energy production industry, the gemstones industry is tied to an "underworld" of illicit markets that has huge potential for generating quick profits for whoever controls either the extraction and production of gemstones or their trade — including, of course, central state authorities, if they are able to impose political order and commercial monopoly (Naylor 2010). "Blood diamonds" that have been used illicitly to fuel civil wars and political instability in Africa have been well studied since the 1990s (Grant and Taylor 2004). In the last decade few reports have been published about the Myanmar government's increasing control over the mining industry and gemstones trade — or about the revenues generated by it — but the few have had a strong impact. Large-scale abuses occurring in Myanmar's mining areas (appalling working conditions, forced labour, child labour, and human rights violations) have also been widely documented by journalists and by trans-national civil society and activist groups.[10] Kachin jadeite mines have received particular attention in recent years (AKSYU 2008). International campaigns advocating a global boycott of Burmese gemstones in order to prevent the potential revenues getting into the hands of the Myanmar ruling elite have multiplied, and were eventually successful in pushing key Western governments to adopt such sanctions.

Scope and Mechanisms of Western Sanctions on Myanmar Gems

Since the Clinton Administration first introduced economic sanctions against Myanmar in 1997, a vast and multi-dimensional arsenal of restrictive measures has been implemented by Washington. United States-based Burmese financial assets have been frozen, banking services to Myanmar leaders prohibited, an extensive list of visa bans enacted, and restrictions on Myanmar imports increased. Since their inception, sanctions have represented a credible set of policy instruments — whether successful or not — to United States policy-makers, whose aim was to show that America "was doing something" and supported Burmese democrats (Steinberg 2010).

The first sanctions imposed by the Clinton Administration (May 1997) were followed by two other sets of economic sanctions, imposed by the Administration of George Bush Jr.: the *Burmese Freedom and Democracy Act of 2003* (BFDA, passed in July 2003) and the *Tom Lantos Block Burmese JADE (Junta's Anti-Democratic Effort) Act of 2008* (Block Burmese JADE Act, passed in July 2008). Following the tragic Depayin event in May 2003 and the subsequent third arrest of Aung San Suu Kyi, the BFDA imposed from 2004 a ban on the importation to the United States of any Myanmar product — including gemstones. However, the ban did not include Myanmar-originated goods that had transited through third countries such as Thailand or China, a manifest flaw that undermined its very rationale. The Block Burmese JADE Act attempted to counter that loophole — notably for gemstones, hence its name. Inspired by Californian congressman Tom Lantos (who passed away in February 2008), the bill was introduced in October 2007 and approved by the House of Representatives in November 2007.[11] However, it took nearly another year for the bill to be fully implemented, and the Block Burmese JADE Act was finally passed in July 2008.[12] This law was primarily designed to avoid the laundering in third countries of Burmese gemstones before the latter were sold on United States soil. Canada also followed the U.S. model: the *Special Economic Measures Act*, which was enacted in December 2007, prohibits all financial dealings with any Myanmar companies or banks, and prohibits all Canadian exports and imports (including of gemstones) to and from Myanmar.[13]

For their part, the Europeans debated amongst themselves along identical lines to define their own sanctions against Myanmar, but proposed different legal frameworks. The EU Common Position 1996/635/CFSP, which was first adopted in October 1996, remains their working basis.[14] It has been revised and/or strengthened every year since; sanctions were suspended on 23 April 2012.[15] While not as strongly formulated as the Clinton and Bush Administrations' proposals for a strict embargo of Myanmar products, the EU Common Position considerably limits any economic and financial cooperation with Myanmar by its member states, and includes the suspension of bilateral or multilateral partnerships. It restricts the import or export of Myanmar-made products, and freezes the Myanmar leaders' financial assets within the European Union (not a large amount) (Egreteau 2010). Expanded in 2007 after the "Saffron Revolution", the Common Position more specifically targets the mining, timber, and gems industries (Camroux and Egreteau 2010).

Three years after being strengthened, and with a more manifest gemstones target, Western sanctions have been facing growing criticism internationally. They have, at the same time, come up against a concurrent boom in gem production and cross-border trade in and around Burma — which has fostered strong scepticism about their relevance. In March 2008, when the focus on Burmese gemstones had just been formulated by European Union and United States policy-makers, the Myanmar government admitted that its profit from the annual gem emporium had been a mere US$153 million. In March 2011, profit from the same international event skyrocketed to US$2.88 billion according to official figures (although one should be cautious about accepting the official data at face value and be aware that it may have numerological undertones).

Early on, the revised 2007 EU Common Position was questioned by academics (Howse 2008; Egreteau 2010). The commerce in gemstones between Europe and Myanmar has long been marginal, and the renowned Belgium gem industry is quite disconnected from its Myanmar counterpart — unlike the gem industries in China, Thailand, and, to a lesser extent, India. Overseas Chinese who have settled in Europe (and the United States), and who are very fond of Burmese jade jewelry, have continued to use China-based traders to import Burmese stones. From the beginning, the foreseeable negligible impact that EU and U.S. gem-focused sanctions would have on Myanmar has been documented (Steinberg 2010, p. 182), and was later attested by internal governmental reports (USGAO 2009). Imports of Burmese gems to the United States have certainly declined — if not been halted — but the Block Burmese JADE Act has had no wider impact on the global Burmese gem market.

While the European Union, United States, and Canada have imposed trade sanctions against Myanmar, Australia has imposed only limited financial sanctions and has restricted entry to Australia for members of the Myanmar regime and some of their business associates (Wilson 2011). Australia has not, however, imposed any specific sanctions to target Burmese gems — hence Burmese jade is sold openly in Sydney's Chinatown, for instance.[16]

Neither New Zealand nor Japan has imposed sanctions on Burmese gems, but neither is a valuable market for Burmese stones. China remains the driving force behind the Myanmar jade industry, while Thailand and India are acquiring a greater foothold in the trading of Myanmar rubies, gold, and sapphires.

THE LOCAL VIEW: CASE STUDY OF THE JADE MARKET IN RUILI, YUNNAN

China has always been the key player in Burma's jade business (although that is not the case with respect to rubies). The borders between Yunnan and northern Myanmar have been notably porous for centuries, and still today there is large-scale smuggling of commodities, including gemstones. Examination of the bustling jade market in the Yunnan cross-border town of Ruili can, therefore, provide a case-study that illustrates the futility of Western sanctions against the Myanmar gem industry — at least in their current framework. Since 2003 the author has made several fieldtrips to Ruili; the latest, in March and August 2011, and May 2012 have provided most of the material for this chapter.

The Rise of a Border Enclave

For centuries, mule caravans trading "Asian" commodities have crisscrossed what is today northern Myanmar and southwest China. A southern branch of the ancient Silk Road even passed through Yunnan and Myanmar on its way to Assam and Bengal. Ming and Qing emperors were as fond of jade as Chinese people of the twenty-first century are (Chang 2003; Sun 2011). Many towns in the region have at different times benefited from the trade in Burmese gemstones, including Tengchong (formerly Tengyueh), Mangshi (Luxi), and Baoshan in China, or Bhamo and Myitkyina in northern Myanmar, but since the early 1990s it is the Yunnan border town of Ruili (facing the Myanmar town of Muse) that has witnessed one of the most extraordinary economic booms of the region. In the first decades after 1949, little exchange took place between Muse (a Burmese Army outpost, which faced, only a few kilometres away, a stronghold of the insurgent Communist Party of Burma (CPB)), and the Chinese hamlet of Ruili, in Yunnan's Dehong Prefecture (Lintner 1989, p. 359). However, after the powerful CPB collapsed in 1989, and with Deng Xiaoping's China pushing for more bilateral trade with the post-Ne Win Myanmar regime, new economic opportunities were created along the Sino-Myanmar borders — opportunities that included the rise of underground networks and criminal armed insurgents.

Yunnan fortune-seekers, businessmen, and jacks-of-all-trades began to flood southward into Ruili in the early 1990s, and then into the northern parts of Myanmar such as Mandalay, in search of fame and easy wealth (Mya Maung 1994). While various "Chinese" trading networks were spreading into Burma's military-controlled areas as well as into border zones dominated by ethnic ceasefire groups (notably Kachin, Pa'O, and Shan), Kachin, Shan, and Burmese Muslim traders who had till then been based in Mandalay, Taunggyi, or Mogok, began to venture northwards, gradually setting up new businesses in Ruili, and then in Jiegao (five kilometres south of Ruili, right at the border facing Muse), a special economic zone created by the Chinese authorities in 1995.[17] In less than a decade Ruili became the perfect entrepôt for all sorts of goods and the epicentre of all Yunnan–Myanmar trans-border businesses — both legal and illegal — a role the towns of Namhkam (Burma) and Tengchong (Yunnan) had played until the twentieth century.

With its underworld of casinos, drugs, and prostitution, for more than a decade Ruili enjoyed an infamous reputation as a "Wild Wild East" city. However, from the early 2000s the Chinese authorities initiated a harsh crackdown on most of the illicit activities that since 1989 had been enriching Ruili, as the author observed.[18] Far less visible today than they used to be (although they have not completely disappeared), underground and criminal networks are bound to become lesser sources of revenue for Ruili, which is now aiming to become one of Asia's exclusive international centres for jade commerce — according to the local authorities.[19] In fact, with the growing Sino-Myanmar economic interaction (a US$2.6 billion bilateral trade in 2009–10), Ruili cannot but benefit immensely from its geographical position along the "Burma Road" linking Mandalay and Kunming (Guo 2010, Le Bail and Tournier 2010). Yunnan province as a whole is also likely to prosper in the next decade on the foundation of its "greener jade" reputation, according to Chinese academics (Lin and Li 2005).

Kinship, Diaspora Networks, and the Creation of an Immigrant Niche of Traders

While it was fortune-seekers from Yunnan who poured into a booming Ruili during the 1990s in search of new opportunities, including criminal opportunities, since the year 2000 a new wave of migration of Chinese businessmen from beyond Yunnan (from cities such as Shanghai, Shenzhen, and Guangzhou), has been observed. Encouraged by administrative advantages, many have come to Ruili to invest, mostly in the jade and tourism sectors.[20] Beside this new type of Chinese migration, an interesting melting-pot of trading communities derived from various Burmese ethnic groups has formed in and around Ruili over the past two decades. These include Kachin and Jingpo (a major Kachin sub-group, many of whom have settled in Yunnan), as well as Shan and *Shan Tayoke* (or "Shan Chinese"), Burmans, and Burmese Muslims of Indian origin, from Mandalay, Yangon, Taunggyi, or Lashio (Egreteau 2011). They hold various types of Chinese visa, border pass, or residency certificate, ranging from the cheapest one-day pass to the nine-month residency permit (depending on their negotiating skills and connections with the Chinese immigration and police local officials). Locals estimate that, as at May 2012, about 30,000 to 40,000 Myanmar dealers are allowed to trade in and around both Jiegao and Ruili.[21] Of these, an estimated 3,000 to 5,000 are Burmese Muslims, including roughly 1,000 Rohingya. The latter, a stateless, downtrodden, and persecuted Sunni minority from the swampy Bangladesh–Myanmar borderlands (Lewa 2008), have, interestingly, developed quite substantial jade businesses and commercial retail shops in Ruili and Baoshan.[22]

The extreme diversity of the Burmese ethnic communities of traders settled in Ruili enables them to act as "middlemen". The 1970s conceptual framework of the "middleman minority" (Bonacich 1973), and the subsequent literature on the "ethnic enclave" or "ethnic economy" (Light and others 1994), and "immigrant niche" (Waldinger 1994), although dated, seem to fit the case of Ruili. Useful brokers in the trading activities of a border area, middlemen minorities master several languages, use ethnic-based networks, as well as kin and community labour forces, while maintaining cultural characteristics distinct from those of the locals — and are therefore more or less segregated from host societies. Jewish, Chinese, and Indian communities have been most studied by international academics, as lightly outlined by Joel Kotkin and his "global tribes" (Kotkin 1993). The Burmese ethnic communities of traders based in Ruili do indeed speak various languages, and they act mostly as "go-betweens" between overtly dominant Chinese jade traders — who control the lion's share of the local jade industry — and the Burmese owners of gem and jade mines inside Burma. Their networks are based around kinship and ethno-religious solidarities: Kachin/Jingpo, Shan/Shan Tayoke, or Burmese Muslims with their far-reaching networks in Yangon and Mandalay, but also in Malaysia, Taiwan, and the Persian Gulf.[23]

All transnational networks associated with the Burmese gem and jade industry (extraction, production, polishing, and trade) appear to be completely outside Western specific trading networks and capital flows. Ruili — despite its remote location — has become in recent years a valuable "immigrant niche", the epicenter of the diaspora linkages these traders have been using to expand their activities beyond Yunnan and Myanmar. Myanmar and Chinese traders from Ruili have broadened their commercial influence (to cities such as Hong Kong, Shanghai, Taipei, Bangkok, or Kuala Lumpur) by making the most of their existing kin-based networks north of Mandalay. Interviews revealed, for instance, that Burmese Muslim dealers most benefit from their personal interactions — with, for example, a sister who owns a shop in Ruili, a brother involved in Mandalay's jade market, an uncle living in the Hpa'kant or Mogok mines areas, a cousin who is a clerk in a Yangon bank, or a nephew who drives trucks between Mandalay and Muse.[24] These private, kin-based trans-national and diasporic networks are, consequently, extremely difficult to trace and control, for whoever aims to legally curb their activities.

"SANCTIONS? WHAT SANCTIONS?"

Some Recent Findings from Ruili

Today, about six thousand shops in Ruili and Jiegao are more or less involved in gem and jade businesses, from the import of raw boulders to the polishing of stones and the sale of fashion jewels.[25] More than rubies, timber, or various illicit commodities still produced in Myanmar, jade and jadeite have since the mid-2000s become the major foundation of Ruili's economy. The biggest local association, the Ruili Gem Traders' Association, boasted five thousand members in 2011, mostly Chinese and Myanmar nationals.[26]

The thirty-odd discussions the author held during his latest fieldtrips in March and August 2011, and May 2012 highlighted a rather mocking attitude on the part of the gem traders towards international sanctions targeting Burmese jadestones. An earlier fieldtrip in July 2009 — less than a year after the implementation of U.S. and EU "smart sanctions" on gems — had revealed some pessimism among the same Ruili-based jade dealers at that time. The number of transactions, as well as the value of the trade in gems and jade, were reportedly far lower than before 2008.[27]

The shutting-down of smaller mines and gem production factories inside Myanmar had been reported,[28] and similar patterns had been observed in Thailand, with ruby and sapphire trading networks affected.[29]

However, rather than being a direct consequence of Western sanctions, it appeared this locally-felt downturn had been a result of the global economic and financial crisis of 2007–09, which had considerably affected overall demand for gemstones, including demand from China. By March 2011, after eighteen months of relative difficulty, the cross-border gem and jade trade was again flourishing in Ruili, with skyrocketing profits now being openly acknowledged. Over a period of twelve months, jewellery trading worth RMB (Yuan) 2 billion (or US$300 million in 2011) was recorded in Ruili alone, according to a claim by local Customs authorities.[30] A jade-oriented economy is indeed thriving locally. Chinese young people from Kunming and beyond are increasingly migrating to Ruili to be employed in shops and factories refining Burmese raw stones and polishing jewels, or to work in the rising local tourist sector.[31] After a re-adjustment phase in 2008–09, Western sanctions appeared to have slipped into irrelevance in these off-limits bustling border regions.

The logic of geography explains a lot. With Myanmar licit and illicit commodities traded directly across the Yunnan-Myanmar border (70 per cent of the China-Myanmar trade goes through the major Customs checkpoint at Jiegao) thus avoiding major international financial and commercial networks, trans-border flows can hardly be controlled by external organizations. The historical porosity and the volatility of the Sino-Myanmar border areas that are plagued with political instability and inter-ethnic strife add to the conundrum. Locals can cross the border between Yunnan and Myanmar at any time for a meagre fee, whether for business and/or leisure purposes — and gemstones, as well as drugs, can be easily hidden and then turned into cash. They also serve as a safer replacement for Myanmar paper money. Smuggling activities have produced a vast underground commerce which represents a valuable share of Ruili's gem and jade industry, in spite of regular crackdowns by the Chinese authorities (Lin and Li 2005; Set Aung 2011).

The patterns of the Burmese gemstone industry, from extraction to marketing and consumption, hinder a stronger impact by any Western policy focus. Myanmar's mining industry is more and more controlled by companies run by businessmen who have close links with Myanmar's military-led government, with a myriad of local small extractors, and the gem trade is increasingly based on transnational kinship networks, with Myanmar and Chinese dealers having secured a quasi-monopoly. The jade business in the region has almost become a bilateral affair; a few (a very few) middlemen operate between Chinese buyers and Myanmar sellers. Western hands are nowhere to be seen — as jade holds little interest for Westerners. As long as overseas Chinese jade enthusiasts (including in Hong Kong, Taiwan, Singapore, Bangkok, or even Sydney) remain the driving force behind the trade, Western sanctions are doomed to miss their Burmese gem target.

The Global View: From Blunt Sanctioning to Better Monitoring?

EU and U.S. sanctions focused on Burma's gemstones have not prevented an amazing increase in the size of the Burmese gem and jade trade since 2008 — nor, therefore, greater profits for the Myanmar state and its associates. Rather than looking merely to impose sanctions on this trade, Western governments and lobby-groups should consider trying to establish multilateral negotiations for better monitoring of the whole Myanmar gem industry. Ending sanctions can be a tough political exercise. Drawing negative responses from Western public opinion and involving changes to complex legislative mechanisms, it is sometimes more costly politically and economically to end sanctions than to perpetuate them or merely "suspend" them, as in April 2012 (Dorussen and Mo 2001), hence the author's suggestion to establish parallel instruments for monitoring the targeted industry rather than to bluntly punish it.

In comparison with the EU Common Position that was revised in November 2007, the American Block Burmese JADE Act passed in July 2008 was specifically designed to emulate the model offered in the early 2000s by the fight to stop the trade in African "blood diamonds". The "Kimberley Process" was initiated by the international community in 2003 to establish an international certification scheme to trace diamonds worldwide and thus eradicate the illicit trade that had funded civil wars in Africa (Wexler 2010). The Process has since come to include representatives of gem-producing nations, transnational civil society groups, and, more importantly, of the diamond industry itself (starting with the powerful De Beers company) who have voluntarily agreed to institute a degree of self-regulation. The Kimberley Process has proved relatively successful — although not in every African gem-producing country[32] — and has noticeably restricted the illicit financing of internal conflicts through diamond trading (Grant and Taylor 2004). Academics have already considered the extension of the Kimberley Process to the whole of the world's gemstones industry (Harrington 2009).

Imposing a Kimberley Process-style mechanism on Myanmar's gem market sounds rational. On examination, however, the idea proves to be quite tricky. First, the Myanmar gem and jade industry is far less cohesive than its African diamond counterpart, which is dominated by few "majors". Myriads of extractors, sellers, and buyers, as well as medium-size corporations (which are increasingly state-run) are involved in Burmese gem mining and production, with different international trading networks used for rubies and jadestones, and there are many different consumer societies and nations willing to acquire them (Clark 1999). Second, Burmese gems are not directly involved in the perpetuation of conflict in Myanmar, the way diamonds were in Angola, Sierra Leone, or Congo. What activists have relentlessly denounced in the case of Myanmar is, rather, the profits that have been scooped up by its military-led authoritarian state.

Although working conditions in mines are appalling, with forced labour, child labour, and human rights abuses, and there are disquieting environmental issues, a local gem-based economy prospers legally in Myanmar, and is recognized and openly promoted by other countries in the region, starting with China, India, and Thailand. It is estimated that overall nearly half a million Burmese people are working in various sectors of the gem industry (through extracting, refining, retailing, and trading activities) — far more than, for instance, in another controversial Myanmar industry, the oil and gas sector.[33]

Establishing a Kimberley Process for Myanmar would need concrete cooperation from all parties (including the Myanmar government, Myanmar businessmen, and ethnic ceasefire groups), the voluntary participation of China, the establishment of legal enforcement mechanisms, and far better knowledge about the patterns of the whole Myanmar gem industry — production, trade, and circulation. While it might be easier to realize such a process for Burmese rubies — after all, Myanmar is home to as much of world ruby production as South Africa's De Beers controls of diamond production (Harrington 2009, pp. 355–56; Wexler 2010, p. 1734) — it might prove extremely difficult to do the same for the volatile jade trade. The role of the United States would be less crucial in relation to Burmese gems than it is for diamonds (half of the world's diamond production is sold in the United States); China is the main state actor in the Burmese jade trade. Nevertheless, mechanisms aimed to create independent supra-national regulatory bodies and to foster better monitoring of the Myanmar gem industry should be considered.

For countries that are considering the imposition of sanctions aimed at the Burmese gem trade, there is a tension between trying on the one hand to balance the need to protect people who live under the yoke of ruthless authorities and corrupt oligarchs (and to protect their threatened environment), with, on the other hand, the positive socio-economic contribution in the form of employment and income that the gemstone industry nonetheless provides to Myanmar society, especially at the local level. Externally-imposed sanctions often kill an industry (Kudo 2008a). There have been some reports of undesired counter-effects (or "collateral damage") as a result of the Western sanctions.

During recent interviews, for instance, local Myanmar and Chinese traders in Ruili admitted they have been affected by the financial sanctions imposed by the West on Myanmar banks, because the sanctions have caused limitations on transactions deeper inside Myanmar (where Chinese banks have not (yet) set up businesses to circumvent sanctions), as well as hindering trans-national remittances. This anecdotal evidence indicates that sanctions have in fact had some limited impact — but, paradoxically, not on their main target. The positive effect for Myanmar and Myanmar society of the money transferred back to Myanmar by Burmese communities in Thailand has been well researched (Turnell, Vicary and Bradford 2008), although in-depth studies of other Burmese remittances networks, in China for instance, are lacking. Recent interviews revealed that many Burmese Muslim and Rohingya merchants living in Ruili and Baoshan were using remittances facilities provided by the Kanbawza Bank based in Muse to send money back to their communities. A Western sanctions target, Kanbawza Bank also has branches in Mandalay and Sittwe, and it appears that Rohingya communities move substantial amounts of money for their families or associates through these branches.[34] Some traders complained about the Western pressure on that specific bank, because it limits their ability to transfer money throughout Myanmar. These examples support the argument for an international focus based on the assumption that monitoring and better understanding a crucial industry, rather than punishing a regime and its business associates, would do more good than harm.

CONCLUSION

Since the 1990s, sanctions policies against Myanmar have been endlessly debated by activists, social scientists, and policy-makers alike. After 2008, the revision of sanctions to incorporate a "smarter" arsenal that targeted Myanmar energy, timber, and gem resources revitalized the Western approach. Yet, as this author argues, the focus on Burmese gemstones has proved to have little real effect: the objectives of both the 2008 U.S. Block Burmese JADE Act and the strengthened EU Common Position of 2007 embodied miscalculation — especially if the rising importance of jadeite within Myanmar's global gem industry and the critical Chinese driving force behind it are taken into consideration. This does not imply that international monitoring of Myanmar gem production and trade should be abandoned. Rather, new international and independent regulatory bodies can be set up to better track Burmese gemstones and to encourage the adoption of responsible corporate practices at all levels of this thriving industry: extraction and production, retailing, and transnational trading. Any consideration of further refinements should involve all parties, starting with the Myanmar producers and Chinese, Thai, and Indian dealers — not only Westerners who are remote from the industry. The most achievable first step could be to focus on the production and trade of Burmese rubies, as monitoring of the trade in jadeite would require much deeper knowledge of that specific industry in and around Burma. In any case, the international (read, Western) community should keep its focus on Burmese gemstones, but disconnect it from its persistent desire to punish rulers and cronies in Naypyitaw.

Notes

1. The author wishes to thank the organizers of the 2011 Myanmar/Burma Update, as well as AusAID for the invitation and conference trip funding. Insightful comments provided by Trevor Wilson, Romain Caillaud, fellow panelists, and the audience during the conference were much appreciated.
2. Research and fieldwork in Yunnan borderlands have been generously supported by the Hong Kong-based *Hang Seng Bank Golden Jubilee Fund for Research*, a two-year grant awarded (2010–12) to the author in February 2010. The author

is indebted to Dong Yu-fei (Swift) for his research assistance on Chinese-language material.

3. The term "jade" is traditionally used to define two different minerals, jadeite and nephrite, but only jadeite is of gem value.

4. Author's interview with the president of the Ruili Gems Traders' Association (RGTA), Ruili, 28 February 2011.

5. Xinhua, "Myanmar enhances gem mining in 18 years", 11 January 2006 <http://english.people.com.cn/200601/11/eng20060111_234572.html> (accessed 29 May 2012).

6. *Myanmar Times*, "Gem auction set for March 10", 7–13 March 2011 <http://www.mmtimes.com/2011/business/565/biz56502.html> (accessed 29 May 2012).

7. *New Light of Myanmar*, "Myanmar jade with best quality in the world", 9 March 2011 <http://myanmargeneva.org/NLM2011/eng/3Mar/n110309.pdf> (accessed 29 May 2012); Reuters, "Myanmar gems sale nets record $2.8 billion – official", 25 March 2011 <http://www.reuters.com/article/2011/03/25/us-myanmar-gems-idUSTRE72O2FI20110325> (accessed 29 May 2012).

8. Xinhua, "Myanmar expects more visitors at next gems emporium", 14 February 2011 <http://news.xinhuanet.com/english2010/world/2011-02/14/c_13731827.htm> (accessed 29 May 2012); Reuters, "Drop in sales at latest Myanmar gems fair", 14 July 2011 <http://www.reuters.com/article/2011/07/14/myanmar-gems-idUSL3E7IE0Y020110714> (accessed 29 May 2012).

9. Xinhua, "Myanmar's gem sale experiences slumping trend", 23 March 2012, <http://news.xinhuanet.com/english/business/2012-03/23/c_131485114.htm> (accessed 29 May 2012).

10. Human Rights Watch, "Burma's Gem Trade and Human Rights Abuses", 29 July 2008 <http://www.hrw.org/news/2008/07/29/burma-s-gem-trade-and-human-rights-abuses> (accessed 29 May 2012). See also Sisodia, Rajeshree, "Jade trade in Myanmar thrives on exploitation, rights abuses", *The National (UAE)*, 30 September 2008 <http://www.thenational.ae/news/world/asia-pacific/jade-trade-in-myanmar-thrives-on-exploitation-rights-abuses> (accessed 29 May 2012).

11. Reuters, "U.S. bill targets Myanmar earnings from gems", 18 October 2007 <http://www.reuters.com/article/2007/10/18/us-myanmar-usa-gems-idUSN1828922920071018> (accessed 29 May 2012); *New York Times*, "U.S. House backs crackdown on Myanmar gem trade", 12 November 2007 <http://www.nytimes.com/2007/12/12/world/asia/12iht-myanmar.1.8706991.html> (accessed 29 May 2012).

12. Agence France Presse, "US enforces law barring Myanmar gems", 27 October 2008 <http://afp.google.com/article/ALeqM5h42cl7UFsCsidxGTWxvSmoyfzZVQ> (accessed 29 May 2012).

13. In 2006, bilateral trade was evaluated at US$9 million. See Reuters, "Canada says will impose tougher Myanmar sanctions", 14 November 2007 <http://www.reuters.com/article/2007/11/14/idUSN14207937> (accessed 29 May 2012).
14. *Official Journal of the European Communities*, No. L287, 8 November 1996, p. 1.
15. Agence France Presse, "EU extends Myanmar sanctions but opens doors", EUbusiness, 12 April 2011 <http://www.eubusiness.com/news-eu/myanmar-politics.9jh> (accessed 29 May 2012).
16. See the report by Australia's Department of Foreign Affairs and Trade, available at <http://www.dfat.gov.au/un/unsc_sanctions/burma.html> (accessed 10 July 2011).
17. *South China Morning Post*, "Opening Economic Zone at Burmese Border approved", 27 October 1995.
18. Author's regular fieldtrips to Ruili since 2003.
19. Author's interview with the president of the Ruili Gems Traders' Association (RGTA), Ruili, 15 May 2012.
20. Author's discussion with a Chinese businessman from CapitalAsia, a Shanghai-based firm, Ruili, 27 February 2011.
21. Author's interview with the president, RGTA, Ruili, 28 February 2011.
22. Author's interviews in Ruili and Baoshan with several Rohingya traders originally from the townships of Buthidaung and Maungdaw (Rakhine State), March and August 2011 and May 2012.
23. Ibid. Many Rohingya jade dealers met have indeed travelled quite a lot, mostly between Dhaka, Kuala Lumpur, Bangkok, Dubai, and even Shanghai.
24. Author's interviews, Ruili, March and August 2011 and May 2012.
25. The market of Jiegao focuses on raw jade and massive boulders trade, while Ruili, five kilometres away, is already specialized in polished and fashioned jewels or jadestones.
26. Author's interview with the president, RGTA, Ruili, 15 May 2012.
27. Author's interview, Ruili's central jade market, July 2009.
28. Thuyein Kyaw-zaw, "Burma's gem mines face closure", BBC Burmese Service News, 17 March 2009 <http://news.bbc.co.uk/2/hi/7947914.stm> (accessed 29 May 2012).
29. *Irrawaddy*, "Sanctions affecting Burmese gems trade", 22 January 2008 <http://www2.irrawaddy.org/article.php?art_id=10005> (accessed 29 May 2012); *Bangkok Post*, "Burmese gems may haunt Thai jewelers", 19 March 2008 <http://www.readbangkokpost.com/business/burmamyanmar/burmese_gemstones_sold_in_thai.php> (accessed 29 May 2012).
30. Xinhua, "Jewelry industry developed in Ruili, China's Yunnan", 30 May 2011 <http://english.people.com.cn/90001/90783/7394133.html> (accessed 29 May 2012).

31. Author's interview with a 25-year old Chinese student from Kunming, trying her luck as tourist guide, Ruili, March 2011.
32. *Economist*, "Zimbabwe and its diamonds: forever dirty", 2 July 2011 <http://www.economist.com/node/18898238> (accessed 29 May 2012).
33. *Bangkok Post*, "Burmese gems may haunt Thai jewelers"; Thuyein Kyaw-zaw, "Burma's gem mines face closure".
34. Author's interviews, Ruili and Baoshan, August 2011 and May 2012.

References

All Kachin Students and Youth Union. *Blood Jade: Burmese Gemstones and the Beijing Games*. Chiang Mai: 8808 For Burma, 2008.

Bonacich, Edna. "A Theory of Middleman Minority". *American Sociological Review* 38, no. 5 (1973): 583–94.

Camroux, David and Renaud Egreteau. "Normative Europe meets the Burmese Garrison State: Processes, Policies, Blockages and Future Possibilities". In *Ruling Myanmar: From Cyclone Nargis to National Elections*, edited by Nick Cheesman, Monique Skidmore and Trevor Wilson. Singapore: Institute for Southeast Asian Studies, 2010.

Clark, Carol. *Seeing Red: A View from Inside the Ruby Trade*. Bangkok: White Lotus, 1999.

Chang, Wen-chin. "Three Yunnanese Jade Traders from Tengchong". *Kolor: Journal on Moving Communities* 3, no. 1 (2003): 15–34.

———. "*Guanxi* and Regulation in Networks: The Yunnanese Jade Trade between Burma and Thailand, 1962–88". *Journal of Southeast Asian Studies* 35, no. 3 (2004): 479–501.

———. "The Trading Culture of Jade Stones among the Yunnanese in Burma and Thailand, 1962–88". *Journal of Chinese Overseas* 2, no. 2 (2006): 269–93.

———. "Venturing into 'Barbarous' Regions: Transborder Trade among Migrant Yunnanese between Thailand and Burma, 1960s–1980s". *Journal of Asian Studies* 68, no. 2 (2009): 543–72.

Dorussen, Han and Jongryn Mo. "Ending Economic Sanctions: Audience Costs and Rent-seeking as Commitment Strategies". *Journal of Conflict Resolution* 45, no. 4 (2001): 395–426.

Egreteau, Renaud. "Intra-European Bargaining and the 'Tower of Babel' EU Approach to the Burmese Conundrum". *East Asia (An International Quarterly)* 27, no. 1 (2010): 15–33.

———. "Burmese Indians in Contemporary Burma: Heritage, Influence, and Perceptions since 1988". *Asian Ethnicity* 12, no. 1 (2011): 33–54.

Ehrmann, Martin. "Gem Mining in Burma". *Gems & Gemology* 9 (1957): 3–30.

Elliott, Kimberly Ann. "The Sanctions Glass: Half Full or Completely Empty?". *International Security* 23, no. 1 (1998): 50–65.

Galtung, Johan. "On the Effects of International Economic Sanctions: With Examples from the Case of Rhodesia". *World Politics* 19, no. 3 (1967): 378–416.

Grant, J. Andrew and Ian Taylor. "Global Governance and Conflict Diamonds: The Kimberley Process and the Quest for Clean Gems". *Round Table* 93, no. 375 (2004): 385–401.

Guo, Xiaolin. "Boom on the Way from Ruili to Mandalay". In *Myanmar/Burma: Inside Challenges, Outside Interests*, edited by Lex Rieffel. Washington, D.C.: Brookings Institution Press, 2010.

Harrington, Alexandra R. "Faceting the Future: The Need for and Proposal of the Adoption of a Kimberley Process-Styled Legitimacy Certification Scheme for the Global Gemstone Market". *Transnational Law and Contemporary Problem* 18 (2009): 353–417.

Howse, Robert L. "Are EU Trade Sanctions on Burma Compatible with WTO Law?". *Michigan Journal of International Law* 29 (2008): 165–96.

Hughes, Richard W. "Burma's Jade Mines: An Annotated Occidental History". *Journal of Geo-Literary Society* 14, no. 1 (1999): 15–35.

Hughes, Richard W. et al. "Burmese Jade: The Inscrutable Gem". *Gems & Gemology* 36, no. 1 (2000): 2–25.

Kessel, Joseph. *The Valley of Rubies*. New York: David McKay & Co., 1961.

Khin Maung Nyunt. 1996. "History of Myanmar Jade Trade till 1938". In *Traditions in Current Perspective: Proceedings of the Conference on Myanmar and Southeast Asian Studies, 15–17 November 1995*, pp. 247–82. Yangon: Universities Historical Research Centre, 1996.

Kotkin, Joel. *Tribes: How Race, Religion and Identity Determine Success in the New Global Economy*. London: Random House, 1993.

Kudo, Toshihiro. "The Impact of U.S. Sanctions on the Myanmar Garment Industry". *Asian Survey* 48, no. 6 (2008a): 997–1017.

———. "Myanmar's Economic Relations with China: Who Benefits and Who Pays?". In *Dictatorship, Disorder, and Decline in Myanmar*, edited by Monique Skidmore and Trevor Wilson. Canberra: ANU E-Press, 2008b.

Le Bail, Hélène and Abel Tournier. *From Kunming to Mandalay: The New Burma Road*. Asie, Visions No. 25. Paris: Institut francais des relations internationales (IFRI), 2010.

Lewa, Chris. "Asia's New Boat People". *Forced Migrations Review* 30 (2008): 40–42.

Light, Ivan, et al. "Beyond the Ethnic Enclave Economy". *Social Problems* 41, no. 1 (1994): 65–80.

Lin, You-bin and Li Ling-hua. "Developing the superiority of Gemstone Industry in Yunnan Province". *Journal of Yunnan University of Finance and Economics* 21, no. 1 (2005): 98–102 (in Chinese).

Lintner, Bertil. "Burma's Jade Trail". *Gemological Digest* 2, no. 4 (1989): 24–31.

———. "The Volatile Yunnan Frontier". *Jane's Intelligence Review* 6, no. 2 (1994): 84.

———. *Burma in Revolt: Opium and Insurgency since 1948*. Chiang Mai: Silkworm Books, 1999.

Marinov, Nikolay. "Do Economic Sanctions Destabilize Country Leaders?". *American Journal of Political Science* 49, no. 3 (2005): 564–76.

Mya Maung. "On the Road to Mandalay: A Case Study of the Sinonization of Upper Burma". *Asian Survey* 34, no. 5 (2004): 447–59.

Naylor, Thomas. "The Underworld of Gemstones: Part 1, Under the Rainbow". *Crime, Law and Social Change* 5, no. 2 (2010): 131–58.

Pape, Robert. "Why Economic Sanctions Do Not Work". *International Security* 22, no. 2 (1997): 90–136.

———. "Why Economic Sanctions Still Do Not Work". *International Security* 23, no. 1 (1998): 66–77.

Pedersen, Morten. *Promoting Human Rights in Burma: A Critique of Western Sanctions Policy*. Lanham: Rowman & Littlefield Publishers, 2008.

Samuels, S.K. *Burma Ruby: A History of Mogok's Rubies from Antiquity to the Present*. Tucson, Arizona: SKS Enterprises, 2003.

Set Aung, Winston. *Informal Trade and Underground Economy in Myanmar: Costs and Benefits*. Bangkok: IRASEC-Observatory Occasional Paper No. 4, 2011.

Steinberg, David I. "The United States and Myanmar: a 'Boutique Issue'?". *International Affairs* 86, no. 1 (2010): 175–94.

Sun, Laichen. "From Baoshi to Feicui: Qing-Burmese Jade Trade, c. 1644–1800". In *Chinese Circulations: Capital, Commodities and Networks in Southeast Asia*, edited by Eric Tagliacozzo, Wen-chin Chang and Wang Gungwu. Durham: Duke University Press, 2011.

Turrell, Robert V. "Conquest and Concession: The Case of the Burma Ruby Mines". *Modern Asian Studies* 22, no. 1 (1988): 141–63.

Turnell, Sean, A. Vicary and W. Bradford. "Migrant-worker Remittances and Burma: An Economic Analysis of Survey Results". In *Dictatorship, Disorder, and Decline in Myanmar*, Monique Skidmore and Trevor Wilson. Canberra: ANU E Press, 2008.

U.S. Government Accountability Office (USGAO). "U.S. Agencies Have Taken Some Steps but Serious Impediments Remain To Restricting Trade in Burmese Rubies and Jadeite". GAO 09-987. Washington, D.C.: Government Accountability Office, 30 September 2009 <http://www.gao.gov/products/GAO-09-987>. Accessed 29 May 2012.

Waldinger, Roger. "The Making of an Immigrant Niche". *International Migration Review* 28, no. 1 (1994): 3–30.

Wallensteen, Peter. "Characteristics of Economic Sanctions". *Journal of Peace Research* 5, no. 3 (1968): 248–67.

Walsh, John. "Robert Gordon and the Rubies of Mogok: Industrial Capitalism, Imperialism and Technology in Conjunction". *Asian Culture and History* 3, no. 1 (2011): 94–100.

Wexler, Lesley. "Regulating Resource Curses: Institutional Design and Evolution of the Blood Diamond Regime". *Cardozo Law Review* 31, no. 5 (2010): 1717–80.

Wilson, Trevor. "The Costs, Achievements and Collateral Effects of Australia's Financial Sanctions Against Burma (Myanmar)", Asiarights Blog, Australian National University, 4 July 2011 <http://asiapacific.anu.edu.au/blogs/asiarights/2011/07/>. Accessed 9 June 2012.

IV

Economic Update

7

TAKING STOCK OF MYANMAR'S ECONOMY IN 2011

Khin Maung Nyo

The year 2011 may prove to have been a milestone for the Myanmar economy because until 30 March the State Peace and Development Council (SPDC) military government managed the economy, but after that date a new "civilian" government, exercising power under Myanmar's 2008 Constitution, took office. Even though both governments claimed to support a market-oriented economy, the new government seems to have shifted away from some of the policy stances of the former government. This is an appropriate time, then, to take stock of the results of previous government action and make some comparisons with initiatives of the new government that try to solve problems inherited from the SPDC military government.

Generally, people were quite impressed when they learnt about the inaugural address made by the new president, Thein Sein, to the parliament (*NLM* 2011a). However, this speech closely reflected what the (government-backed) Union Social and Development Party (USDP) party had promised during the 2010 election campaign. In most points the president's speech reiterated the basic principles of a market economy, but the people of Myanmar, who thirst for economic reform and were unhappy with the administration of the old government, were able to see some hints of change. There are, on the other hand, some cynics who doubt the political will and capacity of the new administration to carry out change.

MYANMAR'S STATUS AS A LEAST DEVELOPED COUNTRY

Myanmar was designated a Least Developed Country (LDC) in 1987, but after so many years since then, it should have graduated from the LDC list. Myanmar needed to meet three criteria in order to graduate. Two of these it is already able to satisfy: for example, Myanmar's Human Assets Index in 2009 was 66.0, and its Economic Vulnerability index was 37.4. However, gross national income (GNI) per capita in 2009 was only US$306, leaving Myanmar still qualifying as an LDC. Myanmar's low rate of economic growth keeps it at that status.

A quarter of Myanmar's population is still living under the poverty line, even though some improvement has been seen in recent years. As usual, double-digit inflation and negative real interest rates have resulted in severe and continuous government deficit budgets and contributed to this outcome. Moreover, in Myanmar it is difficult to establish a business because of the high cost of infrastructure, high transaction costs, and high barriers to entry. Bank loans are not easily accessible, as banks operate at a very rudimentary level. Attempts to establish a stock market are still in the planning stages.

Public expenditure on education and health is very low, accounting for less than 5 per cent of the budget. Consequently, public services in these areas are poor and unreliable. Even minor treatment at a hospital can be a risk to life. There is no effective and efficient mechanism to deal with emergency situations.

Nevertheless, Mr Cheick Sidi Diarra, the UN's High Representative for the Least Developed Countries, Landlocked Developing Countries and Small Island Developing States, speaking on the sidelines of a development conference in Istanbul, Turkey, on 12 May 2011, said that Myanmar could benefit greatly in the coming decade from adopting development policies in line with the Istanbul Program of Action for the Least Developed Countries. These include raising a "trust fund" for future generations by setting aside up to 20 per cent of the country's national income and dedicating another 25 per cent of the national income to infrastructure development and human capital enhancement, with the remaining 55 per cent going to the "functions of the state". Other policies include focusing on boosting productive capacity in order to attract foreign investment — such as building infrastructure, investing in human capital, and transferring knowledge.

Myanmar has not received "preferential treatment" from the World Bank, the International Monetary Fund, or the Asian Development Bank (ADB) for two decades, and receives less official development assistance than other LDCs. Mr Diarra said he thought Myanmar was in an excellent position to graduate from the LDC list by the end of the Istanbul Plan of Action's duration, in 2020 (Nyunt Win 2011).

Possibilities for Improvement of LDC Status

In 2010, Myanmar saw an unprecedented wave of Foreign Direct Investment (FDI) wash over the country. From 1988 until the end of the 2009–10 financial year, a total of about US$16 billion had been invested in Myanmar, mainly in oil and gas, hydropower, and mining projects. In the twelve months from 31 March 2010, the total amount of FDI more than doubled, with nearly US$20 billion being recorded by the government's Central Statistical Organization. China alone signed off on projects totalling US$14 billion.

In the past two years the Myanmar government has given the green light to several major infrastructure and energy projects, including the oil terminal and deep-sea port at Kyaukphyu in Rakhine State, a number of hydroelectric power plants such as the Baluchaung scheme and Myitsone dam, and the US$50 billion Dawei Special Economic Zone in Tanintharyi Region (*Myanmar Times* 2011).

Myanmar will implement the action plan of its Information and Communications Technology (ICT) Master Plan 2011–15,[1] aimed at developing the information and communications technology sector. The 2011–15 ICT Master Plan, drawn up jointly by experts from Myanmar and South Korea, covers five main areas — ICT infrastructure, ICT industry, ICT human resources development, e-education, and ICT legal framework. The government has claimed that the first ICT plan for 2005–10, drawn up in 2005, has been accomplished. The implementation has raised Myanmar's tele-density from one per cent in 2005 to 5.4 per cent in 2011, according to media reports (*Flower News Journal*, 24 July 2011).

FROM SMUGGLERS TO ENTREPRENEURS
AND CRONIES

Under Myanmar's socialist economic system (1964–88), profit-making became illegal and entrepreneurs were virtually regarded as smugglers. Several operations were conducted against private traders, claiming that such people were exploiting other ignorant people. The profit-making concept was taboo, even at the government-operated business school. Economics professors taught their businessmen students to avoid areas of business where government monopolistic enterprises operated so that their own enterprises might succeed. In practice, however, those who competed with state-owned enterprises did well, because of the poor management, operation, and marketing of state firms.

One Myanmar professor presented a paper for his doctorate degree which suggested that trying to suppress the black market, which provided the everyday needs of the Myanmar people, would bring about the destruction of government mechanisms. However, when the State Law and Order Reconstruction Council (SLORC) assumed state power in 1988, former smugglers came to be regarded as entrepreneurs. These new entrepreneurs, who had accumulated their wealth under the Socialist era, then tried to get access and rights to the extraction and exploration of natural resources such as timber and minerals. As the post-1988 government created private businessmen, these two groups mingled with each other for their mutual interest.

In addition, government officials, whose low salaries could not keep up with double-digit inflation, enjoyed the fruits of the market economy by getting their hands dirty. Their family members established private enterprises and were able to gain access to limited resources, privileges, and internal networks through their official connections. Initially, government officials were novices at business and were manipulated by private businessmen. Later, while some family members were directly engaged in the regulation of business, other family members joined the business community. This new business community — whose members later came to be described as "cronies" — was able to influence some government decisions and regulations which benefited them monetarily.

The mingling of army and business interests became evident in the changing behaviour of both sides. Entrepreneurs enjoyed the VIP treatment and "red carpet" welcomes usually accorded to military officials, and military officers came to think in terms of commercial benefit to themselves. Businessmen, who already shouldered a heavy burden of bribery to senior officials, transferred their load to their employees by paying low salaries. Many Myanmar businesses are operated by family members who may have neither the interest nor the skill to run a business well. However, accumulation of great wealth is possible when they bid for privatized state assets and estates.

Over the almost three decades since the Myanmar government first introduced a market-oriented policy, the nature and education status of the people who were active entrepreneurs changed remarkably: initially many were almost illiterate, with only a basic education; then gradually graduates joined the ranks; and in recent years a third generation of entrepreneurs who have been trained abroad in modern management, marketing, and financial management, but who have been unable to utilize their knowledge because of the lack of development of business practices in Myanmar, has emerged.

One example of how the Myanmar government maintained its influence over private business is that the executives of some non-government business organizations were appointed by ministers or other senior authorities: for example, members of the Central Executive Committee of the Union of Myanmar Federation of Chambers of Commerce and Industry and of the Myanmar Women Entrepreneurs Association were appointed by the Ministry of Commerce. These appointees were able to monopolize markets and deliver poor service at relatively high prices. This practice led one famous Myanmar economist to make the bold remark that because of the combined impact of cronies and corrupt officials, no specific improvements could be expected. Not surprisingly, this kind of rent-seeking behaviour became a target for political parties at the 2010 elections. Accordingly, the new president will need to take some initiative to discourage corruption and monopolistic behaviour.

Under the new Myanmar government, older senior officials are finding it difficult to adopt a new way of doing business, as they are accustomed to act only in response to direction from their superiors. One side-effect of this change is that reporters and editors at state-owned newspapers now find it difficult to fill space in their papers. Formerly, there were many news reports about official trips by senior military officials who were directing "this or that", but there was no investigative reporting at all, and no news about events and hardships at the grass-roots level of society. News about private sector developments usually appeared in weekly journals or as advertisements in state-owned daily newspapers. Now the journalists are sailing in uncharted waters.

Under the previous administration, business deals could be made by agreement with local military officials. However, power-sharing arrangements between the new Union Assembly (*Pyidaungsu Hluttaw*) and local authorities have not yet been clearly defined. That is why new ventures and transactions have not emerged following the Myanmar New Year holiday in April 2011.

Uncertainty is still in the air and is the order of the day, while the transition to a new government and administration is taking place only slowly. Will companies do their business as usual on the basis of who they know and not what they know? One business student, who found he did not have enough time for academic studies as well as for carrying out business dealings with the authorities, commented that business management classes could not teach students how to develop business connections, how to find a comfortable way of paying bribes, and how to get special privileges for their firms. One certainty out of this multi-faceted uncertainty is that everybody, including the ordinary people, is waiting for the right moment to launch into business activities which for more than twenty years they have not been allowed to undertake.

CHANGES IN THE BUSINESS ENVIRONMENT

During the years of the government-initiated transformation to a market economy, some real changes have occurred. Myanmar consumers have become more sophisticated, and their style of shopping has shifted away from shopping at local markets towards shopping at big malls. Door-to-door distribution of commodities has also emerged during this period. Imported products, especially from Thailand and China, have begun to replace locally-made products, which are relatively poor in quality. Packaging standards have improved. Awareness and concern about safety of products have increased among producers and consumers because of the more active performance by the (Myanmar) Food and Drug Agency.

As employment and income have increased, especially in the private sector, demand for and use of ICT products, as well as for health and beauty products, has increased remarkably. In general, Myanmar consumers have become more materialistic as the semi-governmental media broadcast programmes that encourage consumerism. Following three bomb blasts at shopping malls, concern about security grew and numerous security devices were imported. However, the Myanmar market is still a seller's market, as no regular flow of goods can be guaranteed. It is dominated by monopolistic and oligopolistic firms. Prices are relatively high, and quality and service suffer. Some changes in specific sectors are set out below.

Real Estate Market

Investment in the real estate market is the best option for profit-making under current market conditions — better than investment in the car and bullion markets — but people can buy real estate only when they have enough disposable money. The price of real estate in the six Yangon downtown townships has reached an amazing height, with both businessmen and construction companies competing for the properties (Htar Htar Khin and Kyaw Hsu Mon 2011).

The six busiest townships in downtown Yangon are Kyauktada, Latha, Pazundaung, Lanmadaw, Pabedan and Botataung, although the price of real estate varies from township to township, as does demand from buyers. Kyauktada and Pabedan enjoy a greater demand and prices there are highest. The ground floors of some apartments in these two townships are attractive for businesses and shops and are hard to come by.

According to Mr Serge Pun,[2] a well-known entrepreneur who has business interests in Myanmar and other parts of Asia:

> The buoyant property market is due to the positive sentiments in Myanmar, which can be attributed to the constitutionally elected Myanmar government late last year. The new Myanmar government's promises of better governance and administration of policy has gone down well both domestically and with international investors, especially in the area of infrastructure, setting the economy on a growth path."[3]

From early in June 2011, however, the property market became sluggish, because of the expiration of the property tax in August. The Property Tax Law applies to both buyers and sellers. Before 2007, 50 per cent of a property's price was levied as profit tax, but in 2007 the Internal Revenue Department announced that the rate would change to 12 per cent for sales above K5 billion (US$6.25 million at the current exchange rate) and 15 per cent for sales below K5 billion. Under the protection of this law, money launderers entered the real estate market and bought many high-priced properties. Since 2008 the price of real estate has skyrocketed. After each gem emporium, Chinese-Shan traders have bought properties by paying the asking price without bargaining, if they liked the property. This way, the asking price became the market price.

The government has sold many state-owned properties by auction and tender but these sales had no significant impact in terms of deflating the market because the prices received were high. The Padomma Theatre in Sanchaung Township, owned by the Ministry of Culture, was sold by tender for K500 billion (US$625 million at the current exchange rate) in February 2001, but because the buyers had difficulty in paying the bidding price on time and were unable to resell at a higher price in the market, they surrendered the site to the government (Nyi Thit 2011). According to a Joint Secretary of the Privatization Commission, about one billion dollars' worth of state assets and enterprises have already been sold (*Snapshot Journal*, 28 June 2011).

Rapidly increasing prices for real estate have caused other problems. Property prices in some major locations have increased six-fold within five years, due to financially powerful investors who are speculating in the real estate market, either with their own financial resources or with money they have managed to inject into the market through various means. Unreasonably high property prices have also exacerbated housing problems for the middle class, company staff, and factory workers, and have undermined efforts to build low-cost housing for them (*Weekly Eleven*, no date).

Furthermore, high property prices are a hurdle for start-up enterprises because they raise the amount of initial capital that is needed and operating costs rise. Since the late 1990s, university students (who could no longer rent accommodation in public hostels because none existed near the new, more remote, university campuses) and low-paid workers have faced difficulties through being forced to live in high-rent private housing. As government investment focused on developing physical infrastructural, the price of real estate, especially in locations near new projects, has become a target for investors.[4]

In 2011, the government sold tens of thousands of cars it had seized in recent years because they had been imported illegally. As a result, car prices, which for years had been highly inflated because of tight import restrictions, fell by as much as 50 per cent, though they were still higher than in neighbouring countries. However, from early in August 2011, after people realized that illegally imported motor vehicles would no longer be taxed and legalized, the prices of cars again began to increase (*Weekly Eleven*, August 2011).

Labour Market

Burmese democracy icon Aung San Suu Kyi sent a message to the Davos World Economic Forum in February 2011 and called for investment from abroad that would be sensitive to labour rights and environmental issues.[5] Some critics interpreted her message as referring to China, which is the biggest investor in Burma and which neglects labour rights and environmental issues. If Burma were to have access to foreign investment and technology from developed countries that usually emphasize developing wider benefits than just pure economic benefit, Burmese workers would suffer less.

Since slow economic development cannot provide opportunities for business development and labour market development, many people in Myanmar try to find better paid jobs abroad. This results in a scarcity of labour in Myanmar, especially of relatively skilled workers.

Within Myanmar's garment industry there are frequent labour disputes between factory owners and workers, mostly related to low wages and the lack of any guarantee of workers' rights. The majority of garment factories are owned by Chinese and Korean nationals. This market is a seller's market in which labourers with low skills can easily get a job. However, poor industrial relations makes this sector unstable and it has become a battleground for owners and workers.

Another interpretation of labour disputes relates to the lack of any mechanism for reflecting workers' concerns and protecting their rights. Without such a mechanism, the "managers" who act as middlemen between foreign owners and local workers have not been able to bring the two conflicting sides to understand and be aware of each other's needs and limitations. If there were some way to negotiate settlement of disputes between management and workers, the number of demonstrations and riots might decrease. In fact, this suggestion does not relate only to workers: others, such as farmers and ordinary citizens, should have a mechanism through which they can voice their concerns and be allowed to participate in affairs and decisions that affect their daily life and livelihood.

Right now, with Japan's economy having been hit by the earthquake and tsunami and by nuclear power problems, Myanmar's textile industry is worried about the security of their market in Japan, which has been taking around 60 per cent of Myanmar's total textile exports. Earlier, orders for garments had increased and workers had hoped their wages would increase proportionately. If factory owners were able to identify their interests with those of their workers, fewer disputes would end in confrontation.

Human Resource Development

During his visit to universities in Mandalay on 26 July 2011, Vice President Dr Sai Maukkham gave a speech about weaknesses in human resource development in the education and health sectors. He pointed out that although the number of graduates being produced by the universities is higher than before, the quality of their education has gradually dropped. The level of qualification of faculty members has also declined. Experienced educational experts were invited to give workshops to address how all aspects of education could be improved in order to bring about the necessary reforms. The Vice President explained that the workshops would focus on strategies such as improving the ratio of highly-qualified faculty members to students; adopting a student-centred approach; increasing undergraduate courses by one more academic year; avoiding the need for students to hire outside tutors; reconsidering the supplementary examination system because it reduces the motivation for students to study right from the start of the academic year; and moving away from the system that allowed students to get two masters degrees within three years. He noted that many students put too much reliance on faculty members when they do research work, and lack self-reliance, and he pointed to the need to open more private schools and universities, and to introduce a system of scholarship awards and stipends (*NLM*, 2011*b*).

The number and type of media outlets has increased during the last few years, and the demand for reporters has risen, creating many job opportunities for young people, especially in towns outside the major centres. Some private media organizations move to try and set up daily newspapers as soon as the government permits them to do so, but say it is a problem to recruit qualified local journalists. "We find it difficult to recruit competent and devoted local reporters in small towns", said one publisher (*Weekly Eleven*, no date).[6]

The Foreign Exchange Market

According to economists and business leaders, the national government is expected to adopt a more flexible approach to exchange rates in response to the appreciation of the Myanmar kyat. The government has been looking at both short-term and long-term ways to "solve" the problem of the strong local currency, which in June 2011 hit a five-year high of K750 to the U.S. dollar. Recently the Myanmar government held discussions with economists and businessmen, and listened to their advice on the best way to solve the issue of the high exchange rate. The former government took a "hard" approach to the currency exchange rate, but the present government has a flexible and pragmatic outlook, and also wants a foreign exchange policy that encourages trade.

Myanmar uses multiple exchange rates, with state imports booked at the official rate of K5.5 to the U.S. dollar. However, private sector businesses use the market rate, which appreciated from a record low of about K1400 in 2007 to K750 in early June 2010. It has since stabilized at about K800. The strong kyat has significantly affected exporters, who spend kyat to produce commodities but earn U.S. dollars in return, and it has made some export items, particularly agriculture and fisheries products, unprofitable on international markets.

Business owners were hoping for a more stable exchange rate, and said the appreciation of the kyat had "severely hurt the business community" (Win Ko Ko Latt 2011). However, any realignment of the different exchange rates into a single rate will need considerable time and expertise, although assistance could be requested from international financial organizations. Exchange rate reform could be part of a broader macroeconomic reform rather than of short-term emergency measures.

The Financial and Banking Sector

The former government always produced a deficit budget which was financed by monetization, except during the last few years, when part of the deficit was financed by issuing treasury bonds. Under the new government, budget policy has moved towards reducing the deficit in order to control inflation, and is aimed at producing a balanced budget in the near future. State and Regional governments may prepare their budget plans separately.[7]

Although some improvements in tax administration are well regarded and appreciated by international and regional organizations such as the ADB, there remains much room for improvement; for example, taxes such as the Export Tax create obstacles for exporters and work against export promotion policies.[8] Corruption and tax evasion is still rampant. Tax administrators need to be exposed to international tax practices and knowledge.

Under the banking law adopted in 1990, the State Law and Order Restoration Council permitted foreign banks to open in Myanmar. However, their only role is to liaise between local and foreign clients for trade and commerce. No foreign bank is allowed to carry out local business. Among the numerous foreign banks which had opened their offices in Myanmar, forty-nine have left the country due to the government's reluctance to liberalize the banking sector, though most of them still maintain their licences.

While the foreign banks are not authorized to carry out local money transactions, the local private banks are also not permitted to handle foreign exchange, including remittances from overseas. Formally, three state-owned banks, Myanma Economic Bank (MEB), the Myanma Investment and Commercial Bank (MICB), and the Myanma Foreign Trade Bank (MFTB) are the only active players allowed to carry out foreign currency transactions. Among these, the Myanma Foreign Trade Bank deals with remittances.

In general, the deduction of 10 per cent of every remittance as a service charge for transactions made by the state-owned bank discourages overseas Myanmar nationals from choosing formal channels for sending money back home. Instead, informal channels have been popular choices despite strict legal and regulatory control of these kinds of business activities. Today, the majority of overseas Myanmar workers remit money to their home town by using informal *hundi* services.[9]

Myanmar banks have a number of weaknesses, and they lag well behind regional and global banks in terms of capitalization, application of banking technology, scale of operations, staff skills, scope, and financial products. There is an urgent need to strengthen and upgrade all aspects of bank operations. International best practice should be adopted, and a fair and competitive environment provided. Restrictions and discrimination need to be removed and the system needs to move towards market-based practices, and to create a favourable business and regulatory environment. A securities market and an equity market should be established. It is essential for the development of the banking sector that the central bank be independent of government influence or interference (Sein Maung 2006).

GOVERNMENT FAILURES AND MARKET FAILURES

As a least developed country, Myanmar faces a number of failures by the government as well as market failures, and these need to be corrected if Myanmar is to become a "modern developed country". For example, to comply with Association of Southeast Asian Nations (ASEAN) standards on lorries and trucks, restrictions on loading capacity were introduced in early March 2011.[10] However, this caused increases in the cost of transporting commodities and, accordingly, in the prices of these commodities. To lessen the burden of transportation charges, the government revoked existing restrictions enforced at toll gates on lorries and trucks. (Weekly Eleven, 30 June 2011). It was reported in July 2011 that, after recognizing that there was a shortage of trucks, the government was considering allowing entrepreneurs to import trucks and lorries (Weekly Eleven, 14 July 2011).

Myanmar's military government nationalized most industries after it took power in a 1962 coup and the government has controlled the lion's share of the economy since. In 1995 the government began a privatization scheme: ports, airlines, highways, mines, dams, factories, warehouses, government buildings, and cinemas have all gone on the block. Private firms may now run schools and hospitals. In 2010, four new banks were opened, the first new banks since around the time of Myanmar's banking crisis in 2003.

The Economist magazine has commented that the Myanmar privatization programme seemed to be a hurried asset-stripping exercise by the generals and their cronies, which had echoes of Russia's 1990s fire sale: the valuations of the assets are not published, nor is the price they fetch; buildings are listed for auction but sales are done in private, so that a handful of pro-junta tycoons are benefiting royally.[11] Such privatization could also have the effect of injecting some competition into what is an almost Soviet-style economic system, and might herald a shift in direction. Reformers in the government might be hoping to follow a path similar to that of China or Vietnam, where the economy has been liberalized but the ruling party has remained firmly in charge and has tolerated little dissent

(*New York Times*, 2010). After learning some lessons from situations where previous procedures were not transparent, the new government is now, as of August 2011, trying to privatize Yangon's commuter circuit train in a more transparent and credible manner (Si Thu 2011).

Since 2000, the cost of using GSM phones provided by Myanmar Post and Telecommunication has been exorbitant. The cost of a SIM card used to be around US$1,500 and only a few people had access to them. Now, around 500,000 GSM phones are in use. In February 2011 the price of a SIM card had reduced to around US$500 (*Weekly Eleven*, 30 June 2011), and where the responsible government agency can supply only a hundred SIM cards daily, private companies can supply thousands of cards within a few minutes. With regard to the Internet, however, in Myanmar its quality remains poor and accessibility is still limited.

CHALLENGES FROM AFTA AND CHINA

Businesses across Southeast Asia are preparing for the challenges presented by the ASEAN Free Trade Agreement (AFTA). In the case of Burma, the government has the largest role to play in making the country's businesses more competitive. There is, for example, almost no macroeconomic framework within the country that could provide businesses with the stability and data needed to make long-term investment decisions Furthermore, with the exception of the regime's business cronies, local entrepreneurs have very limited access to capital markets, and there is no transparency about government revenue and expenditure. With the formation of the new government, some observers had hoped that the government budget for 2011, as well as following budgets, would be published in detail for everyone to see and analyse, as a way of helping to create a climate of transparency, accountability, and a fair playing field.

Despite these serious obstacles, the Burmese business community must embrace the obligations of the ASEAN Free Trade Agreement. Where possible, Burmese businesses must be able to strive to become part of the new local and regional value chain and to grasp whatever new logistical opportunities AFTA may offer.

One of ASEAN's concerns is the entry of cheap Chinese products. Burma, however, has already had experience with Chinese products. Most imported items already carry a tax rate of less than 5 per cent; no remarkable change could be expected from a zero tariff or from the removal of non-tariff barriers. Under AFTA, consumers may enjoy some tax-free goods. The biggest challenge for Burmese businesses will not be external business threats; the most serious problem will continue to be with the government itself.

CONCLUSION

At the 2009 ANU Myanmar/Burma Update Conference, Professor Suiwah Leung commented on Myanmar's economic policies as follows: "The policy paralysis in the (Myanmar) government has been such that, when the world economy emerges from the current recession, Myanmar will be further behind in the competitiveness stakes than before the crisis". Two basic problems she identified as follows: "The Myanmar leadership, on the other hand, seems to have focused on rent-seeking"; and "the constraints on Myanmar's economic development are more policy-induced than arising from economic sanctions". Finally, looking ahead, she suggested, "The challenge in Myanmar seems to be the alignment of interests and institutions in favour of domestic economic reforms".[12]

There are vast areas in Myanmar that need fundamental improvement: productivity, standards and quality, environmental friendliness, market exposure, and modern business management; in addition, formal business structures and networking groups should be established.

These are areas where the government could, if it chose, create a business-friendly environment, by favouring the rule of law, and ensuring transparency and consistency of policies. In addition, the updating of infrastructure could reduce unnecessary transaction and operating costs. The proposed one-stop service for Special Economic Zones could be adapted to serve local enterprises, especially small and medium businesses, which also need start-up capital at low interest rates. Ultimately, it is the new Burmese government that must put its house in order. AFTA will provide a test for Burmese businesses and whether they can compete in the region — but more than that, it will be a test for the new government that the military rulers have created.

Notes

1. No official statement is available; as reported in *Flower News Journal* (Yangon). See also Xinhua, "Myanmar to Implement ICT Master Plan 2011–15", *CriEnglish*.

com, 24 July 2011 <http://english.cri.cn/6966/2011/07/24/2821s650091.htm> (accessed 30 May 2012).

2. Serge Pun is a prominent Chinese-Myanmar businessman who set up Serge Pun & Associates (Myanmar) Limited ("SPA") Group in Yangon in 1991. He later became CEO of First Myanmar Investment (FMI) company (1992), Yoma Bank (1993), and Yoma Strategic Holdings (2006), and has significant property interests in Yangon and elsewhere. Bloomberg Businessweek, "Yoma Strategic Hldgs Ltd (Yoma: Singapore), Executive Profile Serge Pun". See <http://investing.businessweek.com/research/stocks/people/person.asp?personId=28911455&ticker=YOMA:SP&previousCapId=2446002&previousTitle=Hong%20Kong%20Exchanges%20%26%20Clearing%20Ltd> (accessed 10 August 2011).

3. "Yoma Set To Benefit from Property Market: Rebound in Myanmar", Media release, YOMA Strategic Holdings Ltd, Singapore, 15 July 2011 <http://www.yomastrategic.com/pdf/Yoma_Set_to_Benefit_from_Property_Market_Rebound_in_Myanmar.pdf> (accessed 10 August 2011).

4. "Tax on sale of Burmese real estate to be increased?". *Mizzima News*, 5 August 2011 <http://www.mizzima.com/business/5734-tax-on-sale-of-burmese-real-estate-to-be-increased.html> (accessed 30 May 2012).

5. The text of this statement is available on the CNN Website. Paul Armstrong, "Suu Kyi to Davos: Myanmar must reconnect with world", CNN, 29 January 2011 <http://edition.cnn.com/2011/WORLD/europe/01/28/davos.suu.kyi/index.html> (accessed 10 August 2011).

6. See *Weekly Eleven*, no date, <http://eversion.news-eleven.com/index.php?option=com_content&view=article&id=1391:shortage-of-local-reporters-a-blow-to-journals&catid=43:biweekly-eleven-eversion&Itemid=110> (accessed 10 August 2011).

7. "Budget deficits to be handled with effective management to avert possible hindrance to national and regional development", *New Light of Myanmar*, 22 June 2011 <http://www.myanmar.com/newspaper/nlm/Jun22_02.html> (accessed 30 May 2012).

8. According to the Asian Development Bank, the fiscal deficit narrowed to about 3.5 per cent of gross domestic product in fiscal year 2007. The rapid growth in tax revenues is a result of improvements to tax administration since 2004, and state enterprises have been increasingly allowed to raise prices closer to market rates. See <http://www.adb.org/documents/books/ado/2009/MYA.pdf> (accessed 10 August 2010).

9. See Sean Turnell, A. Vicary and W. Bradford, "Migrant Worker Remittances and Burma: An Economic Analysis of Survey Results", in *Dictatorship, Disorder and Decline in Myanmar*, edited by Monique Skidmore and Trevor Wilson (Canberra: ANU E-Press, 2008); also, Nwet Kay Khine, "Remittance flows from

Thailand to Mawlamyine, Mon State, Myanmar" (Bangkok: unpublished paper, Chulalongkorn University, undated) <http://humansecurityconf.polsci.chula. ac.th/Documents/Presentations/Nwet.pdf> (accessed 31 May 2012).

10. No official public announcement was made; the new policy was enforced at the toll gates on the highways into Myanmar.

11. "A beautiful feeling: In Myanmar, where good things happen to bad people, most things are going the junta's way", *Economist*, 5 August 2010 <http://www. economist.com/node/16743025?story_id=16743025> (accessed 24 August 2011).

12. Extracts from discussion opening points, Suiwah Leung (courtesy of conference convenors).

References

Htar Htar Khin and Kyaw Hsu Mon. "Real estate industry braces for tax increase". *Myanmar Times*, 11–17 July 2011.

Myanmar Times. "President signs key economic, development deals with China". *Myanmar Times*, 6–12 June 2011. <http://www.mmtimes.com/2011/ business/578/biz57801.html>. Accessed 31 May 2012.

New Light of Myanmar (NLM). "President U Thein Sein delivers inaugural address to Pyidaungsu Hluttaw". *New Light of Myanmar*, 31 March 2011a. <http://www. burmanet.org/news/2011/03/31/the-new-light-of-myanmar-president-u-thein-sein-delivers-inaugural-address-to-pyidaungsu-hluttaw/>. Accessed 31 May 2012.

———. "Medical institutions to keep in touch with ASEAN, international community and other related organizations for sustainable development". *New Light of Myanmar*, 27 July 2011b, pp. 8–9. <http://www.burmalibrary. org/docs11/NLM2011-07-27.pdf>. Accessed 31 May 2012.

New York Times. "Myanmar's Ruling Junta Is Selling State's Assets". *New York Times*, 7 March 2010 <http://www.nytimes.com/2010/03/08/world/asia/ 08myanmar.html>. Accessed 31 May 2012.

Nwet Kay Khine. "Remittance flows from Thailand to Mawlamyine, Mon State, Myanmar". Bangkok: Unpublished paper, Chulalongkorn University, n.d. <http://humansecurityconf.polsci.chula.ac.th/Documents/Presentations/ Nwet.pdf>. Accessed 31 May 2012.

Nyi Thit. "Will the Burmese real estate bubble burst soon?". *Mizzima News*, 11 July 2011. <http://www.mizzima.com/business/5576-will-the-burmese-real-estate-bubble-burst-soon.html>. Accessed 31 May 2012.

Nyunt Win. "Escape from poverty on horizon". *Myanmar Times*, 577, 30 May 5 June 2011. <http://www.mmtimes.com/2011/news/577/news57702.html>. Accessed 31 May 2012.

Sein Maung. "The role of private banks in Myanmar Economic Development". Presentation at Myanmar Fisheries Federation, 1 July 2006.

Si Thu. "Rangoon Circular Railway Privatization Discussed". *Irrawaddy,* 27 July 2011. <www.irrawaddy.org/article.php?art_id=21778>. Accessed 10 August 2011.

Srivastava, Pradeep. "Myanmar". In *Asian Development Outlook.* Manila: Asian Development Bank, 2009.

Turnell, Sean, A. Vicary and W. Bradford. "Migrant-worker Remittances and Burma: An Economic Analysis of Survey Results". In *Dictatorship, Disorder, and Decline in Myanmar,* edited by Monique Skidmore and Trevor Wilson. Canberra: ANU E Press, 2008.

Win Ko Ko Latt. "Government set to reform foreign exchange policy". *Myanmar Times,* 582, 4–10 July 2011. <http://www.mmtimes.com/2011/news/582/news58202.html>. Accessed 31 May 2012.

8

REFORM AND ITS LIMITS IN MYANMAR'S FISCAL STATE

Sean Turnell

In 2011 Myanmar's economy remains in stalled transition. Twenty years from the first tentative steps away from rigid state control, the reform momentum that appeared promising in the early 1990s has dissipated into an uncertain redistribution of economic power amongst state, state-connected, and private entities. The installation of a nominally civilian government in Myanmar in March 2011 has as yet done little in concrete terms to change this basic equation, even as there have been some intriguing developments in the realm of policy "advice". As has long been the case, however, all is clouded by a broader uncertainty with respect to Myanmar's fundamental political and economic institutions.

In this chapter we examine some of the more important economic developments that have taken place in Myanmar in recent times, but with a particular focus upon institutional developments in policy advocacy, upon Myanmar's public finances, and on capital formation in the private sector. Considered, accordingly, are issues concerned with state spending, "hidden" state accounts, developments in private banking, as well as the illicit capital outflows that further compromise Myanmar's ability to mobilize the financial resources that could turn its economy around.

ECONOMIC REFORM

It is now more than twenty years since Myanmar took its first tentative steps away from the *dirigiste* model that imprisoned its economy following the military takeover in 1962. These steps, manifest in a series of laws enacted from 1990, allowed for the re-emergence of large private sector enterprises, for the formation of private banks, for the opening-up of the economy to trade and foreign investment, and for other activities necessary for a functioning market economy. The new freedoms triggered a brief period of economic growth and new institution building, but even before the decade was out this (modest) circle of progress and reform had run its course. Indeed, by the mid-1990s Myanmar's ruling authorities had begun to reverse some of the earlier openings, while a severe banking crisis in 2003 tarnished both the reform narrative and its advocates. Meanwhile, Myanmar's emergence from the mid-2000s as a significant exporter of natural gas provided "economic rents" of a sort and volume that sapped any remaining will or incentive for government-directed reform. As a consequence, and in striking contrast to its peers and neighbours (even authoritarian states), Myanmar has not embarked upon a single significant measure of economic reform for nearly two decades.[1]

Myanmar's "New" Government

On 30 March 2011 Myanmar's ruling junta, the self-styled "State Peace and Development Council" (SPDC), formally dissolved itself and handed over nominal power to a new "elected" administration comprising a parliament and executive presidency. In political terms, this administration is regarded by many observers as little more than "new wine in an old bottle" (to use but the most popular of the many metaphors employed), but some hope has been entertained that the new arrangements could bring about movement on the economic front. Such hopes are yet to be made manifest. So far, at time of writing, no significant measures have been enacted, nor are there any concrete economic reforms currently in prospect.[2]

Certain institutional and personnel changes permitted by Myanmar's new governing arrangements may give greater cause for hope, although even with these changes, the expectations are for yet-to-be-realized *potentials* for policy, rather than — so far — for anything more tangible. Within the new ministerial line-up in March 2011, for instance, came the appointment in the Commerce portfolio of Win Myint, immediate past president (appointed) of the Union of Myanmar Federation of Chambers of Commerce and Industry (UMFCCI), who in his former role had made guarded references to the need for policy reform.[3] Also appointed were relatively "liberal" ministers for Labour (Aung Kyi, who held the same role in the SPDC regime, and who was the principal interlocutor between the SPDC and Daw Aung San Suu Kyi), and for Hotels and Tourism (Tint Hsan, a leading business figure with connections to the military regime). Against these potentially encouraging appointments, however, is the broader composition of the ministerial line-up in Myanmar's new administration — most of whom are either former military officers or ministers from the previous SPDC regime. Whilst this does not necessarily disqualify them as agents of change, it does point to the limited pool from which Myanmar's new leadership is drawn, and requires from observers a certain prudence in discerning genuine reforms from those that may be merely a façade.

Below ministerial level, Myanmar's new political arrangements have brought with them institutional changes, including the elevation of the Myanmar Investment Commission (MIC) over the (subsequently abolished) Trade Council as the principal body charged with promoting trade and investment.[4] This has removed at least one layer of bureaucracy, and already seems to have had the effect of speeding up decision-making with respect to investment approvals and the issuing of export/import licences.[5] Similarly reformist has been the breaking-up of the monopoly that once embraced the cooking oil import business. On the other hand, such modest reform gestures have been accompanied by policy regression in other areas, including the re-imposition of diesel rationing, the on-again/off-again restrictions on the export of rice, the continuing suspension of "on arrival" tourist visas, the ever-widening array of (official and unofficial) taxes on enterprise, and the perennial favouring (and disfavouring) of businesses on the basis of political connections. Meanwhile, the government continues to restrict the trade in many of Myanmar's most significant commodities, reserving export/import rights either to state-owned enterprises or to entities granted special concessions. Such commodities include teak, sugar, sesame, peanuts, petroleum, gold, gems, jade, wolfram, tungsten, silver, zinc, cotton, antiquities, and rubber.

One of the most high-profile of the institutional changes initiated under Myanmar's new government has been the creation of three presidential "advisory boards", each comprised of three persons, on politics, on legal matters, and on the economy. The economic advisory board, headed by

U Myint (and including two other Myanmar economists, Winston Set Aung and Dr Sein Hla Bo[6]) has been the most active thus far. U Myint, formerly a professor of economics at the University of Rangoon, Head of Research at the UN's Economic and Social Commission for Asia and the Pacific (ESCAP), and a leading figure in various roles concerned with Myanmar's external economic relations — is not only an economist of international standing but also a figure respected across Myanmar's political divide. The author of numerous innovative proposals for economic reform in Myanmar, U Myint has taken on the mandate of crafting policies and institutions to restore the country's traditional role as a major world rice exporter as a key step towards reducing poverty through agricultural and rural development.

At the centre of U Myint's drive for reform is the idea for a "Myanmar Development Resource Institute" (MDRI) to impel the reform process (U Myint 2011, p. 2). To be founded on the idea that the private sector must be the driver of Myanmar's growth and development, with the state playing a "facilitating and support role", MDRI is aimed at reversing the traditional role of the state in Myanmar — moving away from the role "of interfering and telling" people what to do, towards a role of helping them "do what they know is in their own best interest". MDRI is also envisaged as a haven of candour and transparency in a country that has experienced little of either. In a paper setting out his vision for MDRI and for reform more broadly, U Myint noted that in Myanmar it had been the "tendency for academics and researchers to engage in self-censorship in preparing studies and in expressing views and comments about economic and social issues …" (p. 8). This, he said, needed to change, as "[h]onesty and transparency are essential to gain trust and confidence of the people". As a way to better ensure that these virtues were achieved, and to cultivate its "independence and close links with the business and academic community", U Myint took the further step of recommending that MDRI be located in Yangon rather than in the new capital, Naypyitaw.

The proposal to establish MDRI was announced in May 2011 at a much-publicized "National Workshop on Rural Development and Poverty Alleviation". This meeting was nevertheless a vehicle for an unusual degree of candour with respect to Myanmar's economic situation. U Myint himself provided the "theme paper" for the gathering which, in its definition of poverty, pointedly referred to recent work by certain economists on expanding the meaning of "severe deprivation" to include the lack of access to information (U Myint 2011, para. 12). The paper also highlighted the importance of macroeconomic stability (and the need to eliminate "market-distorting interventions"), of "proper regulation and supervision of the financial system", and, perhaps most bluntly of all, of the "transparent use of public funds" (U Myint 2011, paras 48–49). More fundamentally, the paper advocated land reform that would implicitly give farmers full transferable rights over their land, and urged the government to move beyond the fixation of previous governments on creating physical infrastructure in favour of "directing more attention towards evolving better policies, institutional arrangements, and implementation programmes ..." (U Myint 2011, para. 89).

Of course, whatever the recommendations of meetings such as the above, of bodies like MDRI, or even whatever might be the intentions of Myanmar's new governing apparatus, economic reform will ultimately succeed or fail according to the realities of where power truly lies in Myanmar, and according to what financial and other resources are available. At the poverty workshop, Myanmar's new president, Thein Sein, repeated earlier assurances about the need for economic reform (while remaining vague on details), but his willingness and ability to engage in meaningful economic reform (much less political reform) cannot but be open to considerable doubt. The extent to which power in Myanmar resides today in the presidency, the vice-presidencies, the ministries, the parliament, the ruling political party (the Union Solidarity Development Party or USDP, created by the former regime), or the military broadly — or remains (in whole or in part) with former SPDC Chairman Senior General Than Shwe and the senior leadership of the military — is very unclear. But either way, the structure of Myanmar's state fiscal arrangements, and the degree to which these emaciate other sectors of the economy, will be a significant hurdle to any broad programme of economic reform that is not accompanied by fairly dramatic political change. It is to such issues that we now turn.

BURMA'S FISCAL STATE

Government Spending

In early 2011, for the first time in many years, Myanmar's state budget (for 2010–11, together with projections for 2011–12) was made public.[7]

Table 8.1 below aggregates the relevant numbers for 2010–11, the proportion of total spending allocated to each line ministry, and — for the purposes of international relativities — the U.S. dollar equivalent for each item.

Not surprisingly perhaps, the most noteworthy feature of Myanmar's state budget was the dominance of military spending. Expenditure on defence in 2010–2011 was greater than expenditure on all other items combined, and consumed just over half of the budget. However, even as high as expenditure on defence is acknowledged to be, specific allocations to defence almost certainly understate the military's claims on Myanmar's financial resources. It has long been the practice in Myanmar to embed some military spending in the budgets of other ministries, but in addition, the defence forces claim special access to foreign exchange as well as to other earnings of enterprises connected to the military (most notably the two giant military conglomerates, Union of Myanmar Economic Holdings and Myanmar Economic Corporation) (Selth 2002, 2009, 2010).

Other spending lines in the announced budget likewise contain few surprises. After defence, "construction" is the second-largest area of expenditure, and includes on-going costs associated with the building of Naypyitaw, as well as infrastructure more broadly. Spending on electricity

TABLE 8.1
State Spending by Ministerial Category, 2010–11

Ministry	2010–11 (Kyat millions)	Percentage of Total	US$ Equivalent 2011 ($m)
Defence	1,323,066	51%	1,557
Construction	295,963	11%	348
Education	266,906	10%	314
Agriculture	199,444	8%	235
Electricity	78,233	3%	92
Health	73,387	3%	86
Finance & Revenue	14,683	1%	18
Rail	4,487	—	5
Energy	232	—	1
Other	337,827	13%	398
TOTAL	**2,594,228**	**100%**	**3,052**

Source: Myanmar Central Statistical Organization (2011), and author's calculations.

generation, other "energy" sources, and on rail was low for 2010–11, ahead of greatly expanded projected spending on these items in the years ahead (more on which below). No longer shocking perhaps, but notable both for its inadequacy and the gloomy future it portends, was spending on health and education. The former, at little more than US$1.60 per capita, ties with the Republic of Congo as the lowest in the world. The equivalent numbers for government health expenditure in Myanmar's ASEAN peers such as Laos (US$7), Cambodia (US$11), and Vietnam (US$31) does not make for flattering comparison.[8]

Alongside "actual" spending data for 2010–11, projections for state spending in 2011–12 (that is, 1 April 2011 to 31 March 2012) were also made public. In this year ahead, aggregate spending on defence is projected to remain roughly unchanged at a proposed K1.3 trillion — although as a proportion of total government spending, it will fall by nearly half if foreshadowed large expenditures on energy and electricity generation are realized. These expenditures, of K1 trillion and K670 billion respectively, represent costs associated with the Myanmar state's share of spending on infrastructure supporting the Shwe gas pipeline and various hydro-electricity schemes that are joint ventures with China (see Table 8.2).

TABLE 8.2
State Spending by Ministerial Category, 2011–12

Ministry	2011–12 (Kyat millions)	Percentage of Total ($m)	US$ Equivalent	Percentage Increase over 2010–11
Defence	1,318,578	21%	1,551	0%
Energy	1,008,640	16%	1,187	434,658%
Electricity	668,520	11%	787	755%
Construction	578,024	9%	680	95%
Finance and Revenue	479,229	8%	564	3,164%
Communications	320,930	5%	378	160,365%
Agriculture	310,217	5%	365	56%
Education	310,020	5%	365	16%
Rail	208,186	3%	245	4,540%
Other	1,039,204	17%	1,223	253%
TOTAL	**6,241,548**	**100%**	**7,345**	**241%**

Source: Myanmar Central Statistical Organization (2011), and author's calculations.

Myanmar's Budget Deficit and Its Financing

With total taxation revenue of about K1.2 trillion for 2010–11, Myanmar's fiscal deficit (the gap between government spending and revenues) amounted to around K1.4 trillion. Without significant earnings from state-owned enterprises (principally the Myanmar Oil and Gas Enterprise, MOGE) that are largely held outside the public accounts (more on which below), this implies a programme of significant borrowing — from the central bank (printing money), from commercial banks, and from the sale of bonds. Table 8.3 reveals the magnitudes and relativities.

As can be seen from the above, "printing money" remained the most important way the Myanmar state finances itself beyond taxes. Such state borrowing from the Central Bank of Myanmar rose 28 per cent to 6.2 trillion kyat in the nine months to December 2010, and accounted for just over 52 per cent of deficit financing. Government borrowing from commercial banks accounted for 38 per cent of the government's borrowing needs, while sales of new bonds took care of 10 per cent. Such borrowing by the government highlights the way Myanmar's commercial banks have become an increasingly important component of the country's fiscal apparatus, and the extent to which this function has "crowded out" their

TABLE 8.3
Financing Myanmar's Fiscal Deficit
(Kyat millions)

Year	Central Bank Lending to Government	Commercial Bank Lending to Government	Commercial Bank Lending to Private Sector	Government Treasury Bonds Outstanding
2001–02	675,040	40,985	416,176	131,918
2002–03	892,581	43,248	608,401	132,895
2003–04	1,262,588	35,546	341,547	110,675
2004–05	1,686,341	89,217	428,931	111,627
2005–06	2,165,154	100,358	570,924	78,961
2006–07	2,762,626	178,519	652,892	117,614
2007–08	3,534,687	381,677	795,227	179,777
2008–09	3,880,765	611,224	907,117	297,358
2009–10	4,892,468	1,103,426	1,171,064	939,243
2010–11*	6,244,733	2,120,189	1,885,503	1,212,844

Note: *as at December 2011.
Sources: IMF (2011); Myanmar Central Statistical Organization (2011).

lending to the private sector. Indeed, Myanmar's private banks are now in the extraordinary position of lending more to the state (53 per cent of the total) than they do to businesses and consumers (47 per cent). As can be seen in Table 8.3, the trend in this direction has been under way for the last five years or so, but the surge in the last year (a period of supposed greater openings for commercial activity) has been as dramatic as it is troubling.

Meanwhile, the significant growth of Myanmar's bond market is *perhaps* a hopeful development in the country's public finances. In the historical experience of many countries, the rise of bond markets has been a precursor to more open government — a function of the fact that bond holders become a potentially powerful constituency with a vested interest in accountability and sound finance as protection against default. Of course, such processes are usually decades in the making, and much depends on who the bond-holders are. In the case of Myanmar, if the buyers are simply the closely controlled banks or connected conglomerates, then there will be little incentive or pressure for reform from this bond-holding cohort. In the absence of information about who the buyers of bonds are (which is not likely to be available anytime soon), greater accountability and a more transparent financial system must remain contingent hopes.

Finally, the substantial increase in Myanmar's proposed public spending for 2011–12 requires some explaining in terms of its financing. Should the Myanmar government go about doing this in its time-honoured ways — printing money, borrowing from the banks — the effects would be inflation that is dramatically higher (and potentially politically destabilizing), and the near complete disappearance of the remaining sources of private capital. Likewise, Myanmar's bond market is unlikely to be able to absorb a 230 per cent increase in securities on issue. What will square the fiscal circle? It is highly likely it will be debt — specifically, the substantial loans to Myanmar from China that were announced in 2010, and again in 2011.[9] These loans, in three tranches of US$4.2 billion (revealed in September 2010), US$2.4 billion (December 2010), and US$765 million (May 2011), were earmarked precisely for the categories revealed in the 2011–12 budget as being subject to substantial spending increases. There is apt to be at least an element of "double counting" in these loan announcements (which were made during visits to China by various of Myanmar's leaders), and a degree of imprecision with respect to the exact numbers concerned. Nevertheless, what is clear is that Myanmar has been taking on increasing amounts of debt in recent times (exclusively sourced from China). In future this indebtedness may cloud the otherwise rosy scenario suggested by the country's gas earnings, while limiting Myanmar's freedom of movement with respect to its giant neighbour.

"State Fund Account" and the "Special Fund Law"

Myanmar's most significant export commodity, and the "should be" source of game-changing state revenues, is the natural gas that is currently being piped through to Thailand. These exports, exclusively traded through the state-owned Myanmar Oil and Gas Enterprise, brought in net revenues in 2010–11 of around US$1.5 billion. If the foreign exchange earnings of other state enterprise exports (including mining and gems of around US$1.3 billion, and of teak and other hardwood of about US$600 million) are added to these, it can be calculated that Myanmar's government accumulated around US$3.6 billion in net foreign exchange in 2010–11 (MCSO 2011).

Revenues of this magnitude, which vastly exceed domestic tax receipts, should have a transformative effect on Myanmar's budget. Indeed, if properly recorded in Myanmar's public accounts, the deficit discussed above would be irrelevant. In other words, in truth Myanmar should have no budget deficit.

The question of "how" a budget deficit is thus otherwise manufactured by Myanmar's governing apparatus is as simple as it is deceptive. Instead of recording Myanmar's foreign exchange earnings at the country's unofficial market exchange rate (currently at around K850:US$1, and the true measure of its purchasing power), they are recorded at the otherwise moribund official exchange (of around K6: US$1). At this rate, Myanmar's state enterprises contributed earnings to the budget of a mere K22 billion — rather than their "true" international earnings of K2.9 trillion. As noted above, such an amount would at one stroke remove Myanmar's budget deficit, if it were so applied. Instead, and via what are effectively "two sets of books" for Myanmar's fiscal state, a greatly diminished financial pie is all that is available to meet the requirements normally assumed by a state to its people. The ample funds left over from this bit of creative book-keeping are meanwhile credited to a so-called "State Fund Account" administered by the Central Bank of Myanmar, but in effect controlled by Myanmar's most senior military and *de facto* (if perhaps not *de jure*) leadership.

The effective confinement of Myanmar's hard currency earnings into the State Fund Account provides the military and connected parties with discretionary funds to use for purposes that might otherwise prove embarrassing if they were recorded — and then allocated — at their true purchasing power. Presumably such uses include military materiel of various guises and other projects of limited economic or social utility. One manifestation of all this is almost certainly the provision of the actual monies allowed for the promulgation of the "Special Funds Law" just before the convening of the new parliament. This law gives the Commander-in-Chief of the Armed Forces in Myanmar the right, not just of absolute control and discretion over "unlimited" funds for the "perpetuation of national sovereignty", but also freedom from any "person or organization" (including the parliament) questioning or seeking to audit their use.[10] No doubt such a law would be on the wish-list of defence chiefs everywhere, but it is hardly conducive to the making of a prudent fiscal policy.

PRIVATE CAPITAL FORMATION

Myanmar Gets Four New Banks

In August 2010 four new private banks commenced operations in Myanmar. These four banks, the first new financial institutions to be created in the country since the establishment of the semi-government Innwa Bank in 1997, were announced under the brand names of "Asia Green Development Bank", "Ayeyarwady Bank", "United Amara Bank", and the "Myanma Apex Bank". Each of the four is a subsidiary of some of Myanmar's most prominent conglomerates, which in turn are controlled by some of its most controversial business "tycoons". These include Tay Za of the Htoo Group (Asia Green Development Bank), Zaw Zaw of Max Myanmar (Ayeyarwady), Nay Aung of IGE Group (United Amara), and Chit Khaing of the Eden Group (Myanma Apex). All the tycoons are present on international sanctions lists, and are otherwise notable for their close association with Myanmar's former ruling regime.[11] One interesting aspect of the new four private banks is the ethnicity of their ownership. In great contrast to the early 1990s "reform" period, when the then novel private banks were owned by Sino-Burmese, these new players are all identifiably "Myanmar" in character.

The four new banks appear extraordinarily ambitious, and all have promised to open branch networks at a greater scale than any hitherto existing private bank.[12] Whilst they are still far short of creating such networks, the new banks have already made an impact. Helping to fuel the phenomenal increase in lending to the state noted previously in this chapter, the new banks are also largely responsible for the rapid growth in private sector lending (even if this lags behind the funds provided to the government). As can be seen from Table 8.3, lending to the private sector increased 60 per cent in the nine months to December 2010. As discussed below, Myanmar's private sector desperately needs greater access to capital, but the speed of this credit growth and its likely destination (much of it ultimately into real estate speculation in Yangon) alarms many of Myanmar's bankers and economists. Amongst the latter there is something of a consensus view that many of the bad lending practices of 2002–03 have returned and, with these, the spectre of another banking crisis.

The new private banks have largely funded their lending through the accumulation of deposits. As can be seen in Table 8.4, bank deposits overall have increased dramatically over the last few years, with a particular spike in 2010–11 (when total deposits grew by 70 per cent), reflecting the arrival of the four new banks. The new banks employ a number of innovative strategies for attracting deposits, such as a mobile service offered by Myanma Apex Bank that visits some of the larger office buildings in downtown Yangon, and collects savings on the spot.

TABLE 8.4
Commercial Banks: Source of Funds

Year	Demand Deposits (Kyat millions)	Time, Savings and Foreign Currency Deposits (Kyat millions)	Foreign Currency Deposits (US$ millions)
2003–04	84,237	386,298	1,861
2004–05	140,707	594,169	1,993
2005–06	210,216	697,736	2,155
2006–07	319,910	901,120	2,185
2007–08	522,085	1,166,838	2,393
2008–09	515,204	1,596,703	2,662
2009–10	692,429	2,314,230	2,901
2010–11	1,339,283	3,745,828	3,051

Source: IMF (2011).

Despite this recent rapid rise in both loans and deposits associated with the new players, banks in Myanmar continue to lag behind those in peer countries (with the exception of Laos) in terms of both deposit accumulation, and in their provision of finance from these. Table 8.5 below shows the relative data for Myanmar and some "peer" countries with respect to domestic credit provided by the banking system — the critical measure in many ways of its contribution to capital accumulation (and, beyond this, to growth and development).

TABLE 8.5
Domestic Credit Provided by Banks (2009), Percentage of GDP

Myanmar	Cambodia	Indonesia	Laos	Philippines	Thailand	Vietnam
16.9	19.0	36.9	10.5	49.4	136.9	123.0

Source: IMF (2011).

Commercial Banking Broadly

Beyond the four new private banks, Myanmar's incumbent commercial banks more or less continue to do little but "subsist". Myanmar's long history of banking crises, de-monetization episodes, and similar confidence-sapping events means that very few people in Myanmar trust banks enough to put their money in banks for the purposes of wealth accumulation or capital formation. Nevertheless, especially for many business people, the private banks provide reasonably efficient payment, transaction, and remittance services. A practice that illustrates all sides of this phenomenon is the way that most real estate transactions are processed. In Myanmar most purchases of houses and commercial buildings are made in cash, since no conventional home loans are made by the banks.[13] The banks do play a role in the buying of real estate, however — as "middlemen" for the settlement of transactions, receiving the cash from the buyer, signalling to the seller that payment has been received, and then settling the final transfer. In this sense, at least, the banks provide the parties to a transaction with an independent broker in the transaction process, while eliminating the need for the physical transfer of vast amounts of cash between parties who may know little of each other. However, such "brokering" business is hardly traditional banking, and nor does it suggest a role for the banks as aggregators and allocators of capital — a role central to the part banks otherwise play in economic development. Of course, and perverse regulations aside (Myanmar's financial sector is inhibited by an array of inappropriate regulations — see Turnell 2009), Myanmar's banks themselves behave in ways that inhibit their collection of deposits. Most commercial banks, for instance, require a new depositor to furnish the name of two guarantors before they can open an account.

The emergence of new banks in Myanmar also masks a political environment that otherwise remains broadly hostile to financial intermediation. The crises surrounding the Kanbawza and Cooperative Banks in 2011 illustrate this point. The largest and second-largest respectively of the older cohort of Myanmar's private banks, in 2010 the Kanbawza and Cooperative Banks became embroiled in a dispute over the ownership of Myanmar Airways International (MAI).[14] This dispute escalated to the point that the less politically-connected of the banks (the Cooperative Bank) struggled to survive a "run" of depositors who were well aware of the dispute and were anxious that their bank was involved in a conflict with a well-placed regime business identity (Kanbawza Chairman Aung Ko Win) from which it might not survive.[15] Ironically perhaps, subsequent to these events (in 2011) Kanbawza itself came under pressure from anxious depositors concerned that the star of Aung Ko Win was also on the wane (in conjunction with that of Kanbawza's perceived patron, Vice Chairman of the former SPDC, General Maung Aye).

Throughout 2010–11, various minor regulatory and other developments that had the potential to cause peripheral effects on the country's commercial banking sector took place. In mid-2010, for instance, the Central Bank of Myanmar allowed private banks to issue what it called "electronic banking cards" that could function as credit cards, debit cards, or (most optimistically) "smart" cards. Thus far such cards have made little impact. Hindered by the costs of laying out the necessary infrastructure (not to mention complications such as the daily electricity shortages and the restrictions on the functioning of the Internet in Myanmar), there also remains great uncertainty with respect to the regulatory environment — although such cards are allowed today, the banks might reasonably doubt that they will be allowed tomorrow. Electronic banking cards are also available for use at *selected* branches of the state-owned Myanmar Economic Bank in Naypyitaw, Yangon, and

Mandalay; however, as with the private bank equivalents, they are yet to appear in any substantial numbers.[16]

Illicit Capital Outflows

In recent years, increasing attention has been directed to the harmful effects on developing countries of illicit capital flight. The proceeds of this flight are typically the product of corruption, criminal activity (especially the narcotics trade), tax evasion, the "underground" economy more broadly, and — of great relevance to Myanmar — the search for financial safe havens against fear of government expropriation. The usual methods for facilitating capital flight are the simple devices of trade mis-pricing (under- and over-invoicing of exports and imports), and the even more simple procedure of physically "carrying" money out of a country. However motivated or achieved, such illicit flows usually involve a net transfer of wealth from the developing world into the banks of developed countries and offshore financial centres. As such, they greatly undermine the process of capital accumulation, and retard growth.

In 2011 a seminal United Nations Development Programme (UNDP) report on illicit capital flows ranked Myanmar as the eighth-largest source of capital flight over the last (almost) twenty years (UNDP 2011, p. 12). According to the report's estimates, which were based upon World Bank data on country "sources and uses of funds" (adjusted for trade mis-pricing), from 1990 to 2008 some US$8.5 billion flowed out of Myanmar. Such capital flight represented an average of 9.1 per cent of the country's gross domestic product (GDP) across the period (compared to a developing country average of 4.8 per cent) (p. 15). This capital flight was also 4.6 times the amount of foreign aid Myanmar received in these years. To put it more graphically, for every dollar of aid received by Myanmar between 1990 and 2008, US$4.60 flowed right back out (p. 14).

CONCLUSION

Concrete economic reform in Myanmar remains hostage to circumstances that inhibit and squander capital accumulation and the mobilization of the country's financial resources. Fiscal deficits, rising debt, a dysfunctional financial sector, and illicit capital outflows all conspire to deny Myanmar the financial wherewithal to set in motion what the better parts of its governing apparatus understand is necessary to turn its economy around. Removing these financial obstacles to economic reform in Myanmar is not a task that can wait. Superficial reforms can and assuredly will proceed in the period ahead, as might opening the country to foreign aid and to foreign loans. These, however, are but appendages to that domestic capital accumulation that history identifies as necessary for genuine growth and development. Change of some sort is under way in Myanmar, but it does not yet constitute a reform moment.

Notes

1. The last significant economic reform measure was the introduction of Burma's (now increasingly endangered) "Foreign Exchange Certificate" system introduced in 1993.
2. Unification of exchange rates was to be implemented administratively on 1 April 2012.
3. This is not, however, to say that Win Myint's own business operations are without criticism. His name and those of companies owned by him have been linked, for instance, to the confiscation of land from farmers on the outskirts of Yangon. See "Businessmen Join USDP Candidate List", *Irrawaddy*, 5 September 2010 <http://www.irrawaddy.org/article.php?art_id=19388> (accessed 2 July 2011).
4. The MIC was founded in 1994, but hitherto its role has been to forward investment applications to the Trade Council. The latter, which was long headed by SPDC Deputy Chairman General Maung Aye, and then by SPDC Secretary-1 (and now one of Burma's two current Vice Presidents) Thiha Thura Lieutenant-General Tin Aung Myint Oo, was notorious for its recalcitrance and corruption.
5. Notwithstanding, business complaints about suffocating bureaucracy and favouritism in the awarding of permits remain, (mostly) privately at least, vociferous.
6. Winston Set Aung is a Burma-based economist who has been involved in many international and regional research institutions in various countries including Myanmar, Vietnam, Cambodia, Lao PDR, Thailand, Malaysia, Bangladesh, and Japan. Sein Hla Bo is an agricultural economist with overseas academic qualifications and extensive government experience in Myanmar.
7. Media outlets reporting on the budget include Joseph Allchin, "Military Prioritized as Burma Expands Airforce", *Democratic Voice of Burma*, 2 March 2011 <http://www.dvb.no/news/military-prioritised-as-burma-expands-airforce/14546> (accessed 3 July 2011); and "Burma's New Budget: More of

the Same", *Mizzima News*, 4 March 2011 <http://www.mizzima.com/edop/editorial/4966-burmas-new-budget-more-of-the-same.html> (accessed 4 July 2011).

8. Health expenditure data sourced from the World Health Organization, <http://www.who.int/research/en/> (accessed 13 July 2011).

9. See Moe Sett and Min Lwin, "China to Loan Burma 30 Billion Yuan", *Irrawaddy*, 21 September 2010 <http://www.irrawaddy.org/article.php?art_id=19520> (accessed 14 July 2011); Joseph Allchin, "China Loans Billions for Gas Pipeline", *Democratic Voice of Burma*, 16 December 2010 <http://www.dvb.no/news/china-loans-billions-for-gas-pipeline/13428> (accessed 14 July 2011); "Myanmar, China Sign Agreement on Bank Loans", *People's Daily*, 28 January 2011 <http://english.peopledaily.com.cn/90001/90778/7275107.html> (accessed 14 July 2011); Ben Blanchard, "Myanmar, China Seal Friendship with Loan Agreements", *Reuters*, 27 May 2011 <http://af.reuters.com/article/energyOilNews/idAFL3E7GR0HL20110527> (accessed 13 July 2011).

10. The "Special Funds Law" was promulgated on 17 January 2011. See Wai Moe, "Than Shwe grants himself power to access 'Special Funds'", *Irrawaddy*, 4 March 2011 <http://irrawaddy.org/article.php?art_id=20878> (accessed 13 July 2011).

11. See "Four Businessmen Granted Private Bank License", *Irrawaddy*, 31 May 2010 <http://www.irrawaddy.org/article.php?art_id=18587> (accessed 4 July 2011); and Kyaw Tha, "Junta cronies get nod to run banks", *Mizzima News*, 3 June 2010 <http://www.mizzima.com/business/4001-junta-cronies-get-nod-to-run-banks-.html> (accessed 4 June 2011). All of the conglomerates are entities that, in the euphemistic label employed by the Reserve Bank of Australia, "benefit from [Burmese] government economic policies". For more on the background of these conglomerates, and the various accusations against them, see U.S. Department of the Treasury, "Treasury Sanctions Additional Financial Operatives of the Burmese Regime", press release, 25 February 2008 <http://www.ustreas.gov/press/releases/hp837.htm> (accessed 3 July 2011); and Reserve Bank of Australia, "Banking (Foreign Exchange) Regulations 1959, Sanctions Against Burma", media release, 22 October 2008 <http://www.rba.gov.au/media-releases/2008/mr-08-23.html> (accessed 3 July 2011). That this latest tranche of banking licences was exclusively granted to such obvious cronies of the former SPDC has likewise caused more than a little unhappiness amongst other business figures in Burma. One such prominent business person complained that it was "... unfair that not every businessman [sic] who has the capital required by the law has the opportunity to do private banking. Only those who are directly dealing with the regime or a helpful to the generals are permitted. This is not a true market economy system. It's a monopoly". "Burma Relaxes Banking Regulations", *Irrawaddy*, 14 June 2010 <http://www.irrawaddy.

org/article.php?art_id=18716> (accessed 1 July 2011). This same article also notes the tensions *amongst* the existing private banks, and the favouritism granted to some against the tight restrictions maintained against new branch openings, and other operational issues of concern to the banks.

12. Each of the new banks has promised to open a minimum of fifty branches.

13. Every so often the business community in Burma calls for the introduction of mortgages and other forms of loans for property purposes. Such calls as yet go unheeded. Of course, the absence of sound property rights in Burma, and the state's ultimate ownership of all land, in any case count against the reliable provision of long-term loans for property. For a recent example of a call to this end nonetheless, see Kyaw Hsu Mon, "Real estate sector hopes for introduction of home loans", *Myanmar Times*, 11–17 October 2010 <http://www.mmtimes.com/2010/business/544/54409biz.html> (accessed 6 July 2011).

14. Yan Pai, "Burmese banks in dispute over airline ownership", 8 January 2011, *Irrawaddy* <http://www.irrawaddy.org/article.php?art_id=20491> (accessed 1 July 2011).

15. Yeni, "Burmese bank rumoured on verge of bankruptcy", *Irrawaddy*, 14 January 2011 <http://www.irrawaddy.org/article.php?art_id=20526> (accessed 1 July 2011). The Chairman of the Cooperative Bank, Khin Maung Aye, was "well connected" to the former SPDC (he was chairman of the Myanmar Banks Association as well as of Cooperative Bank) — but not so well connected as the owner of Kanbawza Bank, Aung Ko Win (regarded as "close" to the then "No. 2" in the SPDC, Vice Senior General Maung Aye). Kanbawza was the largest shareholder in MAI, followed by the Cooperative Bank.

16. Burma faces especially dire problems in the lack of affordable rural credit. This issue, beyond the scope of this paper, has been examined elsewhere by the author (Turnell 2009, 2010).

References

International Monetary Fund. *International Financial Statistics, June 2011*, Washington, D.C.: IMF, 2011.

Myanmar Central Statistical Organization (MCSO). *Selected Monthly Indicators, April 2011*. Naypyidaw: MCSO, 2011. <http://www.csostat.gov.mm/csomonthly.asp>. Accessed 21 July 2011.

Selth, A. *Myanmar's Armed Forces: Power Without Glory*. Norwalk: Eastbridge, 2002.

———. *Myanmar's Armed Forces: Looking Down the Barrel*. Regional Outlook Paper No. 21. Brisbane: Griffith Asia Institute, 2009.

———. *Civil-Military Relations in Myanmar: Portents, Predictions and Possibilities*. Regional Outlook Paper No. 25. Brisbane: Griffith Asia Institute, 2010.

Turnell, S.R. *Fiery Dragons: Banks, Money and Microfinance in Myanmar.* Copenhagen: Nordic Institute of Asian Studies, 2009.

————. "Recapitalizing Myanmar's Rural Credit System". In *Ruling Myanmar: From Cyclone Nargis to National Elections*, edited by N. Cheesman, M. Skidmore and T. Wilson. Singapore: Institute of Southeast Asian Studies, 2010.

U Myint. *Reducing Poverty in Myanmar: The Way Forward.* Theme Paper presented to the National Workshop on Rural Development and Poverty Alleviation in Myanmar, Myanmar International Convention Center, Naypyitaw, 20–22 May 2011. <http://www.encburma.net/index.php/archives/burma-government/566-dr-u-myint-reducing-poverty-in-myanmar-the-way-forward.html>. Accessed 21 July 2011.

Union of Myanmar, State Peace and Development Council. *The Myanmar Special Economic Zone Law, State Peace and Development Council Law no. 8/2011.* Naypyitaw: State Peace and Development Council, 2011.

United Nations Development Programme (UNDP). *Illicit Financial Flows from the Least Developed Countries: 1990–2008.* New York: UNDP, 2011.

9

DEVISING A NEW AGRICULTURAL STRATEGY TO ENHANCE MYANMAR'S RURAL ECONOMY

Tin Htut Oo

In the past two decades, the system of centrally planned agricultural policies that were introduced under the "Burmese Way to Socialism" and that had existed since 1962 has been progressively dismantled, although slowly and incompletely. It would be fair to state that over the two decades since 1988, following the introduction of policy oriented towards the development of a market economy, government control over agricultural cropping decisions has been substantially relaxed, but this happened only gradually and only through ad hoc mechanisms. Economic transformation proceeded, but with frequent reversals of the deregulation process, in response to changes in the global and, in particular, in the domestic economic and political situation.

Although farmers are now freer to make their own cropping decisions, there are still restrictions on the cultivation of rice on paddy land, particularly in relation to the double cropping of rice as summer paddy production on irrigated paddy land. The dominant theme of government policy has been the pursuit of increased production of rice and of another nine cash crops through targeted yields. The government has set specific sector objectives — first, to generate surplus rice; second, for Myanmar to become self-sufficient in edible oil; and third, to increase the production and export of pulses and industrial raw material crops.

One important step was the ending of state procurement of all crop output, including rice but with the exception of some industrial raw material crops (namely, sugarcane, cotton, and jute), by state-owned economic enterprises (SEEs) at prices fixed by the government. This has increased the amount of rice and other major agricultural commodities available in the market, and has induced more private entrepreneurs to enter the trading business. Government subsidies on agricultural inputs, particularly agricultural chemicals, were abolished, and provision of agricultural inputs and machineries by the private sector is now allowed.

Private exports of agricultural produce, with rice and oilseed crops most recently included, has also been permitted, although with certain interventions and controls being made by the government from time to time. However, the liberalization of rice exports that was initiated in 2003 can be viewed as an ad hoc attempt to transform the marketing system (Okamoto 2009). If liberalization of the rice economy in Myanmar is to be successful, a comprehensive policy, with appropriate strategies to ensure both stability of supply and of the price for rice, is needed, together with more reliable statistical data on rice production, stocks and trade, as well as an enhanced system of market information.

The degree of government control over decisions of farmers on cropping, pricing, and marketing has diminished, and the reforms undertaken have substantially altered the policy context in which the agricultural sector operates, but a review of the structure and recent performance of the agricultural sector starkly highlights its unfulfilled potential. With Myanmar's rich physical endowments, considerable scope still exists for a substantial horizontal and vertical expansion of agricultural output. Since the 1960s Myanmar has been unable to fully exploit its agricultural potential. This inability reflects mainly the need for more appropriate policies and strategies, for full adoption of a market economy, and for further institutional reform of public organizations involved in the sector.

Agricultural development remains essential for sustainable, broad-based, and inclusive development of Myanmar, but only if policies aimed at improving the livelihood of farmers and others involved in agriculture are introduced will the comparative advantage and resource base of particular agro-ecologies be more optimally and efficiently achieved. The present approach, of planned crop productivity — which restricts choice, innovation, and diversification — should be transformed to a "livelihood first" approach, with emphasis given to improving individual farm incomes and, correspondingly, the rural economy of Myanmar.

WHY IS IT NECESSARY TO DEVISE A NEW AGRICULTURE STRATEGY?

This section will assess the need to devise a new comprehensive agricultural strategy for Myanmar on the basis of the following five major factors:

1. need to complete the transition to a market economy under the new constitution and government structure;
2. need to transform agriculture policy from its emphasis on production to an emphasis on income and welfare;
3. need to adjust to the increased integration of regional trade;
4. need to reorganize the agriculture sector by building appropriate physical, legal, and institutional infrastructure;
5. need to increase investment in the agriculture sector.

Transition to a Market Economy in Agriculture

Article 35 of the Constitution of the Republic of the Union of Myanmar (2008) clearly stipulates that the economic system of the Union is a market economy system. The government has frequently stated that one of its foremost economic objectives is to build a modern industrialized nation through agricultural development and all-round development of other sectors of the economy.

In order to achieve that policy objective and move towards market-oriented agriculture, some important criteria must be considered. First and foremost, the country's comparative and competitive advantages can play their role only if macroeconomic policies are sound and if trade policy is neutral and does not work against agriculture. Second, government intervention in the agriculture sector should be shifted towards policy measures that aim to tackle market failure and complement the market mechanism. Last but not least, it is essential to implement a growth policy to ensure that growth benefits both the poor as well as the non-poor.

Transforming to Welfare-oriented Agriculture Policies

A fundamental requirement for devising a new agricultural strategy is to move away from the present production-oriented approach towards an approach that aims at improving the livelihood and incomes of people in the agricultural sector. The main focus of the production-oriented approach was to produce low-cost agricultural commodities for local consumption; this approach stemmed originally from the socialist policies of a previous era.

The military government's strategy for achieving growth in the agricultural sector focused on increasing the production of ten major "pillar crops", namely paddy (rice), maize, groundnuts, sesame, sunflowers, black mung bean (*matpe*), green mung bean, pigeon pea, long-staple cotton, and sugarcane, through targeted yields (see Table 9.1). The pursuit of increased paddy production was a dominant theme, and one that still demands most investment and effort.

The five strategies currently employed to achieve increased production are:

1.   accelerated development of new agricultural land;
2.   provision of sufficient irrigation water;
3.   provision and support for agricultural mechanization;
4.   application of modern technologies;
5.   development and utilization of improved crop varieties.

TABLE 9.1
Pillar Crops and Target Yield

No.	Name of crop	Existing Yield (metric tons per hectare) (2009)	Target Yield (metric tons per hectare)	Yield gap
		Column 3	Column 4	5=(Col. 4 – Col. 3)
1	Paddy (Rice)	4.06	5.15	–1.09
2	Long staple cotton	1.46	1.61	–0.15
3	Sugarcane	61.61	74.13	–12.52
4	Black Gram	1.48	1.61	–0.13
5	Green gram	1.24	1.61	–0.37
6	Pigeon pea	1.25	2.02	–0.77
7	Groundnut	1.57	1.40	+0.17
8	Sesame	0.53	1.21	–0.68
9	Sunflower	0.89	1.79	–0.90
10	Maize	3.43	4.93	–1.50

Source: Tin Maung Shwe (2011).

Improvement of farm incomes and alleviation of poverty, which are paramount concerns of the individual, are only of secondary concern to the government in the drive for increased national production that is the main objective of current agriculture policies and strategies. This production-centred strategy has had the effect of restricting choice and discouraging innovation and diversification by producers in the agriculture sector. This is why new strategies that would complement existing policies with a broad-based approach aimed at improving assets and income for farm households and the rural poor need to be devised.

Adjusting to Increasing Regional Trade Integration

Myanmar's participation in regional trade integration under the ASEAN Free Trade Agreement (AFTA), and its involvement in the expansion of infrastructure with neighbouring countries, offer both opportunities and challenges to the Myanmar economy (see Figure 9.1). Regional trade flows have been increasing in quantity, value, and diversity over the last decade. Myanmar's foreign trade is mainly within the Asian region, accounting for more than 70 per cent of total exports and about 90 per cent of total imports. Major trading partners in the region are China, Singapore, Japan, Thailand, Malaysia, and India (Myint Zaw 2010).

Expanding regional trade integration will require Myanmar to put more emphasis on the competitive and comparative advantages of its agricultural commodities. Continued and intensive analysis will be needed to guide a proper sequencing of deregulation and the elimination of remaining policy distortions. As a member of the Association of Southeast Asian Nations (ASEAN), Myanmar will need to put substantial effort into carrying out the reforms that are necessary for achieving a market economy and that will lead to Myanmar's integration into the region.

REORGANIZING AND RESTRUCTURING INSTITUTIONAL AND LEGAL INFRASTRUCTURE IN AGRICULTURE

The shift in paradigm, with the reforms since 1989 and the present policy of transition to a market economy, will obviously bring changes in the role and objectives of public organizations, particularly of state-owned

FIGURE 9.1
Myanmar in Regional Economic Organizations

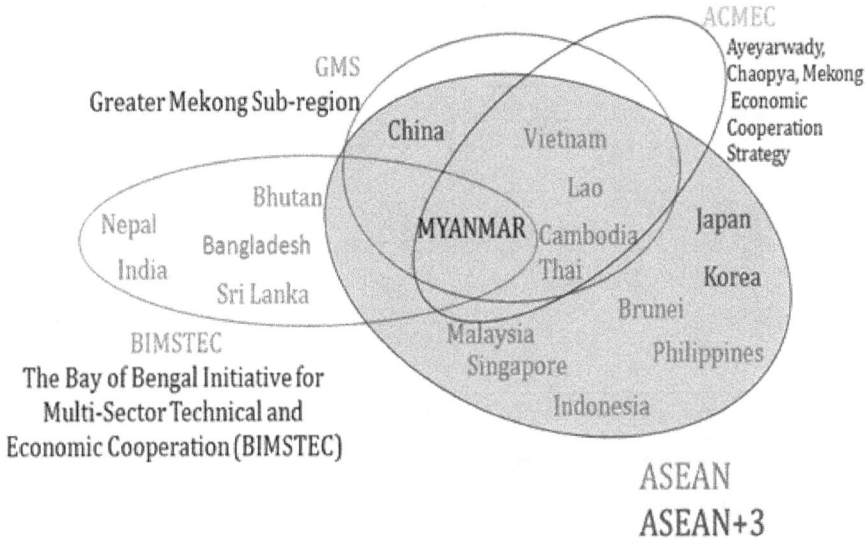

ACMEC
Ayeyarwady,
Chaopya, Mekong
Economic
Cooperation
Strategy

GMS
Greater Mekong Sub-region

China Vietnam

Bhutan   Lao
Nepal   Japan
Bangladesh   MYANMAR Cambodia
India   Thai
Sri Lanka   Korea
                             Brunei
BIMSTEC   Malaysia
The Bay of Bengal Initiative for   Singapore   Philippines
Multi-Sector Technical and   Indonesia
Economic Cooperation (BIMSTEC)

ASEAN
ASEAN+3

Source: Agribusiness and Rural Development Consultants (ARDC).

economic enterprises, in the agriculture sector. However, the specific goals of departments, services, and SEEs in this changed environment, as well as the details of their reorganization and restructuring, still need to be clarified to determine how the new approach can be put into effect.

Furthermore, how the restructuring and privatization of SEEs that undertake economic activities as well as research and development (R&D) and extension services, such as Myanmar Industrial Crops Development Enterprise, will proceed in order to achieve the objective of enhancing economic efficiency is yet to be solved. Lessons learned from other transitional countries have shown that privatization measures should be aimed not at generating the most revenue from sales of state-owned enterprises but at maximizing the economic benefits (World Bank 1999).

Reviewing the organizational set-up of the Ministry of Agriculture and Irrigation (Figure 9.2), the Ministry of Livestock and Fisheries

FIGURE 9.2
Organization Chart: Ministry of Agriculture and Irrigation (MOAI)

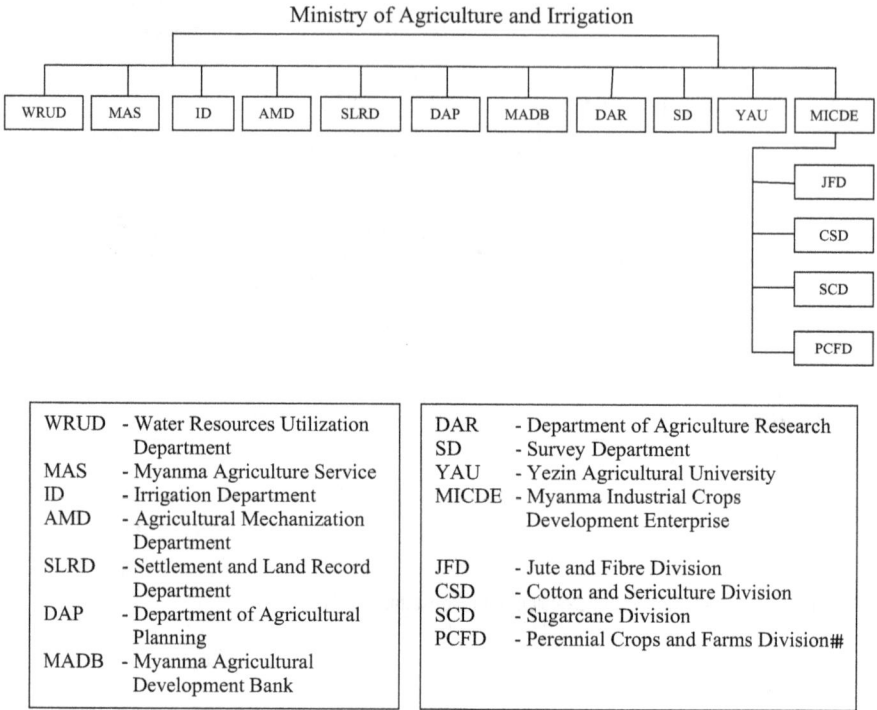

Ministry of Agriculture and Irrigation

WRUD | MAS | ID | AMD | SLRD | DAP | MADB | DAR | SD | YAU | MICDE

JFD
CSD
SCD
PCFD

WRUD	- Water Resources Utilization Department		DAR	- Department of Agriculture Research
MAS	- Myanma Agriculture Service		SD	- Survey Department
ID	- Irrigation Department		YAU	- Yezin Agricultural University
AMD	- Agricultural Mechanization Department		MICDE	- Myanma Industrial Crops Development Enterprise
SLRD	- Settlement and Land Record Department		JFD	- Jute and Fibre Division
DAP	- Department of Agricultural Planning		CSD	- Cotton and Sericulture Division
MADB	- Myanma Agricultural Development Bank		SCD	- Sugarcane Division
			PCFD	- Perennial Crops and Farms Division#

Source: Tin Maung Shwe (2011).

(Figure 9.3), and the Ministry of Forests (Figure 9.4), reveals the lack of much-needed supporting institutions to carry out R&D and to supply extension services for the transfer of technology to the farmers. The functions and organizational set-up of all public organizations in the agriculture sector, particularly organizations under the Ministry of Agriculture and Irrigation and the Ministry of Livestock and Fisheries, should be independently and comprehensively reviewed with the intention of reorganizing and restructuring to meet the new needs that will result from the changes that are occurring.

The formation and organization of private sector associations under the Union of Myanmar Federation of Chambers of Commerce and Industry

FIGURE 9.3
Organization Chart: Ministry of Livestock and Fisheries (MOLF)

Ministry of Livestock and Fisheries

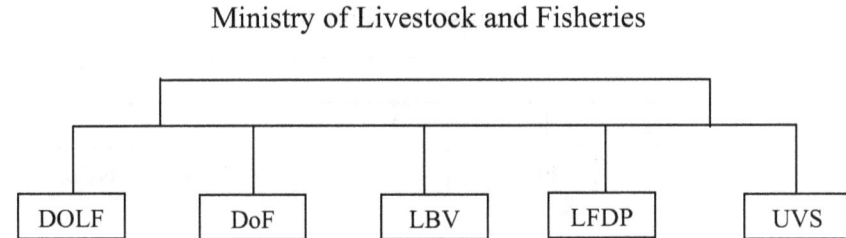

| DOLF | DoF | LBV | LFDP | UVS |

MOLF	- Ministry of Livestock and Fisheries
DOLF	- Directorate of Livestock and Fisheries
DoF	- Department of Fisheries
LBVD	- Livestock Breeding and Veterinary Department
LFDPE	- Livestock Feedstuff and Dairy Products Enterprise
UVS	- University of Veterinary Science

Source: Tin Maung Shwe (2011).

(UMFCCI) is also changing. For example, a number of associations of people connected with rice production, such as the paddy producers' association, rice millers' association, and rice and paddy traders' associations, were reorganized on 2 January 2010 under the umbrella of the newly-established Myanmar Rice Industry Association. Other new associations, such as the Myanmar Fruit and Vegetable Producers and Exporters Association and the Myanmar Agro-Based Food Producers and Exporters Association, have also been formed.

An overview of the existing framework of law and regulation related to the agriculture sector (see Table 9.2), indicates that it is not adequate to fulfil the needs of a market economy, or to ensure the sustainable development of the sector and protect the environment and ecosystems. Some important basic legal frameworks — for areas such as land management and utilization of water resources, establishment of wholesale markets and commodity

FIGURE 9.4
Organization Chart: Ministry of Forestry (MOF)

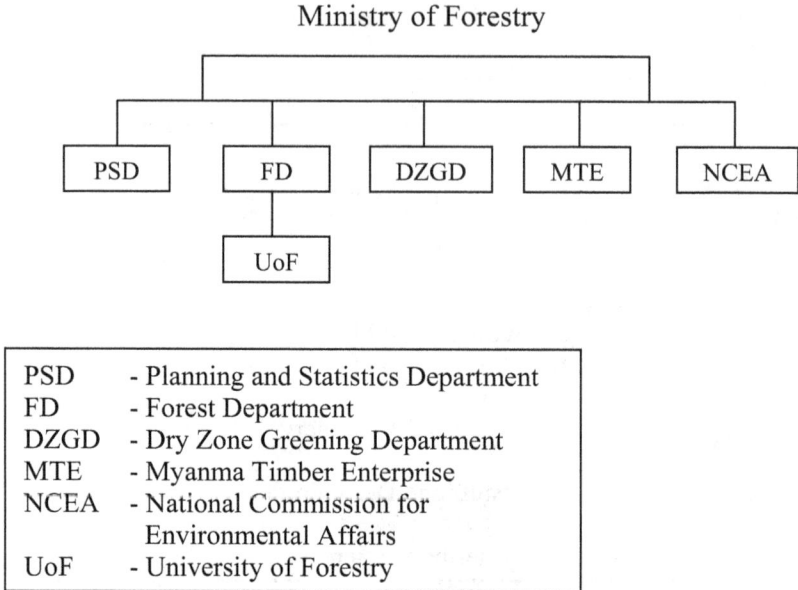

Ministry of Forestry

| PSD | FD | DZGD | MTE | NCEA |

| UoF |

PSD	- Planning and Statistics Department
FD	- Forest Department
DZGD	- Dry Zone Greening Department
MTE	- Myanma Timber Enterprise
NCEA	- National Commission for Environmental Affairs
UoF	- University of Forestry

Source: Tin Maung Shwe (2011).

exchanges, as well as development of standards and specifications for certain commodities, and bio-safety laws — are all urgently required.

Increased Investment in the Agriculture Sector

Budget allocations for the agriculture sector, which is the backbone of the economy, are not only low but are also unevenly distributed within the sector. The average current and capital expenditure allocated to the agriculture sector for the four-year period from 2005–06 to 2008–09 was 4.4 per cent and 6.8 per cent of total budget expenditure respectively (Table 9.3). Out of these funds, the irrigation sub-sector alone received over 32 per cent of total current expenditure and 68 per cent of total capital expenditure; the money was utilized mainly for the construction of new irrigation facilities. As a result, the total expenditure (and capital

TABLE 9.2
Legal Infrastructure in the Agriculture Sector

Laws directly related to Agriculture
- Pesticide Law, 1990
- Myanma Agricultural and Rural Development Bank Law, 1990
- Plant Pest Quarantine Law, 1993
- Fertilizer Law, 2002
- Procedures Relating to the Fertilizer Law, 2007
- Procedures Relating to the Pesticide Law, 2007
- Seed Law, 2011
- Bio-safety Framework and Bio-safety Law (draft stage)
- National Water Vision and Water Law (initial drafting stage)

Some of the Laws, Acts, Rules, and Regulations related to Land Management
- The Waste Lands Claims Act, 1863 (repealed 1992)
- Land and Revenue Act, 1879
- The Land Improvement Loans Act, 1883 (repealed 1992)
- The Land Acquisition Act, 1894
- The Lower Burma Land and Revenue Manual, 1876
- The Upper Burma Land and Revenue Regulation, 1889
- The Lower Burma Town and Village Land Manual 1899
- The Registration Act, 1909
- The Transfer of Immoveable Property Restriction Law, 1987
- Land Nationalization Act, 1953
- Land Nationalization Rules, 1954
- The Disposal of Tenancies Law, 1963
- The Law Amending the Disposal of Tenancies Law, 1965
- The Agriculturist's Right Protection Law, 1963
- Directions of Central Land Committee
- Forest Law, 1992
- The Cantonments Act, 1923
- Duties and Rights of the People's Council and Executive Committee of various levels, 1977
- The State Law and Order Restoration Council's Law No. 8/88
- Duties and Rights of the Central Committee for the Management of Cultivatable Land, Fallow Land and Waste Land and Procedures conferring the right to cultivate land/right to utilize land, 1991

Source: Attorney General's Office, Yangon (1998), and various law books.

expenditure in particular) allocated for other crop sub-sector development, including R&D and transfer of technology, remained very low.

Due to restrictions on economic development aid under the current international economic sanctions, Myanmar receives less in overseas

TABLE 9.3
Total Government Current and Capital Expenditure in Agriculture Sector

Year	Current Expenditure		Capital Expenditure	
	Amount (millions of kyat)	Percentage of Total Government Expenditure	Amount (millions of kyat)	Percentage of Total Government Expenditure
2005–06	54,812	4.6%	61,229	7.8%
2006–07	86,654	4.4%	62,322	5.6%
2007–08	96,634	4.0%	85,114	5.3%

Source: Central Statistical Organization, Yangon, Statistical Yearbook, various years.

development assistance (ODA) than comparable countries in Southeast Asia. World Bank figures for 2009 show that Myanmar received US$7 per capita, compared with US$52 for Cambodia and US$69 for Lao People's Democratic Republic (World Bank Data Catalog).

At the same time, due to an unfavourable investment environment, foreign direct investment (FDI) in the agriculture sector, with the approved amount of US$34.35 million for four enterprises, is the lowest of any sector in the economy, with only 0.11 per cent of the total FDI of US$32 billion in 2010 (based on FDI approvals of only US$34.35 million for four enterprises) (Myint Zaw 2010).

BREAKING THROUGH THE "VICIOUS CYCLE" TO REACH THE "VIRTUOUS CYCLE"

The agriculture sector and the rural economy in Myanmar are still trapped in a vicious cycle due to the inadequacy of the present top-down state-led approach and its focus on crop production. This is illustrated in Figure 9.5. The current approach, with its aim of ensuring food security and self-sufficiency through increased crop production, has not encouraged the establishment of a market-oriented economy, but has instead led to institutional inflexibility and has inhibited change in the rural economy. The net result has been to cause a rise in the costs of agricultural production, with a consequent reduction in the ability of farmers to maintain their livelihood and the continuation of income disparity in rural areas.

If the present vicious cycle is to be turned into a virtuous cycle, it will be essential to devise agriculture policies and strategies with a different

FIGURE 9.5
Vicious Cycle of Agriculture and Rural Economy in Myanmar

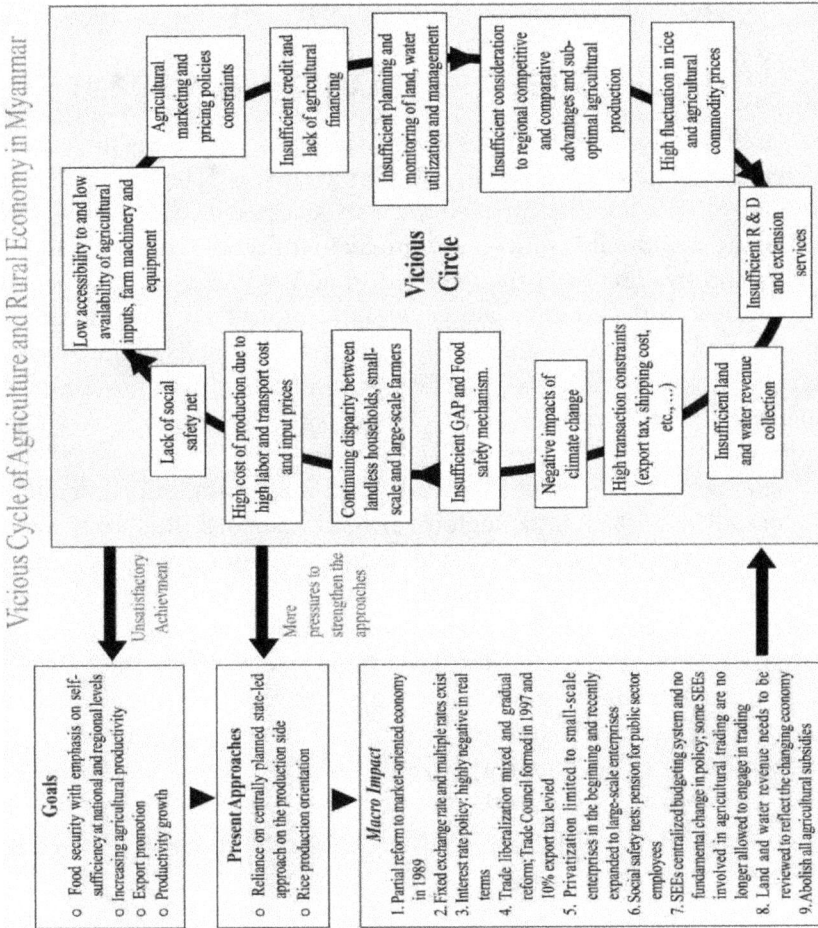

Vicious Cycle of Agriculture and Rural Economy in Myanmar

Goals

o Food security with emphasis on self-sufficiency at national and regional levels
o Increasing agricultural productivity
o Export promotion
o Productivity growth

Unsatisfactory Achievement

Present Approaches

o Reliance on centrally planned state-led approach on the production side
o Rice production orientation

More pressures to strengthen the approaches

Macro Impact

1. Partial reform to market-oriented economy in 1989
2. Fixed exchange rate and multiple rates exist
3. Interest rate policy: highly negative in real terms
4. Trade liberalization mixed and gradual reform; Trade Council formed in 1997 and 10% export tax levied
5. Privatization limited to small-scale enterprises in the beginning and recently expanded to large-scale enterprises
6. Social safety nets: pension for public sector employees
7. SEEs centralized budgeting system and no fundamental change in policy; some SEEs involved in agricultural trading are no longer allowed to engage in trading
8. Land and water revenue needs to be reviewed to reflect the changing economy
9. Abolish all agricultural subsidies

Vicious Circle

- Agricultural marketing and pricing policies constraints
- Insufficient credit and lack of agricultural financing
- Insufficient planning and monitoring of land, water utilization and management
- Insufficient consideration to regional competitive and comparative advantages and sub-optimal agricultural production
- High fluctuation in rice and agricultural commodity prices
- Insufficient R & D and extension services
- Insufficient land and water revenue collection
- High transaction constraints (export tax, shipping cost, etc., ...)
- Negative impacts of climate change
- Insufficient GAP and Food safety mechanism.
- Continuing disparity between landless households, small-scale and large-scale farmers
- High cost of production due to high labor and transport cost and input prices
- Lack of social safety net
- Low accessibility to and low availability of agricultural inputs, farm machinery and equipment

Source: Adapted from Agriculture and Rural Economy Working Group.

approach — an approach that coordinates public and private activities and that is oriented towards improving the lives and incomes of people in the agriculture sector. Only then will it be possible to achieve the objectives of improving food and nutritional security and safety, increasing the income and welfare of individual producers, and maintaining sustainable and inclusive growth of the economy (see Figure 9.6).

A NEW GREEN REVOLUTION MOVEMENT

In the 1970s, as part of Burma's own brand of socialism, the then Burmese government launched a green revolution, known as "The Whole-Township Special High Yielding Programme", in selected townships. Over the following decades this movement spread to the whole country, and higher yields and production were achieved in all the major crops of economic importance in the country. However, after more than three decades, the momentum of the first green revolution has gradually diminished; this is because there has been no nation-wide effort to promote information about, or the utilization of, new technologies, and the provision of regular, high-quality extension services has weakened.

The number of extension staff and subject-matter specialists in almost all the States and Regions of Myanmar has drastically reduced because recruitment activities in all the organizations under the Ministry of Agriculture and Irrigation were halted as part of the process of restructuring SEEs during past years. The present limited numbers of extension staff at the township level have to devote much of their time to routine staff duties and have to carry out their main functions under severe budgetary constraints. In order to regain lost ground, a green revolution-type movement is urgently needed, rather than a business-as-usual approach. For ease of comparison, the main components of the first green revolution and of a possible modern green revolution are shown in Table 9.4.

The Changing Role and Form of Agriculture

Another important reason for the need to devise a new agriculture strategy for this modern era is that there has been rapid change in the "role" and "form" of agriculture in Myanmar. Where in the past the focus was on simply producing enough to feed and clothe the population, now many

FIGURE 5.6

Virtuous Cycle of Agriculture and Rural Economy in Myanmar

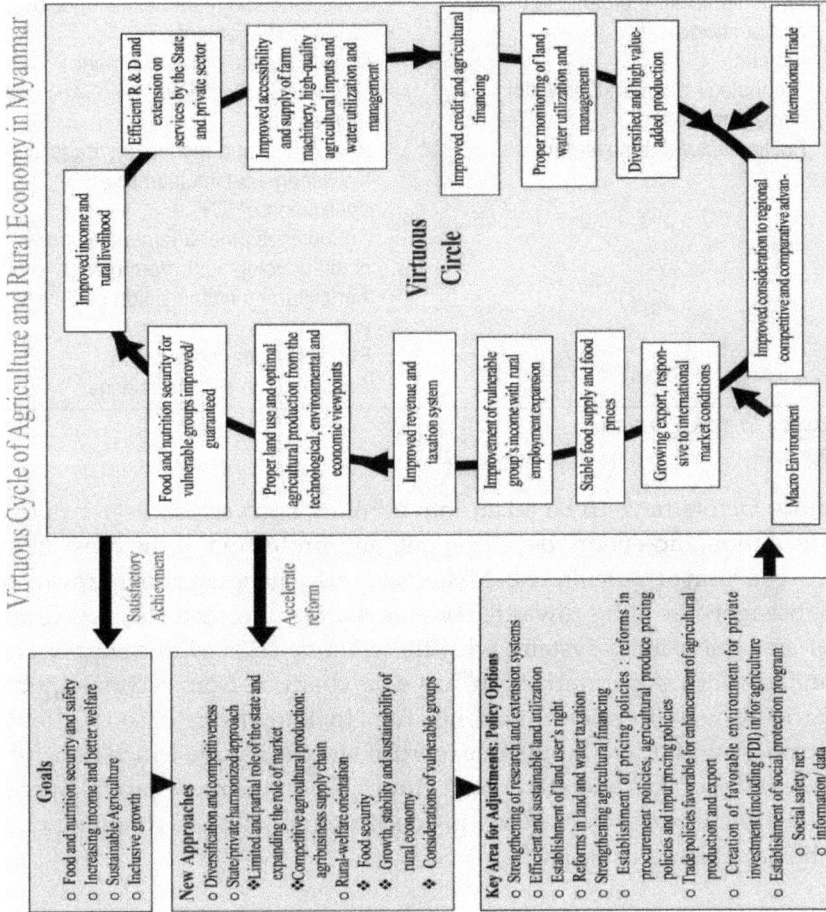

Virtuous Cycle of Agriculture and Rural Economy in Myanmar

Goals

- o Food and nutrition security and safety
- o Increasing income and better welfare
- o Sustainable Agriculture
- o Inclusive growth

New Approaches

- o Diversification and competitiveness
- o State/private harmonized approach
- ✵ Limited and partial role of the state and expanding the role of market
- ✵ Competitive agricultural production: agribusiness supply chain
- o Rural-welfare orientation
- ❖ Food security
- ❖ Growth, stability and sustainability of rural economy
- ❖ Considerations of vulnerable groups

Key Area for Adjustments: Policy Options

- o Strengthening of research and extension systems
- o Efficient and sustainable land utilization
- o Establishment of land user's right
- o Reforms in land and water taxation
- o Strengthening agricultural financing
- o Establishment of pricing policies : reforms in procurement policies, agricultural produce pricing policies and input pricing policies
- o Trade policies favorable for enhancement of agricultural production and export
- o Creation of favorable environment for private investment (including FDI) in for agriculture
- o Establishment of social protection program
  - o Social safety net
  - o information/ data

Satisfactory Achievement

Accelerate reform

Improved income and rural livelihood

Efficient R & D and extension on services by the State and private sector

Improved accessibility and supply of farm machinery, high-quality agricultural inputs and water utilization and management

Improved credit and agricultural financing

Proper monitoring of land, water utilization and management

Diversified and high value-added production

International Trade

Food and nutrition security for vulnerable groups improved/ guaranteed

Proper land use and optimal agricultural production from the technological, environmental and economic viewpoints

Improved revenue and taxation system

Improvement of vulnerable group's income with rural employment expansion

Stable food supply and food prices

Growing export, responsive to international market conditions

Improved consideration to regional competitive and comparative advantage

Macro Environment

Virtuous Circle

Source: Adapted from Agriculture and Rural Economy Working Group.

TABLE 9.4
Main Components of the First and Possible Second Green Revolutions

First Green Revolution: Crop Output Orientation	Possible Second Green Revolution: Income and Livelihood Orientation
• Seed: High Yield Varieties • Agrochemicals: Inorganic fertilizers and pesticides • Irrigation • Technology transfer: Cultivation management • Public sector-led movement	• Agro-ecological zoning • Seed technology and biotechnology • Water management • Soil and nutrient management • Good Agricultural Practice (GAP) and food safety • Knowledge and technology transfer: Knowledge-capital intensive, application of ICT • Agribusiness management: Supply-chain development, from plough to plate • Agricultural mechanization post-harvest and storage • Public-Private coordination • Adaptation to climate change

Source: Compiled by author.

more factors have to be taken into account, such as food safety, poverty alleviation, bio-energy development, and protection of the ecosystem.

The form of agriculture in Myanmar is also changing, moving away from subsistence farming towards commercial farming and the development of an agribusiness system, with the emergence of wider supply chains and modern supermarkets. It has also changed from technology-based agriculture with some mechanization to knowledge-based agriculture business with more inputs of expertise and ingenuity, which depends on natural resources and at the same time has become more capital intensive. The agriculture system needs to adapt in line with the changing climate and to mitigate its impacts.

Change of Landscape in Devising an Agriculture Strategy

In devising an agriculture strategy for Myanmar it is essential to consider not only changes in the role and forms of agriculture, but also changes in the political, technological, and socio-economic landscapes. First, there has been a dramatic change in the political landscape: a centrally-planned socialist economic system characterized by strong political backing and administrative support from the one-party government has given way to an elected multi-party democratic system of government. The implementation of agricultural development programmes is now vested in the Union, State and Regional governments.

Second, the landscape of technology has become more diverse. It is no longer sufficient to introduce high-yielding varieties, improve inputs, and use better technology to increase crop yield. Nowadays what is required is to develop knowledge-based capital-intensive agriculture that will sustain productivity and enhance the livelihood of the rural population.

Third, in a market economy the role of the private sector becomes increasingly important.

One of the most important contributions towards the success of the first green revolution was the participation and strong support of mass politics-backed organizations, particularly the Peasants' Association, which was well established throughout the country up to township level. In the present situation it will be necessary to establish similar mass organizations to represent peasants and farmers, including poor landless rural households, in line with the changing socio-economic situation.

DEVISING A NEW AGRICULTURE STRATEGY TO ENHANCE THE RURAL ECONOMY

The government will need a renewed commitment to comprehensive agricultural restructuring if it is to remove conflicting policies and strategies; promote diversified, sustainable agriculture and a broad-based rural economy; and lay a firm foundation for reducing poverty. Five priority areas are identified for restructuring:

1. land use and management;
2. agricultural production;
3. irrigation, drainage, and water management;
4. agricultural marketing and trade;
5. agricultural financing and credit.

Strategy for Land Use and Management

Efforts to enhance agriculture sector growth and development should concentrate on improving the productivity of land, both land presently under cultivation as well as land being newly developed for cultivation.[1]

Current land tenure policy discourages long-term investment and optimal land use, particularly in paddy land. It also severely limits the ability of farmers to obtain loans and credit from formal financial institutions, since land cannot be used as collateral. One change that the government should introduce as a matter of urgency is to give farmers (the holders of land-use rights) the ability to transfer, sell, lease, or mortgage those land-use rights. This change, which could be carried out under existing law, should protect the right of cultivation. Another change needed is the introduction of a law that would prohibit the confiscation of land for any reason related to the type of crop or produce, and prohibit the unjustified arrest of cultivators. The findings of the 2003 Myanmar Agricultural Sector Review and Investment Strategy Formulation Project provide important insights about the benefits of issuance of land rights to farmers, as follows:

1. The right in itself confers security of tenure and provides assurance to the farmer that investment made in the land will not be lost due to any withdrawal of access rights by the government;
2. The cost of any capital improvements made can be recovered at the time of sale of disposal of rights to another party;
3. The right of access to the land can be used as security for loans.

Before making the changes suggested above, it will be necessary to review thoroughly the current administration and enforcement of existing land use rights, especially in relation to permitting the allocation of fallow land and waste cultivable land to private entrepreneurs for the development of large-scale commercial farms. Any modification of land management laws to allow the transfer, sale, lease, or mortgage of land use rights should not favour those who have grabbed large tracts of land, nor should it discriminate against small holders and the landless poor. Such a strategy for the development of new agricultural land for landless and smallholders deserves to be given priority, as the current policy on land development unduly favours large-scale commercial farming, for which the government also provides soft loans and implicit subsidies.

The lack of consolidated and comprehensive land law — and the existence of a large number of outdated, uncertain, and vague acts, rules, and regulations related to land management — have led to unintentional as well as deliberate abuses of agricultural land use rights. Lack of transparency in the present land management system allows plenty of room for misuse by land management committees at the village-tract level, and even at the village level. Most of the ownership and acquisition issues related to agricultural land arise because of these weaknesses, and from corruption among officials and administrative authorities at various levels, rather than from the policies of the government.

Another essential land management strategy, to be put in place after land-use rights reform, is to adjust existing land tax rates so they reflect current market conditions, in order to encourage efficient land use and ensure equity among land users. Provisions to reduce taxes or allow exemptions when there have been crop losses as a result of natural disaster should be incorporated in the land revenue system.

Last but not least, a policy of creating an environment conducive to the promotion of foreign direct investment for the utilization of agricultural land should be pursued. The agriculture sector has been starved of both the capital and advanced technology that would allow effective and efficient use of available land resources. A conducive climate could be created by establishing a transparent system for setting favourable levels of rent and appropriate periods of tenure for foreign investments for the purpose of utilization of agricultural wasteland, in order to supplement the current low level of public and local private investment and to narrow regional imbalances.

Strategy for Agricultural Production

One essential element of any new agriculture policy will be to ensure a high degree of coordination between the public sector and the private sector.

A policy of allowing farmers to make their own cropping choices should replace the present supply-driven strategy of increasing production of major crops through targeted yields. This would give farmers a chance to maximize any comparative and competitive advantages, and focus on producing in response to demand. One example that suggests some inefficiency in the current approach is the attempt to achieve self-sufficiency in rice production at the national as well as State and Regional level.

An agricultural diversification strategy based on agro-ecological zoning and conservation of the environment, as well as on competitiveness of the products in the domestic and global markets, also deserves being given high priority. For example, the question of whether Myanmar should aim to become again the "rice bowl" of the region highlights the problem of attempting to regain "old glory" rather than aiming to improve the welfare of producers and conserve the environment. A strategy for crop diversification is needed in order to increase production of oilseed crops and other horticultural crops, to cater for the needs generated by expanding urbanization, changing patterns of consumption in the domestic market, and expanding regional trade integration.

Similarly, given the availability of large tracts of land in the country, a strategy to introduce biomass and bio-energy crop production to supply rural energy needs, and at the same time preserve a clean environment, will benefit individual producers as well as the country as a whole. However, promoting new cash crops as well as bio-energy crops, such as *Jatropha curcas*,[2] for reasons of diversification should be based on proven technology and market demand as well as opportunity costs, rather than only on the basis of a top-down political and administrative push, which could jeopardize any well-intended objectives.

A strategy to refocus research and extension towards improving farmers' incomes and allowing choice, rather than government-directed production of crops, is a necessity. The main role of the public sector is to support income improvement and reduction of the risks involved in agricultural production by providing research and development, proper market mechanism and extension services, and better information services. In general, the existing public agriculture institutions in Myanmar have not played this role successfully, as their focus is more on achieving higher yield and increased production of major crops to meet national targets.

A strategy to enhance agricultural mechanization through greater use of appropriate technology and machinery for increasing productivity, improving the quality of produce, and reducing post-harvest losses, is increasingly necessary given the expansion of cropping intensity, which reached 170 per cent in 2008–09 (DAP, various issues).

A strategy to embrace "Green Growth" as way forward needs to be given serious consideration if the government aims to improve the efficiency of agricultural production and protect ecosystems. The application of high inputs and carbon-intensive cropping systems in Myanmar remains relatively low compared to other countries in the region. Myanmar has the advantage of being able to adapt to "Low Carbon Green Growth" as a strategy for achieving sustainable and environmentally-friendly agricultural productivity by improving efficiency in the utilization of land and water resources, energy, and, in particular, carbon.

Strategy for Irrigation, Drainage, and Water Management

All parties involved in use of irrigation water, at all levels of government as well as among water-user groups, must have the vision to aim at ensuring the sustainability of water resources, so there will be sufficient water of acceptable quality to meet the needs of the people in terms of food security, health, livelihood, and environment. This is an essential pre-requisite for developing a new water policy and appropriate strategies. Proper legal infrastructure should be enacted to ensure integrated planning and management of the use of water resources, as several agencies under several ministries are currently involved independently in water resources management sector.

Moreover, strategies for watershed management, dam safety, and environmental impact assessment should be implemented, together with the formation of a peak coordination authority and the establishment of coordination mechanisms at the Union as well as the State and Regional levels.

The most important strategy to overcome the constraints to the efficient utilization of the available supply of irrigation water is the development of irrigation command areas, with responsibility for farm roads, irrigation and drainage canals in the existing reservoir systems, embankment systems, and pump irrigation systems. A total of 233 irrigation works with a planned benefit area of 1.14 million hectares were accomplished during the period between 1988–89 and 2010–11 (Tin Maung Shwe 2011). However, the benefits of a planned irrigable area can only be reaped if all the irrigation works in that area are completed and the irrigation command area network is in operation. It has been noted that the water distribution networks for some of the reservoir projects completed in 2002 have not yet been constructed. (See Table 9.5.)

The management of irrigation operations has been entirely a government responsibility, which has led to considerable inefficiency. In addition, the present decision-making process involves relatively little reference to local needs and requirements. A participatory irrigation water management strategy needs to be established, and this would require the formation and empowerment of water-user groups, who would be involved in making decisions on irrigation. Supervision of State and Regional governments as well as participation by beneficiary groups in this process is an essential element.

TABLE 9.5
Completion of Irrigation Networks from Completed Dams

No.	Name of Reservoir (Township)	Year Completed	Total Irrigable Area (hectares)	Completed Irrigable Area (hectares)
1	Thonze (Tharyarwaddy)	1/2002	18,750	8,029 (82 per cent)
2	Khabaung (Taungoo)	3/2008	41,666	27,708 (66 per cent)
3	Ye' Nwe	3/2006	49,375	1,458 (11 per cent)
4	Baidar (Deik Oo)	5/2002	19,458	8,333 (43 per cent)

Note: Development of water distribution network partially funded by OPEC Fund for International Development (OFID).
Source: Abstracted from Irrigation Department project handouts.

A strategy is needed to develop appropriate charges for provision of water for different types of irrigation facilities, as well as a system for collecting those charges, as part of adapting to the changing economic situation, because the operation and maintenance cost of all irrigation works is subsidized heavily from the public budget. Previously, money collected as charges for provision of irrigation water has normally been counted as revenue, although the amount is minimal and no longer relevant to agricultural operations in the present market economy. It represents a partial recovery of costs for operation and management, but water conservation and efficiency of water use have not been taken into consideration.

Under the new constitution the State and Regional governments are responsible for revenue collection. In the long term, a strategy should be developed to share the cost of projects to supply irrigation water between the Union, State, and Regional governments and beneficiary groups, through appropriate cost-sharing systems and public-private partnership mechanisms.

Strategy for Agricultural Marketing and Trade

Many studies have stated that Myanmar, contrary to the situation in a number of Least Developed Countries, has an agricultural marketing system that functions relatively efficiently and is relatively competitive, operated by the private sector. The presence of commodity exchanges appears to support open trading of many crops, and provides an accessible link between village collectors and township wholesalers, processors and inter-regional wholesalers. There is, however, a need for a strategy to develop an effective legal framework and physical infrastructure for wholesale markets and commodity exchanges, as well as to develop national standards and specifications, and weights and measures, for agricultural commodities.

Liberalization of agricultural markets after 1988 signaled the start of Myanmar's transition to a market economy. An agriculture market information service was established in the early 1990s in the Ministry of Agriculture and Irrigation, but its activities have been, and remain, very limited, and it needs to develop a strategy for strengthening the system for collection and dissemination of agricultural market information to benefit all stakeholders.

A strategy to change the focus of agricultural development towards development of an agribusiness system is needed, in order to enhance the competitiveness of trade in agricultural commodities. Such a system would harmoniously and simultaneously develop on-farm agriculture, as well as corresponding upstream and downstream industries. In order to create a vigorous supply chain for agricultural commodities through development of an agribusiness system, the following strategies should be considered:

1. a strategy to cope with changing domestic and regional markets by increasing food production through adoption of new technologies, including biotechnology and other innovations; improvement of infrastructure such as cold storage facilities; and creation of broader markets that will allow for quality differentiation and more value-added products;
2. a strategy for encouraging smallholder farmers to move up the value chain and enter new markets, through providing assistance with the introduction of new technology and information about new crops and markets.

Strategy for Agricultural Financing and Credit

Recent development forums and workshops have identified the lack of affordable agricultural credit as the most important issue facing poor rural households in Myanmar. Based on comprehensive assessments of current agricultural credit, a portfolio of policies and strategies needs to be implemented to create a favourable economic, legal, and financial regulatory environment to facilitate the provision of efficient agricultural credit and financial services.

The UNESCAP/Government of Myanmar Second Development Partnership Forum, held on 15 December 2009, recommended some key policies and strategies to help reduce the reliance of farm households on exploitive informal lenders, and to lower the costs of borrowing money and increase access to funds (UNESCAP 2010). These included:

1.   to reform both the role of public financial institutions in the provision of agricultural credit and the mechanisms through which credit is provided;
2.   to make available access to greater amounts of credit at slightly positive interest rates;
3.   to expand opportunities for the private sector and cooperatives to become involved in agricultural financing.

A strategy to reform the Myanmar Agricultural Development Bank (MADB), private banks, and underperforming financial intermediaries so they are able to better serve the financial needs of the rural sector is urgently required, as a short- to medium-term measure, due to the current extremely limited availability of credit for investing in increased production in agriculture. MADB lends very small fixed amounts per acre as a seasonal lending programme rather than as a normal banking programme. Private commercial banks are hampered by interest rate caps and regulatory restrictions on lending imposed by the Central Bank.

Developing risk management strategies to cope with the changing climate, the unpredictable global economic situation, and food and commodity price fluctuations, has also emerged as an important issue related to agriculture financing. One issue of particular importance in developing agricultural insurance markets is to allow transfer of extreme weather risks: the government should, for example, explore a strategy for coping with weather index-based insurance against climate change and other agricultural risks.

CONCLUSION

It is not the purpose of this chapter to attempt an in-depth review of the impacts on the agriculture sector of wider macro-economic policies being applied in Myanmar. Nevertheless, it is important to realize that some of these policies do have a powerful and direct impact on the sector. Given the pivotal role of agriculture in the national economy, this sector would be one of the major beneficiaries of macro-economic improvements and stabilization. Current policies where change would be most beneficial for the agriculture sector include:

1. exchange rates and certain taxes — the existing multiple exchange rates, plus export tax and withholding tax, create a 13 percentage point cost, which in effect reduces export earnings and diminishes Myanmar's competitiveness in the trade in agricultural commodities;

2. the cap on interest rates, including on loans offered by the public development banks such as the Myanmar Agricultural Development Bank and the Myanmar Livestock and Fisheries Development Bank;

3. the government's role in relation to economic production, particularly in the provision of public goods and social protections.

The identification and implementation of strategic investments in agriculture and in the rural economy of Myanmar will generate multiple benefits in terms of addressing food security and rural welfare issues. Such investment should also be directed towards efforts to mitigate the effects of climate change and to adapt agricultural production systems. The basic foundation for building a secure future for the country begins with development that manages natural resources, ensures sustainability of the ecosystem, reduces poverty, and promotes better welfare for the nation's citizens.

The Green Revolution movement in the seventies and eighties, that was known as the "Whole-Township Special High Yielding Programme", promoted Myanmar from a situation of almost needing to import food to a situation of being self-reliant in food. There is no doubt that with the right agricultural policies and strategies, another Green Revolution movement, rather than a business-as-usual approach, could once again make Myanmar a "Food Basket" for Asia, the world's most populous and economically dynamic region.

Notes

1. Agricultural land is classified as paddy land (*le'*), upland or dry land (*ya*), alluvial land (*khaing*), garden land (*oo-yin*), tidal land (*dhani*), plus shifting agriculture land (*taung-ya*) and cultivable waste land.

2. Also known as physic nut. The plant was widely cultivated as an alternative
    bio-fuel under government programmes in the early 2000s, but little fuel
    production occurred.

References

Attorney General's Office (AGO). *Myanmar Naing Ngan Upade Myar Hnint Pyin Sin
    Chet Myar Ah Nyeun* [Index to Laws of Myanmar and Amendments]. Yangon:
    Attorney General's Office, 1998.
Central Statistical Organization (CSO). *Statistical Yearbook.* Yangon: Central Statistical
    Organization, various years.
Department of Agricultural Planning (DAP), Ministry of Agriculture and Irrigation.
    Myanmar Agriculture at a Glance. Yangon: Department of Agricultural Planning,
    various issues.
Department of Agricultural Planning (DAP), Ministry of Agriculture and Irrigation.
    Myanmar Agriculture in Brief. Yangon: Department of Agricultural Planning,
    various issues.
Food and Agriculture Organization Regional Office for Asia and the Pacific
    (FAO/RAP). *Selected Indicators of Food and Agriculture Development in Asia-
    Pacific Region 1992–2002.* Bangkok: FAO/RAP, 2003. <http://faorap-apcas.
    org/Selected_Indicators/2003/SI2003.htm>. Accessed 12 March 2012.
————. *Selected Indicators of Food and Agricultural Development in the Asia-Pacific
    Region 1998–2008.* Bangkok: FAO/RAP, October 2009. <http://www.faorap-
    apcas.org/docs/Selected_Indicators/1998-2008/Selected%20Indicator%20Par
    t%20I.pdf>. Accessed 12 March 2012.
————. *Selected Indicators of Food and Agricultural Development in the Asia-Pacific
    Region 1999–2009.* Bangkok: FAO/RAP, October 2010. <http://www.fao.org/
    docrep/013/i1779e/i1779e00.pdf>. Accessed 26 May 2012.
Government of Myanmar and Economic and Social Commission for Asia and the
    Pacific (ESCAP). *Economic Policies for Growth and Poverty Reduction: Lessons from
    the Region and Beyond.* Outcome report. Bangkok: ESCAP, 2010. ST/ESCAP/2578.
    (E.10.II.F.16).
Myint Zaw. "The Role of State and Private Sector in Myanmar Economic
    Development". Myanmar-Korea Economic Forum, organized by Ministry of
    National Planning and Economic Development, and the Embassy of the Republic
    of Korea, Yangon, Chosun Ilbo on 28 September 2010, Seoul.
Okamoto, Ikuko. "Transformation of the Rice Marketing System after Market
    Liberalization in Myanmar". In *The Economic Transition in Myanmar After
    1988: Market Economy versus State Control,* edited by Koichi Fujita, Fumiharu
    Mieno and Ikuko Okamoto. Singapore: NUS Press in association with Kyoto
    University Press, 2009.

Tin Maung Shwe. *Agriculture Development Issues and Strategies*. Background Paper for Development Policy Options in Myanmar. Yangon: Agribusiness and Rural Development Consultants (ARDC), 2011.

United Nations Development Programme (UNDP) and Food and Agriculture Organization (FAO). *Myanmar Agricultural Sector Review Investment Strategy: Volume 1 – Sector Review*. Yangon: UNDP, 2004. <http://www.mm.undp.org/UNDP_Publication_PDF/ASR%20Vol.1%20Sector%20Review.pdf>. Accessed 12 March 2012.

World Bank Data Catalog. "Net ODA received per capita (current US$)". <http://data.worldbank.org/indicator/DT.ODA.ODAT.PC.ZS>. Accessed 7 March 2012.

World Bank. *Myanmar: An Economic And Social Assessment*. Washington, D.C.: Poverty Reduction and Economic Management Unit, East Asia and Pacific Region, World Bank, 1999.

V

The Role of the Media

10

ROLE OF THE MEDIA IN MYANMAR
Can It Be a Watchdog for Corruption?

Nwe Nwe Aye

The mass media today in Myanmar remains largely under the control of the state, although there has been a noticeable degree of relaxation. The state continues to use the media as a tool for advancing the political and socio-economic interests of the ruling regime, as it has since the era of centrally-planned socialism, from 1962 to 1988. Over the past ten years, the military government has gradually allowed participation by the private sector, first in the print media and later in the broadcast media. Yet the government has continued to monopolize the publication of daily newspapers. In the first one hundred days of the new, nominally civilian, government, the situation changed little from the conditions that prevailed under the military regime that ruled the country for over two decades from 1988 to 2010.

In effect, any role the Myanmar media might aspire to in terms of serving as a Fourth Estate remains very constrained, since such necessary conditions as having editorial independence, providing good quality information, and having a broad reach across society, need to develop further (Islam 2002). Neither print media nor audio-visual media are able to fully realize these three characteristics.

This article presents an overview of media development in Myanmar, with an emphasis on the domestic print media, specifically on its role of raising public awareness about corruption and social issues. It will also discuss the possible influence of the growth of domestic broadcast media upon these issues.

PRINT MEDIA: DEVELOPMENT AND CHALLENGES

In Myanmar today, there are three main nationwide daily newspapers, namely *Myanma Ahlin*, *Kyemon* (*The Mirror*) and the *New Light of Myanmar* (an English-language newspaper). Together these can be referred to as "the official press". There are two other daily newspapers, the *Yangon City News* and *Yadanarpon*, which are run by City Development Committees of Yangon and Mandalay respectively. However, their outreach is limited to city readers, and they have very limited distribution outside their respective municipal areas. For the three national dailies, the state-run Myanmar News Agency (MNA) serves as the main source of information.[1] Since the daily papers are published under the umbrella of the Ministry of Information, they are subject to many restrictions, and the types of news stories and issues they can report are very limited. However, MNA, like the state-run television station MRTV (Myanma Radio and Television), is the only news agency that is given access to government meetings and allowed to cover the visits of senior government officials.

In April 2011, the army launched a new daily newspaper named *Myawaddy*. It is more colourful than other newspapers but otherwise it is very similar in content and presentation to its older counterparts. The daily papers have to follow carefully the policy guidelines of the government and are required to cover routine news such as the leadership's inspections of dams, bridges, schools, and hospitals. This can also be viewed as the legacy of the socialist regime and its successor military government. In recent years, the readership and popularity of state-run dailies have significantly declined (see Figure 10.1).

The circulations of state-owned newspapers plummeted in the aftermath of the nation-wide uprisings of 1988 and hit their lowest point in 1991. They went up again in 1992, most probably because of the absence of alternative sources of information in the new political setting. Since 2004,

FIGURE 10.1
Circulation of State-Owned Daily Newspapers, 1986–2007
(in thousands)

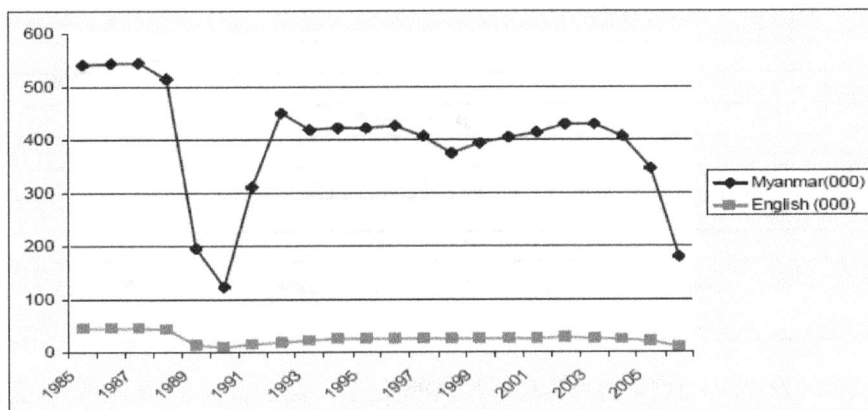

Source: Ministry of Information, Central Statistical Organization, 2008.

as the number of weekly news journals offering alternative outlets has increased, the circulations of state-run newspapers have been falling. The fall could also be connected to an increase of 200 per cent in the cost of subscription fees.

Another explanation for the decline of interest in the official press is that after 1988 Myanmar transformed itself from a centrally-planned to a market-oriented economy. In November 1990 a state-sponsored professional organization, Myanmar Printers and Publishers Association, was formed. The government began to allow private printing houses to be set up and relaxed restrictions on the importation of raw materials for the publishing industry, such as paper and machines. Censorship rules were eased compared to the pre-1990 years and the government issued a number of licences for private weekly journals and monthly magazines (see Figure 10.2).

In 2000, the government permitted the first foreign investment in the local print media, by allowing an Australian investor to publish the *Myanmar Times*, a weekly English-language journal which later (in 2001) became a bilingual paper. With the support of local partners who were

FIGURE 10.2
Number of Private Journals, 1998–2007

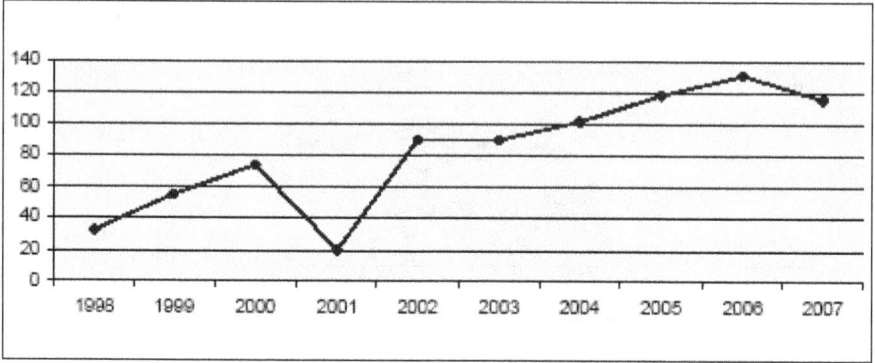

Source: Myanmar Marketing Research and Development.

part of the regime, the *Myanmar Times* enjoyed limited autonomy until 2004, as it was able to bypass the normal censorship procedure. The trend towards increased liberalization was reinforced when a further round of publication licences was granted in the early 2000s.

Individual publishers in the private sector can publish a weekly or monthly periodical only if they have obtained a publication licence from the authorities. Most publication licences have, not coincidentally, been granted to relatives of the military government and their associates (Hsat Linn 2010). However, not everyone who receives a licence has managed to publish a journal and keep it running. In such cases, licences are revoked. Hence, the number of licences does not always reflect the actual number of active periodicals in the market, which could in fact be much fewer.

Table 10.1 shows that the number of general news journals has increased from 28 out of 189 publications in 2009 (15 per cent) to 41 out of 171 publications licensed for publishing in 2011 (24 per cent). This is a significant rise in only two years, and seems to indicate that public interest in general news has increased since local news journals have been able to carry news stories that cannot be found in state-run papers.

Whilst the private print media in Myanmar have gained a certain momentum since 2000, the circulation figures for state-owned daily newspapers and private-owned weekly journals combined are relatively low compared to figures for other countries in the region, with a total of

TABLE 10.1
Journals Licensed for Publishing in 2009 and 2011

	Types of Journals	Feb. 2009	Jan 2011
1	News	28	41
2	International News	5	7
3	Sports	47	39
4	Health	5	6
5	Children	16	6
6	Crime	7	5
7	Mystical	8	4
8	Arts and Knowledge	35	23
9	Religious	2	3
10	Others (Ecology, etc)	36	40
	Total	189	174

Source: Ministry of Information.

only 400,000 copies per week for a population of roughly 59 million. By way of comparison, 2007 figures for Thailand show a circulation of three million copies per day for its 65 million people.

Procedural and Legal Hindrances to Media Development

Myanmar has laws that restrict press freedom. The Registration of Printers and Publishers Law (1962) requires all publishers to submit copies of material that is to be published to the Press Scrutiny and Registration Division (PSRD) of the Ministry of Information prior to publication. Those who print, publish, and circulate opinions detrimental to the "ideology of the state" are liable to seven years' imprisonment. Nearly identical prohibitions of content "detrimental to state interests" can also be found in other laws, such as the State Protection Law (1975), the Television and Video Law (1996), the Computer Science Development Law (1996), and the Internet Law (2000). Furthermore, the government arbitrarily applies the Emergency Provisions Law (1950) and the Official Secrets Act (1932) to suppress freedom of expression.[2]

One of the most significant hindrances for the print media is the degree of censorship imposed by the Press Scrutiny and Registration Division. Senior staff of the PSRD are normally military officers. For reasons avowedly relating to the security of the regime, the PSRD is sensitive about even the mildest criticisms of government policies. This is despite the fact that the vast majority of printing licences are held by military leaders or their cronies, and that the foreign ownership laws further restrict the creation of an open publishing market.

Delays in granting censorship clearance creates room for bribes. As the Minister for Information, U Kyaw Hsan, explained at the first regular session of the Pyithu Hluttaw (parliament) on 10 March 2011, approval of a book or a publication can be delayed indefinitely since it requires inspection by relevant experts for specific subjects in addition to the scrutiny of the PSRD (*NLM* 2011*a*). In some cases, since junior censorship officers do not have the authority to approve certain issues that may be raised, a publication may have to be submitted to the Minister for final approval, depending on the seriousness of the issue (see Figure 10.3).

Although the government has eased some restrictions on the coverage of political issues since April 2010 (when the government started calling for the registration of political parties prior to the elections), the extent to

FIGURE 10.3
Chart of the Censorship Authorities

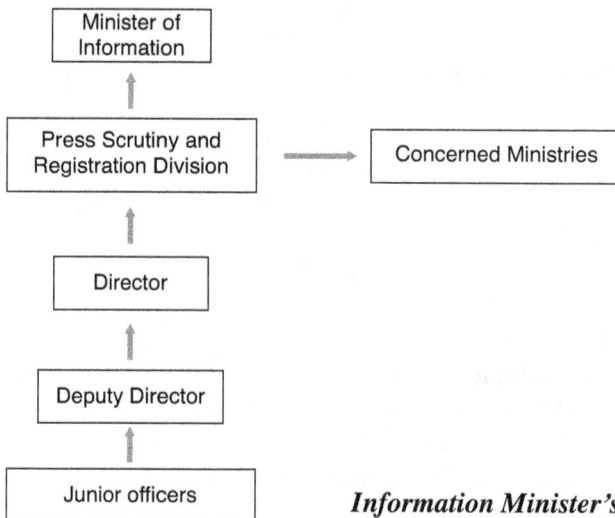

Information Minister's response to a lawmaker at the first regular session of Pyithu Hluttaw on March 10

Note: As at 10 March 2011.

which activities of the organized pro-democracy opposition groups and individuals (such as Aung San Suu Kyi, the National League for Democracy (NLD), and other dissidents) can be reported is limited. Any "negative" reports and commentaries about China, India, ASEAN, and other countries friendly towards the regime (such as Russia and North Korea) are still forbidden. Censors scrutinize the smallest details in wording and layout, as well as the size, content, and location of images.

The combination of these various restrictions imposed on the media has resulted in Myanmar continually being ranked as one of the worst countries for press freedom. Freedom House, an organization that monitors freedom around the world, includes Myanmar among the ten worst-rated countries in the world in 2010 (although it noted that there had been marginal improvements in Burma, due to somewhat more open media access to opposition leader Aung San Suu Kyi following her release from house arrest).[3]

As can been seen in Figure 10.4, which shows the Press Situation Index figures over almost twenty years for several Southeast Asian countries, as calculated by Freedom House, press freedom in Indonesia significantly

FIGURE 10.4
Press Situation Index: Singapore, Cambodia, Indonesia and Myanmar, 1994–2010

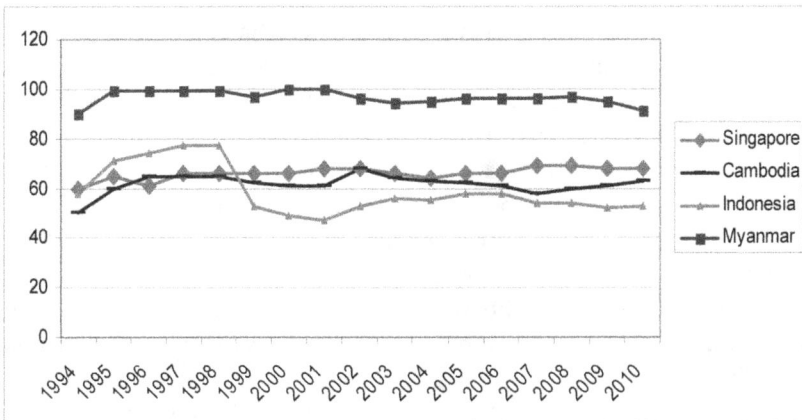

Note: The higher the score, the worse the situation is in terms of freedom of the press. A score of 0-30 is considered "free"; 31-60 equates to "partly free"; and 61-100 is considered "not free".
Source: Freedom House.

improved after the fall of President Suharto in 1998 and has subsequently moved from "Not Free" status to "Partly Free" status. Myanmar, however, remains mostly unchanged over that period.

Reporters Without Borders compiles an annual global Press Freedom Index. In 2010 Indonesia was ranked 117th of 178 countries while Cambodia and Singapore were ranked 128th and 136th respectively in its 2010 Press Freedom Index. Unsurprisingly, Myanmar stood fifth from the bottom with a rank of 174.

According to the 2011–2012 Reporters Without Borders press freedom index, Burma had improved its position, and was ranked 169th out of 179 countries. The organization's report on Myanmar noted, however, that "The government has made a few conciliatory gestures towards the opposition since April 2011, but has so far balked at any significant concessions on media freedom".[4]

HOW CAN RECENT CHANGES IN CENSORSHIP BE UNDERSTOOD?

The Myanmar government began to liberalize the private media in the 2000s partly in order to adapt to the information revolution and globalization. It came to realize, apparently, that many authoritarian (especially communist) regimes, collapsed in the late 1990s due to their inability to make sound policy decisions based on timely information. It seems the regime may have a twofold purpose in opening up the "media space".

First, the government can expect pro-military local journalists in the private sector to conduct public relations on its behalf. With this objective apparently in mind, the government started to privatize the print media from 2000 onwards, and the audio-visual media from 2009. Privatization of some TV channels has also been under way, with one particular channel, MRTV-4, operating under a joint-venture agreement between the Forever Group and the Ministry of Information.

Second, the regime uses the media to keep open lines of communication with its domestic and international rivals and critics. These objectives seem to be in line with the strategic vision to "counter media with media" stated by the Information Minister, then General Kyaw Hsan, in 2005.

After the Press Scrutiny and Registration Division was transferred to the Ministry of Information from the Ministry of Home Affairs in 2005, Myanmar authorities promised a more "flexible" approach to the media in return for a more proactive response by the press in supporting the policies of the government (Wai Phyo Myint 2005).

The Ministry stated then that positive criticism of government ministries and officials would be allowed to some extent. However, no coverage about corrupt activities by high-ranking officials has appeared in any domestic publication, because of continued censorship. Even when stories about corruption scandals were carried by the state-owned media, they were used as a political tool to reaffirm the regime's internal cohesion and to offset external condemnation.

Globalization brought a number of professional journalism networks to Myanmar. As Myanmar journalists increasingly interact with their fellow counterparts in the region, they have come to realize the need to raise public awareness of social and humanitarian issues such as HIV/AIDS, migrant workers, poverty, natural disasters, and corruption. There have been no changes, however, in the government's restrictions on foreign correspondents, and even today the only foreign media representatives allowed to be stationed in Myanmar are representatives of the official Chinese media. It remains difficult for foreign journalists to obtain a journalist visa, and most foreign reporters still enter the country on a tourist visa (a practice quietly tolerated by the authorities).

While the private media are not in a position to directly criticize the government's policies, they try subtly to highlight social problems. For example, every year, private journals include articles about the people's expectation that electricity will become available for twenty-four hours a day as soon as the monsoon starts.[5] The media may highlight the fact that road deaths in Yangon streets have dramatically increased: this subtly suggests the need for more traffic regulation and control. From time to time some journals will include articles about social issues, but present them in general terms as global or regional issues, thus avoiding direct criticism of the government. Human trafficking, for example, might be presented with cautions about the dangers it poses, and in the context of increased migration within the Southeast Asia region.

The Role of the Print Media in Combating Corruption

The role of the private media in Myanmar remains limited to that of providing information. The private media do not noticeably help to encourage public policy debate, let alone fulfil a watchdog role on governance issues such as corruption. Almost all weekly journals are based in Yangon, and there are few local (town or provincial) newspapers. This means that the reporting of corruption cases at the local level is rare, while big corruption scandals at the national level cannot be reported. For example, even in the case of the biggest corruption scandal of recent times, which involved the arrest in 2006 of more than five hundred officials and staff from the Myanmar Customs, Trade, and Tax Departments, the local media were denied the chance to independently report the events. The public had to listen to the Myanmar-language broadcasts from foreign radio stations to receive the news.

After this event, the local media outlets were then used to communicate anti-corruption propaganda on behalf of the military government. The government has said it proposes to amend the anti-corruption law (which dates from 1948), but to date that amendment has yet to be finalized.[6]

Corruption is a criminal offence, the penalty for which can be imprisonment and/or a fine. Relevant laws and legal instruments against corruption-related offences include the *Penal Code*, the *Public Property Protection Law*, the *Money Laundering Law*, and the *Anti-Drug Law*. Burma signed the UN Convention on Corruption in December 2005, but has not yet ratified it. However, most observers agree that in spite of these laws, rampant corruption pervades all levels of the political and administrative systems. Transparency International states: "Little is known on the specific forms and patterns of corruption in the country ... In the absence of sound democratic institutions and an effective system of checks and balances, the legal and institutional frameworks against corruption appear rudimentary and likely to be misused by the junta for political reasons".[7]

In 2006, several government ministries opened telephone hot lines for the public to make complaints about corruption or other abuses by government employees. Citing Myanmar official statistics, China's news agency *Xinhua* reported on 27 March 2007 that the Myanmar government had punished 1,247 service personnel for malpractice in 2005 and 2006 (Xinhua 2007). It is common practice for the government to misuse anti-corruption laws as a means of ousting political opponents. For instance, in 2004 the authorities arrested the former Prime Minister General Khin Nyunt and many of his colleagues and family members, ostensibly for corruption (U.S. Department of State 2008). However, formal charges of corruption were only brought against a very small number of the purged associates of Khin Nyunt, and some of his most trusted officers were later released from prison and reemployed by the new security apparatus.

The laws are thus used selectively or not at all, and are not employed systematically or fairly.

The print media did achieve some success in exposing one particular case of malpractice, in 2009, and this was a step in the right direction. Media reporting was instrumental in persuading the Myanmar Medical Association (MMA) to take action against a senior surgeon who had mis-diagnosed a patient's illness and then operated upon the patient, who died from post-operative complications. The constant attention given by the private media to this tragic incident not only highlighted the perils of Myanmar's deteriorating healthcare system, but also generated a wider debate on medical ethics. When evidence of malpractice became clear, the MMA finally made a decision to suspend the surgeon's licence for five years and asked the clinic where he had been working to pay a substantial compensation to the victim's family (*Irrawaddy* 2009). However, the surgeon was spotted practising again at the same hospital one year after the conviction, demonstrating once again that the wealthy and well-connected have the ability to circumvent the law and avoid any resulting convictions.

In relation to exposing malpractice and corruption, the media outlets in Myanmar to all intents and purposes have their hands tied — at present. Only if the Myanmar government decides to move to root out systemic corruption, and allows the media to report on such issues, whether in the private sector or within the government and bureaucracy, will this situation change.

MEDIA OPENNESS BEFORE AND AFTER THE 2010 ELECTION

Following the announcement of the election laws in March 2010, the censorship authorities allowed weekly journals to include a few pages of political news, mainly stories about newly-formed political parties, politicians, and Myanmar's parliamentary past. In the same month the National League for Democracy announced it would boycott the elections. To the amazement of local journals, this news was approved for publication in weekly periodicals.

After that, many local journalists hoped that the mainstream private media would also be permitted to include stories about opposition parties and candidates, but those hopes were dashed when stories related to the public's scepticism about the fairness of the elections and about the lack of interest of the electorate were rejected. In the end, only positive comments about the elections, which hardly reflected the true opinion of the public, were left on journal pages.

On 31 March 2011 the newly-inaugurated President, U Thein Sein, in his speech to members of the Union Government, stressed the importance of clean government and pledged to fight against corruption. Notably, he said, "To be a clean government, we must abstain from corruption and bribery, which tarnishes the image of the nation and the people". In the same speech, he invited the media's cooperation, while acknowledging their important role:

> We also have to respect the role of the media, the fourth estate ... We are required to inform the people about what they should know and appreciate positive suggestions from the media (*NLM* 2011*b*).

His speech was justifiably regarded as a milestone, because it addressed publicly issues that had once been taboo, and, for the first time in many decades, recognized the role of the media. Many observers, however, will wait to see if the president's words are put into action.

In June 2011, the Press Scrutiny and Registration Division removed pre-publishing censorship for monthly and weekly publications that focus on sports, entertainment, health, information technology, and children's literature. However, there is a catch — publications that no longer require pre-publishing approval may also no longer publish some of the news reports they had included before, especially material of a political nature. Periodicals that focus on general news, religion, economy and business, education, crime, politics, and history remain subject to the previous censorship procedures for the time being.

In a booklet released by the Ministry of Information in June 2011, the Ministry promises to transform existing censorship policies step-by-step in accordance with the Article 354(a) of the new constitution, which guarantees Myanmar citizens the right to express and publish freely their convictions and opinions *so long as they are not contrary to the country's laws* [author's italics]. This has sufficiently emboldened some of the local media to run articles against corruption. As a result, serious comments on general corrupt practices have been published in weekly publications, but few publications have mentioned specific allegations of malpractice against by senior officials. Editors remain uncertain about how much the PSRD will tolerate reporting of corruption allegations against individuals and companies close to the senior military leadership, its cronies, and former military officers.

For example, in early July 2011, a regional commander was reportedly suspended on corruption charges, and this news appeared in the foreign media. The public was intrigued by the story, but uncertainty existed about whether the story was in fact genuine reporting of a corruption issue, or instead a case of allegations being planted in the media as part of an internal power struggle within the upper echelons of the military. News reports on such cases have never, so far, made it to the pages of to the local print media.

When local publishers report allegations of corruption, they put themselves at great risk of threats from some in the private sector. Most recently, the *Hot News Journal* published a story about unsatisfactory service at a well-known private hospital when the hospital failed to send a deceased person to the mortuary immediately. The hospital in question, Shwegondine Specialist Centre, sued *Hot News Journal* for defamation. The case has yet (at time of writing) to be settled. Public interest in the lawsuit is high as the journal is owned by the daughter of a former high-ranking general and hospital shares are held by senior military personalities and their cronies (Nayee Lin Latt 2011).

It is only right that private media should adhere to accepted ethical standards for journalism, but the long-term impact of anti-libel lawsuits on media freedom will have to be closely monitored. The 2008 Constitution links freedom of expression with the rule of law.[8] Hence, media freedom will depend on how the courts in Myanmar interpret the existing laws, and how they enforce them. The judicial branch itself needs to be credible and free from corruption and interference, because the ability of the Fourth Estate to serve as a watchdog rests equally on well-functioning checks and balances in all three branches of government.

BROADCAST AND ELECTRONIC MEDIA: MORE EFFECTIVE MEDIA?

Television and Radio Stations

For people living in rural areas of Myanmar that are not adjacent one of the nation's borders, the most frequently used media are broadcast media such as radio, television, and video (when power can be locally supplied).

Until 1988 there was only one centralized television and radio station in Myanmar, operated by the government. By 2010, the number of television channels had increased to four — Myanmar Radio and Television (MRTV), the military-run Myawaddy TV, Myanmar International, and MRTV-4, a joint venture with Shwe Than Lwin Media Company and the Forever Group. Among the four, MRTV-4 provides the liveliest programming throughout the day.

In terms of information and news, however, all channels have to comply strictly with government policies and guidelines. Accordingly, television is one medium where the government can still exert its control for propaganda purposes.

Since 2009, the government has given permission to a few private companies to run FM (frequency modulation) radio stations, namely, City FM, Mandalay FM, Pyinsawaddy FM, Padamya FM, Shwe FM, Cherry FM, FM Bagan, and the government propaganda tool, Padaukmyay. Each of these FM radio stations has been allowed to cover one or more of the country's eight regions. After years of stagnation, the state-owned Myanmar Radio seems to have lost virtually all its appeal and listeners. By contrast, the new FM stations broadcast music as well as celebrity and sports news, and pay substantial sums of money to access the work of popular entertainers. Yet, as in the case of television, domestic broadcast media are still a long way from being able to report any real news.

The alternative source of information on which the vast majority of the Myanmar public rely is foreign radio stations. Short-wave radios are affordable, and stations such as the British Broadcasting Corporation (BBC) and Voice of America (VOA) have a decades-long history, dating back to Myanmar's parliamentary era, of broadcasting Myanmar (Burmese) language programmes. The BBC Myanmar Service in particular played a crucial role in raising public awareness of the events leading to the 1988 demonstrations. After 1988, two other prominent short-wave stations dedicated to Myanmar issues and news came into existence: they are the independent Democratic Voice of Burma (DVB) based in Oslo, Norway, and Radio Free Asia's (RFA) Burmese programme based in Washington, D.C.[9]

Over the past twenty years, these foreign radio stations have hired competent Myanmar journalists. Although they are often accused of being driven by an anti-government agenda, the stations have increasingly demonstrated their professionalism and integrity. They have produced a number of programmes that would not be possible to produce in Myanmar, such as live broadcasts, policy debates, and in-depth news analyses. Additionally, listeners have the chance to receive news on Myanmar as published in newspapers worldwide. Through the "Letters from Myanmar" section, the radio stations inform the public about different types of corruption taking place at all levels in Myanmar and report upon local grievances.

In general, the authorities in Myanmar collect information centrally in order to understand what is occurring in local areas. News reported about Myanmar by foreign radio stations can often draw their attention. The information can help them identify problems in provincial areas and may lead to further action if corruption seems serious. In many cases, the authorities choose not to respond if such scandals do not seriously threaten the security of the regime. Myanmar language programmes broadcast by overseas radio stations create a flow of information between domestic and international domains. In this respect, international broadcast media can not only help acclimatize Myanmar people to the ideas and practice of free speech, but also play a role in monitoring corruption.

CONCLUSION

Despite severe censorship, the private media in Myanmar are not isolated from the global media community. Myanmar authorities cannot really prevent news stories on corruption from spreading to websites or to radio stations. In Myanmar's unique socio-economic context, international media invariably play an important role in shaping public opinion and bringing an awareness of the activities of the government and of government policies.

For its part, the government seems to be encouraging a greater diversity in media, in particular an increase in audio-visual media. The privatization of radio and TV channels in recent years has sought to continue the flow of government propaganda and also to divert public attention from the woes of daily life in Myanmar by offering more entertainment. Hence, the role of local media is strategically and politically important for the government in its ongoing rivalry with expatriate Myanmar media.[10]

Conversely, the domestic print media play a role in raising public awareness on a number of issues, ranging from environmental degradation, ethnic affairs, and climate change to the spread of diseases and natural disasters. In relation to these issues, most private journals have persistently tried to address larger social issues involving business practices and political leadership.

The media in Myanmar have tremendous potential to encourage the government towards making positive changes in governance. It is likely that the media's role in monitoring corruption and development would significantly increase if the present censorship rules were to be removed. Just as a less corrupt regime could bring press freedom to Myanmar, freer media could also guide the government to become responsive, efficient, and clean.

Notes

1. MNA is under the News and Periodicals Enterprise of the Ministry of Information. It also serves as Myanmar's official international English-language news agency.
2. Freedom House reported that "... [a]t the end of 2010, at least 13 journalists were in prison, according to the Committee to Protect Journalists". Among these were a video reporter who worked for the Democratic Voice of Burma (DVB) and her assistant, both sentenced to twenty years in prison for alleged violations of the Electronic Act and the Export Import Act. See Freedom House, *Burma: Freedom of the Press 2011* <http://www.freedomhouse.org/report/freedom-press/2011/burma> (accessed 14 April 2012). In November 2011, Reporters Without Borders reported that fourteen Democratic Voice of Burma journalists "are still being held" and that two more had been arrested since the start of 2010. See <http://en.rsf.org/report-burma,53.html> (accessed 14 April 2012). In March 2012, following publication of its 2011–2012 press freedom index, Reporters Without Borders stated: "At least four journalists (Zaw Tun, Win Saing, Ne Min and Aung Htun) and one blogger (Kaung Myat Hlaing, also known as Nat Soe) are still detained as they were not included in the 14 January amnesty". Reporters Without Borders, "Will media freedom continue to progress in Burma?", 13 March 2012 <http://en.rsf.org/birmanie-will-media-freedom-continue-to-13-03-2012,42104.html> (accessed 14 April 2012). Sithu Zaya, a DVB journalist who took photographs following bomb explosions at the Yangon water festival in 2010, was sentenced first to eight years in prison under the Immigration Act and the Unlawful Association Act, then to an extra ten years for breaching the Electronics Act. His father was also charged under the Immigration Act, Unlawful Association Act, and Electronics Act and was sentenced to thirteen years' imprisonment. See "DVB journalist sentenced to additional 10 years in prison", *Mizzima News*, 15 September 2011 <http://

www.mizzima.com/news/prisoner-watch/5937-dvb-journalist-sentenced-to-additional-10-years-in-prison.html> (accessed 20 April 2012).

3. Karin Deutsch Karlekar, "Press Freedom in 2010: Signs of change amid repression", Overview Essay, *Freedom of the Press 2011*, published by Freedom House <http://www.freedomhouse.org/report/freedom-press-2011/overview-essay> (accessed 14 April 2012).

4. Reporters Without Borders, "Will media freedom continue to progress in Burma?", 13 March 2012 <http://en.rsf.org/birmanie-will-media-freedom-continue-to-13-03-2012,42104.html> (accessed 14 April 2012).

5. Myanmar relies mainly on hydroelectric power. Outside the rainy season that runs from June to September, most of Myanmar's population gets only six to twelve hours of electricity per day.

6. According to the Asia/Pacific Group on Money Laundering, "Myanmar signed the 2003 UN Convention Against Corruption on 2 December 2005 but it has not ratified or acceded to this Convention. Myanmar has an old Anti-Corruption Act of 1948 which is still in effect. Myanmar officials advised the evaluation team that it is drafting a new Anti-Corruption Law. No time-frame for the enactment and implementation of this law was given to the evaluation team." Asia/Pacific Group on Money Laundering, *APG Mutual Evaluation Report on Myanmar: Against the FATF 40 Recommendations (2003) and 9 Special Recommendations*, as adopted by the APG Plenary 10 July 2008, Paragraph 85 <http://www.apgml.org/documents/docs/17/Myanmar%202008.pdf> (accessed 20 April 2012). See also "Myanmar drafting new anti-corruption law", *People's Daily*, 27 March 2007 <http://english.peopledaily.com.cn/200703/27/eng20070327_361382.html> (accessed 20 April 2012).

7. Transparency International notes that "according to many sources, it is common practice for the ruling generals to misuse anti-corruption laws as a means of ousting political opponents, as when the SPDC arrested then-Prime Minister General Khin Nyunt and many of his colleagues and family members for corruption in 2004". See Transparency International, *Overview of Corruption in Burma/Myanmar*, 2 March 2009, p. 4 <http://www.u4.no/publications/overview-of-corruption-in-burma-myanmar/> (accessed 15 April 2012).

8. Article 354 of Chapter VIII states: "Every citizen shall be at liberty in the exercise of the following rights, if not contrary to the laws, enacted for Union security, prevalence of law and order, community peace and tranquility [*sic*] or public order and morality: (a) to express and publish freely their convictions and opinions; (b) to assemble peacefully without arms and holding procession; (c) to form associations and organizations; (d) to develop their language, literature, culture they cherish, religion they profess, and customs without prejudice to the relations between one national race and another or among national races and to other faiths." Constitution of the Republic of the Union

of Myanmar (2008) <http://www.scribd.com/doc/7694880/Myanmar-Constitution-2008-English-version> (accessed 20 April 2012).

9. Democratic Voice of Burma (DVB) is a non-profit media organization based in Oslo, Norway, and run by Burmese expatriates. DVB makes radio and television broadcasts aimed at providing uncensored news and information about Myanmar, and began broadcasting into Myanmar via shortwave radio in July 1992. Radio Free Asia (RFA) is a private, non-profit corporation that operates a radio station and Internet news service. It was set up under the U.S. International Broadcasting Act of 1994, and began operation in 1996. Burmese language services began in 1997. RFA is supported in part by grants from the federal government of the United States of America.

10. It is to be noted that since about the year 2000, exile and expatriate media have also expanded their services, moving away from print to audio-visual media. Examples are *Mizzima News*, based in New Delhi, and *The Irrawaddy*, based in Chiangmai, Thailand.

References

Callamard, Agnes. "Burma: Role of freedom of expression in democratisation processes". Presentation to the Conference on Media Development in Myanmar, organized by the Ministry of Information and UNESCO, Yangon, Myanmar, 19–20 March 2012. <http://www.article19.org/resources.php/resource/3006/en/burma:-role-of-freedom-of-expression-in-democratisation-processes>. Accessed 15 April 2012.

Constitution of the Republic of the Union of Myanmar. Naypyitaw: Printing and Publishing Enterprise, Ministry of Information, Union of Myanmar, 2008. Available at <http://www.burmalibrary.org/docs5/Myanmar_Constitution-2008-en.pdf>. Accessed 24 April 2012.

Hsat Linn. "Military Cronies Expand Control of Burmese Media". *Irrawaddy*, 29 July 2010. <http://www.irrawaddymedia.com/article.php?art_id=19082>. Accessed 16 April 2012.

Irrawaddy. "Surgeon Suspended After Rangoon Girl's Death". *Irrawaddy*, 3 December 2009. <www.irrawaddy.org/article.php?art_id=17346>. Accessed 15 July 2010.

Islam, Roumeen. "Into the Looking Glass: What the Media Tell and Why". In *The Right to Tell: The Role of Mass Media in Economic Development*, by Roumeen Islam, Simeon Djankov and Caralee McLeish. Washington, D.C.: World Bank Institute, 2002.

Ministry of Information (Myanmar). *Policies, Instructions and Directives to Alter the Practice of Press Scrutiny Norms* (in Myanmar language). June 2011, p. 1.

Nayee Lin Latt. "Interview with Hay Mar (aka) Ma Ma". *Irrawaddy*, 19 July 2011. Reprinted in "The media must point out injustices", *Asia Views*. <http://www. asiaviews.org/index.php?option=com_content&view=article&id=30953%3Ath e-media-must-point-out-injustices&Itemid=43>. Accessed 16 April 2012.

New Light of Myanmar (NLM). "Information, knowledge and entertainment programmes provided". *New Light of Myanmar*, 11 March 2011a. <http://www. burmalibrary.org/docs11/NLM2011-03-11.pdf>. Accessed 1 June 2012.

———. "President U Thein Sein speaks to members of the Union Government, Heads of Union level organizations". *New Light of Myanmar*, 1 April 2011b, pp. 1, 7–10 <http://www.burmalibrary.org/docs11/NLM2011-04-01.pdf>. Accessed 1 June 2012.

Transparency International. *Overview of Corruption in Burma/Myanmar*. 2 March 2009. <http://www.u4.no/publications/overview-of-corruption-in-burma-myanmar/>. Accessed 15 April 2012.

United States Department of State. *2008 Investment Climate Statement — Burma* <http://www.state.gov/e/eb/ifd/2008/100832.htm>. Accessed 15 July 2010.

Wai Phyo Myint. "Publishing Rebounds". *Myanmar Times* 277, 1–7 August 2005.

Xinhua. "Myanmar Drafting New Anti-corruption Law". *People's Daily*, 27 March 2007 <http://english.peopledaily.com.cn/200703/27/eng20070327_361382. html>. Accessed 16 April 2012.

11

THE EMERGENCE OF MYANMAR WEEKLY NEWS JOURNALS AND THEIR DEVELOPMENT IN RECENT YEARS

Pe Myint

WHAT DO JOURNALS TELL THEIR READERS?

When we in Myanmar say a *"gja ne"* (journal) we mean a weekly news magazine or a newspaper that is published weekly, usually in the format of a tabloid and containing about thirty-six to sixty pages.

These papers are important sources of information for the Myanmar people. In such a rumour-ridden country, when someone tells a news story to another person, he will invariably be asked, "Where did you hear that?", or "Are you sure? Who told you so?", and if he replies that he has read it in the so-and-so journal, he will to a certain degree be believed.

The journals do not contain propaganda, like the government newspapers or radio and TV stations, nor do they contain criticism of the government, like opposition media operating abroad, but they do contain interesting local news that is closely related to the daily lives of the people, such as that a number of new telephones are to be sold by the telecommunications department at a lower price than before; that petrol is to be sold by private gas stations; that unwholesome food-colouring materials have been found in pickled tea leaves; or that there have been mudslide and floods in such-and-such an area. That is why people buy journals to read and then spread the information they find there to other people. When the Democratic Voice of Burma (DVB) presented a TV programme called "What are the journals telling? (*gja ne dweigabapjo: neithale:*), I found it to be a most appropriate title, precisely reflecting the interest that Myanmar people have in the weekly newspapers — the JOURNALS.

In this chapter I describe the progress that has been made during the last two years by Myanmar journalists in improving their journals by extending the area of reportage into the previously forbidden territory of politics. First, however, I would like to describe very briefly the state of the news media in Myanmar in the preceding years.

A BRIEF HISTORY OF THE NEWS MEDIA BEFORE 2008

A recent history of the news media in Myanmar should begin with U Ne Win. After seizing power in a military coup in 1962, General Ne Win abolished not only the political parties but also the newspapers, except for a few that were nationalized and turned into government propaganda papers. It is necessary to mention that there was a short period of a few years around 1970 when U Ne Win gave publishing licences to some ex-politicians and senior journalists, such as U Nyo Mya, Thakhin Lwin, and Bo Min Khaung, who produced weekly or fortnightly periodicals, attaching the title of "journal" to their publications. Some of the older readers in Myanmar still reminisce about those journals, which were very popular and influential at the time, but except for the *"Thadingja ne"* (*The News Journal*) edited and published by Ahtau'to Hla Aung, none of them looked like replacements for the defunct private daily newspapers. Thus I believe that it is not unreasonable to say that the news media became a government monopoly business under U Ne Win's socialist regime, which lasted from 1962 to 1988.

By 1988, the situation of the print media was such that:

- There was no private daily newspaper;
- There were a few weeklies, but they did not focus on news;
- There were a number of monthly magazines which focused mainly on literature and topics of general interest.

All of these publications had to pass through a tedious process of pre-publication censorship.

The State Law and Order Restoration Council (SLORC) that took power in 1988 and the State Peace and Development Council (SPDC) that succeeded it (the same regime but with a new name) continued the authoritarian rule of U Ne Win, including the tight control of the media, and for that purpose maintained the censorship apparatus that had been used by their predecessor.

However, due to changes SLORC/SPDC subsequently made in economic policy and political ideology, censorship of such important topics as economics and international affairs was to some degree relaxed. At the same time, perhaps as the result of a positive change in attitude towards business, the number of licences issued to private individuals for the publication of periodicals was gradually increased. The early recipients of those permits were persons who had connections in high places. Later, licences were issued to officials from some government departments who sub-contracted them out to private publishers so as to earn funds for the welfare of their personnel.

The first periodicals published in the 1990s were also called journals, but they were not news journals. Although they appeared weekly, they were more like magazines, focusing on permitted topics such as sports, performance arts, music, entertainment, businesses, health, education, and science and technology. The first journals to present current news, feature articles, and commentaries, and to have pages for advertisements like the daily newspapers, came out in early 2000. The journal that opened up the way for weekly newspapers and today's journals, and that led the way in establishing their present format, was the Myanmar-language version of the *Myanmar Times* (known at that time to be a semi-government paper), the first issue of which was published in 2001.

By 2005 there were about a dozen journals providing news coverage for the Myanmar public, but they had limited access to the government offices that have daily dealings with the public and are important sources of interesting news. Even if the journals were able to discover news stories related to those offices, they were unable to publish the stories without the permission of the office concerned. It was difficult for reporters to get news even from the police stations, law courts, and hospitals. Higher levels of the government were forbidden areas for journalists, and to write about politics was unthinkable. As a result, although they had the usual features of a weekly newspaper, the journals that were published in the middle of last decade were largely lacking in content of any substance.

2008: CHANGE IS IN THE AIR

In 2008, some distinctive changes occurred that were to have a profound effect on journals. These changes concerned the new constitution, which was approved by a referendum held in May 2008, and the general election that was to be held later, in accordance with that constitution. Both the constitution and the election were strongly opposed by many political groups and individuals inside and outside the country. The sounds of "boycott" and "no vote" were loudly heard.

In spite of this, from August 2008 a number of articles supporting the election began to appear in certain journals. This was the first time that political issues had been covered by any weekly news journal, and the development had repercussions among journalists and politicians alike. Previously, journals had frequently printed political articles assigned to them by the authorities. Readers knew that those articles, which almost always criticized and disparaged opposition groups and individuals, were propaganda pieces written by officials and pro-government writers under assumed names, and the articles were not taken seriously.

The articles that appeared in those journals from August 2008 onwards evoked strong responses among the public because they were written by well-known writers. The first to write was Maung Suu Sann, a writer-politician. He had been writing regular columns in a number of journals, and had a large audience. Less than three months after the approval of the draft constitution, Maung Suu Sann began a series of articles that strongly supported the forthcoming elections. He wrote in various journals such as *The Modern, Market News, Yangon Times*, and the *Weekly Eleven*. His stand was severely criticized among the general public, and it was said that some of the journals that had previously accepted his work began refusing to publish his articles. The censors would not permit publication of articles that contained arguments counter to Maung Suu Sann's opinions, but his critics found a space through Internet websites, and for a time there was a hot debate between Maung Suu Sann in the pages of various journals and his opponents through their blogs.

What Maung Suu Sann repeatedly claimed at the time was that the elections were the only way to break the political impasse; that the military should be regarded as sponsors of democracy; and that those who opposed the elections were politically naïve and would have no future. Later in 2008, articles from prominent people who supported Maung Suu Sann's line to varying degrees appeared in the journals. These writers included pre-military regime era politicians such as Thakhin Tin Mya and Maung Chit Hlaing, and writers and editors such as Kyaw Win and Nay Win Maung.

2009: POLITICAL WRITINGS RELATED TO THE ELECTIONS

The enthusiasm of Maung Suu Sann's supporters was on the wane when, in December 2008, Senior General Than Shwe, in an address made at a military graduation ceremony, announced that elections would be held in 2010. That announcement not only reinvigorated the above-mentioned writers, but also enticed other journal editors, who had until then been observing from the sidelines, to start publishing articles about politics.

Still, none of the articles published were news stories related to politics. What the journals were presenting was a variety of articles about topics related to politics — for example, articles on political theory or about previous elections held decades ago, political memoirs, and interviews with former politicians and senior journalists about the past and present political situation and future scenarios.

The most active journal supporting the government line at the time was *The Voice* weekly. Throughout 2009 its editorials, as well as articles by columnist Aung Htut (a pen-name of Nay Win Maung[1]) and a group of other regular writers, repeated the same theme in a variety of ways. In an article written in early 2010, Aung Htut said that he was heartily satisfied to have been able to write his political ideas to the fullest extent, and was grateful to those who had provided him with that opportunity.

Another journal, *The Northern Star*, which was first published in early 2009, openly declared that its aim was to provide voters with proper information so they could make an informed choice about which candidates to vote for. Nevertheless, most of the articles included in it were government propaganda pieces, which Myanmar readers used to call "policy articles", and they made little impression on the public.

Although supporters of the government line were free to advocate in whatever way they like, opponents of the government were not able to write about their views openly because of censorship. They were, however, able to present different opinions by disputing the arguments of the government's supporters on particular issues, and sometimes by leveling pointed criticisms at them. The leading critics at the time were Ludu Sein Win and Maung Wuntha, both of them senior journalists and ex-politicians.

During 2009, the *Yangon Times* journal also created a political affairs section, which was later produced as an eight-page insert with the title *The Political Times*. It looked as if the *Yangon Times* media group had plans to publish a new journal with an emphasis on politics at an appropriate time, which they seemed to expect was soon to come. A number of authors wrote for the political section of the *Yangon Times*, and from the ranks of its regular contributors, Ko Ko Hlaing and Dr Nay Zin Latt were appointed as political advisors to the new president, U Thein Sein, soon after his inauguration in March 2011.

Another journal that developed a serious focus on politics during 2009 was *The True News Journal*. Columnists such as Ludu Sein Win, Maung Wuntha, and Sithu Aung Myint tried to present different views rather than just parrot the pro-government line.

Overall, during 2009 several journals published significant amounts of political material, and the readership became quite interested. Although dissatisfied with the one-sidedness of the content, readers understood that the journals were not able to openly express the views of the political opposition groups.

2010: THE APPEARANCE OF POLITICAL NEWS

After beating about the political bush for the whole of 2009, in 2010 journalists seized the chance to report political news for the first time.

In March 2010 the government enacted a set of electoral and party registration laws, which initiated a series of activities among some politicians who did not boycott the elections. They began to organize, formed parties, registered them, held meetings, issued manifestos, gave press conferences and interviews, and later recruited potential candidates for their constituencies. This flurry of activity was followed by political campaigning by the candidates. Although the major opposition party and a substantial part of the body politic were against the elections, many people took an interest in the pre-election activities of the parties and politicians because that kind of thing had not been seen in the country for twenty years.

The journalists were more enthusiastic about these events than most people — they were having their first taste of political reporting. Reporters from about a dozen journals covered the general elections in all its aspects. Although many of the news stories, interviews, commentaries, cartoons, and editorials were partly or wholly censored, editors and readers alike were satisfied that they had done a good job. In the market, the popularity of the journals that focused on politics rose, and more new journals, as well as some existing non-political journals, moved into the field.

However, in November the euphoria of the journalists was unexpectedly smashed. After the journals reported on the release of Daw Aung San Suu Kyi from house arrest and the public excitement that followed, the Press Scrutiny and Registration Division (PSRD) suspended seven journals for one week each and two journals for two weeks each, for breaking the regulations.

2011 AND SINCE

In the early months of 2011 three events of great importance for the media occurred. First, following the elections of November 2010, officials from the PSRD, together with personnel from the government-controlled writers and journalists association, formed a press council called the Committee for Professional Conduct. Many of the publishers and editors of private journals were included, but the real aims of the committee and the way it will function are not yet clear.

Second were the meetings of the Hluttaw (parliament) held under the new government from March 2011. Journalists were eager to cover the event, the first of its kind for them — but they were denied access even to the premises of the Hluttaw.[2]

The third event was a series of addresses delivered by the new president, U Thein Sein, in March and April. In those speeches U Thein Sein repeatedly remarked upon the importance of the news media and their role as the Fourth Estate, and several journalists hailed this as a good sign for the media.[3] The speeches were followed by an announcement by the PSRD that several journals in non-sensitive categories, such as sports, art and culture, health care, education, and science and technology, would very soon be exempted from the requirement to submit their drafts for pre-publication censorship, but that the news weeklies would have to continue as usual until some indefinite date in the future.

HAS THERE BEEN ANY PROGRESS IN FREEDOM OF EXPRESSION?

Some people in Myanmar believe that there has been some incremental progress in the freedom of the press, and that the relaxation on the part of the censors during the last year, and especially in the last few months, is quite obvious.

To illustrate that view, I have chosen as an example a cartoon by Aw Pi Kyeh, which was published twice by the *True News* journal, at different times and in different sizes (see Figure 11.1).

The small-size cartoon was first published on 25 May 2010, months before the elections. It shows a football player changing his jersey for one with a different number [and presumably intending to go back on the field and continue playing]. It was said that the official responsible for scrutinizing the journal was reprimanded by his superiors for allowing (or perhaps for missing) the cartoon, which ridiculed the military personnel changing into civilian clothes without relinquishing their posts. The larger image was published on 3 May 2011, this time without any problem. After seeing such examples, many people have concluded that there has been tangible progress.

On the other hand, some maintain that the censors have selectively lifted restrictions that are no longer of benefit to them. Their argument is that because of changes in government policy, the officials had come to the view that some regulations had become unnecessary, so they were discarded, while regulations they believed were essential were adhered to as strongly as before.

So, what is my view? I see that as the result of living for nearly five decades under censorship, the censor has taken root in the minds of writers and journalists. Each has their own censorship official in their head, who effectively carries out pre-censorship by strictly removing anything that could possibly annoy the real censors. As a result, self-censorship has become much more restrictive than the official censors. Let's see it in a graphic (see Figure 11.2).

In the diagram, the black segment is the area forbidden by the censor, the white segment is the area where the journalists feel free and have kept

FIGURE 11.1
Cartoon as Published at Different Times

25 May 2010   3 May 2011

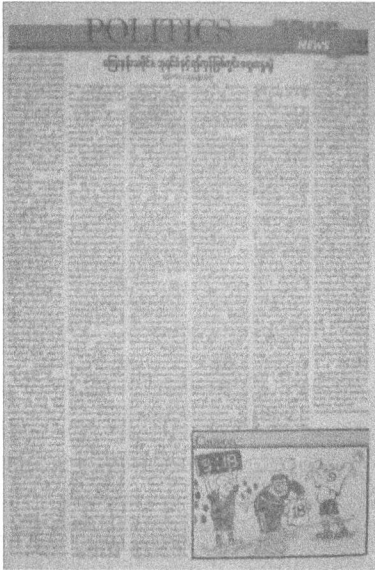 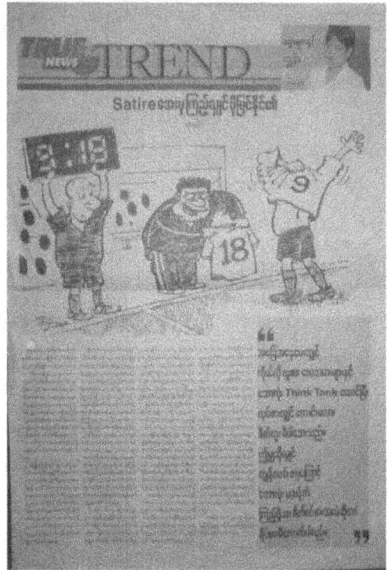

Source: Reproduced with permission of Aw Pi Kyeh.

FIGURE 11.2
Diagram of Self-Censorship

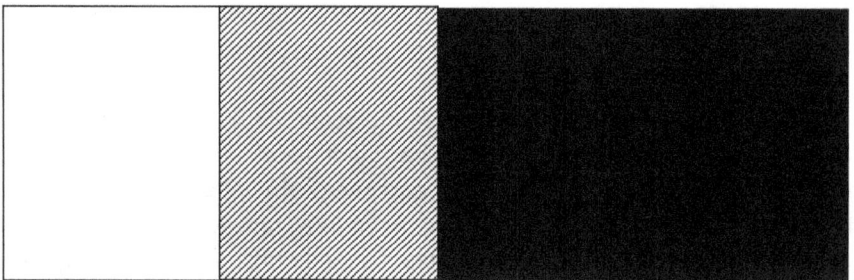

Free Area   Self-censored   Censored Area
Area

themselves within its limits, and the grey segment is the area which they themselves have relinquished in order to appease or to avoid problems with the censor.

What has happened in the last one or two years is that journalists have been trying to reclaim the area they had relinquished, and to some degree they have succeeded. Now they have to deal with the more difficult task of extending into the black area of censorship, so as to reduce that segment to the smallest size possible. As everyone knows, this will depend on events that take place on the Myanmar political stage in the future, and on *that* stage, journalists can — at best — play only supporting roles.

Notes

1. Nay Win Maung was a political activist who worked for reform through his think-tank, Myanmar Egress. He died of a heart attack on 1 January 2012.
2. Access to the parliament for journalists was permitted from the second session of the Hluttaw. Even some foreign journalists were allowed to record interviews from the parliament building before the end of 2011.
3. President Thein Sein's first reference to the need to respect the media as the "fourth estate" was in his 31 March 2011 address to the new government. See "President U Thein Sein speaks to members of the Union Government, Heads of Union level organizations", *New Light of Myanmar*, 1 April 2011, pp. 1, 7–10, <http://www.burmalibrary.org/docs11/NLM2011-04-01.pdf> (accessed 1 June 2012).

VI

The Rule of Law

12

CRITICAL ISSUES FOR THE RULE OF LAW IN MYANMAR

Kyaw Min San

Jurists debate the meaning of the rule of law, and define it from various points of view, yet for centuries the basic principle has rested in the idea that the law applies to all. In *The Republic*, written in the first century BC, Cicero condemned the king who does not abide by the law as a despot who is the foulest and most repellant creature imaginable (Tamanaha 2004, pp. 11–12). The Magna Carta reinforced this idea of the ruler bound to the law along with his subjects.

For some scholars today these traditional ideas of the rule of law would be classed as "rule by law", now that a distinction is being drawn between the two concepts. According to a 2004 report of the UN Secretary-General, rule of law requires measures to ensure adherence to the principles of supremacy of law, equality before the law, accountability to the law, fairness in the application of the law, separation of powers, participation in decision-making, legal certainty, avoidance of arbitrariness, and procedural and legal transparency (United Nations 2004). Similarly, Kleinfeld Belton has argued that the rule of law "is not a single, unified good but is composed of five separate, socially desirable goods, or ends: (1) a government bound by law (2) equality before the law (3) law and order (4) predictable and efficient rulings, and (5) human rights" (Kleinfeld Belton 2005, p. 27).

On the other hand, according to Kirsti Samuels:

> Rule by law requires the use of legal rules in order to assure the uniformity and regularity of an existing legal system. Thus, even an authoritarian legal system, or one which does not protect human rights, will qualify as ruling by law if it uses and enforces legal rules routinely through the use of officials and some form of a judiciary, as long as it achieves a relative degree of certainty and predictability (Samuels 2006, p. 3).

Political science professor Li Shuguang puts it more bluntly: "The difference ... is that, under the rule of law, the law is preeminent and can serve as a check against the abuse of power. Under rule by law, the law is a mere tool for a government, that suppresses in a legalistic fashion" (Tamanaha 2004, p. 3). Indeed, some dictatorial regimes associate rule of law with suppression, and justify their actions on the grounds of law and order, oriented towards an insistence on harmony and security, rather than towards justice and fundamental human freedoms.

The point of view that I adopt in writing this chapter is that the rule of law in its true sense means that everybody is equal before the law and no one is above the law. It means that the government, which is responsible for the writing of law, cannot also be a violator of the law. The rule of law in its true sense can coexist only with democracy, and depends upon respect for citizens' fundamental rights. It means that a fair trial and due process of law are guaranteed according to international standards and norms recognized by the United Nations.

Now Myanmar is in a period of transition to democracy, and the rule of law is of prime importance for the country's future. Newly-elected President U Thein Sein said in his first address to government officers on 31 March 2011 that:

> Another important task is to ensure the rule of law, which is essential for building up a modern and developed democratic nation. It is the duty of not only judicial bodies but also legislative bodies to ensure the rule of law.

> It is required of judicial bodies to carry out judicial tasks in accord with the provisions of the constitution such as openly handling judicial affairs and the right to pass judgment in the presence of the public except legislative constraints [sic], and the rights to defence and appellate jurisdiction in criminal cases (*NLM* 2011, p. 7).

Subsequently, Thura U Shwe Mann, President of the Pyithu Hluttaw (lower house of parliament), reinforced the message by stating in the Yangon Region parliament that, "No one is above the law and all persons must live under the law according to the saying 'No one can stay beyond the law'" (*Weekly Eleven* 2011, p. 3).

The question that we now face is how much can the new government achieve these goals for the rule of law in reality? Although Myanmar is in transition to become a democratic country, other countries in Asia that have made the transition have not succeeded in addressing their rule-of-law problems. The Philippines, for example, is well known as a country more fully democratic than most others in Southeast Asia, but it is still faces rule-of-law problems, and its legal system is also corrupted. So this is the time for Myanmar to consider how to make its democratic transition also effective for developing the rule of law.

There are many critical issues for the rule of law in Myanmar, but in this chapter I will focus only on three of them. The first is the role of the Supreme Court as the highest court in the Union, at the apex of the judicial structure. The second is a lack of authority on the part of the courts and procedures that are unnecessarily complicated, both of which factors are compounded by pressure being exerted on the courts by the administration. The third issue is abuse of power and corruption.

THE STATUS, COMPOSITION, AND BUDGET OF THE SUPREME COURT

In this section, I want to discuss three aspects of the role of the Supreme Court under the provisions of the 2008 Constitution of the Republic of the Union of Myanmar. The first is in regard to the relationship between the Supreme Court and the Courts-Martial; the second relates to the composition of the Supreme Court; and the third concerns its budget.

Under Article 294 of the 2008 Constitution, the Supreme Court of the Union is the highest court of the country. In reality, however, the power of the Supreme Court cannot surpass that of military tribunals (Courts-Martial), because military tribunals have authority to decide military cases as final appeals. According to Article 343(b) of the constitution, in the adjudication of military cases, the decision of the Commander-in-Chief of the Defence Services is final and conclusive. This arrangement appears to pose problems for the rule of law in Myanmar, since it undermines the authority of the Supreme Court as the highest court. It also undermines the separation of powers on which the rule of law is dependent.

In fact, not only can the Supreme Court not overrule the Courts-Martial, but it is also the case that in the present Supreme Court, three judges are understood to have come from the Defence Services. Aside from these three, one of the two remaining judges is understood to have come from the Ministry of National Planning and Economic Development, while the other is from the Ministry of Mines.[1] Therefore, the question arises as to whether or not these five judges have sufficient experience in legal matters. At time of writing, no information about the Supreme Court judges has so far been published in the newspapers, nor have detailed biographies of these judges been made public. Even among legal professionals, the qualities and experience of these judges are not known, so people cannot decide if the qualifications of the judges conform to constitutional requirements and the needs of the courts.

It is my view that highly experienced lawyers and judges should be appointed to the Supreme Court, as provided in Article 301 of the 2008 Constitution, which states that a judge of the Supreme Court shall be a person:

(a) not younger than 50 years and not older than 70 years;
(b) who has qualifications, with the exception of the age limit, prescribed in Section 120 for Pyithu Hluttaw representatives;
(c) whose qualifications do not breach the provisions under the Section 121 which disqualify him from standing for election as a Pyithu Hluttaw representatives;
(d) (i) who has served as a Judge of the High Court of the Region or State for at least five years; or
    (ii) who has served as a Judicial Officer or a Law Officer at least 10 years not lower than that of the Region or State level; or
    (iii) who has practised as an Advocate for at least 20 years; or
    (iv) who is, in the opinion of the President, an eminent jurist;
(e) loyal to the Union and its citizens;
(f) who is not a member of a political party;
(g) who is not a Hluttaw representative.

Incidentally, the president of the Union also appoints judges to the new High Courts of States and Regions, under Article 308(b) of the constitution. Moreover, according to this Article, Region and State legislatures cannot refuse judges nominated by the president. So far as the appointment of judges of these High Courts is concerned, perhaps the chief ministers of respective States and Regions should instead be given the power to appoint judges in their States and Regions, so that the power of the national level does not overwhelm that of the States and Regions.

One other issue that I want to mention briefly in this section is the judiciary budget. Article 297 of the constitution reads, "The Supreme Court of the Union shall submit the judiciary budget to the Union Government in order to include and present it in the Annual Budget Bill of the Union in accord with the provisions of the Constitution". From my point of view, because the Union Government can decide on the question of the judicial budget, it means that the executive can potentially restrict the amount of money going to the judiciary. This arrangement may affect the independence of the courts and damage the rule of law, since control over the courts' purse strings can affect their overall operations. So as to enable more independent jurisdiction of the courts, the Supreme Court should submit the proposed judicial budget to the Union Parliament directly, and the Union Parliament too should decide on the matter directly. Then the courts would be subject to less executive control.

LACK OF AUTHORITY AND EXTERNAL PRESSURE

A second major issue for the rule of law in Myanmar today is that in some cases the courts do not follow the law exactly, because of pressure from the administration, and in some cases the courts do not have the authority to decide matters because, as a result of various rearrangements of laws and institutions, executive agencies have assumed quasi-judicial roles.

In my own experience, in one case that I represented in 2006, I could not argue orally in a divisional court because the court did not follow the letter of the law, due to pressure being applied by the local administration. This happened even though Paragraph 154(12) of the Burma Courts Manual expressly mentions that lawyers must give final arguments orally (Courts Manual 1999, p. 157). In that case, the accused person went to the Myanmar–Thai border, made connection there with an unlawful association, and took K500,000 from this organization. The police charged the accused with crossing borders illegally and with joining an unlawful association, and he was sentenced to twenty-six years' imprisonment. In this case, as a lawyer, I did not get the right to plead orally in the court, even though the law on this matter is clear; the court would only accept a written argument. It is my view that, in order to give meaning to the rule of law in Myanmar, courts should follow the letter of the law exactly, and that cases should be decided in accordance with the law and with principles of justice.

Another example of a similar kind comes from the law reports. According to Sections 24, 25, and 26 of the Evidence Act, a confession to a police officer is inadmissible in court, but in *Union of Myanmar v U Ye Naung and Another* (MLR 1991), the Supreme Court decided that a confession to a military intelligence officer *was* admissible. This ruling, seemingly, was contrary to the procedures prescribed in the Evidence Act, and has damaged the rule of law, because it has given military intelligence officers the authority to obtain confessions. At the time, this decision shocked the Myanmar legal world. Lawyers worried that the move would destroy one of the pillars of the legal system, since it undermined fundamental principles of the Evidence Act.

Subsequently, in *U Ko Gyi v Union of Myanmar* (MLR 2005), the Supreme Court found that an admission made in a military camp by an accused person was insufficient to convict a co-accused of the crime. In this case the reason for the decision was that there was no supporting evidence. In his ruling, the judge wrote:

> It appears that there is only the interrogation record of co-accused Tin Shwe (a.k.a.) Than Htike at Military Intelligence-7 [as evidence]. This case has no other testimonies to link [the accused to the crime] as in the ruling *Union of Myanmar v U Ye Naung & Another,* on which the Yangon Eastern District Court relied. The conviction by Yangon East District court of U Ko Gyi under section 19(a)/21 of the 1993 Narcotic Drugs and Psychotropic Substances Law and the confirmation of Yangon Divisional Court of this judgment are not correct, as there is no circumstantial evidence to support the co-accused Tin Shwe (a.k.a.) Than Htike's admission that the accused U Ko Gyi is guilty (MLR 2005, p. 26; translation by the author).

Although the above decision was a good decision for the accused man, it still did not overturn *Union of Myanmar v U Ye Naung*, because the court described the facts as being different from that case. As a result, the ruling in the *U Ye Naung* case is still recognized. The lack of clarity around the use of evidence, and around the court's jurisdiction to inquire into evidence that a case has generated, can also damage justice and the rule of law, and are matters that both the courts and the new legislatures should consider seriously.

Aside from the types of problems which arise in certain sorts of criminal cases as a result of outside pressure, as described above, in civil matters the shifting of authority to non-judicial agencies and the introduction of unnecessarily complicated procedures are also issues that raise questions about the capacity of state agencies to operate according to the rule of law.

Take the registration of deeds for buying and selling houses: even though this is officially a matter for the registration office of the agriculture department, under a relatively new procedure township committees have been set up for the purpose of assessing tax on the purchase and sale of land and houses. The committees have been formed with six officers apiece: one from the land registration department, one from the revenue department, one from the police department, one from the general administration department, one from the national planning and economic development department, and one from the municipality.

Before the new procedure was introduced, registration to allow individuals to buy and sell land and houses was easy, and there was no need for a committee to evaluate property. Now, the six township officers are supposed to meet as a committee to evaluate houses and land, and then give permission to sell the stamps for the deeds to the lawyers concerned. The lawyers can then access the land registration office under the agriculture department for the purpose of registration. In the process, the state collects 10 per cent of the value in tax. This procedure is much more complicated than previously, and in reality, as the officers concerned are very busy, they find it difficult to meet together to prepare valuations of land and houses for the purpose of taxation. Their difficulties in meeting result in delays, which in turn can result in corruption, since persons who want to sell and buy houses and land without delay find it better to bribe the authorities so that they get a quicker outcome, and also so that the tax assessed on the valuation of their land and houses will be low. Some lawyers take responsibility on behalf of their clients to bribe the concerned authorities so as to smooth out this unnecessarily complicated process.

One of the difficulties associated with vesting committees of administrators with powers over complicated procedures is that it enables officials with personal interests in a case to use the system to cause delays and adopt other tactics to the disadvantage of one party or another. For instance, following the introduction in 1963 of a law to allow for the nationalization of land, the authority to decide on disputes over land was given to land committees at various levels, and these committees were formed with administrative rather than judicial officers. Consequently, courts do not have the authority to decide disputes over land title that they would have in the jurisdictions of other countries.

In one case that I handled, Mrs C. had a dispute with Mr A., a relative of the village head, over land. According to Section 3 of the 1963 Law Protecting Peasants' Rights, no one can prohibit farmers from entering and cultivating land (U Ba Kyaing 1999, p. 60). By law, Mrs C. had the right to cultivate the farmland, but the village head, through his relative, prevented her from cultivating it. Thereafter, Mrs C. faced a delayed process at the land committee and the case, which began in 2008, was still pending in 2010. Throughout this time Mrs C. was not able to cultivate, or even enter, the land. She faces financial loss and her rights to cultivate the land have also been infringed, but because of the present procedures she has been unable to obtain redress.

It is clear from cases like this that there should be changes to many laws so as to simplify complicated procedures and reduce delays and opportunities for abuse. It is also evident that we need to undertake more research to determine how much the rule of law has deteriorated because of interventions from the administration into judicial matters, and take whatever steps are necessary to prevent needless and potentially harmful interventions.

CORRUPTION AND ABUSE OF POWER

The final issue for the rule of law that I want to discuss is bribery and corruption in the court system and police system. Corruption is one of the greatest hindrances to the administration of justice in Myanmar at present. It is widespread, both in the courts and among the police.

In the courts, the clearest manifestation that bribery is rife is that some lawyers and public prosecutors and their clerks work as brokers (*pwe sar* in Burmese). Court clerks also engage in this work, serving as buffers between clients and judges for the purpose of bribery, so that judges can avoid risk by using others to take money. In addition, the filling-out of legal forms under the authority of the court clerks has become a kind of marketplace in the courthouses, and if lawyers or clients do not give money to the clerks, their cases will not proceed smoothly.

What happens in practice, in all aspects of the system, is that where a person (or official) has control over some part of the legal process, that person can demand money in exchange for giving their authorization or taking some action. To give another example, if a plaintiff in a criminal case wants to hire an independent lawyer to appear on his behalf, the lawyer needs to get permission from the public prosecutor, because according to procedural law the public prosecutor is responsible for the plaintiff. To get permission from the public prosecutor, either the client or a lawyer hired by the client may have to offer a bribe.

One reason for the high levels of corruption in the courts is that the salaries of judges, public prosecutors, and police officers are low. Township-level officers receive an average salary of about K100,000 (US$120) per month. It is difficult for a family to survive on this amount; consequently, bribery and corruption are rife in the various levels of the courts, public prosecution departments, and police departments. If bribery and corruption are to be eliminated, it is obvious that judges, public prosecutors, and police officers must be given adequate salaries, access to social security, and be able to enjoy decent living standards.

One practising lawyer told me that the biggest difficulty for him is that he always has to enter the back door of the court, meaning that he has to bribe the judge. Without giving a bribe, there will be no smooth procedure for the party in court. Another highly-experienced lawyer said that he believes bribery and corruption are now prevalent in more than 50 per cent of courts in the present legal system. He said it was his opinion that unless a bribe is given, there is no possibility of winning a case. A third lawyer said that most of the courts in which he practises take bribes from clients, but that some judges make impartial decisions without payment. He also added that bribery at the courts was not under the table but on the table, meaning that judges take bribes as if the laws permit it.[2] From these accounts, it is clear that corruption at various levels of the courts, in both civil and criminal cases, is a continual occurrence in Myanmar.

In one case I handled that concerned cheating, my client was charged under Section 420 of the Penal Code because the other party paid the prosecutor to lodge the charge as a criminal offence rather than as a civil matter. The facts of the case, briefly, are as follows. In 2008, a company that had been established by an armed group in ceasefire agreement with the government started legal action against Mr A., a timber trader. An agent of the company, Mr B., sold timber to Mr A., and Mr A. gave K5 million to Mr B. as part of his payment for the timber. The full amount that Mr. A. needed to give the company was K50 million. Because he had received the advance payment to the company, the agent gave Mr A. the permit that is the necessary legal document produced by the forestry department to allow citizens to take timber from the forestry department and to carry the logs across States. However, the company agent, Mr B., misused the advance payment and then died before the logs were obtained. At that time, the company asked Mr A. to give back the permit. Mr A. in turn asked the company to return the payment he had given to Mr B., but the company refused Mr A.'s demand and commenced criminal charges against him.

Although the company should have brought a civil action against Mr A. to return the documents, the company misused the criminal mechanism as an attempted shortcut to get the permit. Despite the public prosecutor knowing that it was procedurally incorrect, he charged Mr A. with a criminal offence. Fortunately, the court judged the case correctly and acquitted Mr A., but the case lasted nearly two years and Mr A. had to spend money on lawyer's fees and other expenses, such as travelling costs and meals. This meant he was unable to carry on his daily business as a trader of logs.

When I discussed this case with one experienced lawyer, he said that in his experience the line between civil and criminal matters is often a thin one, and it is not easy to differentiate. Some dishonest public prosecutors take advantage of this to use the criminal mechanism to get money, instead of commencing a civil suit, even though the case may be civil in nature. Such misuse of the criminal legal mechanism is another barrier to the rule of law.

Police play the main role in the investigation of criminal cases, and they have authority to detain accused persons on charges that may be brought for the purpose of the payment of bribes rather than as the result of proper investigation. For example, in one case that I handled in 2009, the police brought a case against a woman, Mrs C., alleging that she had stolen a gold chain. In fact, Mrs C. had been conducting an illegal lottery and she had not paid the amount that she needed to pay to the lottery broker, Mrs D. The broker used the police to bring a false charge against Mrs C. in an attempt to get the payment. In that case, however, even though the police had been bribed to bring the false charge, the prosecutor was of good character and the case did not go to court because he released Mrs C. from the charges.

Not only do the police have powers of detention, but they also have powers to release accused persons under Section 169 of the Code of Criminal Procedure, which reads as follows:

> If, upon an investigation under this Chapter, it appears to the officer in charge of the police-station or to the police-officer making the investigation that there is not sufficient evidence or reasonable ground of suspicion to justify forwarding of the accused to a Magistrate, such officer shall, if such person is in custody, release him on his executing a bond, with or without sureties, as such officer may direct, to appear, if and when so required, before a Magistrate when, powered to take cognizance of the offence on a police-report and to try the accused or commit him for trial (Code of Criminal Procedure, p. 62).

In addition, according to Section 157(b) of the Code of Criminal Procedure, the police officer in charge of a police station has authority not to investigate a case if it appears that there are not sufficient grounds for starting an investigation (Code of Criminal Procedure, p. 57). Some dishonest police use these provisions to make money. They exploit detainees who do not know about law and legal procedures and who are worried about the possibility of having to go to court, by threatening and extorting money from them or by promising to get them released instead in return for payment. For example, before the case arrives at court, dishonest police may tell the accused that they can get him or her released if there is not sufficient evidence or by destroying or omitting evidence. Accused people with money who do not want to go to court will bribe the police and public prosecutor, even in the police station or prosecutorial offices, so the case does not go to court.

Bribery and corruption in the courts and among police is causing miscarriage of justice in specific cases and a breakdown of the rule of law nationwide. We need to watch what measures the present government, which says it wants clean government and good governance, will take in order to fight against bribery and corruption and to instill in judges, prosecutors, lawyers, and police the real meaning of the rule of law.

CONCLUSION

Now Myanmar is in a period of transition to democracy and there is hope that the country will have an improved and more transparent legal system in the future. In terms of the three critical issues discussed in this chapter, I would like to make the following recommendations.

The Supreme Court should be the court of final appeal and conclusive for all cases, including military cases. Freedom of expression and fundamental citizens' rights should be granted for the benefit of the country. The courts need to enforce and maintain the fundamental rights as expressed in the constitution, without bias of any kind. Courts should also have the authority to enforce fundamental rights at all levels, not only through application to the Supreme Court, as is presently the case. If citizens have easy and convenient access to justice through the courts without much expense this will be the surest way to give life to the constitutional provisions on citizens' rights. It will also allow for review by higher courts of the lower courts' determinations on issues of rights.

The Supreme Court also needs to monitor constantly to determine whether the lower courts follow the law exactly or not, and should give any guidance necessary for the maintenance of justice and for ensuring that procedural matters are kept simple and transparent. For these purposes, the judicial budget should be adequately funded, and it would be best if the Supreme Court could present its budgetary request directly to the parliament, as noted previously.

The new government should also consider what sort of constitutional process might best ensure the establishment of the rule of law through gradual development of more open and transparent practices. Perhaps, in this respect, it could take Indonesia as a good example. Indonesia is a Southeast Asian country like Myanmar, with certain historical and constitutional parallels, including a politically active military. In recent years Indonesia has made a lot of progress towards establishing the rule of law and reducing the level of corruption in judicial affairs, from which Myanmar also could learn.

As to the issue of corruption, again the government could learn from other governments that have been successful in fighting against bribery and corruption. I think those in Asia deserving of study would be Hong Kong and Singapore. In both places, one of the main factors in addressing these practices was to greatly increase the salaries of judicial and police personnel, to levels even higher than those of other comparable officials. The government of Myanmar, too, needs to consider how to improve the salaries and social security of public servants in order to reduce bribery and corruption. There is a Myanmar saying, "If the stomach is full, moral precepts are kept". What this means is that if people do not have enough food to eat, they cannot possibly maintain a high level of morality. Hence, to fight against corruption, the new government also needs to consider how to promote the living standards of all the people in the country. Then there will be the rule of law and justice and the future of Myanmar will be brighter.

Notes

1. Nominations to the Supreme Court were submitted to the National Assembly by President Thein Sein on 17 February 2011, and were subsequently approved by the Assembly. They are as follows: Chief Justice: Tun Tun Oo, previously deputy chief justice, Naypyitaw Supreme Court; Justices: Tha Htay, former Union Election Commission member; Soe Nyunt, former director, Civil Cases Department, Supreme Court, Naypyitaw; Mya Thein, former director, Management Department, Supreme Court, Naypyitaw); Myint Aung, former Yangon Regional High Court judge; Aung Zaw Thein, former Deputy General Manager, Bonds Management and Planning Department, Naypyitaw; and Myint Han, former Deputy Director, Ministry of Mining.
2. Confidential conversations with author.

References

Code of Criminal Procedure. Ministry of Home Affairs, Myanmar. <http://www.blc-burma.org/index.php?q=node/149>. Accessed 24 April 2012.

Constitution of the Republic of the Union of Myanmar (2008). Naypyitaw: Printing and Publishing Enterprise, Ministry of Information, September 2008. <http://www.burmalibrary.org/docs5/Myanmar_Constitution-2008-en.pdf>. Accessed 24 April 2012.

Courts Manual, 4th ed. Vol. 1. Yangon: Myanmar Supreme Court, 1999.

Kleinfeld Belton, Rachel. "Competing Definitions of the Rule of Law: Implications for Practitioners". Carnegie Papers No. 55. Democracy and Rule of Law Project, Carnegie Endowment for International Peace. Washington, D.C.: Carnegie Endowment for International Peace, January 2005. <http://www.carnegieendowment.org/2005/01/21/competing-definitions-of-rule-of-law-implications-for-practitioners/fhz>. Accessed 24 April 2012.

Myanmar Law Reports (MLR). *Union of Myanmar v. U Ye Naung and Another*. SC 63, 1991.

———. *U Ko Gyi v. Union of Myanmar*. SC 20, 2005.

New Light of Myanmar (NLM). "President U Thein Sein speaks to members of Union Government, heads of Union level organizations". *New Light of Myanmar*, 1 April 2011, pp. 1, 7–10. <http://www.burmalibrary.org/docs11/NLM2011-04-01.pdf>. Accessed 1 June 2012.

Samuels, Kirsti. "Rule of Law Reform in Post-Conflict Countries: Operational Initiatives and Lessons Learnt". Social Development Papers No. 37, Conflict

Prevention and Reconstruction Unit, Social Development Department, World Bank. Washington, D.C.: World Bank, October 2006 <http://siteresources. worldbank.org/INTCPR/Resources/WP37_web.pdf>. Accessed 24 April 2012.

Tamanaha, Brian Z. *On the Rule of Law: History, Politics, Theory.* Cambridge: Cambridge University Press, 2004.

U Ba Kyaing. *Special and Miscellaneous Laws.* 3rd ed. Yangon, 1999.

United Nations Secretary-General. "The Rule of Law and Transitional Justice in Conflict and Post-Conflict Societies". New York: United Nations Security Council, (S/2004/616) 23 August 2004. <http://daccess-dds-ny.un.org/doc/ UNDOC/GEN/N04/395/29/PDF/N0439529.pdf?OpenElement>. Accessed 24 April 2012.

Weekly Eleven. "Tagamya Pwin Ta Kyaung Pyithu Hluttaw Okkata Thura U Shwe Man Pyawgya" [Pyithu Hluttaw Chairman Thura U Shwe Mann Says that the Doors Are Open]. *Weekly Eleven News,* 29 June 2011, pp. 1, 3.

13

MYANMAR'S COURTS AND THE SOUNDS MONEY MAKES

Nick Cheesman

In 2007, Deputy Township Judge U Sein Lwin lost his job and went to jail. His alleged crime was to have solicited bribes so that three women would not become co-accused in a case before him. A prosecutor charged the judge under the 1948 Prevention of Corruption Act, and a court in Taunggyi promptly sentenced him to seven years in prison. The Supreme Court dismissed him from office immediately (Supreme Court 2007*a*).

If the facts of the case were more or less as set out on paper, then, frankly, the judge should have known better. The cases against the three women fell under the Unlawful Associations Act (1908). In other words, their alleged crimes had a political character — and if there is one type of case in which a judge ought under no circumstances solicit or accept bribes in Myanmar, it is a political case.

In contrast with political cases, judges can and do accept money in exchange for adjustments to rulings in most other types of cases. From the accounts of people intimately involved in Myanmar's judicial system, it appears that perhaps the majority of judges are open to offers. Kyaw Min

San in his chapter in this publication writes that one experienced lawyer estimated to him that currently over 50 per cent of courts are riddled with corruption. Others privately reckon that some 70 per cent of judges issue orders in part or in full on the basis of payments received from parties coming before them.

Such estimates should not come as any surprise. While successive governments in Myanmar (and in Burma before it) have rhetorically condemned judicial corruption, instead of stamping out the activities described as corrupt what they have done has, rather, merely encouraged the development of alternative language and practices which enable people to engage in and negotiate the justice trade more effectively.

The official and unofficial languages and practices of the justice trade, the sounds that money makes in and around Myanmar's courts, are the subject of this chapter. To examine them, I draw upon James Scott's study of public and hidden transcripts, where the former consists of gestures, speech, and practices in open interaction between dominant and subordinate groups, whereas the latter takes place beyond direct observation (Scott 1990, pp. 2, 4). Broadly speaking, the anti-corruption speechifying of officeholders, media reports, and government records constitutes the public transcript. The language and methods adopted among legal professionals to describe and negotiate their financial wheeling and dealing constitute the hidden transcript.

I examine these transcripts in two sections. In the following section, I sketch the public transcript on bribery and the judiciary, beginning with a quick survey of earlier periods, and then I concentrate on anti-corruption talk from the 1990s to the present day. In the second section, I look at how the hidden transcript variously accommodates, inverts, and contradicts its public counterpart. I explore a little of the language in the hidden transcript, and briefly illustrate a couple of its methods.

As the public transcript engages with the hidden transcript by conditionally conceding to the interests of subordinates, far from prohibiting the making of money in the courts, it establishes guidelines. In turn, the hidden transcript accommodates and interprets the public transcript to the extent that legal professionals find it in their interests to acquiesce. Beyond this point, the hidden transcript takes on subversive tones, through double meanings, reinterpretation of elite moralizing, and critique. Such dissident talk, however, mostly remains offstage, even when all that it expresses are matters of public knowledge.

HOMILIES, REPRIMANDS, AND ELITE SELF-PORTRAITURE

Scott describes the public transcript as "the *self*-portrait of dominant elites as they would have themselves seen", and, he continues, "While it is unlikely to be merely a skein of lies and misrepresentations, it is, on the other hand, a highly partisan and partial narrative. It is designed to be impressive, to affirm and naturalize the power of dominant elites, and to conceal or euphemize the dirty linen of their rule" (1990, p. 18).

The official narrative on money-making in Myanmar's courts fits Scott's description precisely. The country's rulers portray themselves as benevolent, enlightened men who must constantly exhort their subordinates to aspire to their own high standards. They do not deny the existence of corruption; on the contrary, they acknowledge it and, in a sense, they celebrate it. The existence of something called "corruption" enables the dominant elite to naturalize its own authority. Its anti-corruption talk affirms its inherent superiority: rulers are ethical, subordinates not; rulers establish clean government, while subordinates sully it. This language does not conceal the dirty linen, but euphemizes it by shifting the blame to everyone except those who have seized the mantle of authority.[1]

The modern narrative of corruption and counter-corruption has its roots in the British conquest of Mandalay. The colonial rulers initially treated corruption as in part the residue of earlier power relations based upon patronage, in part a consequence of the presumed inferiority of subject races to European masters. Later, following developments in society and government in Britain, they framed corruption more as a legal and institutional problem of the colony. In 1940 a Rangoon-based committee wrote that corruption was widespread, because of impunity, secrecy, and a lack of courage among superior officers to address it (Bribery and Corruption Enquiry Committee 1941, pp. 44–46).

Once Burma had won its struggle for independence, Prime Minister U Nu declared that national survival depended upon eliminating bribery, which he warned had spread across all sectors of politics, government, and business (U Nu 1951). The parliament passed an act establishing the Bureau of Special Investigation as a counter-corruption agency under the prime minister's office, with a supervisory board answerable to the president (Act No. 50/1951). The Bureau took its mandate head on; however, it was weakened by divisive politics and economic exigencies.

After the 1962 coup, the usurper regime placed the Bureau under a new national intelligence agency. It abolished the supervisory board, and assigned managerial responsibility to the home affairs ministry (Ministry of Home Affairs 2000, p. 277). The bureau's original purpose defeated, it has since operated in effect as a specialized, autonomous police department.

During the period of General Ne Win's military council and its successor one-party legislature, the public transcript on corruption turned increasingly moralistic. Both regimes expressed their resolve to end the exploitation of man by man, and with it, the old "have money, get justice" system (Burma Socialist Programme Party 1980, p. 49). The government classed bribery and misuse of state resources among offences damaging to socialist society and morality, along with gambling, drug use, prostitution, and outrages to the modesty of women and children (Council of People's Justices 1975). No attempt was made to introduce further institutional or legal measures to address profiteering from official positions. According to professionals who worked in the courts at this time, bribery was widespread, although modest in size when compared to the present day, and payment was mostly in kind rather than cash.

Following the collapse of the one-party regime in 1988, successive military-run governments have amplified the moralistic tone of their counter-corruption rhetoric. They have as their recurrent theme that the state is trying its best to eliminate wrongdoing. To the extent that corruption exists, it is a consequence of human weakness. The public transcript turns on the failures of judges, judicial bureaucrats, and others in exploring the moral hazards of their professional activities, and the need for uprightness when shouldering the burden of national responsibilities, so that people can trust and rely upon the justice system. Above all, it avoids systemic critique, which would imply failure on the part of the state to address corruption, and would also imply that senior officials share responsibility for wrongdoing, something the rhetoric now assigns almost exclusively to their subordinates.

The public transcript has changed little in substance over the last two decades, although the manner of its expression has altered somewhat. During the 1990s and early 2000s, former spymaster Lieutenant-General Khin Nyunt regularly chastized judges, judicial bureaucrats, and other personnel at length and in some detail for corrupt practices. In 1993 he said:

I have time and again ordered to take steps to eliminate undesirable things once found around courts, to eradicate malpractice and self-serving behaviour from court environs. However, it is observed that judicial personnel, including judges, prosecutors, and police force personnel at some state, division, district and township courts are colluding and acting as case brokers, telling that they will cut short days in detention if a case is prosecuted, will cut the fine, not to hire a lawyer as that would prolong the case, which lawyer to hire, which judge to approach, etc., and that civil servants and lawyers alike are operating fraudulently outside the boundaries of the law. It is heard that at some courts, detainees expecting to have their case examined on the appointed day can only get brought up to the front of the courtroom from the court holding cell after giving money to the guard. It must be said that because of this type of malpractice and self-serving behaviour, the people lack trust in the judicial system, and are in a kind of loathsome and fearful situation. (*Myanmar Law Reports* 1993, n.p.)

In 2002, Khin Nyunt warned of possible sanctions for wrongdoing, but as usual stressed the need for judges to be supervised well and to comport themselves appropriately.

It is learned that some judges are acting immorally and violating civil service discipline, behaving so as to cause public doubt, and are notorious for taking bribes. Therefore, matters have often arisen where action has been taken against judges not adequately fulfilling their duties, judges violating civil service regulations, and immoral judges. If we review the numbers for actions taken annually, it is known that there were 24 persons in 1999, 28 in 2000 and 66 in 2001. Therefore, be warned that the number of judges against whom actions have been taken and fault laid has been increasing year by year, and it needs to be stressed that superior organizations unceasingly closely supervise and admonish [judges] and that judges also reform themselves. (*Judicial Journal* 2002, p. 14)

In 2004 Khin Nyunt lost his own job due to alleged corruption.[2] His successors have since continued the moralistic counter-corruption narrative, although in a more circumspect manner. In 2007, the then prime minister, General Soe Win, stated that people outside of the courts were commonly discussing the taking of bribes and the behaviour of judges, and that for this reason all judicial personnel needed to be upstanding in their qualities and work practices. He added:

Up to the present day complaint letters are still arriving regarding the judiciary, about weaknesses, omissions, judges' and prosecutors' impoliteness and malpractice in cases sent up for prosecution … [and] that if the weaknesses and flaws are examined, it can be observed that generally they are resulting not from inadequacies and weaknesses in the system, codes of conduct and working procedures, but are flaws and weaknesses of the individual; although it has been found that some weaknesses are not related to individuals' moral character but to lack of expertise, sloppiness, negligence and ill-discipline … (*Myanma Alin* 2007, p. 6)

Prime Minister, General Thein Sein, during 2009 read from literally the same script (or at least from the same scriptwriters, who must have cut and pasted their earlier message, since a paragraph of his speech as reported in the press was a word-for-word repeat of his predecessor's) when he again told assembled judges that the weaknesses were not systemic but individualistic, insisting that "judges are receiving appropriate salaries from the public budget to carry out judicial work, and that therefore it is necessary that they not make verdicts on receipt of bribes" (*Myanma Alin* 2009, p. 3). In March 2011, during his inaugural oration as President U Thein Sein, the former general did not address the problem of judicial corruption explicitly, but he did speak to the importance of the rule of law and avoidance of corrupt practices in order to ensure clean government.[3] At the time of writing, his new administration has made no major announcements or initiatives concerning these issues.

Up to this point, I have restricted my remarks to the contents of the elite-generated public transcript itself — but the transcript can be sustained only when an audience exists that tacitly goes along with it. Where a major official delivers a homily about corruption, it will not do to have a crowd of manifestly uninterested subordinates yawning or dozing off.[4] The assembled body must at least appear attentive and alert. Also, when government newspapers report on efforts to eliminate wrongdoing from the courts, it will not do to have private media outlets revealing that such efforts either do not exist or are futile. They must report in a way that contributes to, rather than undermines, the public transcript, as Nwe Nwe Aye explains in her chapter of this publication.

Judges, judicial bureaucrats, and lawyers in Myanmar conspire with senior figures to sustain the public transcript, both because of warnings against defiance and because of incentives for compliance. From these warnings and incentives, the hidden transcript is derived. I close this section with some comments about the sorts of warnings employed, before turning in the following section to a discussion of the incentives.

The compliance of subordinates is obtained in part through reprimands and threats of disciplinary and legal action. Warnings about disciplinary action, like those Khin Nyunt issued, are not usually made if there are absolutely no grounds to warrant an accusation. Official records show that in most years the Supreme Court removes small numbers of judges for accepting bribes, as well as removing some lawyers for offering them.[5] A few, like Sein Lwin, are prosecuted by the attorney general. Some are demoted, or denied promotion. More are reprimanded. Nevertheless, the number of judges, judicial bureaucrats, and lawyers who are disciplined is miniscule when compared to the incidence of money-making.[6] What is more, the records suggest that what motivates disciplinary action is not of itself concern over the making of money, but concern over the failure of some personnel to maintain the *appearances* required of them.

Since the public transcript identifies the root cause of corruption as immorality, a judge needs to have an air of decorum. He should avoid doing anything that will cause public outrage and make him a liability to the institutions that he represents. Coerced sex with a defendant's sister in the courtroom chambers, as allegedly happened in at least one instance, is far outside acceptable standards (*Myanmar Law Reports* 1994, n.p.). So too are extramarital affairs or "abnormal" relations, particularly where the other person involved is also among judicial personnel.[7] Turning up to court drunk and yelling "incivilities" at judicial staff and the police, as one judge in the delta allegedly was in the habit of doing, is also regarded as inappropriate (Supreme Court 2005).

Similarly, the public transcript encourages professionals to be sensible about *how* they earn from their positions, so as to avoid public recrimination, official reprimand, or worse. Deputy Township Judge U Win Nyunt in Tachilek became one example of how not to operate, when the Supreme Court accused him of soliciting bribes in exchange for rulings. In regard to the act of soliciting bribes itself, Win Nyunt was probably not any different from the majority of judges at his and nearby courts. However, he did so in a manner that was "well known, and furthermore, he went in person to the parties' houses to demand bribes", even after district-level judges had already issued warnings to their subordinates about bribe taking (Supreme Court 2003a). Win Nyunt's crime, the order dismissing him suggests, was not that he took bribes, but that he had not mastered the hidden transcript.

PAY RESPECTS, PAY THE JUDGE OFF

Judges, prosecutors, and lawyers in Myanmar are somewhat hollow authority figures. Since the defeat of judicial independence in the 1960s and

1970s, about which I have written elsewhere (Cheesman 2011), courts have steadily lost credibility. In many trials, the most powerful person present is the police officer bringing the case. Judicial personnel know that they have little sway compared even to their administrative counterparts, as do members of the general public. "Nobody," a retired judge admitted to me, "Looks up to the courts."[8]

The hidden transcript of legal professionals in Myanmar reflects their subordinate status. In many respects, it accommodates and adapts to the public transcript, in tacit acknowledgement that the latter conditionally concedes to their interests. But in doing this, it also adopts and perverts the language of law, making a mockery out of legalism. It inverts the moralistic tone of the public transcript by finding ethical reasons for the taking of bribes. And underneath, it runs a dissident strain through which professionals express bitterness at the hypocrisy of their superiors and the dismal condition of the institutions on which they depend for their livelihoods.

Public transcripts intersect with hidden transcripts at official events, such as refresher training programmes for judges and prosecutors, where euphemism from above is reinterpreted and filtered to down below. The chief justice — in speeches at these events — exhorts subordinates to apply the law cleanly and without bias, and to become people working for the benefit of the country who "do not lose sight of matters concerning state policy" (Supreme Court 2003d).[9] As the chief justice cannot say "If ordered to jail someone, make sure you do it", or "Don't be so stupid as to take bribes in political cases", he instead alludes to the applying of policy. But to make sure that the message has been fully understood, trainers — according to former participants at these programmes — thereafter offer additional nuggets of advice, such as "So as to avoid money problems, it is essential to follow orders from above"; and "If an official wants [the accused] imprisoned, don't be a stickler about the law; convict this time for value next time", meaning that a grateful official will help a cooperative judge by pushing lucrative cases in his direction later. Others offer warnings, such as "If you have to imprison in a political case, don't release for lack of evidence. If you do, it'll be your ruin."[10] Trainers also advise attendees that "To avoid problems, feed your clerks and staff", since well-fed staff will look the other way from their superior's transgressions — unless, of course, they are actively involved as intermediaries.

In any event, all participants are encouraged to heed the maxim "When eating figs, listen for the sound of the slingshot", meaning that just as an inattentive bird can get hit while enjoying the fruit of the tree, an inattentive official can be hit by a complaint if too concentrated upon profiting from his post.

Lawyers, prosecutors, and court clerks employ a wide variety of euphemistic language when discussing the justice trade in their daily work. Some of it is generic slang, such as the expression "to water" something as a reference to the giving of a bribe. For instance, if somebody loses a case, his friend may ask, "Didn't you water it?", or a lawyer may advise a client that if she wants to win a case then, "You'll have to water it well." Other expressions like "no oil without beans" are used to stress to a client that without money being put into a case, it will not get resolved favourably. Among themselves, legal professionals sometimes allude to commonplace expressions, such as "A wise person can earn money", by asking, "Have you got wise?" as a way of asking whether or not the other has received bribes.

These expressions are widely understood and are useful for facilitating straightforward exchanges. Where professionals prefer to communicate among themselves, they may resort instead to perverted legalese, the language of "a politics of disguise ... that takes place in public view but is designed to have a double meaning" (Scott 1990, p. 19). While the bending and inverting of legalese for the most part adapts to the public transcript, it is also subversive, inasmuch as it undermines the legality on which the professionals using it are supposed to rely. It reveals a cynicism that is rooted in disillusionment with the legal system as a whole.

Among this type of legalese, a good example is "Section 870". A lawyer talking with another in front of the courthouse might suggest Section 870 as a means to get the client released from the charges against him. To the by-passer unversed in law, it sounds as if the two are talking about some technical and learned matter. To anyone familiar with the statute books, there is no Section 870 anywhere to be found, the highest being Section 565 of the Criminal Procedure Code. Section 870 is a different type of code: code for three letters of the alphabet that resemble the three Burmese numerals for 8, 7 and 0, which when spelled out mean "to pay respects", a euphemism for a pay-off.[11] Section 870 thus precisely captures the simultaneously integrative yet subversive quality of the hidden transcript among legal professionals, since it inverts the notion of respect for a superior, and respect for the law, by situating both in a money-making discourse that feigns legality. It gives the appearance of respectful adherence to the contents of law while in fact ridiculing them.

Another legalistic euphemism that follows a similar logic is "Part 4". Many legal forms consist of parts that must be completed for the purposes of a case. A court clerk filling out a form may instruct the defence lawyer that Parts 1, 2, and 3 are completed, now it is time to do Part 4. However, the "part" to which she is referring is not in the documents. Rather, it is word play in which the vowel sounds associated with the words "part" and "four" are swapped with one another to take on a meaning that it is time to give something.[12] So far as usage of "Part 4" in the courts is concerned, some lawyers also interpret Parts 1 to 3 as the investigation, the laying of charges, and submissions to the court, with Part 4 being payment of money for the desired verdict.

Sometimes, a euphemism describes a particular practice that enables the making of money in a specific manner. "Double cropping" is a good example. This term comes not from the law but from paddy farming, when cultivators follow a monsoon crop with an irrigated one. In trials, the term designates the practice of lower court judges accepting payments not to acquit but to impose a lesser sentence on conviction and to arrange for the sentence to be overturned or revised upon further payments made on appeal in a higher court.[13] As both the court of first instance and the appeal court make money from the same case, it is a double crop. Simultaneously, both boost the statistics on cases handled, and even at the appeal level a judge has some way to collect money as well as ensuring that an accused person still serves some jail time, so as to keep up statistics on convictions and sentencing.

"Sentence-release" pithily designates a similarly useful method. Sentence-release, like double cropping, enables judges to satisfy competing demands by giving the appearance of efficiency while also making money. Using this technique, judges convict accused persons but hand down sentences that come to less than, or equal to, the total amount of time that the accused has already been in custody awaiting trial. For example, an accused may be brought before a judge charged with a minor theft. From the date of arrest, he may be remanded for two weeks before the case is heard, and then again while the case is tried, which may come to another couple of weeks. If his lawyer has watered the case, but the judge for whatever reason does not want to acquit, she can add up the total number of days that the accused has been in custody already, which in this scenario comes to twenty-eight, and then convict the defendant but impose a four-week sentence with time served deducted, so that the accused is immediately released. The accused goes home, the judge and prosecutor both make money and obtain a conviction to add to their statistics, and the defence lawyer has a satisfied client.

As the counter-corruption discourse proceeds from the singular assertion that legal professionals are unethical because they make money illicitly from their positions, the hidden transcript retorts that the taking of money in exchange for verdicts is sometimes morally superior to the applying of law. For example, in one case that a lawyer was handling just at the time I met him, police had charged the defendant with attempted suicide, which remains an offence under the colonial-era Penal Code. The lawyer went to see the judge assigned to hear the case, and the latter warned that he would probably have to impose a prison term. The lawyer explained that the defendant had attempted suicide because she has seven children whom she could not feed. The judge, who had evidently threatened to imprison the accused so as to open negotiations with the lawyer, agreed to release the accused with a fine, in exchange for a payment equivalent to around 30 U.S. dollars. Because the client had attempted suicide for want of money to feed her kids, not surprisingly she also could not come up with that amount of money. Subsequently, the lawyer — who was handling the case free of charge — again went to talk with the judge, who advised that anyhow, he would release her on fine for "however much she can give", which eventually came to the equivalent of only a few dollars.

This judge, if asked, would perhaps justify the taking of a small amount of money for the release of the accused on grounds that he took pity on her: that this was a better course of action than to apply the law strictly, but also that he cannot just give cases away for nothing, as it will create problems in subsequent negotiations with defendants who can afford to pay. Another judge reasoned, along similar lines, that he took money for rulings because of pity for the accused or his family, compounded by the insistent nagging of lawyers or prosecutors:

> As for bribe money, we don't want to take it. But how can we survive on the monthly salary? I sometimes don't take it ... They [the defence lawyer] say, "Sir, if the accused goes to jail, his whole family will be in trouble. If he goes to jail, his wife will have to prostitute herself. It's already sorted out with the prosecutor. The prosecutor said that if sir says okay then he'll okay it too. He won't go up for revision or appeal," and so on, and so I have to release the accused.[14]

In the hidden transcript, no moral question adheres to whether or not to buy and sell cases, only to how best to conduct transactions. Some lawyers speak favourably of judges who try to identify the party who in their opinion should win a case according to law, and then invite that party to offer something for the correct verdict. One remarked fondly of a judge who refuses to accept bribes when deciding a case, but afterwards is open to the receipt of gifts from the winning party. Through the filter of the hidden transcript, her behaviour does not for this lawyer constitute unethical conduct of the sort condemned in the public transcript, since she decides cases fairly, even if she expects the successful party to understand that she should obtain a reward for doing so.

Although most legal professionals seem to be able to point to peers and superiors whom they admire for their attempts to retain some integrity, few express any respect for those at the apex of the legal system, and fewer still express respect for the system itself. Lawyers share sardonic humour about malfeasance and ineptitude on the part of Supreme Court justices as, for example, by referring to the former long-standing Chief Justice, U Aung Toe as "U Toe Aung", or, roughly, "Mr. Push 'n' Win", meaning that if someone with real authority gave him a shove, they would get whatever verdict they wanted.[15] While this joke is simple and seemingly light-hearted, its inferences go directly to the remark of the former judge quoted above, that nobody respects the courts. His name inverted, the pathetic Chief Justice was the embodiment of a pathetic system, and his high court the height of corruption, as the judge who asked rhetorically how he could survive on a judge's salary noted acerbically:

> The Supreme Court and leadership say, "Don't take bribes. If you don't have enough food, rear livestock, cultivate crops." How can we do that kind of work in Yangon? ... The Supreme Court says don't take bribes. They take hundreds of millions, thousands of millions.

Like the French tenant farmer meeting his landlord, whom Scott quotes, this judge would perhaps have attended events where, on meeting justices of the Supreme Court, he would have forced himself "to appear amiable, in spite of the contempt" he felt for them (Scott 1990, p. 2). For many professionals, such contempt is reserved not only for the Supreme Court bench, but is directed towards the system as a whole. One lawyer said:

> Whether or not a defendant is released ... doesn't depend on the evidence or the lawyer. A penniless defendant can't get released easily. No matter how much a lawyer tries for a penniless defendant, it's pointless. It's not education but money that counts. Lawyers have become brokers between judges and clients.

Another expressed similar sentiments:

> We know in advance who's going to win and who's going to loose a case.
> It's clear. Whoever can't pay the judge will lose. However many precedents
> you rely on in your application [to court], however many legal texts you
> cite, if you don't pay, you're bound to lose. That's why in the period of
> military government, lawyers earning a living from the courts no longer
> closely study the law.

These remarks are the reverse image of officialdom's counter-corruption
rhetoric. They are subversive rather than sanctioned; not disciplinary but
despairing; not euphemistic, but frank. They are not statements that can
be assimilated into the public transcript, since they do not accommodate
its discourse but defy it, through the very fact that they serve no other
purpose than to state the facts. They do not affirm the elite self-portrait
but destroy it, since they ultimately assign the failures of the justice
system to the system itself. They constitute a critique of precisely the sort
that the public transcript prohibits, since they unavoidably place blame
for failure on those in charge. For this reason they are necessarily, and
unremittingly, hidden.

CONCLUSION

The public transcript on corruption in Myanmar's judicial system does not
aim primarily to address practices identified as corrupt, but to affirm an
elite self-portrait in which the dominant group appears innately superior
to its subordinates. Its model of probity is a judicial officer who follows
orders as required, who pretends to subscribe to the values of official
propaganda, and who successfully maintains the appearance of being free
from practices identified as corrupt.

In exchange for going along with the public transcript, the elite grants
conditional concessions to the interests of subordinates. Subordinates
interpret and accommodate these concessions through the language and
practices of the hidden transcript. The hidden transcript sustains its public
counterpart to the extent that legal professionals find it in their interest to
give the appearance of compliance, but the hidden transcript also inverts
and undermines much of the public transcript, even as it seemingly
accommodates it, and underneath it prickles with rancour at the hypocrisy
of senior officials who preach virtue as they practice vice.

Nwe Nwe Aye in her chapter of this publication expresses cautious optimism that the role of the media as a watchdog against corruption will increase as government censorship lessens. From study of the language and methods of money-making in and around the courts, I interpret this to mean that more of the hidden transcript will seep into the public domain through the media. Indeed, a few offstage happenings are already being broadcast on foreign-based radio stations, such as the BBC Burmese Service's *Pyithugyaga Pyithuzaga* programme, which airs listeners' letters and recorded messages about official malfeasance around the country.

If in the future Myanmar's domestic media also become able to report on public complaints of the sort heard on the BBC, it might well be a sign of lessened censorship — but it will not, I would say, indicate that money-making through the courts will be lessened. Even if more of the hidden transcript is taken up by the public transcript, money-making will not dissipate. The incentives are too many, the disincentives too few, and as the business of commerce expands around the country with very little restraint, so too does it penetrate and stimulate the business of the courts. Daily, new language and methods accommodate and conceal new types of transactions. Indeed, by the time this chapter is published, the expressions I have mentioned above to illustrate the hidden transcript might already be redundant. The hidden transcript is always on the move, from one time to the next, from one place to the next. The sounds that money makes in and around Myanmar's courts will not readily diminish. They will merely change their tone.

Notes

1. Moralizing about corruption is of course neither new nor unique to Myanmar. Colin Leys wrote decades ago that "the question of corruption in the contemporary world has so far been taken up almost solely by moralists" (1965, p. 216). To the present day, many anti-corruption campaigns have a strong moralistic tone. Arguably, Myanmar is distinguished by the extent to which moralizing precludes other discourses, and by the extent to which it excludes senior officials from responsibility, except when, for political reasons, an advantage is to be had in doing otherwise.
2. For a summary of the reasons given for Khin Nyunt's removal, see Kyaw Yin Hlaing 2004, pp. 174–75.
3. Kyaw Min San, Nwe Nwe Aye, and Richard Horsey all remark on the president's inaugural speech in their chapters of this publication. See "President U Thein

Sein speaks to members of the Union Government, Heads of Union level organizations", *New Light of Myanmar*, 1 April 2011, pp. 1, 7–10 <http://www.burmalibrary.org/docs11/NLM2011-04-01.pdf> (accessed 1 June 2012).

4. In 2003 two deputy township judges did in fact receive reprimands for "yawning/dozing off … not having interest [and] being distracted" during the Chief Justice's address at a training programme they attended (Supreme Court 2003c).

5. No independent professional body exists for lawyers in Myanmar. The Bar Council consists of the Attorney General and the director-general of his office, the director-general of the Supreme Court, a Supreme Court judge and six lawyers approved by the Supreme Court (Law Amending the Bar Council Act 1989). The Supreme Court has responsibility for issuing orders concerning lawyers, and therefore in this chapter I refer to disciplinary actions against lawyers alongside those against judicial bureaucrats and judges.

6. From a count of the most recent set of records available to me at time of writing, in 2009 the Supreme Court ordered official disciplinary action against a total of 50 judges and 4 judicial bureaucrats, out of which 36 were at the township level. Of these actions, 48 were reprimands, and 4 were demotions. Two deputy township judges were dismissed from office; neither was prosecuted. So far as lawyers are concerned, fewer faced disciplinary action, but the action was more severe. Out of the fifteen lawyers named in the records, three were reprimanded by the Supreme Court. Seven were suspended for periods of two to five years, and six were disbarred from practice. All six disbarred lawyers had been convicted of criminal offences, at least two for political reasons.

7. In 2009 the Supreme Court dismissed a judge after he took a second wife while still married; in 2003 it dismissed a judge who allegedly slept with his court clerk (Supreme Court 2009, 2003b). A deputy district judge it accused of engaging in "abnormal" relations with her senior clerk despite repeated reprimands. The order that she be suspended from promotion for two years does not spell out the abnormality, but indicates that as a woman judge she had a particular responsibility to keep her marital affairs in order (Supreme Court 2007b).

8. All quotes from legal professionals in this chapter I have translated from Burmese. All are from research conducted in the last three years.

9. I am here citing the former Chief Justice, but am referring to the office of chief justice, hence the use of the present tense, since I assume that speeches by the new incumbent — none of which I have yet had an opportunity to read — cover similar ground to those of his predecessor.

10. In the original, "ruin" also is idiomatic speech, meaning literally that the person's rice pot will be broken — a particularly apt idiom given the context.

11. The numerals 8-7-0 resemble the consonants *ga-ya-wa*, hence *gayawa-pyu*, to pay respects.

12. "Part four" is *apaing-le*. When the vowels are switched it becomes *ape-laing*, or literally, "giving line", where "line" connotes an illicit method of working or gaining something. The numerical reference also is sometimes dropped so that the officer requesting payment can simply say something along the lines of, "My part is done; only your part is needed."

13. The practice has a long pedigree. According to the 1940 committee, a "Court may deliberately give judgment against the bribe-giver, knowing, and explaining to him, that it will be reversed on appeal" (Bribery and Corruption Enquiry Committee 1941, pp. 11–12). In the present day, some professionals also use the term "double cropping" to refer to cases where accused persons have to pay twice to complete the process in the lower court; for instance, once to obtain bail and again to obtain acquittal.

14. The monthly salary for a judge at the lowest level was listed in 2009 as K59,000 to K64,000 per month, or a little over US$2 per day. The highest-ranked judicial officer on the circulated salary scale officially received K210,000 to K220,000 per month; at the time, around US$7 per day (figures based on tabulated civil service salaries in Ministry of Finance 2009). As far as I am aware, these figures still applied in 2010–11.

15. For comments on Aung Toe's tenure as chief justice, see Myint Zan's chapter in this publication.

References

Act No. 50/1951. *Atu Sônsanzitsehmu Ôkchoƙye Apwe hnin Atu Sônsanzitse Tana Etupade* [Special Investigation Administrative Board and Bureau of Special Investigation Act].

Bribery and Corruption Enquiry Committee. Report of the Bribery and Corruption Enquiry Committee 1940. Rangoon: Superintendent, Government Printing and Stationery, Burma, 1941.

Burma Socialist Programme Party. "Sanit Thit, Mu Thit, Siyintôn Thit" [New System, New Policy, New Precedents]. In *Pati Yeya Sazaung ba Tayasiyinye hsaingya Saungba-mya* [*Articles on the Judiciary in the Party Affairs Periodical*], 1980.

Cheesman, Nick. "How An Authoritarian Regime in Burma Used Special Courts to Defeat Judicial Independence". *Law and Society Review* 45, no. 4 (2011).

Council of People's Justices. *Hnyun-gyagyet Ahmat 9* [Instruction No. 9], 12 July 1975.

Judicial Journal. "2002 *kunit, Zulaing-la 9 yetne-dwin Thunapyu Tekkatho naik Kyinpa-thaw Tayayôngyoƙ, Shenegyoƙ hnin Pyinè, Taing, Kayaing Tayathugyi-mya, Upade Ayashi-mya hma Tayasiyinye saingya Awwadaganyu-chin Akhan-ana-dwin Naingngandaw Echan-thayaye hnin Pwunbyoye Kaungsi Adwinyehmu-1 Dudiya Bogyoƙkyi Kin Nyun Pyawkya-thi Meingun*" [State Peace and Development Council Secretary-1 Lieutenant General Khin Nyunt's Address on 9 July 2002 at the Institute of Nursing to Supreme Court, Attorney General's Office and State, Division and District Judges and Law Officers Assembled for Receipt of Advice on Judicial Affairs]. *Judicial Journal* 1, no. 14 (2002): 7–20.

Kyaw Yin Hlaing. "Myanmar in 2004: Another Year of Uncertainty". *Asian Survey* 45, no. 1 (2005): 174–79.

Law Amending the Bar Council Act, No. 22/89.

Leys, Colin. "What is the Problem About Corruption?". *Journal of Modern African Studies* 3, no. 2 (1965): 215–300.

Ministry of Finance. *Amein Kyawngyaza Ahmat* 184/2009 [Notification No. 184/2009], 31 December 2009.

Ministry of Home Affairs. *Pyitèye Wungyitana: Thamaing Hmattan hnin Swunsaunggyet-mya [Ministry of Home Affairs: Historical Record and Achievements]*. Yangon: Government of the Union of Myanmar, 2000.

Myanma Alin. *"Tayathugyi-mya thi Kit-amyin, Kit-adwe byin Myawmyinnaing a Shi-ya-mi; Pyithudo ka Leza-yôngyi thaw Theikka, Kogyintaya Shi aung Amyè Saungdein"* [Judges Must Have Views in Keeping with the Times; Always Maintain Morality and Personal Behaviour to Earn the People's Respect and Trust]. *Myanma Alin*, 6 February 2007, pp. 1, 3, 6.

———. *"Tayathugyi-mya thi Naingngandaw Tayayôn-mya ko Kozabyuthu-mya Pyit; Upade Ayashi-mya, Yèdatpwè-do hnin Pubaung-byi Pyithu-mya-ko Upade hnin-anyi Kunyi"* [Judges Are Persons Who Represent the State Courts, Must Cooperate with Law Officers and Police Force to Help People in Accordance with Law]. *Myanma Alin*, 13 May 2009, pp. 3, 20.

Myanmar Law Reports. *"Tayathugyi-mya thi Naingngandaw Tayayôn-mya ko Kozabyuthu-mya Pyit; Upade Ayashi-mya, Yèdatpwè-do hnin Pubaung-byi Pyithu-mya-ko Upade hnin-anyi Kunyi"* [State Law and Order Restoration Council Secretary-1 Lieutenant General Khin Nyunt's Address at the Work Coordination Meeting of State, Divisional and District Judges and Law Officers]. Tayasiyintôn-mya 1993, n.p.

———. *"Pyinè, Taing, Kayaing Tayathugyi-mya hnin Upade Ayashi-mya Lokngan Hnyi-hnaing Asi-awe-dwin Naingngandaw Ngyeinwut-pipya-hmu Tisaukye-apwè, Adwinyehmu-1 Dudiya Bogyokkyi Kin Nyun Pyawkya-thi Lanhnyun-ahmazaga"* [State Law and Order Restoration Council Secretary-1 Lieutenant General Khin Nyunt's Address at the Work Coordination Meeting of State, Divisional and District Judges and Law Officers]. Tayasiyintôn-mya 1994, n.p.

Scott, James C. *Domination and the Arts of Resistance: Hidden Transcripts*. New Haven and London: Yale University Press, 1990.

Supreme Court. Amein Ahmat 44/2003 [Order No. 44/2003], 20 March 2003*a*.

———. Ahmein Ahmat 185/2003 [Order No. 185/2003], 30 October 2003*b*.

———. Ahmein Ahmat 209-10/2003 [Order No. 209-10/2003], 25 November 2003*c*.

———. *Kayaing Azin Tayathugyi-mya Munmanthindan Ahmatsin 1 Thindan Pwinbwè*

Akan-ana-dwin Naingngandaw Tayathugyichok̂ Pyawkya-thi Mein-gun, [Address by Chief Justice at the Opening Ceremony of Refresher Training Program No. 1 for District-level Judges], 5 May 2003*d*.

———. Ahmein Ahmat 41/2005 [Order No. 41/2005], 1 March 2005.

———. Ahmein Ahmat 4/2007 [Order No. 4/2007], 22 January 2007*a*.

———. Ahmein Ahmat 89/2007 [Order No. 89/2007], 17 August 2007*b*.

———. Ahmein Ahmat 70/2009 [Order No. 70/2009], 28 August 2009.

U Nu. 1951 *kuhnit, Mat-la 29 yetne, Yangôn-myo, Latpe-latyu Papyauk-ye Pyaingbwè Subebwè Akan-ana-dwin Wungyi-chok̂ e Mein-gun* [Prime Minister's Address at the Award-giving Ceremony for the Elimination of Bribery Competition, 29 March 1951].

14

THE "NEW" SUPREME COURT AND CONSTITUTIONAL TRIBUNAL
Marginal Improvement or More of the Same?

Myint Zan

On 30 March 2011 a "new" Burmese government was sworn in. A seven-member Supreme Court and nine-member Constitutional Tribunal are among the new organs of state formed under the 2008 Constitution that "came into operation" with the new government.[1] This chapter addresses the issue of whether, under the new government, there has been some improvement in relation to the Burmese judiciary, or whether the situation is much the same as before (that is, during the period from September 1988 until March 2011).

The term "new" is used for both the Supreme Court and for the Constitutional Tribunal. In Burma there have been various "Supreme Courts", or apex courts, since independence.[2] To put these "new" developments into perspective, therefore, it is necessary to give a brief history of the apex courts over the period since independence, if only to explain the use of the term "new". As for the Constitutional Tribunal, it is indeed a new organ of state, since a similar political or legal institution has not previously existed in contemporary Burmese legal history.[3] The first part of this chapter deals with the "new" Supreme Court, the second part with the new Constitutional Tribunal.

THE "NEW" SUPREME COURT, WITH FLASHBACKS TO FORMER COURTS

The Supreme Court formed under Burma's 1947 Constitution, which lasted from 4 January 1948 to 31 March 1962, was Burma's first Supreme Court. From April 1962 a new apex court came into operation, initially with the name of "Chief Court" in English, but in the late 1960s its name was changed back to "Supreme Court". This second apex court lasted from 1 April 1962 to 4 March 1974, when the Council of People's Justices was formed. Soon thereafter the Central Court of Justice (third apex court) was formed. (Both were established under the 1974 Constitution, which had been proclaimed as adopted by the then Revolutionary Council on 3 January 1974.) Like its predecessor, the first Supreme Court, the Central Court of Justice came to an end by military decree, on 18 September 1988 (see Table 14.1).

For the sake of comparison, it is the fourth apex court, which lasted from 28 September 1988 to 30 March 2011, that will be the main focus in gauging whether this newest Myanmar Supreme Court represents "some

TABLE 14.1
Apex Courts In Burma/Myanmar, 1947–2011

Supreme Courts	Name	Start date	End date	Head of Government
First	Supreme Court	January 1948	March 1962	Prime Minister U Nu
Second	Chief Court	April 1962	March 1974	Head, Revolutionary Council, General Ne Win
Third	Central Court of Justice	March 1974	September 1988	President U Ne Win
Fourth	Supreme Court	September 1988	March 2011	Senior General Than Shwe
Fifth	Supreme Court	March 2011	Ongoing	President U Thein Sein

Source: Compiled by author.

improvement" or "more of the same". Comparisons will be made between the methods of appointment and removal of justices, and lack of security of tenure in both periods. Before embarking on this task a brief comparison might be made between the first Supreme Court and the fifth (current) Supreme Court from a historical perspective.

Let us pretend that it is 1948, not long after the formation of the first Supreme Court. What would have been expected of this new apex court? The first 100-day period following the formation the new Supreme Court in 1948 saw significant developments in terms of the exercise of the independence of the judiciary and the protection of civil rights, especially through the issuance of writs. In terms of the quality and learning of the judgements, there were also significant developments and landmark rulings. Therefore, in 1948, there would have been grounds for optimism and great expectations, fully justified, regarding the new Supreme Court.

What is the current prognosis for the new Myanmar Supreme Court in 2011? Have there been hopeful signs and positive developments in the new Supreme Court of 2011, as there were in the first post-independence Supreme Court of 1948? For the new Supreme Court, the answer is categorically in the negative, and assuredly this situation is unlikely to change in the future. A brief comparison with a few landmark cases decided by the first Supreme Court may illustrate this thesis.

One of the peculiar characteristics of the 2011 Supreme Court is that under Section 296(a) of the 2008 Constitution it "has the power to issue … (i) Writ of Habeas Corpus (ii) Writ of Mandamus (iii) Writ of Prohibition (iv) Writ of Quo Warranto (v) Writ of Certiorari". The reintroduction of these writs in the 2008 Constitution is noteworthy because these writs have lain dormant for about five decades. The apex courts under the 1947 Constitution, which guaranteed these writs, did perform their constitutional duties in protecting Burmese citizens and in effecting the release of detained persons through the application of various writs, especially that of habeas corpus. This practice died soon after the 1962 military coup took place.[4]

Will the reintroduction of these writs lead to substantive results, or is the change illusory? On 10 May 1948, the first Supreme Court did concretely and effectively protect the fundamental rights guaranteed under the 1947 Constitution, when Justice E. Maung (1898–1977) granted a habeas corpus application and directed that the detainee be released forthwith (*G.N. Banerjee* case). This bold decision came just four months after the post-independence "first" Supreme Court had been established. It was followed a year later by the decision in the case of *Ma Ahmar v. Commissioner of Police and One*, which ruled categorically that the distribution of leaflets calling the then Prime Minister U Nu's government "murderer Thakin Nu's Fascist government" was held to provide "no justification for preventive detention under the Public Order Preservation Act" and ordered the release of the detainees (BLR 1949, SC, p. 39).

At the time of finalizing this chapter, in April 2012, it has been more than a year since the new Myanmar Supreme Court came into existence on 30 March 2011. No similarly bold ruling on the issuing of habeas corpus, nor any significant case in which the Supreme Court has meaningfully discussed the principles governing habeas corpus or directed the executive authorities accordingly to release detainees, has been made. Apparently none of the more than two thousand political prisoners has been released through writ of habeas corpus. It seems far outside the realms of possibility that the new Supreme Court would exercise judicial independence and order the release of prisoners such as the first and late Burmese Supreme Court did in the early years of independence.

In October 2011 over six thousand prisoners, including among them around 220 prisoners of conscience (though they were not considered by the government to be such), were released by announcement of President U Thein Sein. The release of the prisoners was *not* made as a result of a ruling by the current Myanmar Supreme Court, as was done in 1948 by the former Burmese Supreme Court. Compare the release, by order of the first Supreme Court in 1949, of the distributors of the leaflets that called the then Prime Minister a "Fascist murderer" with the fate of U Ohn Than, who in 2008 received life imprisonment for a solo demonstration he conducted in 2007. In that solo demonstration he stood "silently and held aloft a cardboard sheet calling for the United Nations to intervene and for the armed forces and police personnel to join the people to end the dictatorship" (Cheesman 2009, p. 605). Would a lawyer even now dare to submit a habeas corpus application for U Ohn Than or other prisoners of conscience like him? Would the new Supreme Court even consider his case, far less "order" his release if such an application were ever to reach it? The unlikelihood of a scenario in which U Ohn Than (or similar prisoners of conscience) are released by the new Supreme Court is matched only by the sense of outrage when one compares his case with the release by direction of the Supreme Court more than sixty years ago of those persons detained under the *Public Order Preservation Act*, whose acts were, in comparison, far less innocuous than unfurling a banner making political demands, in that the released detainees of 1949 called the then serving Prime Minister a "Fascist murderer". It is to be noted that U Ohn Than was among the prisoners released in the amnesty of January 2012. In that "amnesty" and in the earlier amnesties of May and October 2011, when President U Thein Sein directed the release of prisoners, only a minority were prisoners of conscience — a description which, incidentally, the government still denies. The release of these prisoners was ostensibly an act of "good will" or *cetana* on the part of the executive government, and not the result of an independent exercise of its jurisdiction by the current Myanmar Supreme Court.

Hence there appear to have been many more grounds for optimism in relation to the then "new" Supreme Court of 1948 than there are in relation to the new Myanmar Supreme Court of 2011. But one should not go too much into the misty past for the sake of analyzing and commenting on the current Supreme Court. This orientation towards the past is bound to give rise only to a "dirge of regrets".[5] The focus of the remainder of this chapter will be on a comparison of the features of the Supreme Court of the period 1988 to 2011 with those of the current Myanmar Supreme Court, with special attention being given to the appointment process, tenure (or lack thereof) of the judges, and the removal of judges.

Appointment and Tenure of Judges in the New Supreme Court and its Immediate Predecessor

No specific provisions existed for the removal, termination, impeachment, or retirement of judges of the Supreme Court during the period of the fourth Supreme Court.[6] Nevertheless, it is clear from actual practice that the ruling military councils could remove the judges of the Supreme Court by decree or announcement, even though these actions were expressed in the euphemism that they were "permitted to retire".[7]

The 2008 Constitution does contain provisions regarding the nomination and appointment of Supreme Court judges by the president. The Supreme Court nominees must be approved by the legislature, although legislative approval is at best only token.[8] Section 299(c)(i) of the 2008 Constitution reads:

> The President shall submit the nomination of the suitable person to be appointed as the Chief Justice of the Union to the Pyidaungsu Hluttaw

and seek its approval. [The Pyidaungsu Hluttaw is a joint session of the two houses of the legislature, the Amyotha Hluttaw (upper house) and the Pyithu Hluttaw (lower house).]

However, Section 299(c)(ii) immediately adds:

> The Pyidaungsu Hluttaw shall have no right to refuse the person nominated by the President for the appointment of Chief Justice of the Union ... unless it can clearly be proved that the persons [sic] do not meet the qualifications for the post prescribed in Section 301.

Sections 299(d)(i) and (ii) of the 2008 Constitution contain almost identical provisions in relation to the nomination and appointment of Supreme Court judges, and again the Pyidaungsu Hluttaw has "no right to refuse the person nominated by the President for the appointment of ... Judges of the Supreme Court of the Union ....".

There are also provisions in the 2008 Constitution that can be weakly construed as guaranteeing "tenure" for the Chief Justice and Supreme Court judges. Section 303 states:

> The Chief Justice of the Union and Judges of the Supreme Court of the Union shall hold office up to the age of 70 years unless one of the following occurs:
> (a) resignation on his own volition;
> (b) being impeached in accord with the provisions under the constitution and removed from office;
> (c) being found to be unable to continue to serve due to permanent disability caused by either physical or mental defect according to the findings of the medical board formed by law;
> (d) death.

Hence, in comparison with the period between September 1988 and March 2011, when by law and in practice no explicit stipulation existed regarding the age to which a Chief Justice or a Judge could serve, under the 2008 Constitution, there is — subject to the above qualifications — "tenure" for the judges of the Supreme Court and the Chief Justice in the current Myanmar Supreme Court. The specific mention of the age limit for the Chief Justice and the Supreme Court judges under the 2008 Constitution contrasts strongly with the situation during the period before the 2008 Constitution came into force. When Chief Justice U Aung Toe was appointed as Chief Justice by a decree of the State Law and Order Restoration Council (SLORC) in September 1988, he was over sixty years of age, and he was over eighty years old when his retirement took effect upon the formation of the new Supreme Court. (See Table 14.2 for dates of office of heads of apex courts from 1948 till the present.) U Aung Toe served as Chief Justice for a total of twenty-two-and-a-half years, making him the longest-serving head of the judiciary in post-independence Burmese history. In contrast, under the provisions of the 2008 Constitution, the youngest age for a nominee for Chief Justice or a Supreme Court judge is fifty years, and when the Chief Justice or Supreme Court judge turns seventy, retirement is compulsory. Hence the maximum number of years a Chief Justice or a Supreme Court judge can serve in the post under the provisions of the 2008 Constitution is twenty.

Prima facie, in terms of appointment and tenure this would appear to be a marginal improvement over the pre-2008 Constitution period. An indulgent, but unrealistic, view might be that there is even a substantial improvement, since (1) there is a sort of legislative "approval" of the president's nominees for Chief Justice and Supreme Court judges, and (2) there is tenure for both the Chief Justice and Supreme Court judges until the age of seventy (so long as the Chief Justice or the judges do not resign, are not impeached and removed from office, are not found to be physically or mentally incompetent by a medical board formed by law, and do not die in office).

As regards the first aspect, legislative approval, the 2008 Constitution itself is explicit that the "Pyidaungsu Hluttaw has no right to refuse the persons nominated by the President" to be either a Chief Justice or a Supreme Court judge, unless the persons do not meet the qualifications stated in the constitution. Moreover, Union Solidarity Development Party (USDP) members constitute nearly 80 per cent of the legislature overall, and 25 per cent of the members of both houses of the legislature are military appointees. At most, no more than 10 per cent of the members of both houses of the legislature belong to what can be called "opposition parties". Even among the non-military, non-USDP members of the legislature, there have not been any murmurs of equivocation, far less disagreement, regarding the president's nominees for Chief Justice and Supreme Court judges, nor, indeed, for any of his nominees in the various organs of government. All were appointed in the first session of the Pyidaungsu Hluttaw that was held from 31 January to 30 March 2011.

Therefore, in the category of appointment and tenure of Supreme Court judges, the apparent improvement, when analysed critically, is marginal. In order to fully discuss the issue of "tenure" of judges of the current Myanmar Supreme Court, the impeachment and removal

TABLE 14.2
Heads of Apex Courts in Burma/Myanmar, 1947–2011

Apex Court Period	Head of Court	Title	Period of Tenure	Law Qualifications
First Court 4 January 1948– 31 March 1962	Sir Ba U (1887–1963)	Chief Justice	4 January 1948– 12 March 1952	MA, LLB (Cambridge) Barrister at Law
	U Thein Maung (1890–1975)	Chief Justice	12 March 1952– 17 July 1957	BA (Calcutta); BA MA, LLB (Cambridge); Barrister at Law
	U Myint Thein (1900–1994)	Chief Justice	17 July 1957– 31 March 1962	MA, LLB (Cambridge) Barrister at Law
Second Court 1 April 1962– 4 March 1974	U Bo Gyi (1898-1982)	Chief Judge	1 April 1962– 5 June 1965	BA, BL (Rangoon)
	Dr. Maung Maung (1925–1994)	Chief Judge, later Chief Justice	5 June 1965– 12 July 1972	BA, BL (Rangoon); LL.D. (Utrecht); J.S.D (Yale); Barrister at Law
	U Hla Thin	Chief Justice	12 July 1972– 4 March 1974	BA, BL (Rangoon)

Third Court 4 March 1974–18 September 1988	Thura U Aung Pe	Chairman, Council of People's Justices	4 March 1974–9 November 1981	
	U Moung Moung Kyaw Win (1909–1982)	Chairman, Council of People's Justices	9 November 1981–30 July 1982	BA (Hons), MA (Hons) (Rangoon) Barrister at law
	U Tin Aung Hein (deceased)	Chairman, Council of People's Justices	30 July 1982–18 September 1988	BA, BL (Rangoon)
Fourth Court 28 September 1988–30 March 2011	U Aung Toe (born 1925)	Chief Justice	28 September 1988–30 March 2011	BA, BL (Rangoon)
Fifth Court 30 March 2011–continuing	U Tun Tun Oo (born 1956)	Union Chief Justice	30 March 2011–27 August 2012	BA (Law), LLB, (Rangoon)
	U Soe Thein	Chief Justice	28 August 2012–continuing	

Source: Compiled by the author with the assistance of Nick Cheesman.

provisions relating to the Chief Justice and Supreme Court judges also need to be considered.

Are Impeachment Provisions for Supreme Court Judges in the 2008 Constitution an Improvement?

In the period of the fourth apex court, from September 1988 to March 2011, there was nothing explicit in the relevant laws to the effect that the ruling military councils could remove Supreme Court judges by whim or fiat, even though that was what actually occurred. However, under Section 302 of the 2008 Constitution, specific steps are laid down for impeaching Supreme Court judges, and should the impeachment be successful, for removing them from office.

Under Section 302(b) and (c), impeachment proceedings can be commenced either by the president or by the "representatives of the Pyithu Hluttaw or the Amyotha Hluttaw" (lower and upper houses respectively). Inasmuch as the 1947 Constitution also contains impeachment provisions, a brief comparison with some of the relevant provisions may be instructive. Under Sections 143(3) and 143(4) of the 1947 Constitution, impeachment proceedings against a Supreme Court judge could only be commenced after "a notice of resolution signed by not less than one fourth of the total membership of that Chamber [of Parliament]". This meant that only members of the parliament could initiate impeachment proceedings against Supreme Court judges. Under the 2008 Constitution, in contrast, not only can the president appoint the Chief Justice and the Supreme Court judges, but the president can, by himself, also initiate impeachment proceedings against them. Since more than 75 per cent of members in the Pyidaungsu Hluttaw are from the USDP (of which President U Thein Sein was a high-ranking member), and because of the number of military appointees in both houses, once impeachment proceedings have commenced against either the Chief Justice or the Supreme Court judges, there is a very strong likelihood that they would succeed and the Chief Justice or judge would be removed.

Aside from these considerations, it is a fact that the lack of independence of the judiciary has been a fixed and permanent feature in the non-shifting political scene in Burma over the past few decades. Any appointee to the Supreme Court would have learned from the experiences, trends, and lessons of the past that "failure of a judge to deport herself according to regime interests will at best result in unemployment" (Cheesman 2009, p. 612).

Moreover, three out of the seven Supreme Court judges appointed in the first session of the Pyidaungsu Hluttaw are ex-military officers or have military backgrounds.[9] The previous lack of independence of the judiciary, as well as the fact that both the president and the Chief Justice appointed by him have military backgrounds, indicate that the guardian of the 2008 Constitution — arguably one of the most praetorian in the world, and definitely in Southeast Asia — is the military rather than the judiciary.[10] To put it another way, even if the judiciary is considered to be one of the guardians of the 2008 Constitution, the judiciary's role would be subordinate to the military, since the constitution explicitly and categorically assigns the leading role to the Defence Forces. Judges could be impeached for violating any provisions of the constitution, which includes as a cardinal feature the leading role of the military.

In these respects, the provisions of the 2008 Constitution for impeachment of judges mean that the independence of the judiciary remains theoretical. Supreme Court judges appointed under the 2008 Constitution would, categorically, not act like at least some of the justices of the long-defunct first Supreme Court established under the 1947 Constitution, in asserting their independence from executive actions. Such a course of action, considered normal in systems where there is judicial independence, could well be considered to violate the provisions of the 2008 Constitution. For these reasons, it could be said that the ostensible improvement of the "new" Supreme Court over that of the old is more apparent than real. If anything, from a certain perspective the position of the Supreme Court could perhaps be considered to be worse, since the constitution entrenches, formalizes, and constitutionalizes military rule.

A considered analysis of the new Supreme Court in comparison to its predecessor during the period prior to the establishment of the 2008 Constitution is that, at best, it could be considered that there has been a marginal improvement. Nevertheless, even that categorization has to be hedged with qualification, and even this qualified prognosis may prove to be optimistic.

THE NEW CONSTITUTIONAL TRIBUNAL

Unlike the "new" Myanmar Supreme Court, the Union Constitutional Tribunal described in Sections 320 to 336 of the 2008 Constitution is a completely new body. Its newness will not, however, lead to a new level of protection of the rights of the people. Well-meaning but (at least in this context) naïve foreign non-governmental organizations have touted hopes regarding the future operation of the Constitutional Tribunal. The detailed provisions regarding formation of the Constitutional Tribunal and the appointment of its members can be referred to in the 2008 Constitution and they will not be commented on here.[11] Instead, a critique of what can be described as fond hopes or deep misconceptions of how the Constitutional Tribunal might operate will be made here.

Constitutional Tribunal and the (Non) Issue of Immunity: Great Expectations or Waiting for Godot?

In an otherwise very critical report entitled *Impunity Prolonged: Burma and its 2008 Constitution,* prepared by the International Center for Transitional Justice, it was stated that:

> [t]he constitutional tribunal has sole authority to interpret the constitution. While it is impossible to know how the tribunal might address immunity issues, the fact that it will be made up of nine members — three chosen by the president and three chosen by both houses in the Legislature — who cannot belong to a political party suggests at least a move in the right direction. As noted above, the immunity clause in the 2008 Constitution is ambiguous and may be open to interpretation by Burma's courts. The clause could also be challenged in various serious criminal cases because amnesty for such crimes would either violate international law or contravene Burma's treaty obligations (2009, p. 35).

The report misconceives the nature of the Constitutional Tribunal and does not take into account the political and judicial realities prevalent in Burma for virtually all of the last five decades. It is beyond the bounds of possibility that the Constitutional Tribunal would interpret Section 445 of the 2008 Constitution, the so-called immunity clause.[12] Which member of the Constitutional Tribunal would dare to decide that certain acts of the State Law and Order Restoration Council and the State Peace and Development Council (SPDC) or their members are not covered by the immunity clause? The threat of impeachment — or perhaps (much) worse — would be a sufficient deterrent for all members of the Constitutional Tribunal and, for that matter, of the Supreme Court, not to entertain such explosive, and indeed (for the protagonists) potentially dangerous, ideas. In the far-fetched scenario that the constitutional provisions and laws concerning the Defence Forces — which under Sections 20(b) and 343(a) and 343(b) of the 2008 Constitution lie solely within the jurisdiction of the Courts-Martial — might be submitted to the Constitutional Tribunal, the Tribunal may simply decline to exercise jurisdiction.

Moreover, Section 322 of the 2008 Constitution lists the "functions and duties of the Constitutional Tribunal" in seven different sub-sections, and even though Section 322(a) mentions that the Constitutional Tribunal's jurisdiction includes "interpreting the provisions under the Constitution", the scope and application of certain constitutional provisions may be beyond the jurisdiction of the Constitutional Tribunal. This is so not only because the provisions concerning Courts Martial are separate from those concerning the Constitutional Tribunal — and under section 294 the Courts Martial have exclusive jurisdiction in matters concerning the military — but also because according to the 2008 Constitution, the military has (a) "the right to independently administer and adjudicate all affairs of the armed forces" [Section 20(b)]; (b) the Courts-Martial are separate from all the other Courts, including the Supreme Court and the Constitutional Tribunal (Section 293); and (c) "[i]n the adjudication of military justice ... the decision of the Defence Services Chief is final and conclusive" (Section 343).

Let us pretend that an extremely unlikely (and theoretical) scenario were to emerge whereby a legal issue arose as to whether the actions of members of the military councils fall within the execution of their respective duties or not. A reading of the constitution's provisions concerning both the Constitutional Tribunal and the Courts-Martial — as well as consideration of actual practice on the ground based on previous trends — would indicate that it is the Courts-Martial rather than the Constitutional Tribunal that would decide the issue.

Also, under Section 325, only the President, the Speaker of the Pyidaungsu Hluttaw, the Speaker of the Pyithu Hluttaw, the Speaker of the Amyotha Hluttaw, the Chief Justice of the Union, and the Chairperson of the Union Election Commission "have the right to submit matters directly to obtain the interpretation, resolution and opinion of the Constitutional Tribunal of the Union". Given that all the persons who currently hold the above posts are former military officers, it is extremely unlikely that these persons will initiate any issue pertaining to the immunity provisions contained in Section 445 of the constitution.

Section 326 of the 2008 Constitution states that the Chief Ministers of the Region or the State, the Speaker of Region or State Hluttaw, the Chairperson of the Self-Administered Division Leading Body or the

Self-Administered Zone Leading Body, and representatives numbering at least 10 per cent of all the representatives of the Pyithu Hluttaw or the Amyotha Hluttaw also "have the right to submit matters to obtain the interpretation, resolution and opinion of the Constitutional Tribunal" but they can do so only "in accord with the prescribed procedures". In the current two houses of the legislature, the non-pro-government parties together constitute barely 15 per cent of members, and it is only this small percentage of members who might in theory be minded to bring up the issues of the interpretation, scope, and application of the immunity clause or the constitutionality of laws. Even this scenario is far-fetched under current circumstances; since members can only submit such matters in accordance with the prescribed procedures, it is likely there would be significant procedural hurdles even if they were to decide to bring the issue before the Constitutional Tribunal.[13]

Finally, if against great odds a challenge were to be lodged before the Constitutional Tribunal over the constitutionality of the repressive laws that were not made by the post-1988 military councils, starting with colonial legislation such as the 1947 *Public Order Preservation Act* and post-colonial legislation such as the 1975 *Law Protecting the State from Hostile, Subversive Elements*, the outcome would be very predictable: the constitutionality of the legislation would be upheld.[14] The Constitutional Tribunal may hold that it has no jurisdiction to deal with the issue, that an application does not raise constitutional questions, is irrelevant, and that the very fact of raising the issue is even abusive of the "constitutional" process. Hence the mere fact of the existence of the Constitutional Tribunal should not raise hopes regarding the issue of immunity from prosecution effectively enjoyed by the military.

Those who have the audacity to hope that the Constitutional Tribunal would deal with and interpret the immunity provisions of the 2008 Constitution are engaging in wishful thinking, comparable to the antagonists in Samuel Beckett's famous play, *Waiting for Godot*. There is nothing in the provisions of the 2008 Constitution that would call for any expectation of moves in the right direction, towards a Constitutional Tribunal that would guarantee human rights and would be as activist as other (in comparison) progressive constitutional tribunals in foreign countries. There is no chance that the Constitutional Tribunal would accept any "challenge[s] in various serious criminal cases" (such as regarding immunity of members of the previous military councils). *A fortiori*, seeking a holding decision or a resolution by the Constitutional Tribunal that "amnesty for such crimes would either violate international law or contravene Burma's treaty obligations", as suggested in the International Center for Transitional Justice report (2009, p. 35), is like pursuing a mirage metaphorically as well as literally.

There is nothing in the provisions of the 2008 Constitution that would call for any expectations that "moves in the right direction" might take place in the Constitutional Tribunal as suggested in the report from the International Center for Transitional Justice. This is because (1) various serious criminal cases or charges would not, could not factually, politically (and therefore) legally be made against any top military officials in relation to the categories of crimes mentioned in the report; (2) procedural, substantive, and security obstacles would be daunting for those involved in making a submission for a resolution on this matter, and even if they succeeded in actually putting up the submission, the Constitutional Tribunal would not agree to consider the submission; and (3) even if the Constitutional Tribunal were to accept or consider the submission, any ruling it made would not hold that certain alleged acts of military officials are not covered by the immunity provisions.

CONCLUSION

The two new judicial institutions that were formed under the 2008 Constitution have at least given rise to some projections about the future, if not exactly to positive hopes or entirely optimistic expectations, even if only in the academic literature (see for example Manley 2010, Nardi 2011). In regard to the future prospects of the Supreme Court, this author has taken an approach that is mainly oriented to the past, and on the basis of his analysis of the formal provisions of the 2008 Constitution, feels able to make a cautious statement, hedged with qualifications, that possibly a "marginal improvement" can be discerned.

As far as the Constitutional Tribunal is concerned, it is indeed a new institution and therefore the analysis is "future oriented". Does the existence of the Constitutional Tribunal indicate a change for the better, or only a marginal improvement? To paraphrase a phrase in the play *Waiting for Godot* ("… meanwhile nothing happens"), meanwhile nothing has happened that would indicate any improvement in terms of the protection of civil and political rights by either the Supreme Court or the new Constitutional

Tribunal. Any marginal improvement can be found only in the formalities of tenure of the Supreme Court judges (but not of the members of the Constitutional Tribunal). The Constitutional Tribunal is a new institution and that is all there is to it. As has been argued above, the newness of the Constitutional Tribunal can only be considered as a positive development by an overly optimistic — and naïve — analysis. The famous first line of A. P. Hartley's novel *The Go-Between* is "The past is a foreign country. They do things differently there." When looking back at the late ('first') Supreme Court of the 1947 Constitution, where things *were* done differently, it is hard to believe that those rulings, as well as the functions and operations of previous Burmese apex courts, did indeed occur in the same country. Hence, to the author, the (Burmese judicial) past (of the first Supreme Court period) is (metaphorically) and substantively a foreign country.

As far as the new Constitutional Tribunal is concerned, the future will not be a foreign country at all — meaning that the comparatively positive developments that can be discerned in other progressive and relatively new constitutional courts in other countries, such as in South Korea (see Healey 2000), and South Africa (see Dickson 1997, Gibson and Caldeira 2003), will not be replicated in Burma. Perhaps even such a comparison is only of academic interest, and unreflective of reality. With the Burmese judicial past being in a "foreign country" and future interpretations, resolutions, and opinions of the Constitutional Tribunal not likely to be similar to decisions made by similar bodies in other countries, any prognosis of marginal improvement can only be made with great caution. Substantive improvements in the Burmese judicial scene will not be forthcoming. Any hopes or expectations to the contrary remind one of the Burmese expression about the saga of the golden deer which, misperceiving a mirage to be water, chases it to no avail.

Notes

1. The 2008 Constitution, unlike its predecessor, the defunct 1974 Constitution, does not use the term "organs of State power". However, more than seven years before the "organs" of the new government were sworn in on 30 March 2011, the "seven-step road map" (apparently to a "disciplined" democracy) was announced on 30 August 2003. Its last step reads: "Building a modern, developed and democratic nation by the state leaders elected by the Hluttaw and the government and other central organs formed by the Hluttaw" (*NLM*, 31 August 2003). Hence the use of the term "organs of power" is not

inappropriate. Also, the phrase "comes into operation" appears many times in the English translation of the 2008 Constitution.

2. See also Myint Zan (2004).

3. The author eschews — indeed he rejects — the delineation of the political and the legal as entirely separate fields of concern. The new Constitutional Tribunal is primarily a political institution. For the author's previous observations pertaining to the subject of law and politics, see Myint Zan (1994) and (2000).

4. For a detailed and perceptive analysis of one among the writs (habeas corpus) supposedly issuable by the new Supreme Court, see Cheesman (2010).

5. In the first part of a two-part article published in the *Working People's Daily*, the late Dr Htin Aung supplicated the "Princess Learned in the Law" and at the start of the conversation informed her that he had come to her not to "burden you with my regrets but to report to you the changes that have taken place in the structure of the judiciary and the profession of law under [the then] newly constituted Socialist Republic of the Union of Burma" (Htin Aung 1974, p. 2).

6. The State Law and Order Restoration Council passed the Judiciary Law (Law No. 2, 1988) in part for this purpose. The State Peace and Development Council repealed the law on 27 June 2000 with the announcement of a new law. Under Chapter III, Section 3 of the Judiciary Law 2000, "[t]he State Peace and Development Council shall constitute [*sic*] the Supreme Court with 1 Chief Justice, 2 Deputy Chief Justices and from a minimum of 7 to a maximum of 12 Judges".

7. On 13 November 1998 the State Peace and Development Council announced that five out of the six Supreme Court judges were "permitted to retire" (Cheesman 2009, p. 612). Only the then Chief Justice U Aung Toe retained his position. Since the independence of the judiciary had been completely destroyed years before 1998, this event did not cause a stir in foreign newspapers, or in academic and professional literature. Compare the lack of interest in the removal of four judges of the then Myanmar (fourth) Supreme Court in 1998 with the criticisms and concerns expressed ten years earlier over the removal of five apex court judges in Malaysia, in what was called the 1988 Malaysian judicial crisis (see for example, Abbas and Das 1989, Addruse 1990).

8. I have specifically used the word "legislature" rather than "parliament". The two legislative bodies formed under the 2008 Constitution do not constitute a parliament in the ordinary and natural meaning of the word. The use of the word "parliament" may be appropriate, in a comparative sense, for some other legislatures in the Asian region, for example, those in India, Malaysia, and Bangladesh. In those countries the term "parliamentary democracy" is appropriate, or at least less inappropriate. So far as Burma is concerned, however, the governmental and also the legislative system under the 2008

Constitution is not parliamentary, just as the governmental and legislative
system embodied in the 1974 Constitution was not parliamentary, and nor has
the term "parliament" been used in official or semi-official usage to describe the
legislatures formed under the 1974 Constitution and the 2008 Constitution.

9. Interview with a Burmese advocate, Canberra, May 2011.

10. Section 20(f) of the 2008 Constitution states: "The Defence Services is mainly
responsible for safeguarding the Constitution". My own translation would be,
"The Defense Services' main duty is to safeguard the Constitution", which,
in my view, conveys a more proximate indication of the military's role as the
"safe-guarder" of the 2008 Constitution. It is also noteworthy that this section
is not under Chapter 7 of the 2008 Constitution, "The Defence Services", but
under Chapter 1, "Basic Principles of the Union", to indicate its paramount
and controlling importance. On the praetorian nature of the 2008 Constitution,
see Myint Zan (2008, p. 195), where comparisons were made with other less
praetorian regimes in Southeast Asia and other regions.

11. Sections 46, 293, 294, and 320–336 of the 2008 Constitution deal with the
Constitutional Tribunal. Section 46 states: "A Constitutional Tribunal shall be
set up to interpret the provisions of the Constitution, to scrutinize whether or
not laws enacted by the Pyidaungsu Hluttaw, the Region Hluttaws and the
State Hluttaws and functions of executive authorities of Pyidaungsu, Regions,
States and Self-Administered Areas are in conformity with the Constitution,
to decide on disputes relating to the Constitution between Pyidaungsu and
Regions, between Pyidaungsu and States, among Regions, among States, and
between Regions or States and Self-Administered Areas and among Self-
Administered Areas themselves, and to perform other duties prescribed in
this Constitution."

12. Section 445 of the 2008 Constitution states: "All policy guidelines, laws,
rules, regulations, notifications and declarations of the State Law and Order
Restoration Council and the State Peace and Development Council or actions,
rights and responsibilities of the State Law and Order Restoration Council and
the State Peace and Development Council shall devolve on the Republic of the
Union of Myanmar. No proceeding shall be instituted against the said Councils
or any member thereof or any member of the Government, in respect of any
act done in the execution of their respective duties."

13. There are cumbersome rules regarding the simple asking of questions in the two
Hluttaws, where Hluttaw representatives are reminded not to ask "irrelevant
questions". If the relatively simple and generally innocuous questions regarding
amnesty for political prisoners (proposed by the opposition National Democratic
Front in the first session of the legislature) have to pass through cumbersome
procedures, one could only envisage how much more cumbersome and
intricate procedures to raise such sensitive an issue as the (non) immunity of
the members of the previous military councils would be.

14. Section 445 of the 2008 Constitution is explicit not only in regard to the laws but also in regard to "policy guidelines, rules, regulations, notifications and declarations of State Law and Order Restoration Council and State Peace and Development Council". Though a legalistic interpretation of this provision does not automatically preclude an eventual ruling that a few of these laws are unconstitutional, no court in Burma during the 1974 Constitution period ruled that any of the laws passed by the Revolutionary Council were unconstitutional, and in any case, no court under the 1974 Constitution had the capacity or jurisdiction to do so. Even though the Constitutional Tribunal has the capacity to interpret provisions under the 2008 Constitution, it is very unlikely that it would follow a different path and rule that laws such as the 1975 Law Protecting the State from Hostile, Subversive Elements were unconstitutional.

References

Cases cited

G.N. Banerjee (Applicant) v. The Superintendent, Insein Jail Annexe, Insein (Respondent). Burma Law Reports (BLR) 1948, Supreme Court, p. 199.

Ma Ahmar v. Commissioner of Police and One. Burma Law Reports (BLR) 1949, Supreme Court, p. 39.

Other References

Abbas, Tun Salleh and K. Das. *May Day for Justice*. New York: Magnus Books, 1989.

Addruse, Raja Aziz. *Conduct Unbecoming: In Defence of Tun Mohd. Salleh Abbas*. Kuala Lumpur: Walrus, 1990.

Cheesman, Nick. "Thin Rule of Law or Un-rule of Law in Myanmar?" *Pacific Affairs* 82, no. 4 (2009): 597–613.

———. "The Incongruous Return of Habeas Corpus to Myanmar". In *Ruling Myanmar: From Cyclone Nargis to National Elections*, edited by Nick Cheesman, Monique Skidmore and Trevor Wilson. Singapore: Institute of Southeast Asian Studies, 2010.

Constitution of the Republic of the Union of Myanmar. Naypyitaw: Printing and Publishing Enterprise, Ministry of Information, Union of Myanmar, 2008. Available at <http://www.burmalibrary.org/docs5/Myanmar_Constitution-2008-en.pdf>. Accessed 24 April 2012.

Dickson, Brice. "Protecting Human Rights Through a Constitutional Court: The Case of South Africa". *Fordham Law Review* 66 (1997): 531–66.

Gibson, James L. and Gregory A. Caldeira. "Defenders of Democracy? Legitimacy and Popular Acceptance and the South African Constitutional Court". *Journal of Politics* 65, no. 1 (2003): 1–39.

Hartley, A. P. *The Go-Between*. London: Hamish Hamilton, 1953.

Healey, Gavin. 2000. "Judicial Activism in the New Constitutional Court of Korea". *Columbia Journal of Asian Law* 14 (2000): 213–34.

Htin Aung, Maung. "A Conversation with the Princess Learned in the Law (Part 1)". *Working People's Daily*, 28 March 1974, p. 2.

International Center for Transitional Justice. *Impunity Prolonged: Burma and its 2008 Constitution*. New York: International Center for Transitional Justice, 2009. <http://ictj.org/publication/impunity-prolonged-burma-and-its-2008-constitution>. Accessed 30 April 2012.

Manley, Stewart. "Exploring the Paradox of Limitation Clauses: How Restrictions on Basic Freedoms in the 2008 Myanmar Constitution May Strengthen Human Rights Protections". *Australian Journal of Human Rights* 14, no. 1 (2010): 155–92.

Myint Zan. "The Mabo Judgment: Third Thoughts and Associated Cases". *Malaysian Law News*, February 1994, pp. 29–33.

———. "Of Consummation, Matrimonial Promises, Fault and Parallel Wives: The Role of Original Texts, Interpretation, Policy and Ideology in Pre- and Post-1962 Burmese Case Law". *Columbia Journal of Asian Law* 14, no. 1 (2000): 153–212.

———. "A Comparison of the First and Fiftieth Year of Independent Burma's Law Reports". *Victoria University of Wellington Law Review* (2004) <http://www.austlii.edu.au/nz/journals/VUWLRev/2004/14.html>.

———. "Myanmar (Burma): From Parliamentary System to Constitutionless and Constitutionalized One-Party and Military Rule". In *Constitutionalism in Southeast Asia*, vol. 2, edited by Clauspeter Hill and Jorg Menzel. Singapore: Konrad Adenauer Stiftung, 2008.

Nardi, Dominic. "Discipline-Flourishing Constitutional Review: A Legal and Political Analysis of Myanmar's New Constitutional Tribunal". *Australian Journal of Asian Law* 12 (2011): 1–32.

New Light of Myanmar (NLM). "Prime Minister General Khin Nyunt clarifies future policies and programmes of State". *New Light of Myanmar*, 31 August 2003. <http://www.ibiblio.org/obl/docs/Roadmap-KN.htm>. Accessed 2 June 2012.

VII

The Continued Importance of International Assistance

15

RETHINKING INTERNATIONAL ASSISTANCE TO MYANMAR IN A TIME OF TRANSITION

Morten B. Pedersen

Myanmar's new government is taking the country in new directions. Early statements by President Thein Sein have been surprisingly frank and honest in their assessment of the country's deep-seated problems, and have committed the government to a wide-ranging agenda of social, political, and economic reform. Although nagging questions remain about how far it will ultimately be willing and — not least — able to go, subsequent government actions appear to have started Myanmar down a path of meaningful political transition and socio-economic transformation.

The sudden movement within Myanmar presents a challenge for an international community whose long-standing absence from the country has left it ill-prepared to understand and effectively respond to the changes taking place. Diplomats are scrambling to catch up, but in many ways it is the aid community that has the biggest steps to take. While recent new aid commitments by Australia and other Western donors are a good start, the overall aid agenda remains decidedly under-ambitious. Aid is still viewed mainly in humanitarian terms rather than as the transformative tool that it both can and must be at a time like this. This is not to suggest that international assistance provides the solution to Myanmar's manifold problems, but simply that it offers important opportunities to actively help move the country forward. Indeed, at this point, aid may be the most important lever that the international community has in Myanmar.

This chapter reviews past achievements of international assistance to Myanmar and considers its future potential viewed from the vantage point of May 2011. It also outlines a second-generation aid agenda for Australia and like-minded donors. The analysis is based primarily on hundreds of confidential interviews conducted by the author in Myanmar between 1997 and 2011; complementary public sources are referenced where available.

PAST ACHIEVEMENTS

The dominant story of international assistance to Myanmar over the past twenty years has been one of onerous government restrictions and limited donor support. Since nearly all agencies and programmes in the country are humanitarian in focus, their developmental impact has, naturally, been limited. However, there is a more positive, if rarely told, story about the crucial role international aid agencies have played in lifting the veil of ignorance about Myanmar's humanitarian crisis, supporting basic needs, protecting vulnerable groups, improving national policy and capacities and, quite possibly, encouraging broader structural change. Importantly, international aid agencies that persisted through the long, difficult years of internal restrictions and external sanctions have built contacts and confidence with local stakeholders, putting them in a key position to contribute to the current transition process. The examples that follow are by no means exhaustive and are intended to convey a general sense of the impact of international assistance over the past twenty years.

Lifting the Veil of Ignorance

When aid agencies began tentatively entering Myanmar in the early 1990s, little was known about the humanitarian situation in the country. Official statistics had long served as a propaganda tool for a government primarily concerned with legitimacy. Exiles and solidarity groups had begun producing penetrating reports on human rights conditions in the conflict-affected border areas, but had no access to other parts of the country, and in any case showed little interest in information that might weaken their political agenda of isolating the military regime. Many were openly hostile to any talk of expanding aid beyond small-scale cross-border assistance to internally displaced communities. As a result, the suffering of millions of other families went largely unnoticed.

That this regrettable situation changed is due in large part to the efforts by aid agencies working within Myanmar to collect and disseminate increasingly reliable, systematic, and comprehensive data on the socio-economic deprivation of the general population. It took a decade, but eventually UN-sponsored national health surveys, coupled with increasingly robust advocacy by reputable international NGOs, became too embarrassing for the government and donors alike to ignore, and by 2001 the first substantial increments of international assistance finally began flowing in. The International Crisis Group in 2002 described the role of the aid community in lifting this veil of ignorance as perhaps its single most important contribution to development in Myanmar (ICG 2002). Since then, aid organizations have shifted their focus to the actual implementation of development programmes, but we should not forget than even getting to this point was a hard-won battle in a country where political conflict has long overshadowed government developmental objectives and where few of the main contestants of power have paid more than rhetorical attention to popular welfare.

Supporting Basic Needs

With improved, if still limited, government cooperation and donor support, aid agencies have been able to implement a wide range of humanitarian programmes and take them up to full-scale operations in a few priority areas. Although the sustainability of much of this work is limited while the root causes of poverty remain, the benefits to individuals and households are very "real".

The best results have been achieved in health, which has been the dominant focus of international assistance in the two decades since aid agencies began operations in Myanmar. One of the most visible achievements is the national immunization campaigns conducted by the United Nations Children's Fund (UNICEF) and the World Health Organization (WHO) in cooperation with the Myanmar government and government-organized non-government organizations (NGOs), which have increased immunization rates to over 80 per cent for six vaccine-preventable diseases. These same structures have also made significant progress in the distribution of micro-nutrients, such as iodine, iron, and Vitamin A, to combat malnutrition, and in the expansion of access to safe water and sanitation. Since the late 1990s, significant efforts have been made also to combat the three major diseases: HIV/AIDS, malaria, and tuberculosis. The multi-agency HIV/AIDS programme can reasonably be credited with halting the tide of Myanmar's HIV/AIDS epidemic, which is among the worst in Asia and initially gave rise to numerous doomsday predictions. Major progress has also been made on malaria treatment, due in large part to the efforts of a single agency, Médécins Sans Frontieres (MSF)/Holland, and its network of local Myanmar doctors. Overall, humanitarian agencies delivering health information and consultations, medicines, improved water and sanitation, and other basic health-related services, either directly or in cooperation with local partners, have helped hundreds of thousands, if not millions, of Myanmar's poor to survive in good health rather than suffer unnecessary illness or death.

Few other sectors have received substantial aid. However, in recent years, as agencies have expanded their activities into areas such as micro-finance and agricultural extension services and support, they have also begun contributing significantly to creating broader livelihood opportunities for vulnerable communities across the country. The micro-finance project implemented by PACT as part of the UNDP's Human Development Initiative has been described as "among the 20 most successful large micro-finance projects in the world" (Birgegard 2010). Significant contributions to improving food security and livelihoods have been made also through smaller-scale but innovative programmes, such as International Development Enterprises/Myanmar's social marketing of simple agricultural tools (O'Neil 2009) and the Metta Foundation's Farmer Field Schools. (Metta is a local NGO but has an international advisory board and receives large-scale international funding).

Protecting Vulnerable Groups

In addition to delivering basic needs, significant efforts have been made to protect vulnerable communities against state repression. In the Northern Rakhine area, a dozen agencies have been working under the umbrella of the United Nations High Commission for Refugees (UNHCR) to protect the rights of the Rohingya, a Muslim minority group; in the eastern part of Shan State a similar coalition led by the United Nations Office on Drugs and Crime (UNODC) has been helping disenfranchised opium farmers cope with a local government-imposed opium ban. Another example is the efforts by the Food and Agriculture Organization (FAO), the United Nations Development Programme (UNDP), CARE, and others, using existing community forestry laws, to secure land tenure for local communities and protect them against illegal land confiscations. Although these activities have had limited effect on formal policies or institutions, they provide an important check on arbitrary personal power exercised by corrupt local officials (Duffield 2008), which is a cause of much suffering all around the country and a main source of community resentment against the government. In fact, many Burmese community leaders argue that the mere presence of international organizations often helps to constrain the abusive behaviour of local officials who fear exposure.

Improving National Policy and Planning

While most humanitarian work leaves the over-arching structures of injustice in place, foreign aid agencies have over time increasingly emphasized developing substantive contacts with national and local authorities as well as close partnerships with Myanmar NGOs, and this has helped improve government policy, build local capacity, and generally improve the long-term viability of aid programmes.

Again, the largest impact has been in the health area. With strong international support, the Myanmar government has established National Strategic Plans for each of the three priority diseases — HIV/AIDS, malaria, and tuberculosis. These Plans are generally perceived as reflecting international best practice and have been successfully leveraged to attract Global Fund and other major grants. Importantly, each of these Plans has been developed through participatory processes, involving also local NGOs and representatives of beneficiary groups. This is unprecedented in Myanmar, and quite revolutionary in a country where even pro-democracy groups tend to work in a highly top-down fashion with little consultation with their constituencies. While much work is left to be done, in some areas such as harm reduction among injecting drug users and public-private partnership on DOTS (Directly Observed Treatment Short course) tuberculosis treatment courses, international experts describe the Myanmar government's approach as being more progressive than in many more democratic countries (Stallworthy 2005).

Outside the area of health, the policy impact of aid agencies has been more sporadic, yet important results have been reached even in highly sensitive areas. The International Labour Organization (ILO), for example, has made significant progress on issues of forced labour and, in conjunction with UNICEF, on the use of child soldiers. The introduction of new laws and regulations banning such practices, along with a growing number of official actions on cases of abuse, is slowly chipping away at the long-standing culture of impunity (Horsey forthcoming). Forced labour has dramatically decreased within the civilian government system, although less so within the army, which is a law unto itself.

In a recent survey of international assistance to Myanmar, Allan (2010) cites several other examples of positive policy impact, including human trafficking, drug control, agricultural extension work, forestry policy, and resettlement of people displaced by Cyclone Nargis. "These stories of success", he concludes, "are neither isolated to a specific area, nor as rare as one might imagine based on the popular press." One could add to this that significant results have been achieved in most areas that have actually received significant international attention, suggesting that even more would have been possible had it not been for severe donor limitations on funding and operational modalities.

Building Local Capacities

Donor restrictions have largely blocked aid agencies from providing training for government officials and members of para-statal organizations. However, substantial capacity-building has been taking place among the local staff of international organizations, as well as within internationally-supported local civil society organizations and at the community level.

According to the then head of Population Services International (PSI), international aid agencies in 2005 employed 3,500 local staff. Such staff, he argued, are exposed "to modern management styles and techniques in a country where people have had little exposure to outside companies and organizations. ... [t]his is real capacity building: the experience of participating in a social organization that is entrepreneurial and results-oriented, in which performance and talents determine promotion and authority." (Stallworthy 2005; author's italics). By 2009, the number of local employees of international aid organizations had increased to 10,000 (*Open Letter* 2009), and it continues to rise. Along with broader educational schemes, including overseas scholarship programmes, this has built a cadre of competent administrators, trainers, and technical experts, which will be crucial for the success of the current transition.

International work with independent civil society was almost non-existent during the 1990s, except for a few prominent organizations engaged in peace and development work in the new ceasefire areas. This situation began changing with the influx of HIV/AIDS funding from 2001 onwards, and since the tragic disaster of Cyclone Nargis in 2008, international-local NGO partnerships have become a major feature of the aid landscape. With limited funding available locally, international aid is a major funding source for most local NGOs of any size. Increasingly this has been complemented with training and "mentoring", as well as with support for networking among local organizations (Dorning 2006). In some cases, local staff of international NGOs have "branched out" to set up their own organizations. While the total number and overall capacity of local NGOs remain relatively small, they have come to play a crucial "connecting" role in the delivery of social services, especially for the poorest of the poor, who often need assistance to access the state system. Some NGOs have also taken on advocacy roles and look set to gain increasing prominence in the freer political system now emerging.

The final element of the trinity of local organizations benefitting from international support and training is community-level beneficiary groups. Contrary to conventional wisdom that participatory programmes are impossible in authoritarian systems, many international agencies have had significant success with setting up various forms of user groups as the focal point for participatory development processes, with group members usually drawn from among the most vulnerable people of the area. This, in turn, has helped empower people to take charge of their own lives, supporting processes of bottom-up "democratization" that will be crucial for the current reforms to become meaningful at the local level (South 2004).

Encouraging Military Reformers?

It has often been argued that the types of impact discussed above are but a drop in an ocean of misery and structural disempowerment. This would seem to reflect a callous disregard for the many, many individual lives that have, unquestionably, been touched, and often saved, by international assistance. It also ignores an intriguing question about the link between international engagement and the dramatic structural changes that we are seeing now. Set against the backdrop of Western sanctions and isolation, international aid agencies have played a unique role in exposing military commanders and government officials to the outside world and "showcasing" what a better relationship with the West could mean. Is it a coincidence that the former military intelligence chief, General Khin Nyunt, who had long been at the forefront of Myanmar's post-1988 re-engagement with the international community, in the early 2000s oversaw a period of, at that time, unprecedented though limited liberalization? Similarly, is it likely that the new generation of reformers in the current government would have so easily reconnected with their long-standing detractors in Western capitals and so quickly invited international support for their reform programme, had they not, over the past twenty years, come to know a different side of the West through personal contacts and experiences with the aid community? While the ongoing transition is undoubtedly driven primarily by domestic imperatives, international agencies may well have a stronger claim than their erstwhile critics in the pro-sanctions movement to having encouraged the changes now taking place by breaking the siege mentality of the military leadership and demonstrating alternative development paths.

FUTURE POTENTIAL

Huge challenges will remain if principled aid is to be increased on a large scale. For nationalists in the regime who are highly sensitive to any perceived encroachment on Myanmar's sovereignty, foreign aid is a bitter pill to swallow (ICG 2002). Even among more progressive officials, decades of self-imposed and, since 1988, externally enforced, isolation has left a legacy of wariness towards outsiders and limited capacity to engage effectively with the international aid community. Dysfunctional national government systems only add to the difficulty of effectively assisting development in the country.

Nonetheless, there is much untapped potential. The past twenty years have seen a significant expansion in the number of international agencies working inside Myanmar, as well as in the type of activities they are able to undertake and the areas of the country they can reach (ICG 2006). The generous international response to the devastation caused by Cyclone Nargis in 2008 was a particularly important turning point, both because it built further linkages, goodwill, and trust between the government and the aid community, and because it opened the eyes of the world to the many Myanmar individuals and groups that have been working quietly, away from the headlines of popular uprisings and opposition politics, to improve the country (ICG 2008; Centre for Peace and Conflict Studies 2009; Kramer 2011). New linkages with Myanmar civil society groups are improving the ability of both the international community and domestic groups to work for change in the many small and fluid spaces that exist within the porous authoritarian state structures (Macan-Markar 2010; Wallis and Jaquet 2011).

The ongoing political transition has clear potential to carry these positive developments further, and even to elevate aid to a whole new level (provided that donors are willing to take some risks for potentially very high rewards). Although it is early days yet, there are strong reasons to expect that the changes already taking place will accelerate and expand. First of all, there has been a generational transition. Senior General Than Shwe, whose personal whims and fancies have to a large degree defined Myanmar politics and governance for much of the past two decades, has retired from all formal government and military positions, as has his deputy, Vice Senior General Maung Aye. They have been replaced with a new generation of generals who are ten to twenty years younger. The new president, Thein Sein, is generally well respected by those who know him, and has shown himself over the years to be unassuming, fairly open-minded, and indeed "clean", something that is highly unusual in a regime otherwise riddled with corruption. He is not a strong leader, but neither is he alone within the new generation in wanting change. While few if any of the new leaders are convinced democrats, authoritarians too can have an interest in improving governance, opening up to the world, and even reaching an accommodation with former foes, as the experiences of a number of neighbouring countries show. In fact, early reforms in those directions in a country like Myanmar are more likely to result from military "soft-liners" seeking to build a new basis for power and legitimacy than from any opposition effort.

Individual leaders aside, this is a new government, and is clearly perceived as such by the incumbents even if critics have dismissed it as nothing more than "old wine in new bottles". Like new governments anywhere, it will be looking now to establish its legitimacy — and with very "thin" democratic credentials it is likely to try to do so by proving itself in governance terms. Early statements by President Thein Sein have not only been relatively conciliatory towards the opposition, but have been heavily focused on the need for governance reform: the new head of state has pledged to clean up the government, to reform the economy, to step up investments in health and education — and he has explicitly called for international assistance in undertaking these tasks. This is a very different tone from that of the previous regime, when everyone was supposed to vilify the opposition and celebrate the self-sufficiency and great achievements of the military government. The new government is clearly still struggling to get organized, but it is notable that the president has appointed a number of specialist advisors, including one of the country's most respected economists, U Myint, who is fiercely independent and, indeed, an advisor to Aung San Suu Kyi. This, again, is highly unusual for military government in Myanmar, which has traditionally been closed, secretive, and anti-intellectual.

Looking ahead, there is now in place a range of new, civilian institutions — and formal institutions, once established, have a tendency to change the interests of the people involved, to become new power centres, and ultimately to become "real". The introduction of a civilian head of state, separate from the commander-in-chief, is important. Future presidents, whatever their background, will be running the government, not the army, and are likely therefore to pay more attention to civilian affairs, including health, education, and economic development more generally, than was the case under the previous regime, which was essentially a security administration. The new parliament and political parties are significant too, even if they are for the moment subject to strong executive power. Already the multiplication of voices and interests formally involved in policy-making has brought increased transparency, and with that the prospect of improved accountability (ICG 2011). The operation of these new institutions, including the new local governments and the holding of regular elections, will have the effect of reintroducing a degree of politics into a government that was previously run by command.

Although political and ethnic conflicts continue to pose serious barriers to both national development in general and re-engagement by international donors more specifically, these changes in governance priorities and processes represent a major shift in a situation that has been frozen for a long time — and promise to build momentum for broader reforms in the coming months and years. In this situation, aid agencies that for many years have been putting in the "hard yards" making friends and developing their understanding of the local context are finding themselves in a unique position to contribute to new change processes. The ILO provides an instructive example of how strong leadership and commitment have propelled some agencies to the frontline of the changes currently taking place. Once the enemy of the regime and subject to intense criticism and even death threats by government sycophants, the labour agency in recent months has been sought out by government officials to help with developing new, international-standard labour legislation. Not all agencies have done equally well, but Save the Children, MSF/Holland, and Population Services International are among several trail-blazing agencies that for years have been fighting off critics (even from within their own ranks), to emerge now fully vindicated and with a crucial role to play in the coming years. The same can be said for smaller organizations working in niche areas, such as Hope International (peace building), Burnet Institute (civil society support), and International Development Enterprises/Myanmar (social entrepreneurship), and for a number of key individuals. With domestic reforms moving forward and donors looking to dramatically increase aid, these agencies will take on a crucial role building bridges between two heretofore largely separate worlds.

A "SECOND-GENERATION" AID AGENDA

With major internal changes under way in Myanmar, it is time for donors to move beyond past, essentially ideological, debates over democracy-led versus development-led transformation that have little to do with realities on the ground, and instead focus in a more practical and targeted way on the actual "drivers of change". There is a need now to focus on the government and the way it governs — not to the exclusion of other issues, but as the key to the kind of transformative changes that everyone has been clamouring for and which may now finally be within reach. This would also be in accord with global donor principles for best practice in fragile states, which in the case of Myanmar have largely been ignored by donors but which have long been applicable there too (Pedersen 2009).

It is possible to say, although with significant caveats, that the ongoing political transition presents the single biggest opportunity in fifty years to shift Myanmar onto a different development path. In order to make the most of this situation and encourage consolidation of the political level changes that are under way, donors need to get off the fence and commit to a more "normal" developmental approach. The all-important objective now must be to help rebuild the state, including its relations with society. More specifically, this is the time to pursue a "second-generation" aid agenda incorporating three core programmes (see 1–3 below) and three cross-cutting themes (see A–C below).

1. *Initiate a World Bank-led Poverty Reduction Strategy process.* Improving the economy is absolutely vital for addressing Myanmar's interlinked political, humanitarian, and human rights crises. There is now an opportunity to introduce significant economic reforms, but a strong international lead is urgently needed, which probably only the World Bank can provide. Re-engagement through a Poverty Reduction Strategy process would provide an entry-point for discussing overall macro-economic and structural reforms while at the same time offering meaningful incentives for the Myanmar government to cooperate. Importantly, such an initiative would not depend on a wholesale restructuring of the economy. Myanmar is still fundamentally a rich country and much could be achieved simply by relaxing the state's stranglehold on economic life and supporting independent economic actors.

2. *Assist the growth of "peace economies" in former conflict-affected regions.* The sixty-year-old civil war lies at the root of Myanmar's "complex emergency". Peace is ultimately a political project, in which international actors (with the possible exception of China) have no real influence. But donors could help to address the grinding poverty, high unemployment, and shattered dreams of the young people, which are major destabilizing factors in many ethnic minority regions today. In areas where open conflict has ended, strong efforts will be needed to revive normal economic activities and to improve market access to central Myanmar and neighbouring countries, and to expand social services.

3. *Take a more systemic approach to supporting social services delivery.* The new government has indicated that health and education will be given increased priority — and each of these areas is critical for government legitimacy, as well as for national development and poverty alleviation. This is a major task, but the existing multi-donor funds for health and education, respectively, provide useful platforms for a more coherent and ambitious "systems

strengthening" approach that would give the Myanmar government a leading policy role while at the same time supporting diverse delivery mechanisms based on comparative advantages.

A. *Encourage inclusive governance processes.* Some might question why support for democracy is not included as one of the core programmes above. The issue of democracy, however, remains a vexed one. As much as the country is crying out for an antidote to half a century of dictatorial rule, the risks of expanding the space for free expression (and dissent) before developing the institutions necessary to fulfil pent-up popular expectations are high. Moreover, traditional democracy aid could easily backfire in Myanmar's highly nationalistic environment, certainly at this early stage in the transition process when spoilers remain powerful. While donors need to pay careful attention to the new "democratic" institutions to see what opportunities for engagement and support may arise, the smarter approach would be more generally to encourage and assist inclusive governance processes at all levels of government and in all areas of international assistance. This goes to the heart of democratic, and indeed "good", governance without the risk of upsetting the fragile political balance.

B. *Mainstream human rights and protection into all humanitarian and development activities.* Democracy without civil liberties is as hollow as economic growth without social justice, and both are all too common features of new democracies elsewhere in Asia and the world. Many aid agencies today hesitate to get involved in human rights work, fearing that it could cause a backlash from the authorities and disrupt their "core activities". Nevertheless, it has to be acknowledged that human rights abuses are a prime obstacle to development and poverty reduction in Myanmar, not only in the regions where there is armed conflict but all across the country. Importantly, existing work on areas such as forced labour, child soldiers (and child rights more generally), human trafficking, and land rights has clearly demonstrated that progress *is* possible.

C. *Invest heavily in capacity-building.* Whatever the objective, little is achievable in Myanmar today without simultaneously attending to the shortage of human and institutional resources. The repressive, top-down, and anti-intellectual governance style of past military governments, coupled with the collapse of the education system and the huge brain-drain that Myanmar has suffered over the years, means that basic governance capacity is lacking in most areas, both inside and outside the government. This is not to deny the skill and commitment of many individuals, but it is a systemic problem that will require capacity-building to be a central component of any and all of the programmes discussed above.

POSTSCRIPT

As this volume goes to press in May 2012, what seemed just a few months ago to be mainly a promise of change has morphed into the beginnings of a far more fundamental transformation of Myanmar politics and governance than anyone had imagined. The National League for Democracy (NLD), which boycotted the 2010 elections in protest over the non-democratic nature of the new constitution, has re-registered as a political party and will soon enter parliament as the biggest opposition party, after sweeping the recent by-elections by winning 43 of the 45 seats that had been vacated. (Aung San Suu Kyi, the leader of the NLD, won her seat with 85 per cent of the vote.) This will further energize the new parliament, which has already become a highly active forum for law- and policy-making, as well as for scrutiny of government actions, where even members of the government party and the military faction play an often-constructive role. Wider political liberalization has seen the emergence of a much more vigorous media, and has emboldened civil society to step up advocacy on important issues of public concern. Most importantly perhaps, there has been a seemingly decisive break-through in the peace negotiations with ethnic armed groups, which for the first time since Independence in 1948 raises a real possibility of country-wide peace, although much remains to be resolved for this to consolidate.

This picture of positive change is marred by continued violent clashes in some parts of Kachin and Shan states. Moreover, below the political level, bureaucratic inertia, incompetence, and major budgetary shortfalls continue to frustrate the implementation of new laws and policies, confirming the crucial importance not only of political and economic reforms, but also of fundamental behavioural and cultural change. However, with clear evidence of top-level political commitment to reform, the case for a new aid strategy has been bolstered. Indeed, any further donor hesitance to fully engage on a robust second-generation aid agenda would significantly retard the ability of progressive actors on the ground to respond to new opportunities in many of the areas outlined above.

Most urgently, there is a need to support state-building to stabilize the current reform drive and ensure ineffective policies and administrative shortcomings do not hold the country back at a time when so much now seems possible.

References

Allan, David. "Positive Engagement in Myanmar: Some Current Examples and Thoughts for the Future". In *Ruling Myanmar: From Cyclone Nargis to National Elections*, edited by Nick Cheesman, Monique Skidmore and Trevor Wilson. Singapore: Institute of Southeast Asian Studies, 2010.

Birgegard, Lars. "Poverty in Burma is Appalling". *Democratic Voice of Burma*, 31 August 2010 <http://www.dvb.no/analysis/poverty-in-burma-is-appalling/11499>. Accessed 3 June 2012.

Centre for Peace and Conflict Studies (Phnom Penh). *Listening to Voices from Inside: Myanmar Civil Society's Response to Cyclone Nargis.* <http://www.centrepeaceconflictstudies.org/fileadmin/downloads/pdfs/Cyclone_Nargis_and_Myanmar_Civil_Society_Response__1_.pdf>. Accessed 3 June 2012.

Dorning, Karl. "Creating an Environment for Participation: International NGOs and the Growth of Civil Society in Burma/Myanmar". In *Myanmar's Long Road to National Reconciliation*, edited by Trevor Wilson. Singapore: Institute of Southeast Asian Studies, 2006.

Duffield, M. "On the Edge of 'No Man's Land': Chronic Emergency in Myanmar". Working Paper No. 01-08. Global Insecurities Centre, University of Bristol, 2008.

Horsey, Richard. "The ILO and Forced Labour in Myanmar". In *Principled Engagement: Negotiating Human Rights in Pariah States*, edited by Morten B. Pedersen and David Kinley. Tokyo: United Nations University Press, forthcoming.

International Crisis Croup (ICG). *Myanmar: Major Reform Underway.* Asia Briefing No. 127, 22 September 2011. <http://www.crisisgroup.org/en/regions/asia/south-east-asia/burma-myanmar/B127-myanmar-major-reform-underway.aspx>. Accessed 10 April 2012.

————. *Burma/Myanmar after Nargis: Time to Normalise Aid Relations*, Asia Report No. 161, 20 October 2008. <http://www.crisisgroup.org/en/regions/asia/south-east-asia/burma-myanmar/161-burma-myanmar-after-nargis-time-to-normalise-aid-relations.aspx>. Accessed 10 April 2012.

————. *Myanmar: New Threats to Humanitarian Aid*, Asia Briefing No. 58, 8 December 2006. <http://www.crisisgroup.org/en/regions/asia/south-east-asia/burma-myanmar/B058-myanmar-new-threats-to-humanitarian-aid.aspx>. Accessed 10 April 2012.

————. *Myanmar: Sanctions, Engagement, or Another Way Forward.* Asia Report No. 78, 26 April 2004. <http://www.crisisgroup.org/en/regions/asia/south-

east-asia/burma-myanmar/078-myanmar-sanctions-engagement-or-another-way-forward.aspx>. Accessed 10 April 2012.

————. *Myanmar: The Politics of Humanitarian Aid*, Asia Report No. 32, 2 April 2002. <http://www.crisisgroup.org/en/regions/asia/south-east-asia/burma-myanmar/032-myanmar-the-politics-of-humanitarian-aid.aspx>. Accessed 10 April 2012.

————. *Myanmar: The Military Regime's View of the World*. Asia Report No. 28, 7 December 2001. <http://www.crisisgroup.org/en/regions/asia/south-east-asia/burma-myanmar/028-myanmar-the-military-regimes-view-of-the-world.aspx>. Accessed 10 April 2012.

Kramer, Tom. *Civil Society Gaining Ground*. Amsterdam: Trans National Institute. <http://www.tni.org/sites/www.tni.org/files/download/tni-2011-civil societygainingground-web2.pdf>. Accessed 10 April 2012.

Macan-Markar, Marwaan. "Donors View Civil Society in New Light after Nargis". *Inter Press Service*, 2 May 2010. <http://ipsnews.net/news.asp?idnews=51283>. Accessed 10 April 2012.

O'Neil, Robert. "Designs on Development". *Harvard Kennedy School Magazine*, Spring 2009. <http://www.hks.harvard.edu/news-events/news/alumni/jim-and-debbie-taylor>. Accessed 9 June 2012.

Open Letter from Non Governmental Organizations on U.S. Policy Toward Burma. 2009. Available on <http://www.refugeesinternational.org/node/3809>. Accessed 3 June 2012.

Pedersen, Morten B. "Burma/Myanmar: Aid, State Fragility and the Emerging Principles for Good Donor Engagement in Fragile States". Discussion paper presented at AusAID, Canberra, January 2010.

————. "Myanmar, the International Community, and Human Rights (with Particular Attention to the Role of Foreign Aid)". In *Finding Dollars, Sense, and Legitimacy In Myanmar*, edited by Susan Levenstein. Washington, D.C.: Woodrow Wilson International Center for Scholars, 2010.

South, Ashley. "Political Transition in Myanmar: A New Model for Democratization". *Contemporary Southeast Asia* 26, no. 2 (2004): 233–55.

Stallworthy, Guy. "NGO Perspective on Assistance in Burma/Myanmar". Paper prepared for the EC Burma Day Conference, European Commission, Brussels, 5 April 2005. <http://www.burmalibrary.org/docs3/Burma_Day-Stallworthy2.html>. Accessed 10 April 2012.

Wallis, Kim and Carine Jaquet. "Local NGOs in Myanmar: Vibrant but Vulnerable". *Humanitarian Exchange Magazine* 51, July 2011.

16

EU-MYANMAR RELATIONS IN A CHANGING WORLD
Time for Paradigm Shift

Thaung Tun

Relations between the European Union (EU) and Myanmar in 2011 are at their lowest ebb. The EU has maintained restrictive measures against Myanmar for over two decades, citing as justification egregious violations of human rights in the country and the lack of progress towards democratization. However, recent developments in Myanmar and the new environment in the EU present a window of opportunity for both Myanmar and the EU to drop the hubris of the past two decades and attempt a different approach.

In April 2011, at the annual review of the EU's sanctions policy on Myanmar, Germany, Italy, Spain, and Austria reportedly pushed for a new and pragmatic approach, while the United Kingdom, the Czech Republic, and others urged that sanctions be maintained. In the end, the sanctions were renewed, but a small concession was made by lifting the travel ban on some civilian leaders of Myanmar for one year, and a decision was taken to keep diplomatic channels open. An existing ban on EU officials visiting Myanmar was also lifted. But much more needs to be done.

A letter dated 11 March 2011 that was sent by the Myanmar-based Group of Democratic Party Friends (GDPF) to the EU, urging it to lift the sanctions, reflects the growing opposition within Myanmar to the sanctions regime. The GDPF has also called on the EU to restore Myanmar's Generalized System of Preferences (GSP) status.[1]

THE EVOLVING SITUATION IN MYANMAR: EU RESPONSES

Myanmar in 2011 is at a defining moment in its history. Elections have been held and the transition from military rule to a form of civilian government and constitutional rule has been initiated. On 30 March 2011, a new civilian government was sworn in. On the same day, the State Peace and Development Council (SPDC), the military council that had ruled Myanmar for over two decades, was disbanded. Senior General Than Shwe, the head of the armed forces, and his deputy, Vice Senior General Maung Aye, have relinquished their posts. The National League for Democracy (NLD) leader, Aung San Suu Kyi, has also been released from house arrest.

The More It Changes, the More It Remains the Same?

Elections were held on 7 November 2010. Those elections may not have measured up to the standards of free and fair elections in established democratic nations, but dismissing them out of hand, as many in the West have tended to do, is not objective. The fact remains that thirty-seven political parties took part in the process. They chose to participate, not out of a misguided belief that the elections organized by the military would be totally free and fair, but because it represented a sea change. While the candidates may be less than happy with the way in which the electoral process was carried out, they see some saving grace in that the establishment of new administrative structures could result in more political and economic space as the system takes root.

Some insist that the change in Myanmar is nothing but a smokescreen for continued military rule. The more it changes, the more it remains the same, they claim. Others believe that the transformation serves a useful purpose. They remain optimistic despite the retention of a number of former ministers and active-duty military officers in the new cabinet. The steps that have been taken, however small and tentative, cannot be discounted, considering that the country has been under one military administration or another since gaining independence in 1948. The decision of the new president to appoint civilians such as the former Chairman of the Union of Myanmar Federation of Chambers of Commerce and Industry to the cabinet is seen as significant.[2] Observers anticipate that more changes could follow with the generational shift in the leadership of the armed forces. General Min Aung Hlaing, a 53-year-old, has succeeded Senior General Than Shwe, who is 78, as Commander-in-Chief of the *Tatmadaw* (the Myanmar Armed Forces).

It is still too early to pass judgment on the effectiveness of the new parliament, but considering the significant number of proposals submitted and questions posed at the maiden session, it could become a useful forum, particularly at the State and Region level. Forty-six questions and 17 proposals were submitted in the lower house, while 33 questions and 16 proposals were submitted in the upper house. This was followed up by four days of questions and proposals in the Pyidaungsu Hluttaw (Union Parliament), the combined assemblies. What is noteworthy is that for the first time in decades, representatives from opposition parties and the military are rubbing shoulders. More importantly, representatives now have the possibility of raising questions regarding issues that concern their communities. The ministers have been pressed to respond to questions ranging from possible amnesty for prisoners to reasons why mobile phone costs are so excessive. This situation would have been unthinkable under the military regime. While the new legislatures are unlikely to make much difference to the lives of ordinary citizens in the immediate future, they are likely to lead to more political and economic space in the long run.

ECONOMIC DEVELOPMENTS OCCURRING DESPITE EU SANCTIONS

Notwithstanding the wide-ranging sanctions imposed by the EU and other Western countries, Myanmar has continued to attract investments from abroad. Foreign investment proposals soared to US$20 billion during the fiscal year 2010–11, a significant increase over the previous year, with the bulk of the funds coming from China. Chinese corporations are involved in a significant number of hydropower, mining, and oil and gas projects across the country. These projects include construction of dams, a railroad, and a large pipeline project across Myanmar, from the Bay of Bengal to Kunming, aimed at satisfying the increasing appetite for oil and gas in China's landlocked Yunnan province.[3]

On 27 April 2011, Myanmar and China signed a memorandum of understanding on a rail transport project extending from Kyaukphyu on the Bay of Bengal to Muse on the Myanmar-China border. The project is expected to be completed in three years. It will run in parallel with the ongoing China-Myanmar gas pipeline project from Kyaukphyu to Kunming in Yunnan Province. It is anticipated that the rail link will vastly improve China's ability to transport energy resources from suppliers in the Middle East and Myanmar. More importantly, it could provide an alternative route for transporting strategic resources and thus minimize the risk of over-dependence on sea lanes. Thailand, too, has increased its investment in Myanmar. The two countries have signed a framework agreement on building a deep seaport, industrial zone, and road and rail link to Thailand. The joint venture project area lies adjacent to the town of Dawei, in southern Myanmar. The proponents are Italian-Thai Construction Company (which built the Skytrain in Bangkok) and the Myanmar Port Authority. The project is to be carried out in three phases over a period of ten years on a build-operate-transfer (BOT) basis. The project, which includes a special economic zone, is estimated to cost US$13 billion.

Myanmar and India have also agreed on a multimodal transport project that will link the two countries. In April 2008, India and Myanmar signed an agreement on the US$110 million Kaladan multi-modal transit-cum-transport project, which would connect India's land-locked northeast with the southern coast of Myanmar. The project, funded by India, includes upgrading the port at Sittwe on the western coast of Myanmar as well as development of a 225 km-long waterway between the port of Sittwe and Kaletwa along the Kaladan River, which flows into Myanmar from the Indian province of Mizoram. The project also includes construction of a 62 km-long road from Setpyitpyin to Lawngtlai (a district in southwestern Mizoram, India), where the road will merge with India's National Highway 54. The Kaladan project will substantially reduce the transport time and the cost of transport between Kolkata and India's northeastern states.

When completed, the project will give India's northeastern provinces access to the sea and an opportunity to develop greater economic linkages with Southeast Asia. With the development of Sittwe port and the waterway towards India, Mizoram will be able to import rice directly from Myanmar, and this will further enhance border trade between the two countries. Sittwe will become a hub for traders and businessmen from northeast India to explore markets in Thailand, Malaysia, and Singapore, and vice-versa. More importantly, the opening of the Kaladan waterways will connect Myanmar and India as never before.

EU MISSING OUT BECAUSE OF ECONOMIC SANCTIONS

While Myanmar's neighbours, China, India, and Thailand, are becoming increasingly involved in Myanmar, the EU's influence has waned considerably. If the EU fails to take stock of the situation and does not adopt a more proactive stance, it will not only miss economic opportunities as Myanmar opens its doors to foreign investment, but will also find itself without leverage in a country that is strategically located between China and India. Until 1988, the EU enjoyed mutually beneficial relations with Myanmar as the U.K., Germany, and France were at the forefront of international assistance and development programmes in the country. However, relations deteriorated following the takeover by the armed forces in 1988. The EU took the regime to task for its iron-fisted policy in dealing with dissent, and in 1990 imposed an arms embargo. Subsequently, sanctions were instituted. The sanctions regime is anchored in the European Council's "Common Position", which was adopted on 28 October 1996. The Common Position reaffirmed the Council's decision of 1990 to expel all military personnel attached to Myanmar embassies in EU member states and to withdraw all military personnel attached to EU diplomatic missions in Myanmar, as well as an arms embargo. It introduced a visa ban on senior Myanmar government officials and their associates, a ban on non-humanitarian aid, an asset freeze, and a limited investment ban. In 2007, the EU further extended the ban to include investment in, or export of, equipment for the timber, mining, and gems industries.

EU Political Sanctions

The EU's involvement in Myanmar is two-pronged, one political and the other humanitarian. The political component is primary, and is aimed at "supporting the national reconciliation process, the introduction of a democratic order and the respect for human rights". The second component is aimed at supporting the most vulnerable members of society through humanitarian aid.

The EU has struggled to manage its policy options towards Myanmar, partly because the public policy environment was complex. Meaningful dialogue between the EU and Myanmar has not occurred, owing to a lack of engagement and the fixation of European countries with the issue of human rights. The complex structure of the EU is another contributing factor, as it is difficult for outsiders to fathom the workings of the organization. The leading institutions of the EU — the European Commission, the Council of the European Union, and the European Parliament — sometimes appear to produce dissonant voices. It is important, therefore, for Myanmar to appreciate that each of these institutions has a different mandate and represents different stake-holders, reflecting the diversity of the EU and the democratic system it represents. It should be noted that although the EU may adopt a common position on an issue like Myanmar, it is still an economic and political union of twenty-seven member-states. There are nuances in the position of each member state.

The EU essentially operates through seven institutions:

- The European Commission, which represents the voice of common interest, is composed of twenty-seven Commissioners for different policy areas, one from each member state. Theoretically, the Commissioners do not represent individual countries but the EU as a whole. The Commission is the executive branch of the EU and can be regarded as a government. In most policy matters, it takes the initiative to propose legislation. It is thus a key player with a substantial degree of independence.
- The Council of Ministers represents the member states;
- The European Council is the summit of Heads of State and Government along with the President of the European Commission;
- The European Parliament represents the voice of ordinary citizens at the grass-roots level. The 736 members of the European Parliament are directly elected by the people. The Parliament forms one half of the EU's legislature, the Council of the EU being the other half. The Parliament and the Council form and pass legislation jointly;
- The European Court of Justice which is the voice of law;
- The European Central Bank which is responsible for monetary policy covering the seventeen member states of the Eurozone;
- The Court of Auditors, which monitors the management of the EU budget.

EFFECTIVENESS OF THE EU'S MYANMAR POLICY

It is increasingly evident that two decades of EU sanctions have not only failed to nudge the military government towards wholesale democratic reforms but have also had a negative impact on small and medium businesses, resulting in hardships for ordinary Myanmar citizens. The EU's reliance on a single-strand policy that focuses mainly on human rights has greatly hindered the ability of European policy-makers and parliamentarians alike to adopt a multi-faceted approach that would open the way for the EU to play a more effective role. Ironically, the EU's internal practices have themselves become obstacles to finding an adequate policy towards Myanmar. The Common Position on Myanmar adopted by the European Council is often the lowest common denominator. It is the position of "the Most Interested Member State" that determines what course of action is to be pursued. Thus the EU policy line follows the domestic and foreign priority of that member state. Over the years, it has become clear that the EU is not monolithic. The dividing line between pro-engagement member states such as France and Germany and the pro-sanctions group led by the U.K. and the Netherlands has determined the policy on Myanmar at various levels in the Union.

The situation is further compounded by the fact that many Members of the European Parliament (MEP) involved in the Myanmar issue are closely associated with the British Parliament. Understandably, their attitude towards Myanmar is influenced by the fact that Aung San Suu Kyi's husband, Dr Michael Aris, was British. On many occasions, this fact has unfortunately led British MEPs to be particularly strident on Myanmar. Different advocacy groups and labour unions have also maintained pressure on the European Parliament (EP). As a result, the EP remains the harshest critic of the military regime.

However, constant criticism has only strengthened the resolve of the Myanmar military to run Myanmar in their own way. Despite the embargoes and restrictions, the Myanmar Government has been able to further consolidate its position, particularly in the last decade, as it has been able to draw on substantial revenues from the sale of gas to Thailand. More importantly, it enjoys excellent relations with both China and India, two of the world's fastest growing economies.

In practical terms as well, the EU's policy of further isolating a country that is one of the most self-contained countries in the world is counter-productive. The move to discourage tourists from visiting Myanmar and bar investments in labour-intensive industries has resulted in the loss of livelihood for tens of thousands of workers. According to the Myanmar Garment Manufacturers Association, the decision to tighten sanctions left more than 85,000 garment industry workers jobless. It was estimated that 95 to 98 per cent of these workers were women, mostly aged between 18 and 35.[4] Sanctions are unacceptable from a humanitarian point of view as well since their effectiveness necessarily entails considerable human suffering, while the likelihood of their achieving political objectives is low. This is quite apparent in the case of Myanmar. Sanctions hurt the population at large. On the other hand, the EU attempt to provide humanitarian aid in an impartial manner through the European Community Humanitarian Office (ECHO) has had no problems. ECHO has been funding relief programmes in Myanmar since 1994 to the tune of €110 million. ECHO opened an office in Yangon in 2005 to facilitate the delivery of European humanitarian aid, and ECHO's success demonstrates what can be done in Myanmar if there is sufficient mutual confidence.

Notwithstanding, the EU continues to maintain sanctions as a weapon of choice. Sanctions are politically less problematic, and less costly, than military intervention. Myanmar considers the sanctions unjust and morally indefensible. The Myanmar government perceives the EU as employing sanctions for political gain at home and using Myanmar as an easy whipping boy. Critics would argue that the EU is particularly harsh on Myanmar in order to make a point to larger powers against which it cannot envisage the use of sanctions. The perception is strengthened by the fact that the EU employs different yardsticks for different countries, depending on strategic considerations. Myanmar sees this approach as a bullying tactic that is actually counter-productive. It has not worked for the past two decades.

Advocacy and Lobby Groups and the Media

In the EU policy-making system, national governments and the EU institutions are not the only players in the policy-making process. Non-governmental organizations (NGOs), civil advocacy groups, and the media all play influential roles. European NGOs and civil advocacy groups are among the most organized and well funded in the world. Their record in winning both moral support and funding for their causes is impressive. Numerous think-tanks and exile groups also form part of the system.

Organizations such as the UK-based Amnesty International, the Brussels-based International Confederation of Free Trade Unions (ICFTU), and the Burma Campaign UK are also part of the equation. The ascendency of modern communications technology and the coming-of-age of the Internet mean that information can be disseminated quickly and effectively.

The media has always had a big role in shaping public opinion in Europe, but this has grown significantly in both scale and importance in recent decades. Lobby groups and interest groups often take advantage of the media to present their case. Interest groups also find a welcome reception in the offices of the MEPs, who share the same concerns and are ready to support such popular causes as human rights and democracy. Those who wish to influence the outcome of the debate in the European Parliament concentrate their efforts on the rapporteurs of the committees concerned. Additionally, ordinary citizens and interest groups have no trouble in getting access to the European Parliament in Brussels.

To a large extent the national governments of the member-states of the EU still retain their dominant position in the EU political process, particularly when politically sensitive measures are involved. Each member has its interest and seeks to convey this through national governments. Invariably, different countries have different interests based on their size and strategic importance. Historical and colonial ties often shape the outlook of a particular member country towards a third country. Thus the U.K. is linked to Myanmar, just as Spain is to Cuba, and France to its former colonies in Africa.

Member countries also have specialists who are able to network and to interact among themselves. They maintain contact daily. Each member state also has a Permanent Representative to the EU in Brussels. They are an important link in the policy coordination process. In recent years, the role of the Permanent Representative has grown as the EU has become a global player, and policy-makers increasingly use Brussels to further their political and economic objectives. Although the European Council is the institution where all foreign policy decisions are adopted formally, the Committee of Permanent Representatives of the member-states has a key role to play, as it prepares the agenda of the Council meetings and influences the outcome of the meetings. Decisions are usually taken in the Committee of Permanent Representatives before they are presented to the Council for approval. While the EU decision process allows for deliberation of an issue at various levels, in practice it is based on consensus. The country holding the presidency generally has responsibility for coordinating the EU's foreign policy. In the past, when the presidency was rotated every six months, achieving consensus in policy towards a third country presented difficulties. It is too early to say how the new presidency will affect the EU's approach to Myanmar, and how the new administration in Naypitaw will react.

Creation of the European External Action Service

In the past, the EU lacked a lead organization to oversee its relations with other countries. The Commissioner for External Relations, the EU High Representative for Common Foreign and Security Policy, the rotating EU presidency, and the various EU members' Ministries of Foreign Affairs vied with one another in the formulation of a strategy towards a third country. However, one of the innovations of the new Lisbon Treaty is the creation of a new European External Action Service (EEAS), intended as a diplomatic corps that will oversee not only Europe's huge aid and humanitarian budget but also relations with countries around the world. With the advent of the EEAS on 1 January 2011, the EU is likely to have a more coordinated foreign relations approach. The new body is slated to oversee Europe's relations with countries around the world. Again, it is too early to say whether this will result in a substantive change of policy towards Myanmar.

CONCLUSION

In light of the transformations taking place in Myanmar and the recent changes in the EU, it is opportune for both sides to take a different approach. In keeping with the EU's policy of encouraging trade and helping the least developed countries to improve their infrastructure, thus developing their productive potential and making their public administration institutions more efficient, it should reconsider its sanctions policy. It is only when the masses are lifted out of poverty and the gap between the rich and the poor is narrowed that democracy can thrive.

The advent of a new administration in Myanmar and developments in the EU present a window of opportunity for both Myanmar and the EU to attempt a different approach to nurture mutually beneficial relations. External assistance could help Myanmar develop at a faster pace and turn its faltering steps towards democracy into firm strides.

In this context, the low amount of official development assistance (ODA) which Myanmar receives each year is an indicator of the pressures that the country has had to bear. In 2007, the total of all ODA given to Myanmar was US$4 per head. The figure rose to US$11 in 2008, largely due to the international relief aid following Cyclone Nargis. Even then it was substantially below the per capita amount received by Myanmar's neighbours in 2007 — Viet Nam received US$29, Cambodia US$46, and Laos US$68. The challenge for Myanmar is compounded as neither the World Bank nor the International Monetary Fund (IMF) is currently assisting Myanmar. The same is true of the Asian Development Bank (ADB). If the EU is serious about helping the people of Myanmar, it should commit itself to a comprehensive approach, including a rethink of the sanctions policy, an offer of structural and technical aid, the development of human resources and the promotion of investment and trade.

As a first step, the EU should move to reinstate the General System of Preferences for Myanmar. In the first instance, GSP privileges were withdrawn from Myanmar as it was believed that forced labour prevailed in the country. While the possible use of porters by the military in the field remains a concern (and the ILO is grappling with that issue), the government has been taking steps to redress the situation. Why then deny GSP privileges to the private sector in Myanmar, particularly if it is generally accepted that the GSP encourages sustainable development and good governance in vulnerable developing countries? At the time of writing, 176 countries benefit from preferential access under the GSP. The "Everything but Arms" (EBA) regulation under the GSP scheme offers free market access, without duties and quotas, to the forty-nine least developed countries. Myanmar belongs to the group of least developed countries but has been denied this privilege. Restitution of GSP privileges will not resolve Myanmar's economic problems but it would go a long way towards relieving the pressure on the privately-owned garment factories and fisheries businesses that provide jobs for thousands of workers.

Areas where external assistance could help Myanmar turn faltering steps into firmer strides, and where the EU obviously has relevant experience, include *inter alia*:

- basic human needs: support the government's efforts to provide primary health care and basic education;
- development of human resources;

- modernization of the civil service;
- establishment of legal and institutional underpinnings for a market economy;
- reform of the agriculture sector;
- promotion of trade and tourism.

An effective development assistance programme must begin with the recognition that the situation in Myanmar is complex, and must take into account the political, economic, and cultural realities on the ground. The success of the tripartite cooperation among Myanmar, ASEAN, and the United Nations in the aftermath of Cyclone Nargis, which devastated parts of Myanmar in 2008, illustrates how a win-win situation can be achieved with mutual confidence and understanding.

The EU needs to take note of the changes taking place in Myanmar and live up to its role as a global player. Myanmar, for its part, needs to initiate steps to inspire confidence in its political and economic transition, and demonstrate its commitment to reform. Myanmar may be a resource-rich country but it needs foreign direct investment and technology transfer from the developed countries to jump-start its economy if it is to catch up with the fast-growing economies in its region.

Notes

1. The GDPF is an alliance of ten democratic political parties in Myanmar which won seats in the November 2010 elections. The alliance expressed concern about sanctions and restrictive policies of a generalized nature which affect the population in labour-intensive industries such as garments and seafood, and which broadly discourage tourism, trade, and investment, to the detriment of the well-being of the population at large. "If the EU grants GSP status to Burma again, ordinary people will gain great advantages", said Dr Than Nyein, the chairman of the National Democratic Force party. "Moreover, small and medium-sized businesses will get into the European market. If our goods are exempted from duty, we will have great opportunities".

2. U Win Myint, a well-known businessman, was appointed Minister for Commerce.

3. Burma received a record US$20 billion in foreign investment in the fiscal year ending March 2011. Neighbouring China was the biggest foreign investor, and most of its investment is directed to power projects. China invested US$8.27 billion, followed by Hong Kong with US$5.39 billion, and Thailand with US$2.94 billion, according to the Ministry of National Planning Development.

4. *Myanmar Times*, 562, 14–20 February 2011.

References

Camroux, David and Renaud Egreteau. "Normative Europe meets the Burmese garrison state: Processes, policies, blockages and future possibilities". In *Ruling Myanmar: From Cyclone Nargis to National Elections*, edited by N. Cheesman, M. Skidmore and T. Wilson. Singapore: Institute of Southeast Asian Studies, 2010.

Egreteau, Renaud. "Intra-European Bargaining and the Tower of Babel: EU's Approach to the Burmese Conundrum". *East Asia* 27, no. 1 (2010).

Frittin, Agnes and Christopher O'Hara. "The Myanmar-EU Roadmap: New Possibilities in a Changing Myanmar". Institute for Security and Development Policy (ISDP), Stockholm. *ISDP Policy Brief*, No. 52, 24 January 2011. <http://www.isdp.eu/publications/index.php?option=com_jombib&task=showbib&id=5917>. Accessed 3 June 2012.

Frittin, Agnes and Niklas Swanström. "Offering Trade Benefits for More Inclusive Elections: EU Trade Sanctions against Myanmar Hit the Wrong Targets". Institute for Security and Development Policy (ISDP), Stockholm. *ISDP Policy Brief*, No. 32, 2 June 2010. <http://www.isdp.eu/images/stories/isdp-main-pdf/2010_frittin-swanstrom_offering-trade-benefits.pdf>. Accessed 3 June 2012.

Mälarstedt, Andreas and Ebba Mårtensson. "From Sanctions to Engagement: The Need for a New Policy towards Myanmar". Institute for Security and Development Policy (ISDP), Stockholm. *ISDP Policy Brief*, No. 50, 12 January 2011. <http://www.isdp.eu/publications/index.php?option=com_jombib&task=showbib&id=5883>. Accessed 3 June 2012.

Pedersen, Morten. *Promoting Human Rights in Burma: A Critique of Western Sanctions Policy*. Lanham, MD: Rowman & Littlefield Publishers, 2008.

Smith. Karen E. *European Union Foreign Policy in a Changing World*. Cambridge UK: Polity, 2003.

Steinberg, David. "International Rivalries in Burma — The Rise of Economic Competition". *Asian Survey* 30, no. 6 (1990).

17

PROSPECTS FOR A POLICY OF ENGAGEMENT WITH MYANMAR
A Multilateral Development Bank Perspective

Adam Simpson[*]

The Asian Development Bank (ADB) is the region's most significant multilateral development bank (MDB), providing financing and expertise that supports projects and programmes across Southeast Asia. Since the mid-1980s, however, neither the ADB nor the World Bank has provided significant direct assistance to Myanmar.[†] Although it is in arrears to both banks — approximately US$450 million to the ADB and US$373 million to the World Bank — these arrears could be waived, as has been done for other countries, if a political consensus of donor countries was reached. The real reason for the lack of engagement stems from the sanctions regimes against Myanmar of the major Western donor countries, particularly the United States. Through its Greater Mekong Subregion (GMS) project,[1] the ADB still provides small amounts of indirect technical assistance to non-government actors in Myanmar, but because of the sanctions, this is relatively insignificant compared with the direct assistance provided to other non-democratic GMS states such as Laos and Vietnam. Much of this indirect assistance relates to proposed "economic corridors" such as the East-West Economic Corridor (EWEC), a GMS Flagship Initiative that aims to facilitate trade and investment and reduce poverty across Myanmar, Thailand, Laos, and Vietnam (Asian Development Bank 2010*d*; 2010*e*).

While the MDBs and Western interests stay away, the economy of Myanmar has been dominated by Asian corporations, primarily from China and Thailand, investing in Myanmar's burgeoning cross-border energy market (Simpson 2013*b*). These investments are undertaken with little social or environmental assessment, making the ADB's procedures, such as its social and environmental safeguards (Asian Development Bank 2009*b*), virtuous in comparison. Any kind of investment in Myanmar is difficult, however, due to the challenging international and domestic political environments that face both private and public actors (Cheesman, Skidmore and Wilson 2010; Roberts 2010). The long-term effectiveness of MDBs can be dependent on the perceived integrity of their reputations as good institutional citizens, and as public organizations they face a large array of competing interests and elements that require consideration. In particular, they are judged on their ability to raise communities out of poverty. As the regional bank, the ADB has the potential to make a significant contribution to Myanmar's future poverty alleviation and development, but the bank has been criticized for promoting inequitable development even in less authoritarian environments (see, for example, Oehlers 2006; Raman 2009; Rosser 2009; Simpson 2007), so the challenge to promote equitable development in Myanmar remains significant.

To engage successfully with Myanmar, the ADB must satisfy both its donors and the Myanmar government that it is promoting development in the country. Western donor governments, however, also require evidence of positive political change before they will agree to fund projects in Myanmar. The ADB has, therefore, been hesitant to engage in Myanmar's domestic political debates, yet it has met with opposition leader Aung San Suu Kyi, who is potentially open to ADB engagement if it demonstrably benefits the general population. These activities could include assisting the exchange rate unification process or updating the country's agricultural programme, although the GMS economic corridors programme has the advantage of an existing framework and greater integration with the region. Most activist groups argue, however, that the ADB should avoid further engagement until there are significant improvements in human rights in the country (Bourne 2011). Although the long-running civil conflict still rages in the east of the country, and new areas of conflict such as in Kachin State have opened up, the domestic political environment in Myanmar has eased significantly following the flawed national elections in November 2010.

These elections resulted in the transfer of formal political power from a military junta to a "civilian" government, although many of the most powerful new politicians are former generals. There are still limitations on political and economic freedoms in Myanmar that would qualify it as authoritarian under some measures, but according to past and present International Labour Organization (ILO) Liaison Officers based in Yangon, there is now a "new level of scrutiny" of government that has accompanied the new parliament (Horsey 2011, p. 4).[2] Throughout 2011 the new government, led by President Thein Sein, instigated a number of progressive democratic reforms and the entrance to parliament of Aung San Suu Kyi and other National League for Democracy members in by-elections in April 2012 bolstered the reform process. Given the dominance of the military in all sectors throughout the country, there are unlikely to be any other more significant shifts in the domestic political system in the near future, so the best prospects for improved governance are to leverage change through the present political openings (Pedersen 2011, pp. 64–65). While there are undoubted difficulties with the operations of MDBs in authoritarian states, the risks of unjust outcomes when considering ADB funding in Myanmar must be balanced against the current unchecked investment environment. The ADB's policies and processes have also improved considerably since its much maligned engagement with Vietnam in 1993 (Raman 2009, p. 286), largely as a result of civil society and academic critiques. While the possibilities for promoting equitable development and genuine transparency and democracy in Myanmar may be limited, the recent strategies of the ADB and its Western donor governments have proved ineffectual. This chapter therefore discusses the opportunities and pitfalls associated with potential ADB investment in Myanmar, particularly in relation to Greater Mekong Subregion programmes such as the East-West Economic Corridor. It argues that, despite the risks, the ADB should pursue its stated goal of poverty reduction through full engagement with Myanmar, accompanied by the ADB's full social and environmental safeguards and the democratic oversight of civil society and donor governments.

THE ASIAN DEVELOPMENT BANK

As distributors of state funds, MDBs are essentially inter-governmental organizations, and therefore their approach to development can be seen as an extension of government policies. The ADB's shares are dominated by the United States and Japan, each of whom has almost 13 per cent of the voting rights, while other regional economic powers Australia, China, India, and Indonesia have approximately 5 per cent each (Asian Development Bank 2009a). With a strong presence both in the bank and the region, however, the United States plays a central role in determining ADB directions, and its policy of isolating Myanmar over much of the last two decades has ensured that little overt ADB funding has entered Myanmar over this time. Despite Myanmar's demonstrable need for development funding, most Western-dominated funding agencies, such as the United Nations Development Programme (UNDP), have been severely restricted in their activities there (International Crisis Group 2011, p. 10).

The role of the ADB in "fragile states" or "weakly performing countries" is, however, contentious; Rosser (2009, p. 377), for example, argues that the ADB has adopted a coercive neo-liberal approach "driven primarily by a concern to manage the risks to developed countries posed by instability, conflict, crime and disease in fragile states, rather than developmental considerations". If this is really the overriding concern of the ADB, then developed countries obviously see little risk of contagion from the maladies facing Myanmar, as Myanmar has received no funding under this programme despite satisfying many of the requirements — having weak governance, weak rule of law, and civil unrest, particularly in ethnic areas. Likewise, although it has been a UN-designated Least Developed Country (LDC) since 1987, Myanmar remains absent from participation in the Asian Development Fund (ADF), which was set up specifically by the ADB to fund both fragile states and other developing member countries to "promote poverty reduction and improvements in the quality of life in the poorer countries of the Asia and Pacific region" (Asian Development Bank 2010b). Despite Myanmar being ranked 132 out of 169 countries on the Human Development Index (UNDP 2010), it has become something of a pariah state for official ADB funding policy, to the extent that Myanmar's gross national income (GNI) is no longer recorded (although this is also a consequence of Myanmar's fictional statistical reporting (Turnell 2010)). While there is little doubt that numerous political, economic, and environmental constraints affect the ADB's stated aim of poverty reduction throughout the GMS (Oehlers 2006, pp. 466–67), most of this activity has bypassed Myanmar anyway, leaving it largely devoid of funding from public organizations.

The focus on neo-liberal approaches within the ADB and World Bank, as, for example, with the visible extension of market economics in the region promoted through the Nam Theun 2 (NT2) Hydropower Project in Laos, has already been criticized both by activists and academics. The NT2 dam is one of the most significant single infrastructure projects within the GMS and received ADB support (despite on-going misgivings within the organization) through the provision of technical assistance and US$120 million in loans and guarantees (Asian Development Bank 2010a; Simpson 2007). An independent report found that the ADB's involvement in tree plantations in Laos actually increased poverty by replacing villagers' land with monocultures and destroying livelihoods (Lang and Shoemaker 2006). Past analysis also suggests that any future involvement by the ADB in Myanmar is at significant risk of causing "reverse aid", with the cost of ADB-tied procurements to be borne by Myanmar and most of the contracts going to transnational corporations (TNCs) based in donor countries (Raman 2009, p. 299). There is some evidence, however, that the ADB, like the World Bank (Ehrentraut 2011; Park 2010), has attempted to address this sort of criticism, in part by creating a recently revised Accountability Mechanism for local communities potentially adversely affected by ADB-funded development projects (Asian Development Bank 2012).

Despite any procedural improvements, however, any major developments in which the ADB or the World Bank invest within illiberal countries such as Laos and Myanmar are still likely to significantly increase risks for the human and environmental security of local communities, who often face relocation from what are usually ancestral lands. This is an important consideration for the largely animist Karen in the area of eastern Myanmar through which the EWEC travels (Simpson 2004, p. 31). Nevertheless, these risks must be balanced against the risks associated with major projects that proceed without MDB oversight, something that is increasingly likely in view of growing business interest in Myanmar from throughout the region.

MISSING THE BOAT

There is a line-up of Chinese, Thai, Indian, and Singaporean TNCs, as well as many others, waiting to invest in Myanmar. Chinese investments in oil, gas, and hydropower are all significant (Simpson 2008; Turnell 2007) and while domestic activism convinced the Chinese government to suspend (at least temporarily) hydropower projects on the Nu River in China (Mertha 2009, pp. 1002–06; Watts 2011), there is little evidence that this pressure has had any influence on its infrastructure development agenda downstream, although China's Myitsone dam on the Irrawaddy River was likewise suspended by President Thein Sein. While there is a vocal and effective civil society in the United States, and on the Thai–Myanmar border, that has largely argued against engagement with Myanmar,[3] the sanctions regime is unlikely to be extended to public and private actors linked to the Chinese state. In part this is because, until recently, no effective counter-lobby in Washington promoting engagement had gained political traction there.[4] It is also because, as Steinberg (2010, p. 175) notes, Myanmar is a minor issue in world politics, being "small, specialized and fashionable". The priorities for U.S. diplomacy with China are Iran, North Korea, trade, currency appreciation, and climate change, with domestic circumstances in Myanmar being relatively insignificant.

The United States and the European Union (EU) have both had sanctions regimes that must be renewed annually, which allows for relatively easy removal. Sanctions were renewed once again in 2011, although in early 2012 the EU suspended its sanctions for twelve months to encourage the political reform process. Section 5 of the U.S. Burmese Freedom and Democracy Act (2003) calls on the U.S. representative at international financial institutions "to oppose, and vote against the extension by such institution of any loan or financial or technical assistance to Burma", which leaves the ADB and World Bank without U.S. support for any significant engagement, although they both participated in the assessment and recovery activities following Cyclone Nargis in 2008 (Sabandar 2010, pp. 199–200). The U.S. vote at these institutions does not constitute a formal veto, but it influences other Western countries in the ADB. One such ally is Australia, which has only five per cent of the ADB's voting rights but is nevertheless the biggest Western country and donor from the region. Since 2007 Australia has maintained financial sanctions on a list of individuals in the military or close to the regime; following a review in 2008, the list comprised 463 people (Reserve Bank of Australia 2008), but this was reduced to 130 after the April 2012 by-elections. Australia has recently increased its engagement in other respects, with a 50 per cent increase in foreign aid to $49 million in 2010–11 and 2011–12 (Rudd 2011, p. 39). Aid from the United States is also increasing. Nevertheless, as a result of the ADB's sanctions and opposition within the ADB, Myanmar was unable to host the GMS meeting that was due in Yangon in 2010, although it hosted a meeting in late 2011 with the support of Thailand and other ASEAN countries.

Because of the sanctions regime, most ADB staff have not been permitted to visit Myanmar unless accompanying an International Monetary Fund (IMF) team as part of the IMF's annual Article IV consultations or as part of a GMS programme, which significantly limited any potential influence. The danger that MDBs and the West face in Myanmar, however, is that they will become increasingly irrelevant as Asian interests provide the political and economic linkages that the Myanmar government seeks. There is little doubt that the locus of economic activity in the recent past, and for the foreseeable future, lies predominantly in Asia rather than in the Western world, and that China has been the dominant force in this transformation. What has not been adequately addressed by many organizations and civil society institutions and governments in the West is the impact that this shift has had on the ability of the West to impose its will on less compliant states such as Myanmar. While the United States remains, for now, the global leader in economic and military power and reach, its supremacy in Asia is being whittled away as a result of China's increasing role in the region (Kang 2010; Miller 2010).

Under Obama, the United States has tried to separate its relations with ASEAN in general from its specific policies on Myanmar (Clapp 2010, p. 413), but this, too, is a recognition of retreating U.S. influence. As for advancing human rights in ASEAN, Katsumata (2009) argues that the ability of the West to apply greater material pressure is diminishing with the rise of an East Asian community centred on the ASEAN–China concord. He also argues, however, that pressure within the normative environment, focused on human rights as a pre-requisite for international legitimacy, is likely to have greater success. Despite the military having successfully consolidated its power in Myanmar (Harn Yawnghwe 2010, p. 432; McCarthy 2008; Selth 2008), there is some evidence that this strategy has the potential to initiate incremental change. For example, despite being prepared "to go to the brink" in its relationship with the ILO (Wilson 2006, p. 83), the military regime relented under threat of action in the International Court of Justice and signed a Supplementary Understanding in February 2007 that gave ILO representatives and domestic workers protections hitherto denied.[5]

Both within ASEAN and even within the Myanmar military itself there are concerns over the increasingly dominant influence of China in the region, and this concern may be the main leverage Western countries can apply (Katsumata 2009, p. 630; Roberts 2010; Wilson 2006). The worst outcome for ASEAN would be that Myanmar becomes China's proxy. In this respect, ASEAN needs Myanmar at least as much as, if not more than, Myanmar needs ASEAN. Investments by ASEAN countries in Myanmar have therefore also increased dramatically, with the result that economic sanctions that have been applied by the United States and Europe to disrupt the economic fortunes of Myanmar's elites are largely ineffectual. Despite arguments in favour of isolating the Myanmar regime from activists based largely in the West (Task Force on U.S. Policy toward Burma/Myanmar 2010), this approach has little chance of achieving its goal. Any significant leverage in this regard came to an end when the revenues from the Yadana Gas Pipeline started flowing to Myanmar at the turn of the millennium, ushering in an era of resource-based foreign exchange income that has proved a lifeline for the regime (Simpson 2013b). Although the National League for Democracy (NLD) and other domestic opposition groups continue to support some sanctions, there are signs that some movement may be forthcoming. Aye Tha Aung, secretary of both the Committee Representing the People's Parliament (CRPP) and the Arakan League for Democracy (ALD), acknowledges that sanctions are "not as effective as they should be due to China, India and Thailand" and that if MDBs manage to bring more transparency, engagement with the ADB "could be worth it".[6] Regardless of how the opposition in Myanmar moves, the regime does not need ADB or World Bank funding to maintain its dominant role in the country, although it knows such assistance would promote the country's development, so there is little economic leverage to be gained by continued isolation.

OPPORTUNITIES FOR ENGAGEMENT: ECONOMIC CORRIDORS

The ADB's Greater Mekong Subregion programme is dominated by large-scale transport and energy projects, with a significant element in the programme being the development of a series of economic corridors that criss-cross the region, with the Northern, Western, Southern and East-West Economic Corridors passing through Myanmar. Although the Southern Economic Corridor (SEC) has received a fillip through the proposed Dawei Development Project in southern Myanmar, the East–West Economic

Corridor (EWEC) is in some respects the most developed of the projects, and is therefore the subject of more detailed analysis in this chapter. The East-West Economic Corridor was launched in 1998 as one of the Flagship Initiatives of the Greater Mekong Subregion, and according to the ADB:

> [i]t has adopted a holistic approach to developing a cost-effective way of instituting an efficient transport system for moving goods and people in the subregion, while simultaneously developing telecommunications and energy infrastructure, tourism, and a policy and regulatory environment that facilitates and encourages private sector development (Asian Development Bank 2010e, p. 6).

The EWEC is centred on the East–West Transport Corridor that runs from Da Nang in Vietnam, through Laos and Thailand, to Myawaddy in Karen State on the Myanmar side of the Thai border, then through Thingannyinaung and Kawkareik to Mawlamyine on the Myanmar coast (see Figure 17.1). Progress on Myanmar projects linked to the EWEC has been limited, in part due to a lack of expertise in the Myanmar government, but also in part to its *ad hoc* and arbitrary policy-making. Significant port expansion at the "gateway node" of Mawlamyine was expected under earlier agreements with the government, but was listed under "little or no implementation" in the most recent EWEC report (Asian Development Bank 2001; 2010e, pp. 10–11). Similarly, industrial zones were announced in Mawlamyine and Myawaddy (Lubeigt 2006), but Mawlamyine is not even mentioned in the latest report, while Myawaddy has been constrained, according to the ADB, by the Myanmar government's "restrictive policies on businesses, especially foreign-owned ones" (Asian Development Bank 2010e, p. 72).

It is not only government incompetence that has restricted activity, but also the practicalities of construction in Karen State itself. In the updated *Vientiane Plan of Action for GMS Development* the twenty-first transport project listed is the Thingannyinaung-Kawkareik leg of the EWEC in Myanmar, which is to be undertaken with Thai funding (Greater Mekong Subregion 2010, p. 6). Thai assistance had already ensured that the relatively flat 18-kilometre stretch of road west from Myawaddy to Thingannyinaung was completed in 2006 and that by mid-2007 a 40-kilometre stretch through the Dawna mountain range to Kawkareik had been surveyed and designed (Greater Mekong Subregion 2010, p. 92). Until this road is built, traffic on the existing road can travel in only one direction at a time, with the direction changing each day, but the insurgent Karen National Union (KNU) and its armed wing, the Karen National Liberation Army (KNLA), is active

FIGURE 17.1
Southern and East-West Economic Corridors

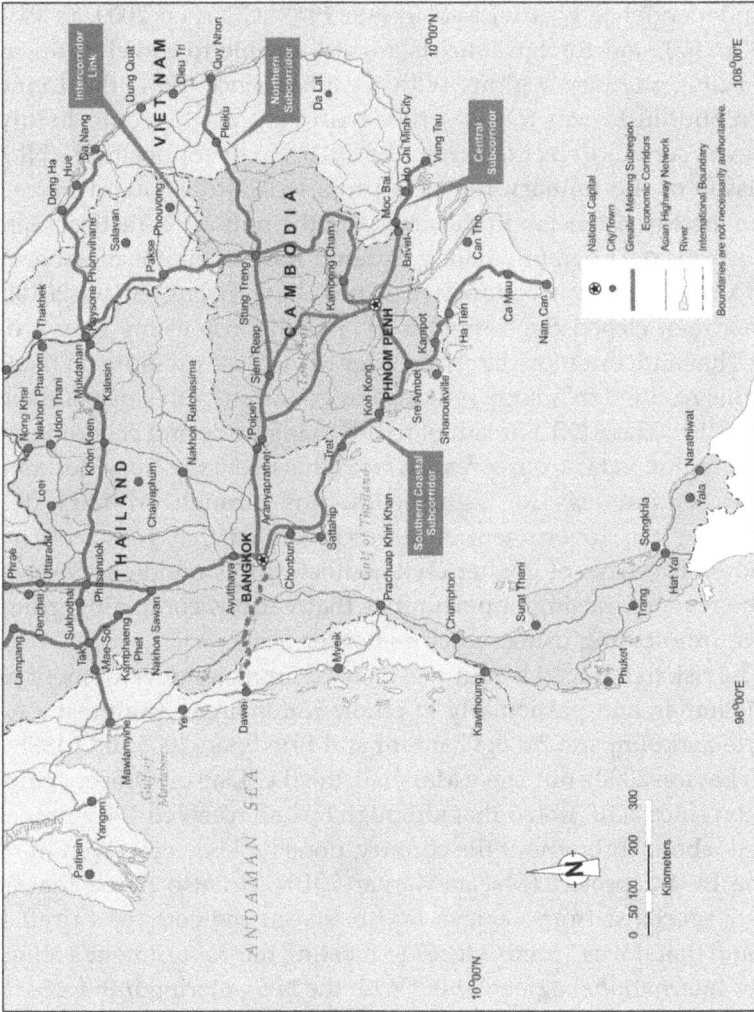

Source: Asian Development Bank (2010c). Reproduced with permission of the Asian Development Bank.

in these mountains and, according to exiled Karen activists, any further construction awaits KNU approval.[7]

This stretch of the road, and much of the Myanmar leg of the road corridor, has been fraught with civil conflict ever since the KNU's demand for independence was refused in late 1948 (Charney 2009, p. 74; South 2009, p. 37), and foreign tourists are still unable to travel in this region. The ruling military regime, with its allies since 1994, the Democratic Karen Buddhist Army (DKBA), nominally controls this route. In July 2010, however, serious defections from the DKBA to the opposition KNLA over the issue of the military regime's proposed Border Guard Force (BGF) led to increased tension in the area, and the military's Tactical Operation Command in Thingannyinaung ordered the remaining members of the DKBA not to carry weapons when travelling (Weng 2010a; 2010b). The regime then closed the border at Myawaddy, ostensibly over a dispute with Thailand, but more likely in order to increase pressure on the DKBA, and this resulted in a large build-up of goods on both sides of the border (Yeni 2010). The ADB's dream of free-flowing trade and economic activity in this region is far from a reality, with this normally busy border closed almost continuously for eighteen months through arbitrary decision-making by the government and a civil conflict that goes back over six decades. The risks of greater civil conflict in this region are exacerbated by the revenue-raising opportunities that various competing groups can derive from taxing increased cross-border trade.

The risk that forced labour will be used for major development projects in Myanmar, and particularly in ethnic Karen areas, is almost inevitable (Doyle and Simpson 2006; Giannini and Friedman 2005; ILO 1998; KWO 2007; Layton 2000), but Steve Marshall, the ILO Liaison Officer stationed in Yangon since 2007, noted that although he had received 430 complaints of forced labour throughout the country, none had been received in relation to the EWEC project (Macan-Markar 2010). He also noted that an ILO labour specialist from Geneva had overseen the country's draft labour law and that it was "pretty close" to meeting the government's obligations under international agreements.[8] With the law entering into force in early 2012 and the ILO's labour rights brochure now being produced in ethnic languages (only after stiff resistance from the government), Marshall sees the potential for reducing forced labour across Myanmar. Although there are no guarantees of probity in a country like Myanmar, the prospect of having a fully-engaged ADB focus attention on the EWEC has the potential to raise labour standards, not only on this project but also for other projects throughout the country.

While the ADB has provided much of the technical assistance for the EWEC transport corridor, its more important role for transnational capital, as with the NT2 dam, is to mitigate international risk. Rather, it has been the Japan Bank for International Cooperation (JBIC), in addition to the Thai contribution in Myanmar, that have provided the main funding across the EWEC, accounting for about 80 per cent of the US$900 million allocated for transport infrastructure. The ADB sees the role of the EWEC as providing an environment that will stimulate sustained private sector-led growth, but it argues that its development financing for the corridor is focused

> on the reduction of poverty, development of rural and border areas, improvements in the earnings of low income and vulnerable groups, including the provision of jobs for women, and the promotion of tourism along the corridor (Asian Development Bank 2010e, pp. 23–24).

These are principled aims, but a 2009 report commissioned by the ADB throws doubts on the ability of a road corridor to achieve some of these goals, particularly in relation to women, where poverty is often concentrated. With a small technical assistance loan paid from the ADB's GMS economic corridor funding (via Singapore), Win Myo Thu, founder of the Myanmar-based non-government organization Economically Progressive Ecosystem Development (ECODEV), studied the impact of regional cross-border road networking development in Myanmar (ECODEV 2010). In particular, he researched the impacts on accessibility and mobility of both women and men and found that, statistically, it helped both areas for men but that it did not help the mobility of women (Win Myo Thu 2010, p. 29).[9]

The provision of cross-border roads may, therefore, exacerbate gender inequalities, which could drive more women into poverty and be a key barrier to achieving the aims set out above. Better highway access to remote areas has also been shown to potentially increase female prostitution, trafficking, and the spread of HIV, with Myanmar's border region areas being highly susceptible (Barcellos and others 2010, p. 9).[10] This report will be publicly available after it is published by the Asian Institute of Technology (AIT), and it demonstrates that policies and programmes will need to be put in place to ensure that "the provision of jobs for women" is selective in the nature of these jobs.

While this report is critical of the project, its actual existence represents a key difference between an ADB-financed project and those solely financed by non-multilateral development bank sources in Myanmar. Although the report doubts the ability of cross-border roads to achieve equitable and just outcomes in relation to poverty reduction for women, it is highly unlikely that it would prevent the project from going ahead. Nevertheless, that the ADB commissioned this report is a vast improvement over private projects in Myanmar, such as that at Dawei, for which there is no legal requirement for any sort of social or environmental impact assessment, and for which *any* assessment, if it exists at all, is likely to be perfunctory. The ADB report will also be published and will be publicly available, which does not happen for private assessments in Myanmar. Exiled Karen activists from the NGO EarthRights International (ERI) suggest that if multilateral development banks do engage with Myanmar, they could bring in more effective governance guidelines than a Chinese or Thai corporation would, which could increase monitoring and advocacy by domestic civil society.[11] They also acknowledged, however, that if the engagement is not done well, it can cause problems. ERI also contributed to a report that recommends:

> [u]ntil the people of Burma can meaningfully participate in development decisions, preconditions for responsible investment are in place, and adverse impacts can be mitigated, then the ADB should refrain from any form of new engagement with Burma (Bourne 2011, p. 8).

The feeling of most civil society activists inside the country, however, is that engagement by MDBs would offer better opportunities for the development of effective governance and a more dynamic civil society, despite the decades of local and international neglect.[12] According to Win Myo Thu, if MDB projects can be used to increase the involvement of local people in decision-making and management, "there are still benefits for governance and participation" even if the project isn't as effective as it could be.[13]

The Southern Economic Corridor (SEC) initially ran from Vung Tao and Quy Nhon in Vietnam through Cambodia to Bangkok in Thailand, but the development of the US$8 billion Dawei Development Project has allowed the SEC to be extended to Dawei (formerly Tavoy) in southern Myanmar. A two-lane cross-border dirt road was completed in 2011, which allowed direct travel between Kanchanaburi (and therefore Bangkok) in Thailand

and Dawei. The Dawei Development Project is being driven largely by the Thai-based Italian-Thai Development Company, which envisions a deep-sea port, petrochemical complex, fertilizer factory, coal-fired power station, and further industrialization along the pristine coast near Dawei, as well as a rail link and, somewhat optimistically, an eight-lane freeway to Thailand (Italian-Thai Development PCL 2010). This project is approximately 250 kilometres south of the proposed terminal of the ADB's EWEC at Mawlamyine, but the size of this project means it has the capacity to significantly impact not only Myanmar's industrial development but also the environmental balance of that entire region. Although the ADB is not directly involved with the Dawei project, ADB staff suggest that the GMS meeting could be used as a trade-off for ensuring increased social and environmental assessments or ADB oversight.

In addition to its geographic location, the attraction of Myanmar for foreign corporations is largely its lack of environmental, labour, and private property rights, which allows this sort of environmentally destructive development to be undertaken in populated areas with little environmental oversight. Villagers displaced from an area receive little, if any, compensation after their forced relocation. As an Italian-Thai representative argued in promoting the project: "Thais would argue about compensation and go to court. That's not the case with this project" (*International Herald Tribune* 2010). Despite these attractions for international capital, the weakness of Myanmar's rather arbitrary justice system also increases both the personal and financial risks associated with investing in Myanmar; Australian businessman Ross Dunkley, the founder and long-time editor of the *Myanmar Times*, was arrested and left languishing in Insein Prison for over a month in 2011 after engaging in conflictual negotiations with his well-connected local business partner.

There may be few labour rights currently in Myanmar, but a lack of development has also reduced the availability of skilled labour. Italian-Thai therefore brought both Thai and Myanmar migrant workers from Thailand for the early stages of the project because they were familiar with working for Thai companies.[14] Reports suggest that the company was paying workers local Myanmar rates on this project, much less than the rates they received in Thailand. Migrant workers from Myanmar are used to organizing in Thailand, despite the obstacles they face (Arnold and Hewison 2005; Hughes 2011, p. 197), and they therefore organized a strike, although reports suggest they were then summarily dismissed. There are therefore great difficulties for the ADB in promoting these economic corridors, because the current absence of labour and environmental regulations in Myanmar is likely to cause problems at a political level for the ADB's major donor governments.

The Southern Economic Corridor, however, runs through a border area that already has a foreign presence attached to the Yadana Gas Pipeline, which is operated by Total, the French oil and gas corporation, and to a new gas pipeline from the Andaman Sea that is being undertaken by PTT Exploration and Production Public Company Ltd of Thailand. Total had invested in the Yadana project prior to the EU's imposition of sanctions, and was therefore exempt. Although the company has faced a transnational campaign to leave the country, and in 2005 settled a French court case over human rights abuses during the pipeline construction (BCUK 2008; Simpson 2007, p. 546), it appears to be fully entrenched in Myanmar and, according to Nicolas Terraz, the country General Manager, has successfully negotiated a long-term relationship with the government whereby Total can raise any issue for discussion provided they "contribute to the economy and they don't enter domestic political debates".[15] Although as an oil and gas company Total has no need for loans from the ADB, the ADB's presence could help with improving general competencies in the government. The company currently works with the UN to train civil servants in the Ministry of Foreign Affairs in international law, and similar partnerships with the ADB could be extended to the economic bureaucracies to improve overall governance. Terraz contends that the elections ushered in "profound changes" in governance in the country, including a "diversification of actors with even more important institutional changes" but that there exist severe limitations in capacity.

Although there is a sense in some activist circles that ADB engagement has the potential to initiate change, the optimism of the ADB's original pre-investment study of 2001 has certainly waned. With three of the EWEC's four countries governed by authoritarian regimes, and the government in Myanmar being the most opaque of these, it is not surprising that some of the utopian assumptions of the initial study have faltered. The project continues, but even the ADB acknowledges there is much to do:

> With limited data and lack of overall transparency, coupled with the absence of quantitative benchmarks, there remains a clear challenge for member countries to develop ownership, oversight, and accountability on the progress in transforming the EWEC into an economic corridor (Asian Development Bank 2010e, p. 10).

CONCLUSION

This chapter has argued that the ongoing geopolitical re-alignment towards the East is rendering the potency of Western sanctions against Myanmar, and the associated boycott by MDBs, ineffectual. Although the ADB has been criticized over its neo-liberal focus and a lack of transparency and accountability, the ADB's social and environmental safeguards, when compared with those associated with major projects in Myanmar currently being undertaken, look quite effective. For ADB engagement to be successful, however, domestic civil society groups would usually be expected to play a vigorous governance and monitoring role. While civil society activism has grown significantly in the last few years, particularly since Cyclone Nargis (Sabandar 2010), there is near universal agreement amongst activists both inside and outside Myanmar that civil society development in Myanmar has been severely curtailed, not only through repression by the government but also by the absence of significant development activities by MDBs and the international community. Fortunately, however, there is also a highly active and effective exiled transnational activist community that could assist in this important role (Simpson 2013a).

To re-engage successfully with Myanmar, the ADB would require from the government reciprocal commitments on transparency and accountability. These sorts of agreements have been broken by the military regime in the past, but with the re-introduction of elections and a parliament, however flawed, there exists at least some potential to develop more consistent, predictable, and accountable governance in Myanmar. The ILO's protracted negotiations with the Myanmar regime have shown how difficult it is to achieve concessions, but that experience has also shown that concessions are achievable, and that with these concessions come further openings. After slow beginnings in 2007, the ILO has now helped draft for the new parliament a labour law that has support from the most senior levels of the military establishment; and the ILO's small team has run extensive training sessions on labour laws, rights, and responsibilities in the ethnic areas of eastern Myanmar, for local authorities and community committees.[16]

The ADB, however, remains in a quandary: if its funding facilitates a large-scale development project in Myanmar that wouldn't otherwise go ahead, the bank might set criteria for accountability and transparency but the project could end up further entrenching the military and providing opportunities for corruption, the forced relocation of villagers, and forced labour. If the project is likely to go ahead anyway, without ADB funding, the Myanmar government may be unwilling to accept severe limitations and restrictions imposed by the ADB when it has the opportunity to gain much easier, and more significant, funding from China and other neighbours. On the other hand, the desire by the Myanmar government for international legitimacy and acceptance should not be underestimated, nor the domestic appetite for expertise that the ADB could offer on projects and financing.

Although ADB engagement with Myanmar is likely to create a plethora of new risks, there is the potential for a determinedly transparent engagement to minimize those risks and alleviate some that already exist, so that, on balance, there is some hope for improvement in the daily lives of the marginalized and long-suffering people of Myanmar. This policy is not necessarily inconsistent with the maintenance of a sanctions regime that is sharply focused on military equipment or military personnel accused of human rights abuses, but should be seen as complementing those measures in the development of more equitable, transparent, and accountable governance in Myanmar.

Notes

*   The author undertook interviews with ADB staff in Bangkok, and with World Bank staff in Washington, D.C. and Bangkok, during four field trips in 2011 and 2012. Due to the delicate nature of negotiations between the Myanmar regime and MDB country members, most staff from these and some other institutions preferred to remain anonymous or avoid institutional attribution for this chapter.

†   In August 2012, as this publication was going to press, the World Bank announced that its Board would be considering a loan of US$85 million for Myanmar, the first such loan for Myanmar for twenty-five years.

1.   The Greater Mekong Subregion (GMS) is made up of Cambodia, China (specifically Yunnan Province and Guangxi Zhuang Autonomous Region), Lao People's Democratic Republic, Myanmar, Thailand, and Vietnam.

2.   Author's interview with S. Marshall, ILO Liaison Officer, Yangon, 9 May 2011.

3.   Author's interview with Human Rights Watch staff, Washington, D.C., 22 March 2011; Author's interview with Open Society Foundation staff, New York, 25 March 2011; Author's interview with U.S. Campaign for Burma staff, Washington, D.C., 22 March 2011.

4.   Author's interview with U.S. Embassy staff, Yangon, 10 May 2011.

5.   Author's interview with S. Marshall, ILO Liaison Officer, Yangon, 7 January 2011.

6. Author's interview with Aye Tha Aung, secretary of ALD and CRPP, Yangon, 27 December 2010 (translated by Zaw Myat Lin).

7. Author's interview with Naing Htoo, Programme Coordinator, EarthRights International (ERI), Chiang Mai, 10 December 2010.

8. Author's interview with S. Marshall, ILO Liaison Officer, Yangon, 9 May 2011.

9. Author's interview with Win Myo Thu, Managing Director and Founder, ECODEV, Yangon, 5 January 2011.

10. Author's interview with Lwin Lwin Nao, Coordinator of the Information and Documentation Department, Palaung Women's Organization (PWO), Mae Sot, Thailand, 3 December 2010.

11. Author's interview with Naing Htoo, Programme Coordinator, EarthRights International, Chiang Mai, 10 December 2010; Author's interview with Chana Maung, Southeast Asia Office Director, EarthRights International, Chiang Mai, 10 December 2010.

12. Author's interview with Bobby Maung, CEO, Network Activities Group (NAG), Yangon, 7 January 2011; Author's interview with Mael Raynaud, Myanmar Egress, Chiang Mai, 27 November 2010; Author's interview with Debbie Aung Din Taylor, International Development Enterprises (IDE), Yangon, 9 January 2011.

13. Author's interview with Win Myo Thu, ECODEV, Yangon, 5 January 2011.

14. Author's interview with S. Marshall, ILO Liaison Officer, Yangon, 9 May 2011.

15. Author's interview with N. Terraz, General Manager, Total E&P Myanmar, Yangon, 9 May 2011.

16. Author's interview with S. Marshall, ILO Liaison Officer, Yangon, 7 January 2011.

References

Arnold, D. and K. Hewison. "Exploitation in global supply chains: Burmese workers in Mae Sot". *Journal of Contemporary Asia* 35, no. 3 (2005): 319–40.

Asian Development Bank. *Preinvestment Study for the Greater Mekong Subregion East-West Economic Corridor*. Volume 3 of *Industry and Industrial Zones*. Manila: Asian Development Bank, 2001.

———. *Membership*. <http://www.adb.org/about/members> (updated 31 December 2009a). Accessed 8 May 2012.

———. "Safeguard Policy Statement". June 2009b. <http://www.adb.org/documents/safeguard-policy-statement?ref=site/safeguards/main>. Accessed 8 May 2012.

———. "GMS Nam Theun 2 Hydropower Development Project". <http://www2.adb.org/projects/project.asp?id=37734> (updated 3 August 2010a). Accessed 8 May 2012.

————. "About the Asian Development Fund (ADF)". <http://www.adb.org/about/main> (updated 30 September 2010*b*). Accessed 8 May 2012.

————. "GMS Economic Corridors". <http://www.adb.org/GMS/Economic-Corridors/gms-ec.asp> (updated 17 September 2009, 2010*c*). Accessed 20 June 2011.

————. "Greater Mekong Subregion: Projects". <http://www.adb.org/GMS/projects/adb-projects.asp> (updated 15 September 2010*d*). Accessed 10 February 2011.

————. *Strategy and Action Plan for the Greater Mekong Subregion East-West Economic Corridor*. Manila: Asian Development Bank, 2010*e*. <http://www.adb.org/publications/strategy-and-action-plan-greater-mekong-subregion-east-west-economic-corridor>. Accessed 8 May 2012.

————. *Accountability Mechanism Policy 2012*. ADB Policy Paper. March 2012. <http://www.adb.org/documents/accountability-mechanism-policy-2012?ref=site/accountability-mechanism/overview>. Accessed 8 May 2012.

Barcellos, C., P. Feitosa, G.N. Damacena and M.A. Andreazzi. "Highways and outposts: Economic development and health threats in the central Brazilian Amazon region". *International Journal of Health Geographics* 9, no. 30 (2010): 1–10.

Bourne, S. *The ADB in Burma: Behind the Scenes*. Quezon City, Philippines: NGO Forum on the ADB. April 2011. <http://www.forum-adb.org/inner.php?sec=2&id=37>. Accessed 4 July 2011.

Burma Campaign UK (BCUK). "Totalitarian Oil: Fuelling the Oppression in Burma". London: Burma Campaign UK. <http://www.burmacampaign.org.uk/index.php/campaigns/total-oil/10/121> (updated 16 May 2008). Accessed 1 July 2011.

Charney, M.W. *A History of Modern Burma*. Cambridge: Cambridge University Press, 2009.

Cheesman, N., M. Skidmore and T. Wilson, eds. *Ruling Myanmar: From Cyclone Nargis to National Elections*. Singapore: Institute of Southeast Asian Studies, 2010.

Clapp, P. "Prospects for rapprochement between the United States and Myanmar". *Contemporary Southeast Asia* 32, no. 3 (2010): 409–26.

Doyle, T. and A. Simpson. "Traversing more than speed bumps: Green politics under authoritarian regimes in Burma and Iran". *Environmental Politics* 15, no. 5 (November 2006): 750–67.

ECODEV. Economically Progressive Ecosystem Development (ECODEV). <http://ecodev-mm.com/index.htm>. 2010. Accessed 23 February 2011.

Ehrentraut, S. "Decentralization and the promise of indigenous peoples' empowerment: The case of the World Bank in Cambodia". *Pacific Review* 24, no. 1 (2011): 89–113.

Giannini, T. and A. Friedman. *A Report on Forced Labour in Burma*. EarthRights

International. March 2005. <http://earthrights.org/docs/ILO_Forced LaborReportinBurma2005.pdf>. Accessed 17 August 2005; also 15 October 2009.

Greater Mekong Subregion. *Vientiane Plan of Action for GMS Development 2008–2012.* Vientiane: Greater Mekong Subregion. <http://www.adb.org/GMS/POA-Vientiane-2008-2012-asof4Aug.pdf> (updated 4 August 2010). Accessed 5 February 2011.

Harn Yawnghwe. "United States-Myanmar relations: On the threshold of rapprochement? A response". *Contemporary Southeast Asia* 32, no. 3 (December 2010): 427–33.

Horsey, Richard. "The Initial Functioning of the Myanmar Legislatures". Conflict Prevention and Peace Forum Briefing Paper. New York: Social Science Research Council, 17 May 2011.

Hughes, C. "Soldiers, monks, borders: Violence and contestation in the Greater Mekong Sub-region." *Journal of Contemporary Asia* 41, no. 2 (2011): 181–205.

International Crisis Group. *Myanmar's Post-Election Landscape.* Asia Briefing No. 118, 7 March 2011. <http://www.crisisgroup.org/en/regions/asia/south-east-asia/burma-myanmar/B118-myanmars-post-election-landscape.aspx>. Accessed 12 May 2012.

International Herald Tribune. "An industrial project that could change Myanmar". *International Herald Tribune,* 26 November 2010. <http://www.nytimes. com/2010/11/27/world/asia/27iht-myanmar.html>. Accessed 1 Febuary 2011.

International Labour Organization. *Report of the Commission of Inquiry appointed under Article 26 of the Constitution of the International Labour Organization to examine the observance by Myanmar of the Forced Labour Convention 1930 (No. 29).* Geneva, 2 July 1998. <http://www.ilo.org/public/english/standards/relm/gb/docs/ gb273/myanmar.htm>. Accessed 17 October 2004; also 15 June 2011.

Italian–Thai Development PCL. "Dawei Development Project". PowerPoint Presentation, 2010.

Kang, T.G. "Assessing China's approach to regional multilateral security cooperation". *Australian Journal of International Affairs* 64, no. 4 (August 2010): 406–31.

Karen Women's Organization. *State of Terror: The Ongoing Rape, Murder, Torture and Forced Labour Suffered by Women Living Under the Burmese Military Regime in Karen State.* Mae Sariang and Mae Sot, Thailand: Karen Women's Organization, February 2007. <http://www.womenofburma.org/Statement&Release/state_ of_terror_report.pdf>. Accessed 20 June 2011.

Katsumata, H. "ASEAN and human rights: Resisting Western pressure or emulating the West?". *Pacific Review* 22, no. 5 (December 2009): 619–37.

Lang, C. and B. Shoemaker. *Creating Poverty in Laos: The Asian Development Bank and Industrial Tree Plantations*. Briefing Paper, World Rainforest Movement. April 2006. <http://www.wrm.org.uy/>. Accessed 1 February 2010.

Layton, R. "Forced labour in Burma: A summary of the International Labour Organization Report and subsequent developments". *Southern Cross University Law Review* 4 (2000): 148–68.

Lubeigt, G. "Industrial zones in Burma and Burmese labour in Thailand". In *Myanmar: The State, Community and the Environment*, edited by M. Skidmore and T. Wilson. Canberra: Asia Pacific Press, ANU, 2006.

Macan-Markar, M. "Southeast Asian highway hits roadblock in Burma". In *Irrawaddy*, 1 August 2010. <http://www.irrawaddy.org/article.php?art_id=19348>. Accessed 1 March 2011.

McCarthy, S. "Burma and Asean: Estranged bedfellows". *Asian Survey* 48, no. 1 (2008): 911–35.

Mertha, A. "'Fragmented authoritarianism 2.0': Political pluralization in the Chinese policy process". *China Quarterly* 200 (2009): 995–1012.

Miller, K. "Coping with China's financial power: Beijing's financial foreign policy". *Foreign Affairs* 89, no. 4 (July–August 2010): 96–109.

Oehlers, A. "A critique of ADB policies towards the Greater Mekong Sub-Region". *Journal of Contemporary Asia* 36, no. 4 (October 2006): 464–78.

Park, S. *World Bank Group Interactions with Environmentalists: Changing International Organization Identities*. Manchester: Manchester University Press, 2010.

Pedersen, M.B. "The politics of Burma's 'democratic' transition". *Critical Asian Studies* 43, no. 1 (2011): 49–68.

Raman, K.R. "Asian Development Bank, policy conditionalities and the social democratic governance: Kerala Model under pressure?". *Review of International Political Economy* 16, no. 2 (May 2009): 284–308.

Reserve Bank of Australia. *Burma Annex: Burmese Regime Figures and Supporters*. Canberra: Reserve Bank of Australia. <http://www.rba.gov.au/media-releases/2008/mr-08-23-annex.html> (updated 22 October 2008). Accessed 20 June 2011.

Roberts, C. *ASEAN'S Myanmar Crisis: Challenges to the Pursuit of a Security Community*. Singapore: Institute of Southeast Asian Studies, 2010.

Rosser, A. "Risk management, neo-liberalism and coercion: The Asian Development Bank's approach to 'fragile states'". *Australian Journal of International Affairs* 63, no. 3 (2009): 376–89.

Rudd, K. *Australia's International Development Assistance Programme 2011–12*. Canberra: Department of Foreign Affairs and Trade, 10 May 2011. <http://cache.treasury.gov.au/budget/2011–12/content/download/ms_ausaid.pdf?v=1>. Accessed 2 July 2011.

Sabandar, W. "Cyclone Nargis and ASEAN: A window for more meaningful development cooperation in Myanmar". In *Ruling Myanmar: From Cyclone*

Nargis to National Elections, edited by N. Cheesman, M. Skidmore and T. Wilson. Singapore: Institute of Southeast Asian Studies, 2010.

Selth, A. "Burma's 'saffron revolution' and the limits of international influence". *Australian Journal of International Affairs* 62, no. 3 (2008): 281–97.

Simpson, A. "Gas pipelines and green politics in South and Southeast Asia". *Social Alternatives* 23, no. 4 (December 2004): 29–36.

———. "The environment-energy security nexus: Critical analysis of an energy 'love triangle' in Southeast Asia". *Third World Quarterly* 28, no. 3 (April 2007): 539–54.

———. "Gas pipelines and security in South and Southeast Asia: A critical perspective". In *Crucible for Survival: Environmental Security and Justice in the Indian Ocean Region,* edited by T. Doyle and M. Risely. New Brunswick, New Jersey and London: Rutgers University Press, 2008.

———. "An 'activist diaspora' as a response to authoritarianism in Myanmar: The role of transnational activism in promoting political reform". In *State-Society Relations under Authoritarian Rule,* edited by F. Cavatorta and E. Lust. London and New York: Routledge/ECPR Studies in European Political Science, 2013*a.*

———. *Energy, Governance and Security in Thailand and Myanmar (Burma): A Critical Approach to Environmental Politics in the South.* Farnham: Ashgate, 2013*b.*

South, A. *Ethnic Politics in Burma: States of Conflict.* London and New York: Routledge, 2009.

Steinberg, D.I. "The United States and Myanmar: A 'boutique issue'?". *International Affairs* 86, no. 1 (2010): 175–94.

Task Force on U.S. Policy toward Burma/Myanmar. 2010. *Current Realities and Future Possibilities in Burma/Myanmar: Options For U.S. Policy.* New York: Asia Society, March 2010.

Turnell, S. "Myanmar's economy in 2006". In *Myanmar: The State, Community and the Environment,* edited by M. Skidmore and T. Wilson. Canberra: Asia Pacific Press, ANU, 2007.

———. "Finding dollars and sense: Burma's economy in 2010". In *Finding Dollars, Sense and Legitimacy in Burma,* edited by S.L. Levenstein. Washington, D.C.: Woodrow Wilson Centre, 2010. <http://www.wilsoncenter.org/topics/pubs/ASIA_092010_Burma_rpt_for web.pdf>. Accessed 5 March 2011.

United Nations Development Programme. *The Human Development Index (HDI).* New York: United Nations Development Programme, 2010. <http://hdr.undp.org/en/statistics/hdi/>. Accessed 23 February 2011.

Watts, Jonathan. "China's big hydro wins permission for 21.3GW dam in world heritage site". *Guardian,* 1 February 2011. <http://www.guardian.co.uk/environment/2011/feb/01/renewableenergy-china>. Accessed 8 February 2011.

Weng, L. "DKBA banned from carrying weapons when traveling". *Irrawaddy,*

4 August 2010a. <http://www.irrawaddy.org/article.php?art_id=19133>. Accessed 1 March 2011.

————. "DKBA battalions defect to KNLA". *Irrawaddy*, 28 July 2010b. <http://www.irrawaddy.org/article.php?art_id=19077>. Accessed 1 March 2011.

Wilson, T. "Foreign policy as a political tool: Myanmar 2003–2006". In *Myanmar: The State, Community and the Environment*, edited by M. Skidmore and T. Wilson. Canberra: Asia Pacific Press, ANU, 2006.

Win Myo Thu. *Impact of Cross Border Road Development on Rural Livelihoods and Gender Differences*. Yangon: ECODEV, 2010.

Yeni. "Behind closed borders". *Irrawaddy*. 29 July 2010. <http://www.irrawaddy.org/article.php?art_id=19089>. Accessed 1 March 2011.

18

CONTEXT SENSITIVITY BY DEVELOPMENT INGOS IN MYANMAR

Anthony Ware

Myanmar is a difficult country for international non-government organizations (INGOs) to operate in effectively. It has significant humanitarian needs but the domestic and international political environments hamper effective assistance. On the one hand, agencies working in Myanmar face a sometimes obstructive, and often inept, authoritarian government which is suspicious of both their motives and those of international donor governments. On the other hand, aid and development resources and mandates are heavily restricted by international donors disturbed by allegations of human rights violations and concerned that satisfactory policy preconditions for macro-economic development are not in place. This is a "complex political and bureaucratic environment" (ICG 2008), a "politically delicate situation" (CEC 2007), in which the tension in Myanmar's relations with the international community is as large a contributor to the difficulty in delivering humanitarian assistance as Myanmar's domestic policy, capability, and will. The result for INGOs is restrictions on access, funding, and mandates.

This chapter presents analysis of new primary research data collected from INGOs working inside Myanmar between 2009 and mid-2011. In particular, it looks at their contextualization of common development approaches in order to maximize programme effectiveness. The key finding is that INGOs believe that although operating in Myanmar is difficult, their effectiveness is not as heavily restricted as is commonly perceived by people outside the country, provided they deploy appropriate sensitivity to the operational context. This is particularly true for activities that address the impact of extreme poverty in communities, but also applies in areas such as advocacy and capacity-building for the emerging civil society.

There have been many studies of Myanmar politics, and of the pros and cons of sanctions, but while this body of research often mentions the humanitarian impact of the political stalemate, few studies examine INGO effectiveness or how INGOs adapt to attempt poverty alleviation in Myanmar. This research goes well beyond previous studies by Inwood (2008), Igboemeka (2005), and Duffield (2008), presenting analysis of a much larger number of more recent primary interviews within Myanmar. I have previously presented findings from this research regarding the ways INGOs create space to operate in spite of Myanmar government restrictions and the restrictions imposed by the international community on funding and mandates (Ware 2011). Without covering this ground again, this chapter explores how INGOs contextualize their implementation of international development principles to be most sensitive to the particular circumstances in Myanmar. (A more detailed presentation of these findings has also recently been published; see Ware 2012.)

The remainder of this chapter presents the results of this fieldwork with INGOs in Myanmar. The first section explores the ways INGOs contextualize their relationships with other development stakeholders, including officials, donors, and civil society, through consideration of ideas on partnerships, capacity-building, rights-based approaches, advocacy, and accountability. The following section considers the ways INGOs work sensitively in local communities according to ideas of participation, equity, sustainability, and active citizenship. The chapter ends with some conclusions from this research.

CONTEXT SENSITIVITY IN RELATIONS WITH OTHER STAKEHOLDERS

Partnership and Capacity Building — with Civil Society and NGOs

It has long been recognized that INGOs need to move from being service providers to being equal partners with civil society in facilitating development (Paldron 1987). Strengthening civil society is essential for promoting self-help and for overcoming both paternalism and dependency (Frantz 1987). As a result, capacity-building and local organizational development are primary objectives for many development agencies globally (Pettit 2000).

However, a good many INGOs who ascribe to this ethos globally, in Myanmar still implement most of their programmes directly through paid staff. For example, while the global practice of Care International is to minimize the number of their own staff and work primarily through local partners, in Myanmar they have a large staff, and directly implement 95 per cent of their programmes (Agland, Care 2009). Care International is not alone. Médecins du Monde, as another example, directly implement projects in Myanmar to an extent they would not do in other countries, using international staff to run their own HIV/AIDS clinics and programmes.

> We absolutely want to build local capacity of local NGOs, CBO, informal groups, whatever ... And we would like to do hospital cooperation ... [But for now] we are operating as if we are in an emergency situation ... (Lancelot, MDM 2009).

Many INGOs in Myanmar would prefer to focus on technical cooperation or building the capacity of local NGOs, as they do in other countries, but the limiting factor is the lack of capacity of local NGOs in terms of scale, governance, and abilities such as evaluation skills. Some organizations, such as Oxfam, ActionAid, and the Burnet Institute, for example, have made conscious decisions to implement almost all their programmes through local partnerships and to build local capacity rather than coming in themselves from outside, but developing a shared culture, ideals, and beliefs takes time, and the progress of their programmes is much slower.

A common criticism made by local NGOs is that where large INGOs do form partnerships with local organizations, they often "see the local partners as their implementers, not in any sense of true partnership" (Dorning, Burnet 2009). They have a fear that large international agencies will roll over the really good local initiatives that stem from local civil society, using the local organizations simply to implement their own programmes. Oxfam deals with this in part by working with a range of "project partners", while focussing on developing more significantly the capacity of innovative "strategy partners" (Win, Oxfam 2009).

The capacity and development of civil society in Myanmar has long been constrained by government policy (ICG 2001; Liddell 1997; Steinberg

1997). However, over the last five to ten years a very active civil society has emerged at what many describe as below-the-radar level: not registered, not big, but very active (Lancelot, MDM 2009; Lorch 2007). The response to Cyclone Nargis clearly demonstrated the resurgence of this "informal" civil society (CPCS 2008), and since Nargis there has been a large push for partnerships between local and international implementation agencies (Dorning, Burnett 2009). Identifying and building the capacity of potential partner organizations has therefore become a high priority, with the greatest challenges for most INGOs being to find suitable candidates and build the organizational capacity of unregistered organizations, rather than to develop technical skills.

The fact that most local organizations are not registered is an additional obstacle to partnerships. Partnering with smaller unregistered organizations is tricky: "you find funding but you have to carry it for them since institutional donors will not take the risk of investing money in a group that is not registered, that is not controllable" (Lancelot, MDM 2009). Nonetheless, Burmese nationals and local NGOs that were interviewed indicated that they definitely want to see more of these capacity-building partnerships.

Partnership and Capacity Building — with Officials

Building the capacity of government agencies and departments, and strengthening state institutions and civil service, are widely seen as essential for sustained economic development (see, for example, ESCAP/ADB/UNDP 2007). A few UN agencies, such as the Food and Agricultural Organization (FAO), have sufficient mandate and a relationship that is good enough to partner with and build capacity in Myanmar government departments (Imai, FAO 2009), but most agencies, whether UN or INGO, lack such a mandate or funding.

For most INGOs, any partnership with government officials and departments is complex. On the one hand, restrictions applied by donors, boards, and the international community to prevent funds flowing to persons connected with the regime often include officials down to the township (local government) level (Source 1, 2009). On the other hand, many officials are deeply suspicious of the motives of INGOs and their donors (Source 16; Source 31; Source 50, 2009), or are not interested in partnership because they don't want to be controlled by the strings attached to aid (Lancelot, MDM 2009). Nonetheless, most respondents suggest that, at least at a township level, most local authorities are open to partnership and assistance.

Many agencies actively invite township-level officials to training. One bilateral donor spoke of their positive experience providing technical assistance and training for township-level officials in the fight against avian flu. They "found ministries to be very professional and motivated … [with] no leakage of money" (Source 1, 2009). Nevertheless, political forces on both sides work against partnership. One respondent expressed frustration at inequalities they had to perpetrate by not being allowed to pay travel expenses for low-paid civil servants to attend training, when they do pay these expenses for all other participants (Agland, Care 2009). Another found that township officials who were most open and interested were quickly moved to another area (Source 24, 2009).

One INGO implemented a three-way partnership in a community-level livelihood programme, between themselves, a local implementing partner, and a government agency (Source 25, 2009). They provided funding, strategy, and training, while the local partner handled all direct implementation and funding. No funding went to the government, and despite the strained nature of such a relationship, they concluded that including officials in the partnership promoted healthy dialogue and coordination. However, another INGO attempting a similar partnership expressed frustration that such approaches almost co-opt local officials into INGO projects, rather than generate genuine partnership (Agland, Care 2009).

Closer partnership with officials requires access to funds with little in the way of restrictions, something most organizations don't have. The Leprosy Mission International, however, describe in glowing terms the positive outcomes they have had partnering with the right officials (Griffiths, TLMI 2009). For them it began when Cyclone Nargis struck. They quickly realized that the Department of Social Welfare was going to be overloaded with administration of new project applications, so they rang the department and asked what additional equipment they needed to process the administrative mountain they faced. The Leprosy Mission International provided computers, printers, photocopiers, and generators. While they did this with the motive of ensuring that people with disabilities were cared for after the cyclone, they found the strengthened relationship most empowering for their work. They were subsequently invited to help write a protection plan for people with disabilities, and to work with the department on disability access in Naypyitaw. They have now also been asked to help draft disability legislation for the new parliament (Griffiths, TLMI 2011). They argue:

> Relationship building often comes through being willing to recognise and work with the agendas of other people.... No matter who's in charge of the country in the future, the same group of civil servants are going to provide these services, so up-skilling and resourcing them is not necessarily putting money into the hands of restricted people. And by strengthening their hand, it strengthens their ability to do a lot of good things that they want to be doing (Griffiths, TLMI 2009).

Western concerns about corruption in partnership with officials appear ill-founded. One source gave a comparison:

> I have had less problems with corruption in Burma than in Laos or Thailand.... The problem is mostly with business ... there is definitely less corruption when it comes to aid (except exchange rate, big issues) because most locals are concerned about the poverty of the people (Source 31, 2009).

One key Burmese worker with a UN agency argued that INGOs finding ways to partner with officials is an essential component of facilitating the political change the outside world is looking for in Myanmar: "We need to allow them to own the changes at the village level. Only international agencies can offer that; the local people can't" (Source 41, 2009). However, building such partnerships requires "more time and effort building relationships [with officials] than in other countries" (Tumbian, WV 2009).

Thus, despite the obstacles, many INGOs expressly indicate that if they were given more freedom, then partnership and capacity-building with officials and government agencies would be something they would do more frequently.

Duffield (2008) argues that the main role of INGOs in Myanmar is to "push back, contain or modulate the effects of unchecked, arbitrary personal power" by all connected to the regime. Clearly many UN and INGO leaders do not agree. Steve Marshall, the ILO Liaison in Myanmar, argues that one key obstacle to effective development work in Myanmar is the absence of a cohesive civil service which can implement the high-level policy initiatives agencies are currently negotiating with senior officials

(Marshall, ILO 2009). This view sees building the capacity of the civil service as essential. It is clear that restrictions on partnerships with officials cause great frustration for many international agencies. Given the emphasis on partnerships for poverty alleviation in President Thein Sein's inauguration speech (*NLM*, 2011) and subsequent signs of policy development around this goal (U Myint 2011), INGOs are increasingly thinking that this is the right time to explore capacity-building partnerships with the civil service (Herzbruch, LRC 2011).

The danger, of course, in building a close relationship with government officials is that "you may be perceived from the outside as being too close; you have to tread a fine line" (Source 15, 2009). In talking about this, many INGOs' leaders felt the need to defend themselves against being labelled "regime apologists".

Rights-Based Approach

The definition of a "Rights-Based Approach" (RBA) to development varies greatly, but it usually views poverty as the direct result of disempowerment and exclusion, thus seeking to empower rights-holders (citizens) to hold duty-bearers (national governments) to account under international human rights legislation. In particular, the RBA seeks to assist marginalized poor people assert their rights to a fair share of existing resources and power, making the process explicitly political (ACFID 2009; Nyamu-Musembi & Cornwall 2004).

Given the already highly politicized context, the RBA is a contentious topic amongst INGOs in Myanmar. Several organizations interviewed have adopted the RBA as their global approach to development, yet in order to "do no harm" and not put people at risk, until 2011–12 these organizations worked in Myanmar in a more reserved way, advocating for basic services on behalf of communities, arguing that poverty itself is a violation of human rights (for example, Source 24, 2009). The ILO, with their mandate to work against forced labour, already spend most of their time advising citizens of their rights under existing Myanmar law. They suggest that existing national laws provide a reasonable framework in many areas, and that raising the awareness of rights under these laws is a critical part of development. However, even when people understand their legal rights, very few are brave enough to exercise them (Marshall, ILO 2009).

Many interviewees felt a rights-based approach was not appropriate in Myanmar since "the law is in the mouth of the generals; there is nothing down on paper, no real rule of law because what is written can always be manipulated" (Source 16, 2009). Some see the RBA as built on concepts that are not relevant in Myanmar, given that neither the people nor the military leaders believe there are rights: "needs and responsibilities yes, but not rights" (Tegenfeldt, Hope 2009). Others suggest that many ministers and key officials are already "aware of human rights principles, are concerned, and are trying to improve on them ... but they have very little budget in which to operate ... criticism is not helpful when officials genuinely are concerned" (Source 31, 2009).

Inescapably, part of the issue of talking about rights in Myanmar is the fact that the international community regularly couches the most stinging of their rebukes in human rights language, to the extent that the Myanmar government believes human rights allegations are being exploited to destabilize the state, and are being raised for political advantage rather than out of genuine humanitarian concern (for example, see *NLM* 2009). They argue that the end result of human rights activism is that the Myanmar people are further denied their human rights because of restrictions on the right of the country to develop (for example, see Soe Tha 2007). Interestingly, Pedersen (2009) agrees in part, suggesting that "poverty has emerged as the most acutely felt constraint on human rights for the majority of people across the country", thus putting rights obligations in part back on the West, not just on the Myanmar government.

There is a view from at least some local non-government organizations (LNGOs) that "instead of advocating for political rights, international organizations should start working at the grassroots level strengthening the capacity of society" (Source 41, 2009). Overall, those who assess their work as most effective believe RBA goals are better pursued by building relationships with authorities and appealing for assistance non-confrontationally, rather than talking about rights and duties.

Advocacy

INGOs point to a wide range of policy change and development to show that advocacy can work in Myanmar. Allan (2010) describes advances in areas such as human trafficking, drug control, disability strategy, sustainable forestry, and HIV-Malaria-TB prevention. The Leprosy

Mission points to recent invitations for various INGOs to assist in drafting legislation surrounding disability, the elderly, and the protection of women and children as wins for advocacy (Griffiths, TLMI 2011), while President Thein Sein's apparent enthusiasm for the alleviation of extreme rural poverty could also be taken as an advocacy win. However, progress seems as much related to the particular issue involved as it is to the methodology and approach: items related to security or involving budgetary reallocations make less progress, while changes related to technical matters or local needs are more likely to succeed than calls for policy change. For example, despite much advocacy, increases to health and education spending have been minimal.

It is widely agreed that significant progress in development requires major policy change. "It [advocacy] is really the main thing we need to do" (Lancelot, MDM 2009). Yet most INGOs are "particularly hesitant to pursue fully rational advocacy strategies that would do a better job of leading to more complete overall development in any sense" (Source 30, 2009). Several INGOs acknowledged a lack of understanding of government decision-making processes as one cause of this, particularly once decisions need to go higher than regional or ministry level (Source 18; Source 25, 2009). One UN informant argued that, "Most organizations ... don't engage and negotiate boldly enough behind closed doors. When we push back non-confrontationally, but boldly, they generally move closer to a consensus or compromise solution" (Source 42, 2009). Yet interviewees from these same organizations implied the vulnerability of such work by seeking assurances of anonymity for these comments.

Most advocacy in Myanmar is personal and non-confrontational. One respondent spoke of "silent advocacy" (Source 20, 2009), by which she meant private discussions away from the public spotlight. The Myanmar Red Cross speaks of "informal advocacy" or "situation-sensitive advocacy" (Tha Hla Shwe, MRC 2011). Oxfam prefers to speak of advocacy as "building relationships", and notes that success is very dependent upon the individuals involved (Win, Oxfam 2009). Indeed, "the word 'advocacy' itself, in some cases, makes people afraid" (Tumbian, WV 2009).

> Advocacy is not so nearly as helpful a term as dialogue. I would much rather talk about dialogue and engagement than about advocacy. A Western form, a marketing approach, a civil rights-based approach to advocacy is simply inappropriate here, but that does not mean you can't have an advocacy strategy that uses a whole range of tools and techniques to

progress exactly the same messages in a very different way, using very different media (Allan, Spectrum 2009).

The most effective approach appears to be through exploring needs and issues together with officials, with no confrontation and no blame, looking for ways to meet needs together, particularly at the community and township level. "It is more like seeking support or seeking to supplement what the community has already done to help themselves" (Source 24, 2009). World Vision explained this advocacy as "report[ing] needs to the government, so they know and so they can support us by sending their technical people" (Tumbian, WV 2009). Effectively, this approach adopts methods described in the literature for involving elites in poverty alleviation, even when their vested interests lie elsewhere (e.g. see Hossain and Moore 2002).

> Our approach is to make them understand what the reality is … we give them real information, bring them to reality, bring them to the field, so they can understand what the reality of the situation is. Why would you make other people ashamed? If you want to win, don't make other people feel like they have lost (Source 6, 2009).

One respondent emphasized that many officials at the township level are genuinely concerned about many of the same issues as development agencies. Advocacy that directly criticizes concerned individuals who are hamstrung by small budgets is not helpful (Source 31, 2009).

Accountability

Eyben (2008) argues that mutual accountability in international development is not so much about parties holding each other to account for performance against pre-established objectives, as about the messy complexity of relationship and process with mutual responsibility. "Much of what proves with hindsight to be effective aid may well be an outcome of relational approaches." This conception of accountability appears particularly apt in Myanmar, where agencies need to overcome the strained relationship between the West and the Myanmar government in order to operate effectively.

INGOs with the greatest ease of access have strong relationships with authorities, built largely through highly transparent dealings with officials. Many invest significant time and personnel in developing and maintaining relations with government officials (for example, Agland, Care 2009; Griffiths, TLMI 2009; Purnell, WVI 2011; Tegenfeldt, Hope 2009). Transparency is a key: many INGOs are

> even more transparent [than usual] ... The entire thing that is at stake ... is to build trust.... So we are absolutely transparent in everything we do ... we are trying really to build trust with them, that they see the value of us working with them [and] spread that message that international aid ... can really bring development and improvement (Lancelot, MDM 2009).

The Myanmar government is not, of course, particularly transparent in return. However, that is perhaps sometimes more a matter of bureaucratic capacity than intent. "I don't think they want to be non-transparent, but they don't want to be required to give more than they can provide" (Lancelot, MDM 2009).

Interestingly, however, given the level of transparency in direct relationships with officials, INGO reports that are delivered to higher levels of authority are not always as transparent. One INGO country director complained that officials "have literally said to me, use [your figures and information] where you want and when you want, but please, could you report it like this and like this" (Source 18, 2009).

Another explained:

> We tell [departmental contacts] exactly what we are doing and ask for their advice on what to put into our written reports — people in the department advise back what to write up and what not to write up. It creates more trouble for them if we report everything (Source 20, 2009).

Similarly, at least one INGO leader voiced concern that "INGOs here seem to be less open to information sharing [with other INGOs] than we found them in [another country], as if they mimic the government and become less transparent themselves" (Source 18, 2009). One longer-term journalist concurred, suggesting he had noted a much greater reluctance for INGOs to go on record and talk about their activities after the purge in the military leadership in 2004, and that since then they preferred to remain more "under the radar" (Goddard, MT 2009). Following the unprecedented relief cooperation in the wake of Cyclone Nargis, this tendency seems to have improved significantly with, for example, eighteen agencies cooperating very openly in an impact study after the March 2011 earthquake, and recent inter-agency discussion of salary scales for local staff (Herink, WV 2011). Still, it is interesting that these comments were made a full year after the cyclone.

In regard to accountability to donors, many respondents readily agreed that they maintain a very low publicity profile about their Myanmar work in donor countries. "Caution is wise" when it comes to publicising projects outside the country, and some country directors are particularly careful to advise visitors from other parts of their organization not to include anything in their promotional materials that would upset either the Myanmar government or people outside Myanmar. In part, this is in recognition of the government's sensitivity that portrayals of poverty may be exploited by opponents, but it also highlights the complexity of accountability towards donors.

CONTEXT SENSITIVITY IN WORK WITHIN LOCAL COMMUNITIES

Participation

Participation is a central concept in development theory, having "become widely accepted as the minimum requirement for successful and sustained development outcomes" (Clarke, 2009). "Empowerment happens when individuals and organized groups are able to imagine their world differently" and take action to change their circumstances (Eyben et al. 2008).

Political limitations, access issues, and regional conflict mean participation is not always implemented well in Myanmar. One Burmese manager in a UN agency complained that participatory committees set up for most projects "are just user groups that stop at the end of the project, leaving again a vacuum" (Source 41, 2009). Nonetheless, many other more highly participatory "process-led", "human-centred", and "integrated" programmes in Myanmar have created ownership and empowered communities to assess their needs, prioritize, and design their own solutions, often resulting in the emergence of genuine community-based organizations (CBOs).

This finding — that highly participatory development works well in Myanmar — is counter-intuitive given the strongly authoritarian government. One respondent commented:

> I found myself, in my early time here, amazed that we had the flexibility to do what we were doing with so much of this community empowerment work. It puzzled me immensely as to why there was never any kickback (Allan, Spectrum 2009).

Anthropological research by Skidmore (2003, 2004) and Fink (2001) highlights another factor that needs to be taken into account. Their research investigated the psychological impact of military rule in Myanmar, and concluded that people develop an aversion to risk trying new things and are disempowered in decision-making. This perception is mirrored in Aung San Suu Kyi's (1995) writing. "People here are not willing to try things outside areas that are safe" (Goddard, *Myanmar Times* 2009).

Certainly, "fear is a significant component of the landscape here … it is very real" (Tegenfeldt, Hope 2009). There is "a lot of fear of doing new things, or of being seen to be taking the lead on things or pushing things forward … there is kind of a status-quo culture … There is a real fear of being clamped down on" (Wells, Paung Ku 2009). Invitations to become involved in participatory development, therefore, "often meet with scepticism from village leaders … worried what this will mean for their relationship with local authorities" (Source 20, 2009). "People will come together, but they're not used to making decisions for themselves … some of that is due to political repression, and some of it is due to the people just being really poor" (Agland, Care 2009).

Nonetheless, interviewees felt that this fear of the authorities is more immobilizing in the political arena, and perhaps more in urban and peri-urban areas than in village-level development, but that fear and scepticism could be overcome. Process is critical, though, and requires leadership and a demonstration of approval.

> They need the door opened for them by local senior authorities, village or regional, to give them permission before they're willing to move forward.… They need to make sure that the link is there.… They need to be reassured that what they are doing is acceptable. Here it is more than in other places … Here it *needs* to happen (Agland, Care 2009).

Such approval is often provided by a key individual in the village, someone confident in their position (such as a headman or former headman), with high-level relationships, who endorses the process and is able to motivate and inspire others (Griffiths, TLMI 2009).

Good relationships with local officials are often ensured by local partner organizations, who can spend "a lot of time talking to local officials to convince them this is good for the community and not a threat" (Source 20, 2009). In other instances, developing such relationships is a learned skill that is utilized by key community members, rather than the result of deliberate engagement or policy by INGOs or NGO partners: "If you don't liaise with the authorities, then the authorities will follow up what you have been doing anyway, so you might as well try to do the right thing" (Allan, Spectrum 2009). Where possible, it can be fruitful to include officials in projects in such a way that they can consider they helped the work and can take some credit for the results — although it can result in pressure to implement infrastructure projects, tangible outcomes that local authorities can easily take credit for.

Most INGO respondents suggest that they emphasize high levels of participation more strongly in Myanmar than elsewhere. For some it is a deliberate effort to build highly democratic grass-roots practices, to prepare the way for a more democratic national future (Source 24; Source 41, 2009). Most pointed to high levels of volunteerism, self-reliance, self-motivation, and independence within the culture, demonstrated by the local response to Cyclone Nargis, as making highly participatory programmes particularly suitable in Myanmar (Source 24, 2009; Tegenfeldt, Hope 2009; Tumbian, WV 2009; Wells, Paung Ku 2009).

Equity

Equity is a fundamental element of effective participatory development, and requires that the disempowered be given the opportunity to provide input into decision-making processes. Equity is usually emphasized in terms of gender, but more broadly "requires the voices of women, the young, the old, and landless, disabled, and other marginalized groups [alongside] the voices of traditional leaders, religious leaders, and landowners" (Clarke 2009). Equitable development, therefore, also needs to be sensitive to mitigation of fault lines within society which drive exclusion and marginalization (Conflict Sensitivity 2004; Carment and Schnabel 2001).

Equity is a significant issue in Myanmar. "The result of living under such a system of strict hierarchy, is that they are not used to being able to have a say in the development of their own village" (Source 20, 2009). Building equity and genuine participation in such a "deeply fractured society" (Wells, Paung Ku 2009) requires time and deliberate effort to empower the voices of women, minorities, and the marginalized.

Hope International Development Agency is possibly the INGO that most directly addresses these concerns in Myanmar. Its representative argues:

> [Westerners] characterize this country as a peace-loving Buddhist people who have the misfortune to be ruled by some military thugs.... I see

> this, in contrast, as a country that has a long, deep and broad history of violence, and the use of violence and the threat of violence to maintain social control.... It is in the family, it is in community organizations, it is in religious organizations, and of course it is in the military (Tegenfeldt, Hope 2009).

Consequently, most poor people defer to village leaders, religious leaders, or to local members of the regime-connected Union Solidarity Development Association (USDA) or of the military, for example, rather than offering genuine participation. Dealing with the root causes of authoritarianism and marginalization is essential for improving equity in development; empowerment must facilitate personal transformation that results in people coming to see one another in more mutually respectful relationships (Tegenfeldt, Hope 2009). It must help communities develop good communication, negotiation, mediation, and consensus decision-making skills.

In order to improve equity, it is essential not only to address gender issues, but also to reduce suspicion between groups and build participation that demonstrates development is not just for one ethnic, religious, or political group (Tegenfeldt, Hope 2009). For example, one INGO reported coming under pressure several years ago to exclude known supporters of the National League for Democracy (NLD) from eligibility for its microfinance loans (Source 31, 2009). The Myanmar Red Cross came under similar pressure at one point to exclude NLD supporters even when taking blood donations (Tha Hla Shwe, MRC 2011). However, Western INGOs sometimes equally discriminate against members of the regime-affiliated USDA (Salai, Swissaid 2009). It was not uncommon for villages to choose USDA members as part of village development committees, and INGOs were often very concerned about their political affiliation. Given that the USDA has since been converted into the Union Solidarity Development Party, the new ruling party in Myanmar, their concerns were well founded. Clearly, if the election of USDA members was due to deference by community members out of a sense of hierarchy and power, this would be reason for concern.

There is evidence in the literature that good accountability processes and highly democratic decision-making can be a safeguard against elite capture of community-driven development, despite the presence of elites on committees (Fritzen 2007; Labonne and Chase 2009; Platteau and Gaspart 2003). In the same way that INGOs must strive to ensure that committees include women as well as some of the poorest and most vulnerable persons in a community, several respondents were adamant that the principles of equity also mean USDA members must not be excluded simply because of political affiliation (for example, Win, Oxfam 2009). Likewise, considerations of equity mean that village and religious leaders should also be included in participatory processes, not completely sidelined (Tumbian, WV 2009).

Sustainability

In an environment where international agencies are restricted in building the capacity of township officials, it is difficult to ensure that officials are able to maintain village-level development. Sustainable development therefore requires that communities should be able to maintain their own development themselves, beyond the life of the project. A number of agencies thus have a deliberate goal of building equitable, participatory village development committees into community-based organizations, able to continue the process of community empowerment and sustainable development long after the involvement of the international or local agency. These agencies assess this strategy as having been effective in Myanmar:

> We have proven on the ground that the poor, if given opportunity, can fully participate in prioritizing their needs and work together with the project in shaping their lives. ... If these groups are given proper support, guidance and training can be a springboard to the emergence of community-based organizations (Source 41, 2009).

Part of the reason why this is possible appears to be that, rather than most people living a learned dependency, "it is just the complete opposite: most people are not expecting any help from anybody and assume they are just going to have to do it themselves" (Wells, Paung Ku 2009).

However, it takes considerable time to develop the capacity of village committees so they can become firmly-based CBOs. While the approach and programme of each agency is different, agencies interviewed by the author suggested that in their experience it takes between seven (Source 41, 2009) to fifteen years (Tumbian, WV 2009) to develop a functioning CBO in a village community. Two other INGO leaders with prior experience of just-commencing programmes suggested they believed it could be achieved in as little as three years if it was made the central focus of the intervention and done intensively with a facilitator living within the community (Source 24, 2009; Source 30, 2009). It was also noted that success in such a venture "depends largely on whether committee members are assigned by the village, or whether people with a real heart, spirit and genuine leadership character are brought into the committee" (Source 41, 2009).

Active Citizenship

Active citizenship is widely seen as the logical conclusion of highly participatory development, when communities and local NGOs own their development initiatives, advocate for themselves, and hold authorities to account to sustain development (Clarke, 2009). Given the surprising finding that, despite the high degree of authoritarianism in the country, the most effective development programmes in Myanmar are strongly participatory and inclusive, one might suspect effective programmes may also incorporate a high degree of active citizenship.

Respondents were very conscious that empowerment must do no harm and not put people or communities at risk. They are also very aware that most Burmese are very reluctant to challenge authorities at any level (Goddard, *Myanmar Times* 2009), or even to talk about issues they perceive as relating to higher levels of authority (Wells, Paung Ku 2009). Indeed, there is "a lot of evidence that the government views the people as the enemy, that they fear the public, and fear the public doing too much" (Long, *Myanmar Times* 2009).

Speaking about local NGO and CBO networks, Dorning lamented that, "What we can't do here, but would be possible in other countries is … they could become political in themselves, they could lobby for their own constituency" (Dorning, Burnet 2009). Most INGOs discouraged any politicization of their work in villages or of their local partners, and most attempts even to facilitate local NGOs in lobbying donors and international authorities were unsuccessful. Instead, apart from communities actively seeking cooperation from local officials through lines of relationship, INGOs largely assume the role of advocacy on their behalf. Indeed, some INGOs avoid even using the term "empowerment" in their communication with the government (Source 6, 2009).

This finding is consistent with research in places where active citizenship may put people in danger. Clarke (2009), for example, argues that participation has become "fetishised to some degree", such that it is considered the overriding factor in all development interventions, and that consequently active citizenship is also widely assumed to be optimal in all circumstances. Instead, using the example of illegal Burmese workers in Thailand, Clarke argues that active citizenship may not be possible (or optimal) where public participation could endanger lives, and where people do not have the supporting legal and political mechanisms for such a role. In such situations INGOs should assume such a role on their behalf, as they have in Myanmar.

However, since the recent elections and inauguration of the new president and parliament, there appears to be a decided change in the level of local advocacy and active citizenship. Local NGOs have become far bolder in using the public civil space to engage in public debate of policy issues, something previously heavily restricted. For example, discussion of the Kachin State hydroelectricity dams is becoming common even in Yangon; local groups have organized regular seminars in Dawei calling for corporate social responsibility in relation to the deep-sea port; and the Ayeyawady River Awareness campaign by a Yangon-based group is using media and art to raise issues of watershed and environmental management within the Ayeyawady basin (Wells, Paung Ku 2011). This is a new level of locally-led active citizenship within the country, and something INGOs have yet to significantly engage with.

CONCLUSION

This chapter has documented many of the complexities INGOs face in implementing their development programmes sensitively in Myanmar in order to facilitate greater effectiveness. While there is broad consensus that poverty in Myanmar is largely the result of governance failures, the difficulties faced by INGOs relate to restrictions stemming from both the Myanmar government and the international community. Nonetheless, despite the complexity and difficulties, if INGOs operate with appropriate sensitivity to the context, their effectiveness is not as heavily restricted as is commonly perceived by those outside the country. This is particularly true for projects that directly address the impact of extreme poverty on communities, but also applies in areas such as advocacy and developing the capacity of the emerging civil society.

This chapter has summarized the major insights obtained from key development practitioners working in Myanmar about the types of contextualization that make INGO development interventions most effective. The insights from their experience provide something of a blueprint for other organizations working in Myanmar, and offer hope for incremental change and effectiveness in alleviating the impact of extreme poverty in Myanmar. More broadly, this research highlights the clear need for development practitioners to be ready to adapt global development approaches to local circumstances. It points to the lack of substantive research into the contextualization of development, and the tendency of the international and academic community to espouse a global ideal without sufficient emphasis on alternatives and adaptations in implementation.

APPENDIX 1
RESEARCH METHODOLOGY

I conducted semi-structured interviews in person with fifty key practitioners between 2009 and 2011. Most were country directors or programme managers with INGOs and UN organizations based in Myanmar. I also interviewed a number of local NGO leaders, as well as leaders of INGOs who work into Myanmar through partnerships, and a couple of representatives from bilateral donor organizations and journalists. A majority of those interviewed were non-Burmese, reflecting the make-up of senior INGO and UN organization staff.

Most interviews were conducted face-to-face in Myanmar and Thailand, after Cyclone Nargis and the referendum in 2008 but before the 2010 elections were scheduled. Interviews were around one hour in length, and were guided by a loose schedule of open-ended questions. Most interviews were recorded and transcribed. The initial data analysis was verified using a Delphi panel discussion in Yangon during December 2009, with a number of follow-up interviews conducted during June 2011.

All respondents have been given an anonymous reference number (Source 1–50), while about half the participants agreed to allow at least some of their responses to be on the record. The latter are noted by in-text citations providing author, agency, and date.

Interviews Cited

Agland, Brian. Country Director, Care (INGO). Personal interview (recorded), 9 July 2009, Yangon.
Allan, David. Director, Spectrum (LNGO), and former country coordinator of World Concern (INGO). Personal interview (recorded), 16 July 2009, Yangon.
Dorning, Karl. Country Representative, Burnet Institute (INGO). Personal interview (recorded), 10 July 2009, Yangon.
Goddard, Geoffrey. Former Editor, *Myanmar Times*. Personal interview (recorded), 8 July 2009, Yangon.
Griffiths, Mike. Country Director, The Leprosy Mission International (INGO). Personal interview (recorded), 10 July 2009, Yangon.
———. Personal interview, 22 June 2011, Yangon.
Herink, Chris. Country Representative, World Vision Myanmar (INGO). Personal interview, 21 June 2011, Yangon.

Herzbruch, Birke. NGO Liaison Officer, Local Resource Centre. Personal interview, 27 June 2011, Yangon.

Imai, Shin. Representative in Myanmar, Food and Agricultural Organization. Personal interview (recorded), 7 July 2009, Yangon.

Lancelot, Anne. Country Representative, Médecins du Monde (INGO). Personal interview (recorded), 14 July 2009, Yangon.

Long, Douglas. Editor, *Myanmar Times*. Personal interview (recorded), 8 July 2009, Yangon.

Marshall, Steve. Liaison Officer, International Labour Organization. Personal interview (recorded), 29 June 2009, Yangon.

Purnell, David. Senior Director Operations, East Asia Region, World Vision International (INGO regional office). Personal interview, 8 and 22 July 2009, Bangkok.

Salai, Khin Maung Aye. Country Coordinator, Swissaid Myanmar Programme (donor). Personal interview (recorded), 8 July 2009, Yangon.

Source 1. Country Coordinator for a bilateral donor. Personal interview, July 2009, Yangon.

Source 6. Country Representative (INGO). Personal interview (recorded), July 2009, Yangon.

Source 15. Country Director (INGO). Personal interview (recorded), July 2009, Yangon.

Source 16. Senior advisor (INGO). Personal interview (recorded), June 2009, Yangon.

Source 18. Country Representative (INGO). Personal interview (recorded), July 2009, Yangon.

Source 20. Country Programme Manager (INGO). Personal interview (recorded), June 2009, Bangkok.

Source 24. Policy and Project Advisor (INGO). Personal interview (recorded), July 2009, Yangon.

Source 25. Strategic coordinator (INGO). Personal interview (recorded), July 2009, Yangon.

Source 30. Director of local NGO / former country coordinator for an INGO. Personal interview, July 2009, Yangon.

Source 31. Former country representative (faith-based INGO). Personal interview (recorded), March 2009, Melbourne.

Source 41. Former senior manager (Burmese national with a UN agency). Personal interview, July 2009, Yangon.

Source 42. Field Coordinator / Deputy Head (UN agency). Personal interview (recorded), July 2009, Yangon.

Source 50. Former editor, *Myanmar Times*. Personal interview (recorded), March 2009, Melbourne.

Tegenfeldt, David. Senior Advisor, Hope International Development Agency (INGO). Personal interview (recorded), 29 June 2009, Yangon.

Tha Hla Shwe. President, Myanmar Red Cross (government organized non-government organization or GONGO). Personal interview, 21 June 2011, Yangon.

Tumbian, James. Country Representative, World Vision Myanmar (INGO). Personal interview (recorded), 14 July 2009, Yangon.

Wells, Tamas. Project Manager, Paung Ku Project (Save the Children) (INGO). Personal interview (recorded), 7 July 2009, Yangon.

————. Personal interview, 22 June 2011, Yangon.

Win, Chaw Su. Coordinator Strategic Programme and Organization Development, Oxfam (INGO). Personal interview (recorded), 13 July 2009, Yangon.

References

Australian Council for International Development (ACFID). *Millenium Development Rights: How human rights-based approaches are achieving the MDGs: Case-studies from the Australian aid and development sector.* Canberra: ACFID, 2009. <http://www.acfid.asn.au/what-we-do/docs_what-we-do/docs_hrproject/Millenniu m%20Development%20Rights.pdf>. Accessed 15 May 2012.

Allan, David. "Positive Engagement in Myanmar". In *Ruling Myanmar: From Cyclone Nargis to National Elections,* edited by N. Cheesman, M. Skidmore and T. Wilson. Singapore: Institute of Southeast Asian Studies, 2010.

Aung San Suu Kyi. *Freedom from Fear and Other Writings.* London: Penguin Books, 1995.

Carment, David and Albrecht Schnabel. *Building Conflict Prevention Capacity.* Ottawa and Tokyo: International Development Research Centre and United Nations University, 2001. <http://www.idrc.ca/uploads/user-S/10226960610cp-capacity.pdf>. Accessed 14 October 2009.

Centre for Peace and Conflict Studies (CPCS). *Listening to Voices from Inside: Myanmar Civil Society's Response to Cyclone Nargis.* Phnom Penh: Centre for Peace and Conflict Studies, 2008.

Clarke, Matthew. "Over the border and under the radar: Can illegal migrants be active citizens?". *Development in Practice* 19, no. 8 (2009): 1064–77.

Commission of the European Communities (CEC). *Towards a European Consensus on Humanitarian Aid: Report on Responses to Crises — DRC, Pakistan, Lebanon and Burma/Myanmar.* COM(2007) 317 final, SEC(2007) 782. Commission Staff Working Document, 13 June 2007. <http://ec.europa.eu/echo/files/policies/consensus/communication_en.pdf>. Accessed 12 October 2009.

Conflict Sensitivity. *Conflict Sensitive Approaches to Development, Humanitarian Assistance and Peacebuilding.* Conflict Sensitivity Consortium, 2004. <http://www.conflictsensitivity.org>. Accessed 30 September 2009.

Duffield, Mark. *On the Edge of 'No Man's Land': Chronic Emergency in Myanmar.* Working Paper. Department of Politics, University of Bristol, 2008. <http://www.bris.ac.uk/politics/gic/projects>. Accessed 14 October 2009.

Economic and Social Commission for Asia and the Pacific, United Nations Development Programme, and the Asian Development Bank (ESCAP/ADB/UNDP). *Access to Basic Services for the Poor: The Importance of Good Governance.* Report No. ST/ESCAP/2438. Bangkok: United Nations Economic and Social Commission for Asia and the Pacific (ESCAP), United Nations Development Programme (UNDP), and the Asian Development Bank (ADB), 2007. <http://www.mdgasiapacific.org/files/shared_folder/documents/MDG_Access_to_basic_services.pdf>. Accessed 15 May 2012.

Eyben, Rosalind. *Power, Mutual Accountability and Responsibility in the Practice of International Aid: A Relational Approach.* Brighton, UK: Institute of Development Studies, University of Sussex, 2008.

Eyben, Rosalind, Naila Kabeer and Andrea Cornwall. *Conceptualising Empowerment and the Implications for Pro-Poor Growth.* Brighton, UK: Institute of Development Studies, University of Sussex, 2008.

Fink, Christina. *Living Silence: Burma under Military Rule.* London: Zed Books, 2001.

Frantz, Telmo Rudi. "The Role of NGOs in the Strengthening of Civil Society". *World Development* 15, no. 1, Supplement (1987): 121–27.

Fritzen, Scott A. "Can the Design of Community-Driven Development Reduce the Risk of Elite Capture? Evidence from Indonesia". *World Development* 35, no. 8 (2007): 1359–75.

Hossain, Naomi and Mick Moore. *Arguing for the Poor: Elites and Poverty in Developing Countries.* IDS Working Paper 148. University of Sussex, UK: Institute of Development Studies, 2002.

International Crisis Group. *Myanmar: The role of civil society.* Asia Report No. 27, 6 December 2001. <http://www.crisisgroup.org/en/regions/asia/south-east-asia/burma-myanmar/027-myanmar-the-role-of-civil-society.aspx>. Accessed 15 May 2012.

————. *Burma/Myanmar after Nargis: Time to Normalise Aid Relations,* Asia Report No. 161, 20 October 2008. <http://www.crisisgroup.org/en/regions/asia/south-east-asia/burma-myanmar/161-burma-myanmar-after-nargis-time-to-normalise-aid-relations.aspx>. Accessed 10 April 2012.

Igboemeka, Adaeze. *Aid Effectiveness in Burma/Myanmar.* U.K. Department for International Development (DFID), South East Asia, 2005. <http://webarchive.nationalarchives.gov.uk/+/http://www.dfid.gov.uk/mdg/aid-effectiveness/newsletters/burma-report.pdf>. Accessed 15 May 2012.

Inwood, Paul Douglas. "International Humanitarian Assistance to Myanmar". Master of Philosophy in Development Studies thesis, Massey University,

Palmerston North, New Zealand, 2008. <http://mro.massey.ac.nz/bitstream/handle/10179/760/2whole.pdf?sequence=1>. Accessed 15 May 2012.

Labonne, Julien and Robert S. Chase. "Who is at the Wheel When Communities Drive Development? Evidence from the Philippines". *World Development* 37, no. 1 (2009): 219–31.

Liddell, Zunetta. "No Room to Move: Legal Constraints on Civil Society in Burma". In *Strengthening Civil Society in Burma: Possibilities and Dilemmas for International NGOs*, edited by Burma Center Netherlands (BCN) and Transnational Institute (TNI). Amsterdam: Transnational Institute and the Burma Center Nederland, 1997; and Chiangmai: Silkworm Books, 1999.

Lorch, Jasmin. "The (Re)-emergence of Civil Society in Areas of State Weakness". In *Dictatorship, Disorder and Decline in Myanmar*, edited by Monique Skidmore and Trevor Wilson. Canberra: ANU E-Press, 2007.

New Light of Myanmar (NLM). "Habits of exploitation of human rights by certain powerful countries as a pretext for meddling in internal affairs of member states still linger on". *New Light of Myanmar*, 20 July 2009.

————. "President U Thein Sein delivers inaugural address to Pyidaungsu Hluttaw". *New Light of Myanmar*, 31 March 2011. <http://www.burmanet.org/news/2011/03/31/the-new-light-of-myanmar-president-u-thein-sein-delivers-inaugural-address-to-pyidaungsu-hluttaw/>. Accessed 31 May 2012.

Nyamu-Musembi, Celestine and Andrea Cornwall. *What is the "Rights-Based Approach" All About?* IDS Working Paper 234. University of Sussex, UK: Institute of Development Studies, 2004. <http://www.ids.ac.uk/files/Wp234.pdf>. Accessed 15 May 2012.

Paldron, Mario. "Non-Government Development Organizations: From development aid to development cooperation". *World Development* 15, no. 1, Supplement (1987): 69–71.

Pedersen, Morten B. "Setting the Scene: Lessons from Twenty Years of Foreign Aid". Paper prepared for the National Bureau of Asian Research (NBR) forum, "Burma/Myanmar: Views from the Ground and the International Community", held 8 May 2009 at the Senate Office Building, Washington, D.C. <http://www.nbr.org/research/activity.aspx?id=45>. Accessed 26 October 2009.

Pettit, Jethro. "Strengthening Local Organization". *IDS Bulletin* 31, no. 3 (2000).

Platteau, Jean-Philippe and Frédéric Gaspart. "The Risk of Resource Misappropriation in Community-Driven Development". *World Development* 33, no. 10 (2003): 1687–703.

Skidmore, Monique. "Darker than Midnight: Fear, Vulnerability, and Terror Making in Urban Burma (Myanmar)". *American Ethnologist* 30, no. 1 (2003): 5–40.

————. *Karaoke Fascism: Burma and the Politics of Fear*. Philadelphia: University of Pennsylvania Press, 2004.

Soe Tha, U (Minister for National Planning and Economic Development, Government of Myanmar). "Press conference on economic growth of Myanmar, implementation of Millennium Goals and cooperation with UN agencies and internal and international NGOs". Naypyitaw, 17 December 2006. <http://groups.yahoo.com/group/myanmar_information/message/13589>; also at <http://www.myanmar.com/pressconference>. Both accessed 15 May 2012.

Steinberg, David I. "A Void in Myanmar: Civil Society in Burma". In *Strengthening Civil Society in Burma: Possibilities and Dilemmas for International NGOs*, edited by Burma Center Netherlands (BCN) and Transnational Institute (TNI). Amsterdam: Transnational Institute and the Burma Center Netherlands, 1997; and Chiangmai: Silkworm Books, 1999.

U Myint. 2011. *Reducing Poverty in Myanmar: The Way Forward.* Theme Paper presented to the National Workshop on Rural Development and Poverty Alleviation in Myanmar, Myanmar International Convention Center, Naypyitaw, 20–22 May 2011. <http://www.encburma.net/index.php/archives/burma-government/566-dr-u-myint-reducing-poverty-in-myanmar-the-way-forward.html>. Accessed 30 May 2011.

Ware, Anthony. "Facilitating Community Development Projects Within Myanmar: Preliminary Results of International NGO Interviews". In *Communities, Labour and Livelihood in Southeast Asia*, edited by Hanafi Hussin. Kuala Lumpur: University of Malaya, 2011.

————. *Context-Sensitive Development: How International NGOs Operate in Myanmar.* Sterling, VA: Kumarian Press, 2012.

World Faiths Development Dialogue (WFDD). *Cultures, Spirituality and Development.* Oxford, UK: World Faiths Development Dialogue. <http://www.developmentandfaith.org>. Accessed 4 October 2009; [<http://berkleycenter.georgetown.edu/wfdd/publications/list>. Accessed 15 May 2012].

LIST OF ABBREVIATIONS

ACFID	Australian Council for International Development
ADB	Asian Development Bank
ADF	Asian Development Fund
AIT	Asian Institute of Technology
ALD	Arakan League for Democracy
ASEAN	Association of Southeast Asian Nations
BBC	British Broadcasting Corporation
BCUK	Burma Campaign UK
BFDA	*Burmese Freedom and Democracy Act of 2003* (U.S.)
BGF	Border Guard Force
BOT	build-operate-transfer
CBO	community-based organization
CPB	Communist Party of Burma
CRPP	Committee Representing the People's Parliament
DKBA	Democratic Karen Buddhist Army
DOTS	Directly Observed Treatment Short course (for tuberculosis)
DVB	Democratic Voice of Burma
EBA	"Everything but Arms" (EU regulation)
ECHO	European Community Humanitarian Office
ECODEV	Economically Progressive Ecosystem Development
EEAS	European External Action Service
EP	European Parliament
ERI	EarthRights International
EU	European Union
EWEC	East–West Economic Corridor
FAO	Food and Agriculture Organization

FDI	Foreign Direct Investment
GDP	gross domestic product
GDPF	Group of Democratic Party Friends
GMS	Greater Mekong Subregion
GNI	gross national income
GONGO	government organized non-government organization
GSP	General System of Preferences
HIV/AIDS	Human Immuno-deficiency Virus/Acquired Immune Deficiency Syndrome
ICFTU	International Confederation of Free Trade Unions
ICT	information and communications technology
IDE	International Development Enterprises
ILO	International Labour Organization
IMF	International Monetary Fund
INGO	international non-government organization
JBIC	Japan Bank for International Cooperation
KDA	Kachin Defense Army
KIA	Kachin Independence Army
KIO	Kachin Independence Organization
KNLA	Karen National Liberation Army
KNU	Karen National Union
KSPP	Kachin State Progressive Party
LDC	least developed country
LNGO	local non-government organization
MADB	Myanmar Agricultural Development Bank
MAI	Myanmar Airways International
MDB	multilateral development bank
MDGs	Millennium Development Goals
MDRI	Myanmar Development Resource Institute
MEB	Myanma Economic Bank
MEP	Members of the European Parliament
MFTB	Myanma Foreign Trade Bank
MGE	Myanmar Gems Enterprise
MIC	Myanmar Investment Commission
MICB	Myanma Investment and Commercial Bank
MMA	Myanmar Medical Association
MNA	Myanmar News Agency
MOGE	Myanmar Oil and Gas Enterprise

MRTV	Myanma Radio and Television
MSCO	Myanmar Central Statistical Organization
MSF	Médécins Sans Frontieres
NAG	Network Activities Group
NDA–K	New Democratic Army–Kachin
NDF	National Democratic Force
NGO	non-government organization
NLD	National League for Democracy
NLM	*New Light of Myanmar*
ODA	Official Development Assistance
PNO	Pa'O National Organization
PSI	Population Services International
PSRD	Press Scrutiny and Registration Department
R&D	research and development
RBA	rights-based approach
RFA	Radio Free Asia
SEC	Southern Economic Corridor
SEE	state-owned economic enterprise
SLORC	State Law and Order Restoration Council
SPDC	State Peace and Development Council
TNC	transnational corporation
UMFCCI	Union of Myanmar Federation of Chambers of Commerce and Industry
UN	United Nations
UNDP	United Nations Development Programme
UPR	universal periodic review
USDA	Union Solidarity and Development Association
USDP	Union Solidarity and Development Party
VOA	Voice of America

INDEX

Myanmar Airways International, 150
Myanmar Central Bank, 178
Myanmar Development Resource
    Institute (MDRI), 49, 140, 141
Myanmar Economic Bank, 150
Myanmar Economic Corporation, 10,
    17, 142
Myanmar Egress, 17, 213 n.1, 317 n.12
Myanmar Fruit and Vegetable
    Producers and Exporters
    Association, 163
Myanmar Garment Manufacturers
    Association, 294
Myanmar Gems Enterprise, 94, 96
Myanmar Gemstones SLORC Law 8/95,
    94
Myanmar Industrial Crops
    Development Enterprise, 161
Myanmar International (TV), 198
Myanmar Investment Commission,
    139
Myanmar Livestock and Fisheries
    Development Bank, 179
Myanmar Medical Association
    (MMA), 195
Myanmar News Agency, 186, 200 n.1
Myanmar Oil and Gas Enterprise
    (MOGE), 144, 146
Myanmar Port Authority, 290
Myanmar Post and
    Telecommunication, 132
Myanmar Printers and Publishers
    Association, 187
Myanmar Radio, 198
Myanmar Radio and Television
    (MRTV), 186, 198
Myanmar Red Cross, 331, 337, 344
Myanmar Rice Industry Association,
    163
Myanmar Times, 15, 206, 313, 342, 343
    censorship and, 188
    establishment of, 187–88

Myanmar Women Entrepreneurs
    Association, 123
Myanmar-Thailand highway, 29
Myawaddy, 308, 310
Myawaddy (army newspaper), 186
Myawaddy TV, 198
Myint Aung, 229 n.1
Myint Han, 229 n.1
Myint Zan, 12
Myitkyina, 56, 58, 63, 64, 66, 102
Myitsone Dam, 7, 68, 121, 305

N

Naing Htoo, 317 n.7
Nam Theun 2 (NT2) Hydropower
    Project (Laos), 304, 311
Namhkam, 103
Nanyarseik, 92
*Narcotic Drugs and Psychotropic
    Substances Law1993*, 222
national and regional assemblies,
    see legislative assemblies
National Democratic Force, 77, 298 n.1
National Highway 54 (India), 190
National Human Rights Commission,
    11, 13
National League for Democracy
    (NLD), 3, 46, 69, 195, 337
    censorship and, 191
    elections and, 6, 24, 76
    freedom to operate website, 5
    government policy and, 7
    media reporting of, 15
    members in parliament, 302
    Ministry of Home Affairs and, 6
    post-election registration, 6, 284
    reopening of offices, 7
    sanctions and, 7, 307
    splits within, 77
National Workshop on Rural
    Development and Poverty
    Alleviation, 140

www.ingramcontent.com/pod-product-compliance
Lightning Source LLC
Chambersburg PA
CBHW050225270326
41914CB00003BA/572